Dr Peter Marshall is the UK's leading authority on bookkeeping, whose publications bear the accreditations and endorsements of all the professional institutes. What makes his books so popular is not only his comprehensive knowledge of the topic; his status as a trained educational psychologist means he has greater insight into the processes of learning and memory and how to maximise the efficiency of both and pass exams. His other books include *Computerised Book-keeping* and *Mastering Spreadsheet Bookkeeping*, both of which are published by How To Books/Robinson.

Further details of his contributions to the subject can be found on his website masteringbook-keeping.com

Also by Dr Peter Marshall

Computerised Book-keeping

Mastering Spreadsheet Bookkeeping

Other accounting books

Book-keeping and Accounting for the Small Business

Do It Yourself Bookkeeping for Small Businesses

Understanding and Interpreting Company Accounts

Write Your Own Business Plan

The Small Business Start-up Workbook

Investing in Stocks and Shares

Dr Peter Marshall

MASTERING BOOKKEEPING

A complete guide to the principles
and practice of business accounting

**THE INSTITUTE
OF CERTIFIED
BOOKKEEPERS**

AN ACCREDITED TEXTBOOK OF
THE INSTITUTE OF CERTIFIED BOOKKEEPERS

ROBINSON

ROBINSON

First published in Great Britain in 1992 by How To Books

This revised and updated edition published in Great Britain in 2017 by Robinson

Copyright © Dr Peter Marshall, 1992, 2017

1 3 5 7 9 8 6 4 2

The moral right of the author has been asserted.

A CIP catalogue record for this book
is available from the British Library.

ISBN 978-1-47213-703-6

Typeset in Times by Initial Typesetting
Printed and bound in Great Britain by CPI Group (UK) Ltd, Croydon CR0 4YY
Papers used by Robinson are from well-managed forests and other responsible sources

www.littlebrown.co.uk

How To Books are published by Robinson, an imprint of Little, Brown Book
Group. We welcome proposals from authors who have first-hand experience
of their subjects. Please set out the aims of your book, its target market and
its suggested contents in an email to Nikki.Read@howtobooks.co.uk

Contents

Contents

Contents

Contents

Preface

This book was inspired as much by educational science as by bookkeeping. Having had a dual role of business studies writer and educational researcher I have been particularly interested in the way educational science can be applied to this subject, which has, hitherto, been largely missed by the research community.

Other books teach bookkeeping in a spatial way assuming that if students understand the page layouts they will naturally understand how to enter them. That is so for people with relatively spatial learning styles, such as accountants tend to have, but it is not the case for those with a more sequential learning style, such as bookkeepers so often tend to have. This is a cause of much communication difficulty in classrooms. This book tackles this problem head-on by teaching in a sequential – 'set of rules' – manner.

Although this book aims to teach readers the principles of double entry accounting, it must be acknowledged that there are many small businesses (corner shops, cafés, hairdressers, etc) which do not use this. This edition includes a short section on the kinds of deviations from conventional accounting which a reader may encounter.

This book has been designed to cover the requirements of all the principal bookkeeping courses, including ICB, IAB, AAT, the GCSE and A level courses of AQA, OCR, Edexcel, Pitman, LCCI and all the various Open College syllabi in the subject. Moreover, this edition contains a wealth of examination material. In this enhanced and fully updated edition it will provide students with all they need to achieve success in their courses.

Peter Marshall

ICB examination papers and model answers are reproduced by kind permission of the Institute of Certified Bookkeepers. AQA examinations questions are reproduced by kind permission of The Assessment and Qualifications Alliance. OCR questions are reproduced by kind permission of Oxford, Cambridge and RSA Examinations. AAT questions are reproduced by kind permission of The Association of Accounting Technicians. IAB examination papers and model answers are reproduced by kind permission of The International Association of Book-keepers.

1 A period of transition

With the increasing globalisation of trade and industry at all levels it is becoming increasingly necessary to achieve some degree of harmony in accounting practices between countries. The standards that applied in the UK since 1970 i.e. Statements of Standard Accounting Practice (SSAPs) and Financial Reporting Standards (FRSs)) are being gradually phased out and replaced by International Accounting Standards (IASs) and International Financial Reporting Standards (IFRSs). All companies listed on EU Stock Exchanges already use the international standards and in time they will be used by all UK businesses.

Here are some examples of the changes in terminology with which you will have to become familiar. In the international standard terminology, instead of turnover the term *revenue* is used, instead of stock the term *inventory* is used, and debtors and creditors are called *accounts receivable* and *payable*. Provisions tend to be referred to as *allowances*, the profit and loss account is known as the *income statement* and any profit that is brought down to the balance sheet is termed *retained profits*. Debentures are known as *loan notes*, fixed assets are called *non-current assets* and long-term liabilities are called *non-current liabilities*.

2 The role and significance of the professional association

One of the distinguishing characteristics of all professions is the existence of professional associations. Such bodies maintain and improve the reputation of the profession by the regulation of conduct, the improvement of skills and the validation of qualifications.

The Institute of Certified Bookkeepers is based at 1 Northumberland House, Trafalgar Square, London WC2N 5BW, under the Royal Patronage of His Royal Highness Prince Michael of Kent GCVO. The other professional association for bookkeepers is The International Association of Book-keepers (IAB), whose registered office is at Burford House, 44, London Road, Sevenoaks, Kent TN13 1AS.

Bookkeeping became a regulated profession under the Money Laundering Regulations of 2007. As a result of this bookkeepers now have special legal duties imposed upon them, and failure to comply with them has serious legal consequences. All practising bookkeepers must be registered with a supervisory body. Both professional bodies mentioned here are Treasury Appointed Supervisory Bodies under the Money Laundering Act and, as such, will monitor, guide and supervise members to ensure compliance.

In addition, membership also provides proof of proficiency which is recognised worldwide. It offers assistance with career development, not only through the provision of training and qualifications, but also though notification of job vacancies, updates on legislation and advice and guidance on private practice. Members also get the opportunity to meet and associate with others in the same profession in local groups and forums.

www.bookkeepers.org.uk homepage reproduced by kind permission of The Institute of Certified Bookkeepers.

www.iab.org.uk website page reproduced by kind permission of The International Association of Book-keepers.

3 Data security and the Data Protection Act 1998

When a business keeps a substantial number of personal details in computerised accounting records it may be obligated to register with the Information Commissioner. The person who decides how data will be used and for what purpose is referred to in the Act as the data controller while a person on whom data is kept is referred to as a data subject. It is essentially so that the data subjects are aware of what is held and how it is used.

It is not necessary to inform the Information Commissioner if:

- the data controller is only using the data for sending and receiving invoices and statements;
- the data subjects are companies and no individuals can be identified in them;
- the data is only used to process payroll and prepare statutory returns.

However, if a data controller is going to make accounting data available to management or any other department for non-accounting purposes, e.g. marketing, statistical, planning or control purposes, it must register. It must disclose the kind of data held, the purpose for which it will be used and how subjects can access their own data.

LEGAL OBLIGATIONS IN RESPECT OF PERSONAL DATA

Businesses registered under the Data Protection Act 1998 must comply with certain standards of practice contained in Schedule 1 of the Act. These require that the personal data shall:

- be obtained only for specified and lawful purposes and must not be used in any manner incompatible with such purposes;
- be relevant and adequate but not excessive for the purpose for which it has been collected;
- be accurate and kept up to date;
- not be kept for any longer than necessary for the purpose for which it was collected;
- only be processed in accordance with the subject's rights under the Act;
- be protected by appropriate organisational and technical measures against unauthorised and unlawful use, or accidental loss or damage;
- not be taken outside of the country to any country where there is not adequate legal protection of the rights and freedom of data subjects in respect of the processing of their personal data.

In many businesses today accounting information *will* be used for non-accounting purposes so it is very likely that anyone who controls such data will need to register and comply with the Act. To access the full text of the Act click on www.opsi.gov.uk/ads/ads1998/19980029.htm. The Information Commissioner's general website is on www.ico.gov.uk.

4 The flow of documents and processes

This chapter outlines the paper trail between buyer and seller in a typical business transaction and the processes within each firm that each document triggers.

Estimate or quotation
Sometimes it is not possible to give a precise quotation and an estimate is regarded as the best that can be done. The quotation must be for an exact figure while an estimate is only a rough figure. However, the final costs of work or supplies are expected to be within 10% of the estimated figure and courts are likely to be sympathetic to the purchasing party in actions where this figure has been exceeded.

Request for quotations
Often when a business wishes to purchase goods and services from another requests for quotations will be sent out to a number of potential suppliers. Any company interested in competing to supply goods to the business will begin to calculate the lowest prices at which it is prepared to supply the goods or services. It will then prepare a quotation or estimate (according to whichever was requested) and send it to the potential customer.

When the customer receives the estimates or quotations they will compare them all on the basis of prices and perceived quality of the goods or services being offered, taking into account such things as delivery dates and past experience of dealing with that particular supplier.

Purchase order
When a final selection is made the buyer will normally issue a purchase order. This will state the quantity, type of goods, prices and the special conditions of the contract, such as the terms of business, the timescale in which payment is agreed to be made, e.g. strictly 30 days. Delivery instructions and any other special conditions which may apply will be included, e.g. there may be a penalty clause for late completion of work, entitling the buyer of services to compensation of a specific sum, or a specific percentage of the total.

Delivery note
If the supplier accepts this purchase order then a delivery note will normally be made out and sent with the goods. This will normally be in at least triplicate form and will specify the goods.

Some multipart, carbonised sales forms contain three copies of the delivery note and two copies of the sales invoice. The delivery notes, being the bottom two copies, may have the cash columns blocked out. In certain aspects these invoices and delivery notes will be the same, including the boxes for name and address, order number and details of goods, but the cash details will normally be omitted on the delivery notes.

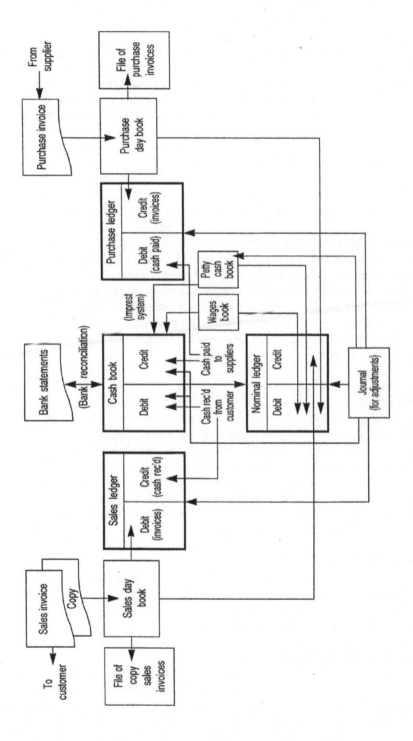

Fig. 1. An overview of business accounts records. Note: The actual records are shown in the boxes. The arrows show the flow of information between the various records. The boxes shown in bold are divisions of the ledger. There is an additional month-end information flow between ledger divisions when cross-referencing is made in folio columns.

The delivery note will be passed to the stores, where it will trigger the packing and shipment of the goods to the customer. At the same time the stock records will be adjusted to show the goods have been booked out from stock and have become the responsibility of the delivery driver and remain so until he or she returns a signed delivery note confirming they have been received by the customer in good order.

Where the order is for services

If the purchase order is for services rather than goods, e.g. building work, then a job order sheet may be produced by the supplying firm and passed to the works department for the manager to allocate the job to a worker or workers.

Customer signs to confirm delivery

When the goods arrive a copy of the delivery note is signed by the customer after he or she has checked the goods are those that were ordered and have been received in good condition. There will usually be a second copy for the customer to file. These retained copies are source documents for updating the stock records, which at the end of the year, after verification against a physical stock check, will be used in the balance sheet as one component of the current assets section (Closing Stock).

Production of an invoice

The signed delivery note will be passed to the sales office of the supplier, where it will trigger the preparation of an invoice. This may have already been prepared as part of a quadruplicate or quintruplicate set and sent to the customer with the delivery note, or it may be sent by post once a signed delivery note is received to confirm the goods it is charging for have been received by the customer.

In a manual system one copy of the invoice will go to the accounts department where its details will be entered into the sales day book. In a fully computerised system the sales day book may automatically be updated with the invoice details when the invoice is produced on the system.

Purchase returns note

Sometimes goods are returned by agreement with the supplier, because they are faulty or not what was ordered. In such a case a purchase returns note will be created by the buyer, which is essentially the opposite of a delivery note, describing the goods being returned and the reason.

Production of a credit note

The receipt of this note will normally, after checking it is justified, trigger the production of a credit note at the supplier's end (which is essentially the opposite of an invoice). When the customer receives this it will be entered in the purchase returns day book and this, in turn, will be posted to the debit side of the relevant bought ledger account to reduce the indebtedness of the company to that particular supplier.

Production of a statement

At the end of the month (or sooner if it is the firm's policy) the sales day book details will be posted to the ledger divisions – the sales account in the nominal ledger and the personal account details in the sales ledger. The ledger divisions will be balanced and the resulting balances will be reproduced in statements and sent to customers, informing them of the amount they owe, whether they are overdue and when they should be paid by. These will also include any interest or penalties that have been agreed for late payment and details of any early settlement discount the customer can claim.

Often these will be age-analysed, i.e. stating which parts of the total amount have been outstanding for one month, which parts of it have been outstanding for two months, and so on. If the debt is overdue for payment a strong demand will normally be annotated, such as *This account is overdue for payment. Please settle by return.* Such demands may become increasingly strong the older a debt becomes.

Statements will not normally give details of the goods or services supplied. Their purpose is merely to deal with the financial indebtedness of the customer, but some statements may show such details.

Often a remittance advice slip will be included with the statements (attached or as a separate slip). It will give the necessary details for the cashier to tie up the payment with the relevant account. This is partly for the convenience of the customer to save them preparing a covering letter to accompany the cheque.

Production of a cheque

The receipt of the statement by the customer is usually what triggers the production of the cheque payable to the supplier and any remittance slip that came with the statement will be filled in and sent with it to the supplier.

The details from the cheque stub will be entered into the cashbook to credit the bank with the funds it is transferring to the supplier and if any early settlement discount has been received it will be posted to the discount received account. The other side of each part of this transaction will be posted to the debit side of the supplier's personal account in the bought ledger, to record that the business has been settled by bank funds, less any discount the suppliers have allowed.

Figure 2 provides a schematic illustration of the flow of documents in a single business transaction and the processes which are triggered by each.

Symmetry of the processes of purchases and sales

This same flow of documents takes place in respect of goods supplied by the firm as for goods supplied to the firm. The roles are just reversed.

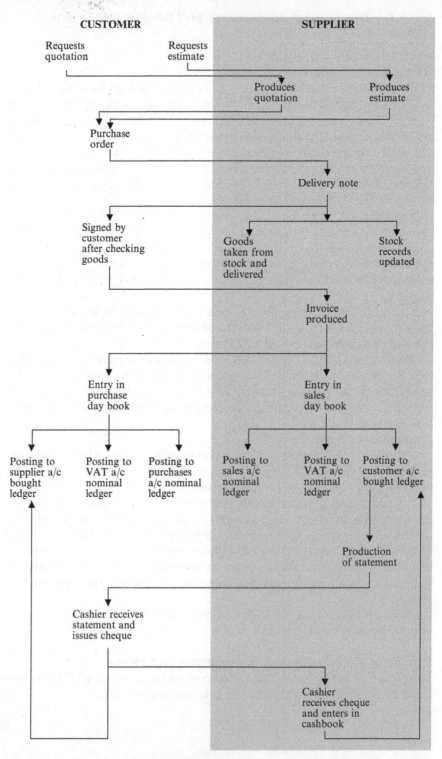

Fig. 2. An illustration of the flow of documents and the processes which each triggers in a transaction between two businesses.

5 What is double entry bookkeeping?

Debit and credit

All transactions have two sides, a **debit** and a **credit**. When a firm sells a TV and sends a bill for payment, for example, on the one hand it has made a sale (which is a credit entry). On the other hand it has gained a liability from the customer (debit entry). That customer is liable to the firm for the money.

The need for two records

Both these transactions need recording separately, because we need:

- a total of sales figures for tax computation and management purposes (to make sure the business is working to plan)

- a cumulative total of money owed by each customer.

A check of accuracy

There is another important advantage of double entry bookkeeping. If both sides of each transaction have been recorded then, at any time, if the sums have been done correctly the debit entries will equal the credit entries. It provides a check of accuracy. An example is as follows:

Example
Suppose A. T. Office Supplies made the following transactions:

Purchased 6 tables for £60.00 from seller A
Purchased 10 chairs for £40.00 from seller B
Sold 1 table for £15.00 to customer A
Sold 1 chair for £24.00 to customer B
Received cheque for £15.00 from customer A
Paid cheque for £60.00 to seller A

The entries would be:

DEBIT	£	CREDIT	£
Purchases	60.00	Seller A	60.00
Purchases	40.00	Seller B	40.00
Customer A	15.00	Sales	39.00
Customer B	24.00		
Bank	15.00	Customer A	15.00
Seller A	60.00	Bank	60.00
	214.00		214.00

JOURNAL

Date 200X	Particulars	Dr.	Cr.
Jan 1	Sundries:		
	Factory premises	69,500	
	Fixtures and fittings	1,000	
	Printing machine	18,000	
	Motor van	5,000	
	Bank	6,500	
	Capital		100,000

Dr.		Factory Premises			Cr.
Date 200X	Particulars	Totals	Date 200X	Particulars	Totals
Jan 1	Opening balance	69,500			

Dr.		Fixtures & Fittings Account			Cr.
Date 200X	Particulars	Totals	Date 200X	Particulars	Totals
Jan 1	Opening balance	1,000			

Dr.		Printing Machine Account			Cr.
Date 200X	Particulars	Totals	Date 200X	Particulars	Totals
Jan 1	Opening balance	18,000			

Dr.		Motor Van Account			Cr.
Date 200X	Particulars	Totals	Date 200X	Particulars	Totals
Jan 1	Opening balance	5,000			

		Capital Account			
Date 200X	Particulars	Totals	Date 200X	Particulars	Totals
			Jan 1	Opening balance	100,000

CASH BOOK

Receipts					Payments				
Date 200X	Particulars	Discount	Cash	Bank	Date	Particulars	Discount	Cash	Bank
Jan 1	Opening balance			6,500					

Fig. 3. An example of the journalising and posting to the ledger of the opening figures.

6   Opening the books of account

Assets, liabilities and capital
When opening the books of a new business for the first time we need to list:

- all its assets

- all its liabilities.

By taking away the value of the liabilities from the assets, we can tell how much **capital** the business has at the beginning. In other words:

assets – liabilities = capital

Or to put it another way:

assets = capital + liabilities

Accounts as an equation
The accounts of a business always represent such an equation, in which one side is always exactly balanced by the other side. This balancing list of opening assets, liabilities and capital should then be posted to (i.e. entered in) the relevant ledger accounts, by way of a very useful account book called the **journal**. We will see how to do this when we come to the journal and ledger sections a little later on.

The page on the left shows a typical first page of the journal of a new small printing business, working from a small workshop, and owning a printing machine and delivery van. As you can see, the firm's assets are £100,000, made up of such things as premises, equipment, and £6,500 cash at bank. We keep a separate account for each of these assets – factory premises account, fixtures and fittings account and so on. The cash account we record in the ledger (cash book division); in the example (bottom left) you can see the £6,500 entered in as an 'opening balance'.

```
┌─────────────────────────────────────────────────────────────┐
│                          Invoice                            │
│                                                             │
│  D. Davidson (Builder)              Delivered to:           │
│  1 Main Road                        Broad Street            │
│  Anytown                            Anytown                 │
│  Lancs                              Lancs                   │
│                                                             │
│  P356   20/12/200X                                          │
│                                                             │
│  20  bags of cement                 10.00       200.00      │
│  15  5 litre tins of white emulsion  1.00        15.00      │
│  32  bags of sand                    5.00       160.00      │
│  40  metres of 100mm x 50mm pinewood 1.00        40.00      │
│                                                 415.00      │
│                    VAT @ 20%                     83.00      │
│                                                 498.00      │
│  E&OE                                                       │
└─────────────────────────────────────────────────────────────┘
```

Fig. 4. Example of an invoice.

```
┌─────────────────────────────────────────────────────────────┐
│                        Credit Note                          │
│                                                             │
│  D. Davidson (Builder)              Delivered to:           │
│  1 Main Road                        Broad Street            │
│  Anytown                            Anytown                 │
│  Lancs                              Lancs                   │
│                                                             │
│  P3756   20/01/200X                                         │
│                                                             │
│  60  Door hinges                     0.50        30.00      │
│                                                  30.00      │
│                    VAT @ 20%                      6.00      │
│                                                  36.00      │
│  E&OE                                                       │
│                                                             │
└─────────────────────────────────────────────────────────────┘
```

Fig. 5. Example of a credit note.
E&OE stands for errors and omissions excepted.

Recording daily details: books of prime entry

Double entry accounts are kept in the ledger, but daily details of transactions are not normally entered directly into it; it would become too cluttered and difficult to use. For convenience we first of all enter all the day-to-day details of transactions in other books, called **books of prime entry**. In modern accounting these books are the:

- purchase day book

- purchase returns day book

- sales day book

- sales returns day book

- journal

- cash book

- petty cash book.

Day books or journals

This group of books can also be called either **day books** or **journals**. We will use the term day books here for the four which are identically ruled and most often referred to as day books, that is the purchase day book, purchase returns day book, sales day book and sales returns day book. The word journal we will keep for the journal proper, because of its individual ruling and the others we will call 'books of prime entry'. It is the four day books as defined here, that we will explain in this section.

Source documents for the bookkeeper

The sources of information we need to enter into the day books are invoices and credit notes. When a firm receives invoices or credit notes for goods it has purchased they are known as purchase invoices and credit notes inwards respectively. When it sends them out, they are called sales invoices and credit notes outwards. Whether the documents refer to sales or purchases, their format is basically the same. After all, what is a purchase invoice to one party in the transaction is a sales invoice to the other, and similarly for credit notes.

> The production of invoices is usually triggered by receipt of signed delivery notes for *goods sold* and by time sheets or some kinds of job completion docket for *services rendered*. Except in very small firms, where such details may be known by heart, product or service descriptions, codes and prices are sourced from sales, or service catalogues, trade terms are dictated by company policy and any special terms which are allowed to particular customers may be listed in a customers special terms file.

DEBIT NOTE

P Donague   Delivery Address: 6 Broad Street
1 Main Road   Anytown
Anytown   Lancs.
Lancs.

Credit note number CN 200X/12/28 – 3

Undercharge of invoice number p356 20/12/200X   10.00

VAT   2.00

Total   <u>12.00</u>

Fig. 6. Example of a debit note.

Debit notes

Sales office clerks occasionally make mistakes and undercharge a customer for goods, so firms usually print the term E&OE on their invoices, which means errors and omissions excepted. This means the firm reserves the right to ask for more money for the goods if they realise they have inadvertently undercharged. If this has to be done the document they use is known as a debit note. An example is given in Figure 6 opposite.

Bookkeeping and confidentiality

Bookkeeping and accounting technicians have a duty to treat all information to which their job exposes them in strictest confidence, disclosing details only to those who have a professional right to know them. Examples are:

- employers, or employees who need the information to carry out their professional role;

- professionals outside the company who work on behalf of the company who need the information to carry out their function;

- any other person to whom their employer, or officer senior to themselves instructs them to disclose information, since it must be assumed that the employer or senior officer will also be working within the confines of such confidentially rules.

PURCHASE DAY BOOK

Date	Supplier	Inv. Fo. No.		Net.Inv Value	VAT 20%	Stationery	Books	Calculators
200X								
Apr 1	Morgan and Baldwyn	4/1	BL6	80.00	16.00	80.00		
3	"			200.00	40.00			200.00
15	S. Jones	4/2	BL5	70.00			70.00	
21	A Singh Wholesale	4/3	BL9	160.00			160.00	
				40.00	8.00	40.00		
30	Morgan and Baldwyn	4/4	BL6	150.00	30.00	150.00		
				700.00	94.00	270.00	230.00	200.00

Fig. 7. How to write up purchases into the purchase day book.

A. Frazer, a retail stationer, makes the following purchases during the month of April 200X:

200X

Apr 1	Morgan and Baldwyn	20 Geometry sets @ £4
3	"	40 Calculators @ £5
15	S. Jones	20 Assorted books @ £3.50
21	A Singh Wholesale	40 Assorted books @ £ £4
		80 Bottles of ink @ £0.50
30	Morgan and Baldwyn	25 De-luxe writing cases @ £6

Figure 7 shows how he writes up the transactions in the purchase day book.

8 The purchase day book

The **purchase day book** is one of the day books mentioned. It is where we first enter up all our purchases on credit. The book itself is not part of 'the accounts': it is just one of the sources from which the accounts will be written up later on.

How to write up the purchase day book
What you need:

- the purchase day book
- the invoices for the period (day, week, etc.).

First, sort the invoices into date order. Next, write or stamp a purchase invoice number on each one. (This is not the invoice number printed on the document when the firm receives it; that is the sales invoice number of the firm which sent it.) The idea is to help the bookkeeper find an invoice easily if he/she has to look up details of an old transaction.

Many firms keep a list of consecutive numbers for this purpose. Others use a two-part number made up of the month number and a number from a consecutive list for that month.

Step by step
1. Write the year of entry once, at the head of entries to be made for that year. There is no need then to keep writing the year against each individual entry. This helps to keep the page neat and uncluttered. Do the same for the month, and then the day, as in the example on the opposite page:

   Apr   1
           3
         15
         21
         30

2. Enter the supplier's name, e.g. Morgan and Baldwyn.

3. Enter your own purchase invoice number e.g. 4/1.

4. Enter net invoice total, e.g. £80.00. (Net means after deduction of any trade discounts and not including VAT; we will come to these later.)

5. Enter the VAT, e.g. £16.00.

6. If analysis columns are in use, also enter the net amount of each invoice under the correct heading, e.g. 'stationery'.

7. When required (e.g. monthly) total each column. You will then be able to post (transfer) the totals to the ledger.

S. JONES (WHOLESALE STATIONERY SUPPLIES) LTD
210 Barton High Street, Barton, Barshire

Credit Note No: SJ /02206   10/2/200X

To authorised return of faulty
desk diaries   200.00

VAT @ 20%   40.00

                                                        240.00

Name of customer
D. Davidson
1 Main Street
Anytown
Lancs.

Fig. 8. Example of a credit note inwards.

PURCHASE RETURNS DAYBOOK

Date	Supplier	C/N No	Net Inv. Value	VAT 20%	Stationery	Books	Cards	Machines
200X								
Feb10	S.Jones	2/1	200.00	40.00	200.00			
14	Morgan & Baldwyn	2/2	270.00			270.00		
25	A. Singh	2/3	230.00	46.00			15.00	215.00
			700.00	86.00	200.00	270.00	15.00	215.00

Fig. 9. Example of the same credit entered into the
purchase returns daybook.

9 The purchase returns day book

Returning unwanted goods

When a firm buys goods or services on credit, it records the details in the purchase day book, as we saw on the previous pages. Sometimes, however, it has to return what it has bought to the supplier. For example the goods may be faulty, or arrived damaged. In this case, the firm obtains a **credit note** from the supplier, and the value of the credit note is then entered up in the purchase returns day book.

All the points which apply to the purchase day book also apply to the purchase returns day book. Even the ruling is identical, though of course the transaction details may be different. So once you have become familiar with the ruling of a typical purchase day book, you will also have a picture of the purchase returns day book in your mind.

Example

Look at the example on the opposite page. We purchased a quantity of desk diaries from S. Jones (Wholesale Stationery Supplies Ltd), and unfortunately found that some of them were faulty. We told them about the problem and they agreed that we could return them. S. Jones then issued us with a credit note for the value of the faulty goods, plus VAT, a total of £240.00. The credit note is dated 10th February. We now enter the details of this credit note in our purchase returns day book as shown opposite.

1. On the far left we enter the date, followed by the name of the supplier.

2. In the third column we enter our own credit note number from our own sequences of numbers, in this case 2/1 meaning February, credit note number one. (We do not enter S. Jones' own number SJ/02206.)

3. In the correct columns we then enter the net amount of the credit, i.e. excluding VAT – £200.00 – and the VAT element of £40.00 in the VAT column.

4. If our purchase returns day book has additional analysis columns, we 'analyse' the net amount into the correct column, in this case stationery.

The additional analysis columns can be useful, because they help us to check the value of each category of goods returned.

Entwhistle & Co – Builders Merchants
Ferry Yard, Anytown, Anyshire

To: D. Davidson (Builder)   2nd January 200X
    1 Main Street
    Anytown
    Lancs

INVOICE No:-   **501**

100 English facing bricks @ 28p	£	28.00
24 breeze blocks @ 50p		12.00
Assorted cut timber		320.00
Screws, nails and ironmongery		40.00
5 rolls vinyl wallpaper @ £ 3		15.00
		415.00
VAT @ 20%		83.00
Total		498.00

Terms strictly 30 days net

Fig. 10. Example of a sales invoice.

SALES DAY BOOK

Date	Customer	Inv. No.	Net.Inv. Value	VAT 20%	Bricklyr Supplies	Carptry Supplies	Decor Supplies	Roofing Supplies
200X								
Jan 2	D. Davidson	SO1	415.00	83.00	40.00	360.00	15.00	
4	Kahn & Kahn	SO2	30.00	6.00		30.00		
5	JBC Roofing	SO3	250.00	50.00				250.00
			695.00	139.00	40.00	390.00	15.00	250.00

Fig. 11. The same sales invoice duly entered into the sales day book.

10   The sales day book

A. Frazer records his sales

Let us suppose that A. Frazer is a business stationery supplier. He makes the following sales on monthly credit account during the month of June 200X:

200X
Jun 1   Edwards' Garage   150 white A4 envelopes = £4.00
                               150 small manilla envelopes = £4.00
    6   A. K. Insurance
            Services   150 large envelopes = £10.00
    8   J.B.C. Roofing   4 calculators @ £12.50 ea
   30   F. Evans   20 note pads = £21.60

Let's suppose that, like many firms, A. Frazer has his sales invoices pre-printed with numbers in a chronological sequence and that the above sales were billed on invoice numbers 961/2/3 and 4. He would write the invoice dates followed by the names of the customers in the first two columns of his sales day book. In the next column he would enter the net invoice values (i.e. excluding VAT), and in the next the amounts of VAT charged on each invoice. Further to the right, he would then 'analyse' the net amounts into handy reference columns. (This analysis will be useful to him later, as he will be able to tell quickly what value of his sales were for stationery, what for calculators, and what for any other categories which he may decide to have analysis columns for.)

Date	Supplier	Inv. No	Net Inv. Value	VAT 20%	Statnry	Calcs.
200X						
Jun 1	Edwards' Garage	961	8.00	1.60	8.00	
6	A.K. Insurance Servs	2	10.00	2.00	10.00	
8	J.B.C. Roofing	3	50.00	10.00		50.00
30	F. Evans	4	21.60	4.32	21.60	
			89.60	17.92	39.60	50.00

Fig. 12. Extract from A. Frazer's sales day book.

```
CREDIT NOTE No: 0135                    8 March 200X

To authorised return of                      £    p
5 × 10 litre cans of white gloss paint       50.00
returned as faulty
VAT @ 20%                                     10.00
                                             60.00

┌                        ┐
  Name of customer
  D. Davidson (Builder)
  1, Main Street
  Anytown
  Lancs
└                        ┘
```

Fig. 13. Example of a credit note inwards.

SALES RETURNS DAY BOOK

Date	Customer	C/N No	Net Inv Value	VAT 20%	Bricklayer Supplies	Carpentry Supplies	Decor Supplies
200X							
Mar 8	D. Davidson	135	50.00	10.00			50.00
10	J.B.C. Roofing	6	60.00	12.00	60.00		
			110.00	22.00	60.00		50.00

Fig. 14. The same credit note outwards duly entered
into the sales returns day book.

11 The sales returns day book

When a customer asks for a credit

When a firm sells goods or services on credit, it records the details in the sales day book, as we saw on the previous pages. Sometimes, however, the customer has to return what he has bought. For example the goods may be faulty, or arrived damaged. In this case, the firm sends a **credit note** to the customer, and the value of the credit note is then entered up in the sales returns day book.

All the points which apply to the sales day book also apply to the sales returns day book, even the ruling is identical, though of course the transaction details may be different. So once you have become familiar with the ruling of a typical sales day book, you will also have a picture of the sales returns day book in your mind.

Example

Look at the example on the opposite page. We sold 50 litres of white gloss paint to D. Davidson (Builders) who unfortunately found them to be faulty. They returned the goods to us and we issued them with a credit note for the value plus VAT, a total of £60.00. The credit note is dated 8 March 200X. We now enter the details of this credit note in our sales returns day book as shown opposite.

1. On the far left we enter the date, followed by the name of the customer.

2. In the third column we enter the credit note number (this is usually pre-printed on credit notes outwards, but if not it must be allocated from a chronological sequence).

3. In the correct columns we then enter the amounts of the credit, i.e. excluding VAT – £50.00 – and the VAT element of £10.00 in the VAT column.

4. If our sales returns day book has additional analysis columns, we 'analyse' the net amount into the correct one, in this case *Decorators' supplies*.

The additional analysis columns can be useful, because they help us to check the value of each category of goods returned.

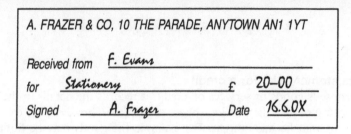

A. FRAZER & CO, 10 THE PARADE, ANYTOWN AN1 1YT

Received from   *F. Evans*

for   *Stationery*   £   *20–00*

Signed   *A. Frazer*   Date   *16.6.0X*

BARSHIRE BANK PLC

Barshire House, Barton   *1.6.* 20 *0X*

Pay   *D. DAVIDSON*

Twenty one pounds only   21.00

A.K. INSURANCE

B. Jones

CASH BOOK

Dr. (Receipts)						(Payments) Cr.				
Date	Particulars	Fo.	Discount	Cash	Bank	Date	Particulars	Fo.	Discount	Cash	Bank
June 1	Balance	b/d		50.00	1,750.00	Jun 1	Razi & Thaung	BL3			40.00
2	Edwards Garage	SL2	2.50		97.50	1	D. Davidson	BL5			21.00
8	Cash Sales	NL2		7.50		9	A.T. Office Supplies	BL4		100.00	
9	C.Jones	SL5			12.50	12	Cash	¢			290.00
12	Bank	¢		290.00		14	Wages	NL8		240.00	
15	J.B.C. Roofing	SL7		110.00		14	Petty Cash	PCB3		50.00	
16	Cash Sales	NL2		20.00		20	M. Bandura	BL6		30.00	
24	Eliot Transport	SL8	5.00		200.00	22	L. Cleaves	BL12	4.87		190.00
24	Morgan & Baldwyn	SL1			42.50	22	Van den Burgh	BL7			200.00
30	Cash	¢			7.50	30	Interest and bank charges				20.00
						30	Bank	¢		7.50	
						30	Balance	c/d		50.00	1,349.00
			7.50	477.50	2,110.00				4.87	477.50	2,110.00

Fig. 15. Examples of cash book entries concerning money received, and a payment by cheque.

12   The cash book

What is the cash book?

The cash book is where we record the firm's cash and cheque transactions. In it we record all the payments coming in and all the payments going out. Like the four day books it is a book of prime entry: it is the first place we record a transaction. However, unlike the day books, it is also a book of account, i.e. part of the ledger. The cash book and petty cash book are the only ones with this dual status.

The cashier is responsible for writing cheques to pay bills, banking money received and for drawing funds for petty cash. Most people are familiar with the process of writing cheques, banking funds and drawing cash from banks so no treatment of this will be given here. Similarly most people understand what payments by standing order and direct debit mean. What they may not be familiar with, however is receiving and making payments by electronic means, e.g. BACS and CHAPS transfers. Both are electronic forms of funds transfer for which a form has to be completed at the bank branch. BACS takes around four working days to reach the recipient, but CHAPS payments are usually received same day.

The advantages of making payments by BACS or CHAPS include:

- No need to write individual cheques.
- The payments are more secure, as they are not physically handled in any form.

The advantages of receiving payments in this way, include:

- The funds are available immediately the instruction is received by recipient's bank branch, as no clearance time is needed.
- They are less time-consuming as the need to visit the bank to pay in a cheque is eliminated.
- No bank paying-in slip has to be filled in.
- The payments are more secure as the funds are not physically handled.

Recording cash and bank transactions

The cash book is where we first record the details of cash and banking transactions. This includes all cash or cheques received from such customers as Mr Jones or JBC Roofing (see opposite) or indeed from anyone else, and all cash or cheques paid out to suppliers or to anyone else (disbursements). Banks debit firms directly for their services – they don't send out invoices for payment of interest and bank charges. The firm must record details of these amounts in the cash book as soon as it knows them, for example from the bank statement which shows them.

Source documents

To write up the cash book we need:

- Cheque book stubs (counterfoils) and paying-in book stubs (counterfoils) for all transactions which involve the bank account.

- Any bank advice slips, bank statements or other information received from the bank from time to time. This might for example include a letter advising that a customer's cheque has been returned unpaid by their bank owing to lack of funds, or information on standing orders, direct debits or bank charges and so on: anything that tells us about any payments going out from, or receipts coming into, the firm's account.

- Cash purchase invoices, receipts for cash paid out, and copies of receipts given for cash paid in.

- Any payment advice slips which arrived with cheques or cash received: these will show for example whether an early settlement discount has been claimed.

Entering debits and credits

All the cash and cheques we receive are entered on the left-hand side of the cash book (debits). All the cheques we write, and cash we pay are entered on the right-hand side (credits).

CASH BOOK

Dr.									Cr.
Date	Particulars	Fo.	Cash	Bank	Date	Particulars	Fo.	Cash	Bank
200X					200X				
Mar 1	Balance	b/d		1,500.00	Mar 28	S. Jones	BL6		48.60
19	Cash sales	NL4	81.00		31	Salaries	NL9		600.00
31	Bank	¢	303.16		31	Cash	¢		303.16
					31	Wages	NL14	384.16	
					31	Balance	c/d	0.00	548.24
			384.16	1,500.00				384.16	1,500.00
Apl 1	Balance	b/d	0.00	548.24					

Fig. 16. Entering details of cash and bank transactions
into the cash book.

13 The cash book: money paid in

Cash book entry step by step

1. Turn to your first receipt counterfoil for the period you are handling (day, week, month). Record, in the first column of the cash book on the far left the date of the transaction. To help keep the page neat and uncluttered, just enter the year once at the top of all the entries for that year. Do the same for the start of each new month.

2. Write the payer's name in the second column (cash sales in the example opposite).

3. The third column is for the folio reference which you will enter later. Leave it blank at this stage.

4. In the fourth column (not used in example) enter the amount of any early settlement discount.

5. In the fifth column (cash) enter the amount of cash received, £81.00.

6. Now turn to your paying-in book counterfoils and do exactly the same – except for one small difference: enter the amounts in the sixth (bank) column this time. Enter in the first (date) column the date of the bank lodgement as shown on the front of the counterfoil. The date written in ink by the payer-in (the cashier) might be different from the bank branch stamp on the counterfoil; the paying-in book might have been written up the day before the lodgment, and lodged in a nightsafe at the bank after the close of business, to be paid in properly the next day. Where there is a difference, you should use the date shown on the bank's stamp.

7. Turn the counterfoil for the period over and look on its reverse side. Each counterfoil represents a payment into the bank of a sum of money in cash and/or cheques; it should bear the names of people from whom the cheques have been received (the drawers). Enter in the second column of the cash book (name column) the first name from this list.

8. Again, the third column is for the folio reference, which you will enter later. Leave it blank for now.

9. Enter in the fourth column (discounts) the details of any discount allowed.

10. Enter in the sixth column the actual amount of the cheque.

11. Repeat steps 6 to 10 for all the cheques in the list.

12. Now enter the cash paid in to the bank, if any.

13. Write the word 'cash' in the second column (since it is the cashier who is paying it in).

14. Enter amount in the sixth column (bank column).

CASH BOOK OF A. FRAZER

Dr.   Cr.

Date 200X	Particulars	Fo.	Discount	Cash	Bank	Date 200X	Particulars	Fo.	Discount	Cash	Bank
Aug1	Balance	b/d		50.00		Aug 1	Balance	b/d			1,100.00
2	Edwards Garage	SL60	0.72		27.88	30	Wages	NL8			800.00
12	Razi & Thaung	SL9	10.07		392.43	30	A.T. Office				
20	Morgan & Baldwyn	SL11			560.63		Suppls	BL5	5.01		195.50
						30	F. Evans	BL6			258.00
31	Balance	c/d			1,372.56	31	Balance	c/d		50.00	
			10.79	50.00	2,353.50				5.01	50.00	2,353.50
Sept 1	Balance	b/d		50.00		Sep 1	Balance	b/d			1,372.56

Fig. 17. A. Frazer's cash book.

Notes

The balance of A. Frazer's cash as at 1st August 200X was £50.00 and there was a bank overdraft of £1,100. On 2nd August a cheque was received from Edwards' Garage for £27.88 in full settlement of its bill of £28.60. On checking, it is found that discount has been properly deducted. On the 12th a cheque was received from Razi and Thaung for £392.43 in full settlement of their a/c in the sum of £402.50, after properly deducting 2½% discount for settlement within 7 days. On the 20th a cheque was received from Morgan and Baldwyn in the sum of £560.63 in full settlement of a/c in the sum of £575.00, after deducting 2½% discount for payment within 7 days. On checking it is found that the cheque is dated 14 days after the invoice date. On the 30th £800.00 cash was drawn for wages, a cheque for £195.50 was paid to A. T. Office Supplies after deducting 2½% for payment within 28 days and a cheque for £258 was paid to F. Evans.

Write up his cash book for the month. (Worked answer below.)

1. No discount has been entered for Morgan and Baldwyn as they were not eligible for the discount they claimed. Only £560.63 would, therefore, be deducted from their ledger account and they would remain indebted to the firm for the remaining £14.37.

2. If the cheque for £195.50 takes into account a 2½% discount then the discount figure will be £5.01, since if £195.50 = 97.5% then 1% =

$$\frac{£195.50}{97.5}$$

    = £2.00½ and 100% = £2.00½ × 100 = £200.50, of which 2½% = £5.01

3. It has been regarded as unnecessary to debit the £800 drawn from the bank to cash since it went straight out again in wages; the debit entry has, thus, been made directly to wages account.

14   The cash book: money paid out

Posting to the credit page

Now we need to do our first piece of double entry bookkeeping. Since the bank has been debited with the money the cashier paid in, the cashier must be credited with the same amount. Otherwise, the cashier will appear to remain indebted for a sum he/she no longer has.

Step by step

1. Enter the date of the paying-in slip in the date column of the right hand (credit page) of the cash book.

2. In the second (name) column, enter the word 'bank', since it is the bank which is taking the money from the cashier.

3. In the fifth (cash) column, enter the amount of the payment. You have now given the cashier credit for that amount – and so you should! They no longer have it: they have given it to the bank.

4. Now let's do the other credit side entries. Take the first of the receipt vouchers for cash paid out for the period (day, week, month). Enter the date (taken from the receipt voucher) in the appropriate column of the right hand page (see step 1 on the previous page).

5. In the second column enter the name of the person to whom the cash was paid.

6. Discount details probably won't be relevant here; such discounts arise from early settlement of credit accounts, usually by cheque rather than by cash. If any such account was settled in cash, the cashier would know about it: they would have been the one to arrange payment. In such cases enter the details in the fourth (discount) column.

7. In the fifth column enter the amount of cash paid out.

8. Turn to the first cheque book counterfoil for the period. In the first column of the right hand (credit) page, enter the cheque date.

9. In the second column enter the name of the payee (the person to whom the cheque is payable).

10. In the fourth column enter details of any discount received. You will find this from the copy of the payment advice slip outwards.

11. In the sixth (bank) column, enter the amount of the cheque.

12. When required, total both the debit and credit columns for both cash and bank. Enter balancing items, so that both sides add up to the same figure, narrating them 'balance c/d'.

13. Bring down the balancing items on the opposite sides as the opening balances for the next period, narrating them 'balance b/d'.

BANK RECONCILIATION
as at 30 June 200X

Balance as per cashbook (in favour)		910.00
Add customer account		
paid directly into the bank:		
Watson		180.00
		1,090.00
Deduct dishonoured cheque:		
Davies		50.00
		1,040.00
Deduct standing order paid but not yet		
recorded in cash book:		
Wilson & Smith		30.00
Updated balance as per cash book		1,010.00
Balance as per bank statement (in favour)		880.00
Deduct cheques drawn but not as yet		
presented for payment:		
Smith	30.00	
Jones	40.00	
Clarke	50.00	120.00
		760.00
Add lodgement 30 June not yet showing		
on bank statement		250.00
Balance as per cash book		1,010.00

Fig. 18. Example of a bank reconciliation.

15 Disagreeing with the bank

Cash book versus bank statement
Every cashier tries to keep the cash book as accurate and up to date as possible. Many receipts and many payments may have to be entered up each day. Then, at regular intervals, the firm receives bank statements from the bank – weekly, monthly or quarterly. Unfortunately, the balance shown on the cash book hardly ever agrees with the one shown on the bank statement! There can be various reasons for this.

Noting unpresented cheques
When you get the bank statement and compare the balance with that shown in your cash book, you'll see that some cheques you drew have not yet been presented to the bank for payment: they simply don't appear on the bank statement at all, as yet. The cashier enters cheque transactions within a day or two of handling the cheques; but it could be days or even weeks before the payee presents them to your bank for payment.

Noting bank lodgements
Payments into the bank will have been recorded in the cash book, but if they haven't yet been recorded by the bank they won't appear on the bank statement. This could happen, for example, if a bank statement was sent out between the time the cashier lodged the bankings in the night safe and the time he/she actually paid them in over the counter.

Automatic payments
Payments by direct debit or standing order may have been omitted by the cashier, but they will still appear on the bank statement.

Bank charges and interest
A cashier may know nothing about these until the bank statement arrives, containing the details.

Returned cheques
A customer's cheque may have been returned unpaid – 'bounced' in popular jargon. The cash book will show the money having been received, but the bank won't have received funds for the cheque; so the statement will show a contra entry.

Errors
The cashier could simply have made an error. Bank errors can happen, but they are rare.

BANK RECONCILIATION AS AT (*date...*)

	£ p	
Balance as per cash book	320.00	(in favour)
Add customer's account		
paid by telephone banking (M. Bandura)	40.00	
	360.00	(in favour)
Deduct dishonoured cheque (D. Davidson)	10.00	
	350.00	(in favour)
Deduct bank charges	50.00	
Updated balance as per cash book	300.00	(in favour)
Balance as per bank statement	500.00	(in favour)
Deduct cheque drawn but not yet		
presented for payment: S. Jones	200.00	
Balance as per cash book	300.00	(in favour)

Fig. 19. Worked example of a bank reconciliation statement.

On comparing A. Frazer's bank balance as per bank statement with his bank balance as per cash book, it is found that the former shows £500 in favour while the latter shows £320 in favour. In looking for the reasons we find that a cheque drawn by D. Davidson in favour of the firm in the sum of £10.00 has been dishonoured, a cheque drawn by the firm in favour of S. Jones for £200 has not yet been presented by his bank for payment, bank charges have been made in the sum of £50 and a customer's (M. Bandura's) bill of £40.00 has been paid via telephone banking and the cashier was not aware of this. Figure 19 shows how we would write up a Bank Reconciliation Statement.

16 The bank reconciliation

If a discrepancy arose from just one source it would be easy enough to deal with, but usually there are several discrepancies, some distorting the credit side and some distorting the debit side, and liable to cause confusion.

To remove this confusion, and explain the discrepancies, the cashier draws up a bank reconciliation statement. The cashier, after all, is responsible for the firm's money, so if the bank statement disagrees with the cash book balance, he/she must clearly show the reason why.

There are three ways of reconciling the two accounts:

1. Reconcile cash book to bank statement: starting with the closing cash book balance, and check through step by step towards the bank balance, explaining the discrepancies as we go.

2. Reconcile the bank statement to the cash book: the opposite process (see Figure 19).

3. Correct all the errors and omissions on both the cashier's part and the bank's part, showing how we did it, until we end up with the same balance from both viewpoints. (See Figures 18 and 20.)

The third way is usually the best since it is easier to understand. We'll see how to write up a bank reconciliation statement, step by step, on the following pages.

What you need
- the cash book

- the bank statements for the period (week, month, quarter).

Remember, a page of figures can be bewildering to your reader, who may not understand bookkeeping as well as you, or have the time or patience to make sense of muddled words and figures. Simplicity and clarity should be your goal. Head all your cash columns £ and p to avoid having to write these symbols against every single entry. Likewise, when writing dates record the month once only, followed by the individual days. Put a clear heading against the left of each line of your figures. You will probably need two cash columns, one for sub-totalling particular types of transactions. For example, if there are three unpresented cheques you would add their values in a left hand column, and place the subtotal in a main right hand column.

```
                    BANK RECONCILIATION AS AT (date...)


                                                    £    p
Balance as per cash book                       780.00 (overdrawn)
Add dishonoured cheque: D. Davidson             10.00
                                               790.00 (overdrawn)



Add bank charges                                50.00
                                               840.00 (overdrawn)



Deduct customer's account
  paid by telephone banking: M. Bandura         40.00
Updated balance as per cash book               800.00 (overdrawn)


Balance as per bank statement                  600.00 (overdrawn)



Add cheque drawn but not yet
  presented for payment: S. Jones              200.00
Balance as per cash book                       800.00 (overdrawn)
```

Fig. 20. Suppose the same circumstances as in the worked example on page 34 were true except that the balance as per bank statement was £600 overdrawn and the balance as per cash book was £780 overdrawn. This figure shows what the bank reconciliation would look like.

Bank reconciliation step by step

1. Compare the balances of the bank statement and the cash book as at the end of the accounting period you are checking. If they disagree then a bank reconciliation will be needed. Proceed as follows.

2. Can you see on the statement any standing orders (STOs), direct debits (DDRs) or bank charges? These items may not have been recorded in your cashbook as yet. Also, are there any returned ('bounced') cheques? If there are, they will appear as consecutive entries, or at least close together, identical but appearing on opposite sides (Dr and Cr) and will be annotated '₵', 'Contra Entry', or 'Returned Cheque'.

3. Take a sheet of A4 paper and write 'Balance as per cash book'. Place the actual figure next to it on the right hand side of the page. State whether it is 'in favour' or 'overdrawn' (see example overleaf). It is important to use a term such as 'in favour' rather than 'in credit', since 'in credit' is ambiguous here. An 'in credit' bank balance means you are 'in the black', but an 'in credit' balance in the cashbook means you are 'in the red'. The terms 'in favour' and 'overdrawn' overcome this ambiguity, since they mean the same from both viewpoints, the firm's and the bank's.

4. List all the omissions on the cashier's part, in groups, e.g. listing STOs first, then DDRs, then bank charges, etc. Write your additions and deductions as you go to show what difference it would have made to the bank statement if such errors or omissions had not occurred. If you arrive at a figure that is equal to the bank statement balance then the job of reconciliation is done. Write against your final figure 'Corrected balance as per cashbook'. If this does not happen then proceed to reconcile the bank statement to the cashbook as follows.

BANK RECONCILIATION
as at 30 June 200X

Balance as per bank statement (in favour)			880.00
Deduct cheques drawn but not as yet presented for payment:			
	Smith	30.00	
	Jones	40.00	
	Clarke	50.00	
			120.00
			760.00
Add lodgement 30 June not yet showing on bank statement:			250.00
			1,010.00
Deduct customer account paid directly into the bank:			
	Watson		180.00
			830.00
Add dishonoured cheque:			
	Davies		50.00
			880.00
Add standing order paid but not yet recorded in cash book:			
	Wilson and Smith		30.00
Balance as per cash book			910.00

BANK RECONCILIATION
as at 30 June 200X

Balance as per cash book (in favour)			910.00
Add cheques drawn but not as yet presented for payment:			
	Smith	30.00	
	Jones	40.00	
	Clarke	50.00	
			120.00
			1,030.00
Deduct dishonoured cheque:			
	Davies		50.00
			980.00
Deduct lodgement 30 June not yet showing on bank statement:			250.00
			730.00
Deduct standing order paid but not yet recorded in cash book:			
	Wilson and Smith		30.00
			700.00
Add customer account paid directly into the bank:			
	Watson		180.00
Balance as per bank statement (in favour)			880.00

Fig. 21. The bank reconciliation method advised has been chosen for its simplicity and clarity. Above are worked examples of the two alternatives referred to on page 35; use them only if specifically requested by an examiner or employer.

5. Check off each payment listed in the cash book against the bank statement. Tick each one in pencil in the cash book and on the bank statement as you go. As you will see, items on the credit side of your cash book appear on the debit side of the bank statement and vice versa. This is because the same account is seen from two opposite viewpoints: the cash book from the firm's and the bank statement from the bank's.

6. Record next on your sheet the words 'Balance as per bank statement' ('in favour' or 'overdrawn', as appropriate) and place the actual figure next to it, on the right hand side of the page. Then list all the errors and omissions on the bank's part, in groups, e.g. listing unpresented cheques first, and then any unshown lodgements. Write your additions and deductions as you go to show what difference it would have made to the bank statement if such errors or omissions had not occurred.

7. When you have listed all the errors and omissions, if you have done it correctly, the two balances should now match. If so, write against your latest figure 'Balance as per cash book' ('in favour' or 'overdrawn' as appropriate).

Updating the cash book

The items in the first part of the reconciliation statement, i.e. the one that starts with balance as per cash book, represent items that the cashier had not previously known about. Now that they are known about the cashier can update the cash book by making the necessary entries.

Take the worked example in Fig. 19. Suppose the cashbook of A. Frazer and Co., balanced off for the month, appeared as shown in Fig. 22a. The balance as per cash book shows £320 in favour, while the balance as per bank statement shows £500 in favour. The reconciliation statement shown in Fig. 19 explains the differences. We can update the cash book by making the entries listed in the second part of the reconciliation, as this shows the entries that belong in but have not yet been made in the cash book. This is demonstrated in Fig. 22b.

So much for updating the accounts in accordance with the first part of the reconciliation statement, but what about the second part, the one that starts with the balance as per bank statement? Don't worry about that part. It would only update the bank statement and that is merely a copy from an account that is not ours to update. It is the bank's. We don't include the bank statement balance at all in the accounts. Even in the balance sheet the cash figure comes from the balance as per cash book. In any case, by the time the next statement arrives the figures missing from the current one will have been included.

CASHBOOK

200X		Cash	Bank Dr £		200X		Cash	Bank Cr £
Jun 1	Balance b/d		300.00		Jun 1	I. Bodlavich		80.00
	L. Gregory		410.00			F. Khan		120.00
	D. Davidson		10.00		Jun 26	S. Jones		200.00
						Balance c/d		320.00
			720.00					720.00
	Balance b/d		320.00					

Fig. 22a. The cashbook before updating.

CASHBOOK

200X		Cash	Bank Dr £		200X		Cash	Bank Cr £
Jun 1	Balance b/d		300.00		Jun 1	I. Bodlavich		80.00
	L. Gregory		410.00			F. Khan		120.00
	D. Davidson		10.00		Jun 26	S. Jones		200.00
	M. Bandura	£	40.00			D. Davidson	£	10.00
						Bank charges		50.00
						Balance c/d		300.00
			760.00					760.00
	Balance b/d		300.00					

The updates after the bank reconciliation

Fig. 22b. The cashbook after updating.

40

16 The bank reconcilation—cont.

You have now crossed from single entry bookkeeping into double entry accounting since the cash book bridges a gap between these two, being both a book of prime entry and part of the double entry system. In most accounts offices the keeping of the cash book is a specialised job. It is the task of the cashier, a position of considerable responsibility and attracting a higher salary than that of a day book clerk. For those of you already working in an accounts office, mastering this section could soon gain you promotion and pay rises.

PETTY CASH BOOK

Dr Receipts	Fo.	Date	Cr Details	Rec	Total	Motor exp.	Travlg	Postage	Statnry	Cleaning
		200X								
50.00	CB5	May 1	Cash							
		1	Petrol	5/1	10.00	10.00				
		2	Fares	5/2	3.20		3.20			
		5	Petrol	5/3	8.00	8.00				
		8	Postage	5/4	9.00			9.00		
		17	Stationery	5/5	1.30				1.30	
		22	Fares	5/6	1.40		1.40			
		25	Fares	5/7	1.40		1.40			
		26	Petrol	5/8	7.00	7.00				
		31	Cleaning	5/9	4.00					4.00
		31	Fares	5/10	1.40		1.40			
		31	Postage	5/11	1.80			1.80		
					48.50	25.00	7.40	10.80	1.30	4.00
						NL8	NL9	NL15	NL17	NL18
48.50	CB6	31	Cash							
		31	Balance c/d		50.00					
98.50					98.50					
50.00		Jun 1	Balance b/d							

Fig. 23. Example of a completed petty cash book page.

SMITHS GARAGES, NORTH CIRCULAR ROAD, NEWTON
Tel: Newton 0798

Date: *9/10/0X*

To: *A, T. Office Supplies*

.... £ *1.60*

Received with thanks. *H. Green*

Fig. 24. Example of a simple cash purchase invoice, showing the supplier, goods or services supplied, date, and payment.

17   The petty cash book

The petty cash float

The petty cashier looks after a small float such as £50 or £100 in notes and coins. It is used to pay for miscellaneous small office expenses such as staff travel and hotel accommodation, window cleaning, or small office items needed quickly. The petty cashier keeps account of all such transactions in the petty cash book.

Using the imprest system

From time to time the cashier will reimburse the petty cashier for the amount he/she has spent on the firm's behalf: the float is replenished to the original amount. This is called an **imprest system**, and the original amount of the float e.g. £50 is called the **imprest amount**.

Without a petty cash book, cash expenditure on lots of very small items would mean making entries in the ledger, for each item of expense. But by using the petty cash book, such items can be analysed into useful columns which can be totalled up monthly, and just these totals – not all the details – posted to the ledger.

Keeping the petty cash secure

The petty cashier is personally responsible for the petty cash, so he/she should:

- keep it locked away

- limit the number of people who have access, preferably to one person

- reconcile cash to records regularly (petty cash vouchers + receipts + cash = imprest value).

A helpful analysis

Even if the firm is small, and the cashier keeps the petty cash book themself, it is still a very useful means of analysing and totalling office expenditure. Otherwise all such expenditure would have to be entered in the cash book and later posted individually to the ledger. The cash book, remember, has an analysis facility for double entry bookkeeping. The analysis columns of the petty cash book act as a book of prime entry for the expenses in which the petty cashier becomes involved. From here they are later posted to the expense accounts in the ledger.

Dual status of the petty cash book

The petty cash book, like the cash book, usually has a dual status: it is both a book of prime entry and part of the ledger. However, some firms treat it purely as a book of prime entry, to record transactions involving notes and coins. They then write up a 'petty cash account' in their general ledger. Here, however, we will treat it as part of the ledger. Unless told otherwise, you should do the same.

Like the other books of prime entry, such as the day books, the petty cash book usually has a few helpful analysis columns. But since it is also part of the ledger, it also needs to have both debit and credit columns.

Receipts	Fo.	Date	Details	Rec. no.	Total	Stnry	Trav. exp.	Tel.	Cleang.
		200X							
50.00	CB1	Jan 1	Bank						
		6	Stationery	1/01	1.50	1.50			
		17	Trvlg exp.	1/02	2.00		2.00		
		26	Telephone	1/03	0.50			0.50	
		28	Wndw clnr	1/04	8.00				8.00
					12.00	1.50	2.00	0.50	8.00
12.00	CB1	31				NL4	NL6	NL8	NL9
		31	Balance c/d		50.00				
62.00					62.00				
50.00		Feb 1	Balance b/d						

Fig. 25.

1. Suppose A. Frazer has only just started up in business and intends to use an imprest system for his petty cash transactions. (The firm's estimated turnover is below the VAT threshold so it does not intend to register as taxable. There is, therefore, no need to account for VAT in the petty cash book.) The transactions during its first month are as follows. Write up his petty cash book for the month.

Jan 1   Received cheque from cashier £50
    6   Paid for staples and glue £1.50
  17   Paid travelling expenses £2.00
  26   Refunded phone-call expenses 50p
  28   Paid window cleaner £8.00
  31   Received cheque from cashier to replenish the fund to the imprest amount of £50.00

2. A. Frazer is a Taxable firm for VAT purposes; this means that the VAT aspects of its transactions have to be recorded in its books. Suppose the firm's Petty Cash transactions for the month of December 200X are as follows. Write up his petty cash book for the month, using the imprest system. Assume, for the purpose of this exercise, that there is currently only one VAT rate in operation and that is 20%.

Opening balance £100.00, Dec 10 paid travelling expenses £20.00, Dec 15 refunded petrol expenses £10.00 and paid cleaner £16.00, Dec 21 bought parcel tape £1.85, Dec 31 received cheque from cashier to replenish the fund to the imprest figure of £100.00.

Receipts fo.		Date	Details	Rec. no.	Total	VAT	Trvlg. exp.	Motor exp.	Wages	Stnry.
		200X								
100.00		Dec 1	Balance b/d							
		10	Trv. exp	12/01	20.00		20.00			
		15	Petrol	12/02	10.00	1.66		9.10		
			Cleaner	12/03	16.00				16.00	
		21	Prcl tape	12/04	1.85	0.30				1.69
					47.85	1.96	20.00	9.10	16.00	1.69
47.85	CB15	31	Balance c/d		100.00	NL11	NL6	NL7	NL5	NL9
147.85					147.85					
		200X								
100.00		Jan 1	Balance c/d							

Fig. 26.

What you need
- the petty cash book

- all the cash purchase invoices for the period.

Preparation: numbering and dating
Sort all your cash purchase invoices (receipts) into date order, and number them. (The numbers already printed on them won't do: they are cash sales invoice numbers of the firms that issued them and no uniformity between them can be expected.) You need to give them consecutive numbers from your own numbering system, so that you can file them chronologically for each period. Many firms keep a list of such numbers for this purpose. Others give them a two part number made up of the month number (e.g. 3 for March) and a number from a consecutive list for that month.

Value Added Tax (VAT)
The VAT may not be shown as a separate item on cash purchase invoices for small amounts. If not, the petty cashier will need to calculate the VAT content, if any, of each invoice total (see page 179). HM Revenue and Customs publish details of current VAT applications and rates, but a little experience will save the petty cashier having to check this every time. To find the VAT content at 20% just multiply the gross figure by 0.1667 and if the VAT rate is 5% multiply the gross figure by 0.0476 instead.

Opening a new petty cashbook
When starting a new petty cash system (i.e. opening a new petty cash book) a sum of money will be entrusted as a float to the petty cashier, let's say £50.00. He/she immediately enters this on the debit (left) side, because he/she now 'owes' the cashier that amount.

PETTY CASH BOOK

Receipts	Fo.	Date	No.	Details	Rec	Total	VAT 20%	Trav. exp.	Stnry	Motor exp.	Post
100.00	CB6	200X Feb 1		Cash							
			1	Fares	2/1	5.00		5.00			
			2	Envelopes	2/2	7.00	1.16		5.96		
			4	Petrol	2/3	8.00	1.33			6.81	
			7	Petrol	2/4	9.00	1.50			7.66	
			16	Postage	2/5	6.00					5.11
			18	Fares	2/6	3.00		3.00			
			19	Fares	2/7	3.00		3.00			
			25	Petrol	2/8	7.00	1.16			5.96	
			26	Postage	2/9	4.50					4.50
			27	Staples	2/10	2.00	0.33		1.70		
			28	String	2/11	3.50	0.58		2.98		
						58.00	6.06	11.00	10.64	20.43	9.61
							NL8	NL6	NL14	NL11	NL9
58.00	CB7		31	Cash							
			31	Balance c/d		100.00					
158.00						158.00					
100.00		Mar 1		Balance b/d							

Fig. 27. Example of a completed page in a petty cash book.

46

18   How to write up the petty cash book—cont.

Step by step

1. Enter in the third column the date that the fund or float was received.

2. Write in the fourth ('particulars') column the word 'cash' or 'bank' as appropriate, depending on whether the float came from the cashier by cash, or from the bank by cheque.

3. Write the imprest amount in the first column (debit cash column). Unless the system is being started from scratch, this stage will have been completed previously. The procedure for all other entries will start from step 4 below.

4. Record from each cash invoice the date, purchase invoice number, purpose of expenditure, gross and net invoice total and VAT, as shown on the page opposite. Enter the net total directly into a suitable analysis column.

5. Whenever necessary (end of period, end of page) total up the two main columns. The cashier should reimburse the petty cash fund for what has been spent, to restore the fund to its original imprest figure. Then balance the two columns, just like any other ledger account: entering a balancing item (the difference between the two totals) to make each side add up to the same amount. That balancing item should be annotated 'balance c/d' (carried down). The counterpart of that balancing item should then be recorded after the totals as the *opening* figure for the *next* period and annotated 'balance b/d' (brought down).

6. Next, total up each analysis column and the VAT column and cross check with the gross invoice total column, to make sure there are no mistakes.

Entering the folio references
Enter folio references for the debit side in the folio column, e.g. CB (cash book)7. Enter those relating to the credit side at the foot of their respective column totals: it is only the *totals* that will be posted to the ledger, e.g. travelling expenses, folio reference NL6 (Nominal Ledger item 6) in the example opposite.

THE JOURNAL

Date	Particulars	Fo.	Dr.	Cr.
200X				
Feb 20	Morgan and Baldwyn	SL15	25.00	
	Sales	NL1		25.00
	To correct error of original entry			
21	Drawings	PL3	70.00	
	Purchases	NL6		70.00
	To record goods taken from stock for private use			
22	Sundries:			
	Motor van 2	NL39	8,000.00	
	Edwards Garage	BL16		8,000.00
	Asset disposal A/C	NL40	3,350.00	
	Motor van 1	NL10		3,350.00
	Edwards Garage	BL16	2,000.00	
	Asset disposal A/C	NL40		2,000.00
	Profit and loss A/C	NL41	1,350.00	
	Asset disposal A/C	NL40		1,350.00
	Edwards Garage	BL16	6,000.00	
	Bank	CB18		6,000.00
	To record the details of the purchase by cheque of a motorvan with part exchange on old motor van.			

Fig. 28. Example of a complete page of journal entry. Note: You would normally expect provision for depreciation account to also feature in such a combination entry as this, but here it does not in the interests of simplicity.

19 The journal

A general purpose record

A book of prime entry, the journal is simply a place for making the first record of any transaction for which no other prime entry book is suitable. It has debit and credit columns, but they are simpler than those of the cash book and petty cash book. The journal itself is not part of the accounts, merely one of the sources from which the accounts are written up later on.

Examples of journal entries

Here are some examples of transactions you would need the journal to record:

- opening figures of a new business (e.g. list of assets)
- bad debts
- depreciation (e.g. of vehicles or equipment)
- purchase and sales of fixed assets (e.g. vehicles or plant)
- correction of errors
- goods taken for private use (as against for sale)
- ledger transfer needed if a book debt were sold.

Information needed for an entry

When entering a transaction into the journal, you need to record these aspects of it:

- date
- accounts affected
- folio references
- amounts (debit and credit)
- reason.

Write a brief explanation against each entry. Separate each new entry from the one above by ruling a horizontal line right across the page (see Figure 28).

Sometimes it is a good idea to make combination double entries, i.e. where there is more than one debit entry per credit entry, or vice versa. This would be appropriate when journalising 'opening figures', which include various assets and liabilities, together with the capital figure to which they relate. A group of entries are recorded on the opposite page with the prefix 'Sundries', which all relate to trading in an old motor van for a new one.

On the next page we will see how to write up the journal step by step.

THE JOURNAL

Date	Particulars	Fo.	Dr.	Cr.
200X				
May 28	L. Cleese	SL6	60.00	
	L. Cleaves	SL10		60.00
	To correct error			
	of commission			
30	Profit and loss A/C	NL30	85.00	
	F. Evans	SL8		85.00
	To write off bad debt			

Fig. 29. Journalising an item in the sales ledger.

1. Journalise the following:
On 28 May 200X it is discovered that L. Cleaves' a/c in the sales ledger has wrongly been debited with the sum of £60. Such sum should have been debited to L. Cleese's a/c instead. Two days later, F. Evans, a debtor of the firm, is declared bankrupt and the firm expects no ultimate settlement of his a/c in the sum of £85.00.

2. Using the following information, calculate the capital, journalise the opening figures and post them to the ledger for A. Frazer, a retail stationer, who started business on 1 April 200X. Cash at bank £1,450.00, cash in hand £50.00, office equipment £1,500.00, land and buildings £54,000, fixtures and fittings £4,000.00, a motor van £3,000.00 and stock £2,000.

THE JOURNAL

Date	Particulars	Fo.	Dr.	Cr.
200X				
	Sundries			
Apr 1	Land and buildings	NL1	54,000.00	
	Fixtures and fittings	NL2	4,000.00	
	Office equipment	NL3	1,500.00	
	Motor van	NL4	3,000.00	
	Stock	NL5	2,000.00	
	Cash at bank	CB1	1,450.00	
	Cash in hand	CB1	50.00	
	Capital	NL6		66,000.00
	To record opening figures			

Fig. 30. Journalising the opening figures.

Using miscellaneous source documents

There are no routine source documents for this job, as there are for example for the purchase day book (purchase invoices) or for the cash book (cheque counterfoils etc). The journal is a miscellany, and its sources will be miscellaneous. They may be documented by nothing more than a rough note, if indeed they are documented at all. For example, the sales manager may pass a memo to the journal clerk saying that a customer has gone into liquidation, so that its debt to the firm will have to be written off. Similarly a roughly pencilled note from the accountant, saying what depreciation should apply to an asset, may be your only source document for an entry.

Writing up the journal step by step

1.   Enter the date in column one (the date column).

2.   Enter the names of the ledger accounts which will be affected by this entry, e.g. Motor van account, or Profit and loss account, as in example 1 opposite. Indent the credit entry (usually the second entry). The folio column gives the 'address' of the account in question in the ledger, for example NL (nominal ledger), CB (cash book), PCB (petty cash book) and SL (sales ledger).

3.   Record the amounts against each ledger account name. Note: these last two steps provide the posting instructions for the ledger clerk. Many debit entries may have a common credit entry, as with opening figures. If so, prefix them with the word 'sundries'.

4.   Explain, briefly but precisely, your reason for the entry, e.g. 'To write off bad debt' or 'To record opening figures'.

5.   When you have finished, underline the entry right across the page.

Filing source documents

When the day books have been written up the source documents should be filed. Bank statements are filed chronologically, purchase invoices alphabetically or numerically (if the latter there is an important caveat). It must be on the basis of a number you allocate, rather than the supplier's invoice number. Sales invoices are numbered by one of the following methods:

*   they are pre-printed with consecutive numbers;

*   the invoice clerk obtains consecutive numbers from a log book;

*   they are given numbers consisting of the year, month and consecutive number of issue in that month in the form of yy/mm/ consecutive number as and when they are produced.

POSTAGE BOOK

Dr.	Date 200X	Particulars	Cr. £ p
92.00	Jan 1	Balance b/d	
	1	Edwards	20
	1	Bandura	26
	1	Jones	26
	1	Northern Electricity	1.30
	1	J.B.C. Roofing	20
	1	Evans	20
	4	Eliot Transport	26
	4	Morgan and Baldwin	26
	5	Entwhistle	2.60
	9	Davidson	26
	10	A.T. Office Supplies	20
	15	Baker	26
	25	Cleaves	26
	25	Gange	26
	25	Entwhistle	26
	28	Keele Engineering	20
	29	Razi and Thaung	2.60
	29	Eliot Transport	20
	29	Inko	20
	30	Kahn and Kahn	26
	31	Keele Engineering	1.30
	31	Evans	20
	31	Jones	20
	31	Baker	20
	31	Edwards	20
12.60	31	$20 \times 36p + 20 \times 27p$	
	31	Balance b/d	92.00
104.60			104.60
92.00	Feb 1	Balance c/d	

Fig. 31. Example of a postage book page.

21 The postage book

This book is like the petty cash book, in that it is a subsidiary account book. It gives a useful record of a fund entrusted to an employee, in this case the postage clerk. This person may have several other junior jobs to do within the office, such as reception/telephonist.

The postage book works much like the petty cash book, except that there is no VAT to deal with, and no analysis columns. It, too, is run on an imprest system, whereby the fund is topped up from time to time to its original level (the imprest amount).

One big difference, however, is that the fund is not kept as notes and coins: cash received by the postage clerk is used immediately to buy postage stamps. The fund exists in the form of stamps, not cash.

It differs even more from the petty cash book, and indeed from any of the other books, because it is not even a book of prime entry, providing sources for ledger posting. So it is really on the edges of the accounting system. The real source of postage data for the ledger is the cash book: this records cash paid into the postage fund.

Nevertheless, it is a useful financial record for the firm. It provides details of a current asset (even if small) in the form of postage stamps; it is the only source document from which this detail can be gleaned. The postage book also provides a record of the financial relationship between the postage clerk and the firm.

You can buy books specifically designed for this purpose, though any general notebook with cash columns can be ruled up to do the job.

Writing up the postage book step by step
You will need:

- the receipt slips for stamps purchased (supplied by the Post Office);

- the stamped letters and/or parcels to be sent out.

Suppose the imprest amount was £92.00.

1. Record the date in the date column, with year/month to start.

2. Record the combined value of any stamps purchased, from the receipt slips, in the first (debit cash) column. In the third ('particulars') column record the breakdown of the stamps purchased, e.g. 20 × 36p and 20 × 27p as in the example opposite.

3. List the addressees' names shown on the envelopes or parcels, in the third column ('particulars'), recording against each in the fourth (credit cash) column the value of the stamps affixed.

4. When desired, the cashier can be asked to replenish the fund to the original imprest amount of £92.00. At such times the two columns should be totalled, treating the imprest figure as the balancing item.

SALES DAY BOOK

Date	Supplier	Inv. no.	Net. inv value	Stationery	Books
200X					
Feb 4	S. Jones	2/1	200.00	200.00	

CB10

CASH BOOK

Date 200X	Particulars	Fo.	Discount	Cash	Bank	Date 200X	Particulars	Fo.	Discount	Cash	Bank
Feb 1	Balance	b/d			9,000.00	Feb 1	Petty cash	PC15			50.00
28	S.Jones	SL17	10.00		190.00	28	Balance	c/d			9,140.00
			10.00		9,190.00						9,190.00
Mar 1	Balance	b/d			9,140.00						

P15

PETTY CASH BOOK

Receipts	Fo.	Date	Details	Rec	Total Exp.	Motor Exp.	Trvlng
		200X					
50.00	CB10	Feb 1	Cash				
		1	Petrol	5/1	10.00	10.00	
		28	Balance c/d		40.00		
50.00					50.00	10.00	
40.00		Mar 1	Balance b/d			NL9	

JOURNAL

Date	Particulars	Fo.	Dr.	Cr.
200X				
Feb 21	Drawings	PL3	70.00	
	Purchases	NL6		70.00
	To record goods taken for private use			

Fig. 32. Examples of entries in books of prime entry to be posted to the ledger (see page 58).

22 The ledger

The firm's official record

The ledger is the 'official' record of a firm's accounts. We sometimes speak of the general ledger, the bought ledger, sales ledger and cash book separately – as if they were separate 'ledgers'. But to an accountant the ledger is a single unit, even if it is made up of physically separate books. The ledger is really a 'system' rather than a book. Whatever form it takes – books or computer disks, etc – 'the ledger' means the master record of all the firm's financial affairs.

Divisions of the ledger

We have already discovered two parts of the ledger – the cash book and the petty cash book – which also happen to be books of prime entry. The only difference in the ruling between that and the other divisions we will now deal with is that the latter are simpler. The cash book has three cash columns on each side; the other divisions of the ledger have only one. (However where ledger posting is done on a computer the format involves three columns, a debit and credit column and a running balance column. This is because the running balance can easily be calculated electronically – it doesn't call on the time and effort of the bookkeeper. In manual systems, working out such running balances is considered a waste of time.)

The other ledger divisions are:

* the general ledger (often called the nominal ledger)

* the personal ledger, subdivided into bought ledger (or purchase ledger) and sales ledger (or debtors ledger)

* a private ledger is sometimes kept, in which capital items are posted, for example proprietor's drawings. It is sometimes kept away from staff because the proprietor considers such information confidential.

The nominal and personal ledger

In the nominal ledger the impersonal aspects of transactions are posted, for example purchases, sales figures, wages, stationery and asset purchases. In the personal ledger the personal side of each transaction is posted, i.e. the credit to suppliers' accounts when the firm has purchased something, and the debit to customers' accounts when the firm has sold something.

Fig. 33. The ledger.

Different accounts within the ledger

Each part of the ledger contains a number of different accounts – one for each expense item, revenue asset or liability, as they will appear in the final accounts. For example, there will be an account for purchases, an account for sales, an account for wages, and a separate account for each asset such as Motor car 1 account, Motor car 2 account or Printing machine account, and so on.

A variety of forms

Though the ruling of each type of book is reasonably standard, both the ledger and books of prime entry are found in a variety of forms. Indeed, they don't have to be 'books' at all. They can be sheets of analysis paper in a loose leaf binder, or written into a computer program so that the rulings appear on a VDU screen. Entries are then made via the keyboard rather than with pen and paper.

In a loose leaf ledger system these divisions (sales, purchases, nominal, etc.) may take the form of cardboard page dividers. If bound books are used, each division may be a physically separate bound book. The personal ledger (purchase ledger/sales ledger) will contain a separate account for each supplier and customer. The arrangement of accounts in each division is flexible.

Post only from books of prime entry

Nothing should ever be posted into the ledger except from the books of prime entry.

Never, for example, post information into the ledger directly from such things as invoices, bank statements, cheque counterfoils, petty cash receipt slips and so on. These are source documents for the books of prime entry.

Recording each transaction twice

We have already seen how each transaction in double entry bookkeeping has two aspects – a debit and a credit. So each transaction has to be recorded in two separate places, on the debit side and on the credit side. It follows that at any moment in time the total number of debit entries must exactly equal the total of credit entries (unless a mistake has been made). In a small office, one ledger clerk will probably handle all the divisions (except perhaps the cash book). In a large firm there may be a separate bought ledger clerk, sales ledger clerk, and so on.

SALES LEDGER

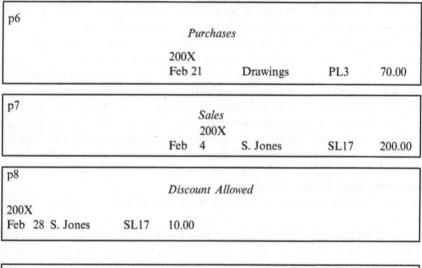

p17

S. Jones

					200X			
Feb	4	Sales	NL7	200.00	Feb	28 Bank	CB10	190.00
						28 Discount allowed	NL8	10.00
				235.00				200.00

NOMINAL LEDGER

p6

Purchases

200X
Feb 21   Drawings   PL3   70.00

p7

Sales
200X
Feb 4   S. Jones   SL17   200.00

p8

Discount Allowed

200X
Feb 28 S. Jones   SL17   10.00

p9

Motor Expenses

200X
Feb 1   Petty cash   PC15   10.00

PRIVATE LEDGER

p3

Drawings

200X
Feb 21 Purchases NL6   70.00

Fig. 34. Postings to the ledger from the prime entries on page 54.

23 Posting to the ledger from the day books

What you will need
- The ledger in all its parts – all the books or sheets that make up the complete ledger or at least the part you are concerned with, e.g. the purchase ledger.

- All the books of prime entry, or those you are concerned with, e.g. the purchase day book.

Posting from the purchase day book to the ledger
1. Turn to the start of the entries in the purchase day book as yet unposted to the ledger. Your first job is to post each purchase invoice (gross) to the credit of the supplier concerned, in their personal ledger account. The personal ledger should have an index of supplier's names, telling you on what page in the ledger you will find their account. (If no account exists, you will need to open one. Just head a new page with the supplier's name, and remember to list it in the index.)

2. In the first (date) column, write the date of entry.

3. Write the name of the account to which the other side of the transaction will be posted, in column 2 ('particulars').

4. In the fourth (cash) column record the gross value, in other words including VAT, of the transaction.

5. Now make the dual aspect of these postings: post the column totals for the net amount (i.e. net goods value) and VAT, to the debit of purchases and VAT accounts respectively. The procedure is the same as for posting the personal side of the transaction, following steps 1 to 4.

Posting from the purchase returns day book to the ledger
This is the reverse of posting from the purchase day book. This time you debit personal accounts in the bought ledger, and credit the VAT account and a purchase returns account in the nominal ledger.

Posting from the sales day book
This is just like posting from the purchase day book, except that you debit personal accounts in the sales ledger, and credit the VAT account and a sales account in the nominal ledger.

Posting from the sales returns day book
This is the reverse of posting from the sales day book: you credit personal accounts in the sales ledger, and debit the VAT account and a sales account in the nominal ledger.

Dr.				A. T. Office Supplies			Cr.
200X				200X			
				May 1	Balance	c/d	380.00
				26	Purchases	NL9	620.00
May	28	Bank	CB17	380.00			
	31	Balance	c/d	620.00			
				1,000.00			1,000.00
				Jun 1	Balance	b/d	620.00

Fig. 35. Postings to the purchase ledger.

1. Postings to the purchase ledger

Suppose that, as at the last day of April 200X, A. Frazer owed A. T. Office Supplies the sum of £380.00. On the 26 May the firm purchased further goods from A. T. Office Supplies for £620. On 28 May the firm paid its April statement by cheque. This is what the ledger postings would look like (*and remember, they have to be recorded in the books of prime entry first*).

2. Postings to the sales ledger

Suppose that K. Gange is a customer of A. Frazer, and at the close of last month (January 200X) his a/c balance stood at £2,100.00. Suppose that on 4 February Gange returned goods to the value of £100.00. On 6 February Gange purchased a further £1,000 worth of goods. On 12 February he paid his January a/c, after deducting the returned goods and a 2½% agreed discount for payment within 14 days. Gange then purchased a further £980.00 worth of goods on 18 February and then £220.00 worth of goods on 26 February. This is what the ledger postings would look like:

Dr.					K. Gange			Cr.
200X					200X			
Feb	1	Balance	b/d	2,100.00	Feb 4	Sales returns	NL19	100.00
	6	Sales	NL18	1,000.00				
					12	Bank	CB6	1,950.00
	18	Sales	NL18	980.00	12	Discount allowed	NL22	50.00
	26	Sales	NL18	220.00	28	Balance	c/d	2,200.00
				4,300.00				4,300.00
Mar	1	Balance	b/d	2,200.00				

Fig. 36. Postings to the sales ledger.

60

24 Posting to the ledger from the cash book

The cash book entries are, by their very nature, one side of the double entry. All you have to do now is to make the other side of the entry:

Step by step

1. Every time you post in the cash book, make an opposite posting to the relevant personal account in the bought or sales ledger as appropriate. The narration against each of these postings will be 'cash' (if the payment was in the cash column of the cash book) or 'bank' (if it was in the bank column). Now you have to post any discounts from the discounts column. Remember, although the cash book is part of the ledger, this column does not have such status; it is a single entry element sitting inside a ledger division, while not exactly being part of it. So the postings from the discounts column must be twofold, just as for any other prime entry source.

2. Post the discounts to the correct personal accounts, making sure they are to the opposite sides to the ones on which they appear in the cash book.

3. Post the column totals to the other side of the 'Discount allowed' or 'Discount received' accounts in the nominal ledger as applicable, to complete your dual posting. Use the name of the account to which the dual posting has gone for this purpose in all ledger posting.

Posting from the petty cash book

The petty cash book may, or may not, be treated as part of the double entry system. If it is, as with the cash book, its entries will themselves already contain one side of the ledger posting; you have only to make the other. However, this one aspect of the dual entry is itself split into various postings to nominal ledger accounts and this is why analysis columns have been used. Their individual totals, together with the VAT column total, provide the figures to be posted to the various accounts denoted by their column headings. The net invoice total column is not posted anywhere.

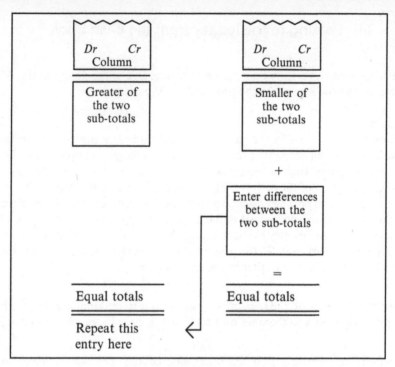

Fig. 37. Balancing the ledger.

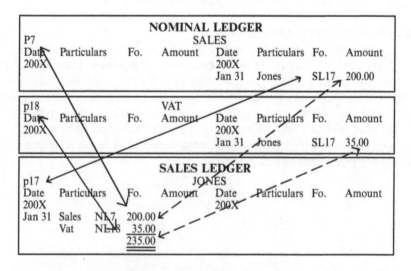

Fig. 38. In the above examples of Folio Column entry you will see that each posting is cross-referenced with another. Note also that the Sales Ledger should not be confused with the 'Sales A/C' in the Nominal Ledger.

25 Balancing the ledger

Periodically, usually once a month, the ledger accounts are balanced.

Balancing the ledger step by step

1. Total up both the debit and credit sides individually. Work out what figure you need to add to the lower figure to equalise the totals. Write against this figure: 'Balance c/d' (carried down).

2. Rule off. Enter the two equal totals and underline twice, to show they are final totals.

3. Enter the same figure on the opposite side below the total box: this will be the opening figure for the new period. Write against it: 'Balance b/d' (brought down). Note: you do not need to do this if the account only contains one item; in such a case no lines are drawn, and no dual totals entered.

The word 'balances' as used here simply means differences.

Completing the folio columns

We have now posted all our entries to the ledger. The next stage before extracting the trial balance is to complete the folio columns against each posting in the ledger. These columns show the ledger 'address' (ledger division and page number) where the counterpart posting has been made. Let's take as an example the folio column beside a posting in the sales account of the nominal ledger; we might perhaps write 'SL8' for the address of a personal account in the sales ledger, i.e. it is on sales ledger page 8. The name of the account in which the counterpart posting has been made is entered in the particulars column of each ledger account, so you could say that this extra cross-referencing is unnecessary. But if the ledger divisions are large, a note of the exact page number could save time. Also filling in the folio columns will help the detection of errors. If the trial balance fails, errors of omission can be spotted by the absence of a folio column posting, because it could mean that no counterpart posting has been made.

Important points to understand

Of all the things students find difficult to grasp in bookkeeping, two in particular stand out.

- The first is knowing whether to debit or credit an account. Which is the debit aspect and which the credit aspect of the transaction? What does it really mean to debit or credit an account?

- The second is knowing which nominal ledger accounts to post the impersonal side of transactions to, i.e.: knowing how to classify expenses and revenues into the right account names in the first place.

As for how to name the overhead expense accounts, with the exception of limited companies (whose final accounts formats are governed by law – see p.137) there is no hard and fast rule. Each firm and each accountancy practice will have defined its own range. The various worked examples of trial balances in this book will give you some idea. The range of asset and liability account names are a little easier to suggest, since the anticipated balance sheet effectively governs the range of accounts which will be set up. There is a good degree of consistency between firms in this respect and the range which tends to be used can be memorised in terms of 4 levels of classification.

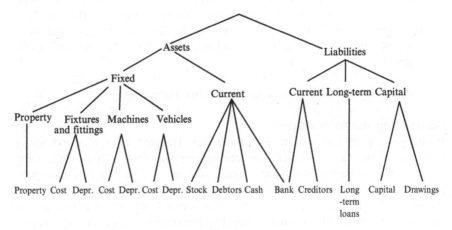

Fig. 39.

You will see that this classification gives us an eventual 15 asset/liability accounts, but there may be more, e.g.: if the firm has more than one machine there will be a separate asset and depreciation account for each of them.

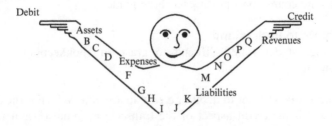

Fig. 40. Let Alf Direct You.

Once you have mastered how to categorise things into assets, expenses, liabilities and revenues then with this simple model in memory you cannot go wrong.

25 Balancing the ledger—cont.

Taking the first point first:

1. The word debit comes from the Latin verb *debere*, meaning 'to owe'; debit is the Latin for he or she owes. In business, a person owes to the proprietor that which was loaned or given to him by the proprietor.

2. The word credit comes from the Latin verb *credere*, meaning 'to trust' or 'to believe'. Our creditors believe in our integrity, and trust us to pay them for goods and services they supply; so they are willing to deliver them without asking for immediate payment.

Perhaps this will help a little in personal ledger accounts; but what about the impersonal accounts of the nominal ledger? Whenever an account has a debit balance it means that it 'owes' the proprietor the value of it (and vice versa for credit balances), as if that account were a person.

RED HOUSE CEMENT WORKS
Mulvy Island Road
Anytown, Anyshire.

Invoice No: 002345

	£ p
100 Bags of cement @ £10	1,000.00
Less 35% trade discount	350.00
	650.00
Plus VAT	130.00
Total	780.00

Terms strictly 30 days net

Fig. 41. Example of the way trade discount may be shown on
a wholesaler's invoice to a retailer.

S. JONES (WHOLESALE STATIONERY SUPPLIES) LTD
210 Barton High Street, Barton, Barshire

Invoice No: 00322   10/2/200X

10 reams of typing paper @ £7	70.00
plus VAT 20%	14.00
	84.00

2½% early settlement discount
Deduct £2.10 if paid within 14
days.

Customer
Razi & Thaung
15 Bolton Road
Finchester

Fig. 42. Example of the way early settlement discount may be shown on an
invoice.

26 Discounts

Trade discounts

A trade discount is one given by wholesalers to retailers, so that the retailers can make a profit on the price at which they sell goods to the public. Example:

Wholesale price of 5 litre tin of paint:	£4.00
Trade discount:	£2.00
Recommended retail price:	£6.00

In this example, the trade discount is $33^1/_3$ of the recommended retail price. However, trade discounts have no place as such in a firm's accounts. They are deducted before any entry is made in any of the books. As far as the wholesaler is concerned, his price to the retailer is simply £4.00, so £4.00 is the amount the wholesaler enters in his sales day book, and the amount the retailer enters in his purchase day book.

Early settlement discounts

These are discounts offered to persuade customers to settle their debts to the firm early. Typically, a discount of 2½% might be offered for payment within 14 days. But the details can vary. Example:

Building materials supplied:	£200.00
Less 2% discount for settlement within 7 days:	£ 4.00
	£196.00

Firms offer such discounts for two reasons: to speed up cash flow and to reduce the chance of debts becoming bad debts (the longer a debt remains outstanding, the more likely it is to become a bad debt).

If you write up your day books daily, you will not know whether or not an early settlement discount will be taken. You will know once the actual payment arrives. So you have to enter the figure without any deduction of discount into your sales day book. When the debt is paid, if a discount has been properly claimed, the credit entry to that customer's account will be 2½% less than the account shows. You then need to enter the discount as a credit to his account and a debit to 'discount allowed account' in the nominal ledger. This will make up the shortfall. It has the same effect as cash on the customer's personal account – and so it should: the offer shown on the invoice is like a 'money off voucher', and we would expect to treat that the same as cash.

Discounts and VAT

An early settlement discount is based on the invoice total (including VAT). Whether it is claimed or not will not alter the net sale value or the VAT amount which will be entered in the books.

CASH BOOK

Dr.   Cr.

Date 200X	Particulars	Fo.	Discount	Cash	Bank	Date 200X	Particulars	Fo.	Discount	Cash	Bank
Mar 1	Balance	b/d		50.00	1,000.00	Mar 13	Eliot		7.64		297.81
13	Morgan & Baldwyn	SL5	13.71		260.34						
20	Edwards' Garage	SL7			193.40						
28	A. Singh	SL9			640.39	31	Balance	c/d		50.00	1,796.32
			13.71	50.00	2,094.13				7.64	50.00	2,094.13
Aprl 1	Balance b/d			50.00	1,796.32						

PURCHASE LEDGER

BL3
Dr.   *Eliot Transport*   Cr.

200X				200X		
				Mar 1	Balance b/d	305.45
Mar 10	Bank	CB8	297.81			
10	Disc recd	NL19	7.64			
			305.45			305.45

SALES LEDGER

SL9
Dr.   *A. Singh*   Cr.

200X				200X			
Mar 1	Balance	b/d	674.10	Mar 1	Bank	CB8	640.39
				31	Balance	c/d	33.71
			674.10				674.10

SL18
Dr.   *Edwards Garage*   Cr.

200X				200X		
Mar 1	Balance	b/d	193.40	Mar 20	Bank	193.40

SL20

Dr.   *Morgan and Baldwin*   Cr.

200X				200X			
Mar 1	Balance	b/d	274.05	Mar 13	Bank	CB8	260.34
				13	Discount All	NL18	13.71
			274.05				274.05

NOMINAL LEDGER

NL18
Dr.   *Discounts Allowed*   Cr.

200X			200X
Mar 31	Debtors	13.71	

NL19
Dr.   *Discounts Received*   Cr.

200X		200X		
		Mar 31	Creditors	7.64

Fig. 43. Recording discounts in cash book and ledger.

Prime entry of discounts in the cash book

You make your prime entry of discounts in the cash book. But the column you use is unlike the other cash columns: it is not a ledger column, just a prime entry 'lodging place'. Entries in the discount column of the cash book, unlike entries in its other (ledger) columns, are not part of a dual posting; the dual posting is made in the 'discount allowed account' in the nominal ledger for the one part, and the personal customer account in the sales ledger for the other (or 'discounts received account' and supplier account, as the case may be). The postings to the discount accounts in the nominal ledger are, of course, column totals rather than individual items.

Entering early settlement discounts

Both the cashier and the ledger clerk will be involved in entering early settlement discounts. When the cheques are first received from customers or sent out to suppliers the cashier will check whether they have been properly claimed by reference to the time limit for early settlement discount and then enter the discounts in the cash book when he/she is entering the other payment details. For this step-by-step process please refer to pages 27 and 29.

At the end of each month the ledger clerk will make the dual postings to the ledger accounts for each item in the discount columns of the cash book.

Step by step

What you will need is the cash book, sales ledger, purchase ledger and nominal ledger.

1. One by one, post each item in the discounts received column to the debit of the named suppliers' purchase ledger accounts.

2. Post the column total for the month to the credit of discounts received account in the nominal ledger.

3. One by one, post each item in the discounts allowed column to the credit of the named customers' sales ledger accounts.

4. Post the column totals to the debit of discounts allowed account in the nominal ledger.

SALES LEDGER

Total Debtors Account

Dr.						Cr.
Balance	b/d	200.00	Cheques		150.00
Sales		300.00	Balance	c/d	350.00
		500.00			500.00

Fig. 44. An example of a total debtors acount.

PURCHASE LEDGER

Total Creditors Account

Dr.					Cr.
Cash paid to			Balance	b/d	2,000.00
suppliers		1,200.00	Purchases		2,200.00
Balance	c/d	3,000.00			
		4,200.00			4,200.00

Fig. 45. An example of a total creditors account.

SALES LEDGER
Sales Ledger Control Account

200X					200X				
Feb 1	Balance	b/d	15,000		Feb 28	Sales returns		200
28	Sales		10,000		28	Bank		11,100
					28	Discounts allowed		400
					28	Bad debts		300
					28	Balance	c/d	13,000
			25,000					25,000

Fig. 46. Example of a more complex sales ledger control account.

27   Control accounts

Useful summaries

A control account is a sort of trial balance for just one ledger division. You write the account at the back of the ledger division concerned. The main idea of control accounts is to subdivide the task of the main trial balance. They also provide useful summaries of data for more effective financial management. For example the boss might want an up-to-date figure for total debtors, to help monitor credit control in the firm. Control accounts are in fact sometimes called total accounts (for example, total creditors account).

Subdividing the work

In a small firm, where one bookkeeper posts all the ledgers, control accounts might be unnecessary. But the double entry system can be quickly expanded if necessary by using control accounts. Individual specialist bookkeepers, such as the bought ledger clerk or sales ledger clerk, could balance their own ledger division using a control total, i.e. a balancing item equal to the difference between all their own debit and credit balances. A head bookkeeper could then build up an overall trial balance just by taking the control account totals. In large firms today, control accounts are vital to the smooth running of the accounting system. Without them, reaching a trial balance would really be a difficult, time-consuming and messy business.

Control accounts are summaries of ledger balances in a division of the ledger. For example, purchase ledger control accounts contain the sum totals of all VAT inclusive purchases, payments to suppliers and discounts received.

The postings go on the same side as they do in the individual ledger accounts. However, to avoid a duplication on one side of the dual posting either the control accounts, or the individual ledger accounts must be left out of the double entry system. If the individual ledger accounts are treated as double entry then the control accounts are not, in which case they are known as memorandum accounts. If, however, the control accounts are treated as part of double entry system then the individual ledger accounts which they summarise are known as subsidiary ledger accounts and are not part of the double entry system.

Though they are most commonly used for the sales and purchase ledger divisions, control accounts can be used for any ledger divisions, e.g. cash or petty cash. Furthermore, the layout is the same and they are administered in the same way, so once you know how they are used for one type of account you know how they are used for others.

Advantages of using control accounts

The principal advantage of using control accounts is to reduce the need to deal with many sales, or purchase ledger balances to a single sales, or purchase ledger balance. This way interim and final accounts can be drawn up more quickly.

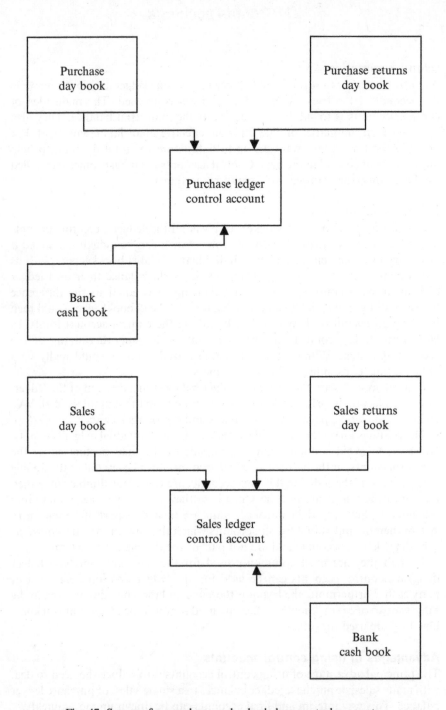

Fig. 47. Sources for purchase and sales ledger control accounts.

A second advantage is that the control account balances can be used as a check on the accuracy of individual ledger account postings, especially if the control accounts are posted by a different bookkeeper to the one who puts the individual sales and purchase ledger accounts. This is usually the case in large companies. It is unlikely that the same posting errors will be made by both clerks.

Thirdly, subdividing a ledger means errors are easier to find because each division is self-contained in double entry terms.

Fourthly, fraud is made more difficult. Illegal transfers of money are more likely to be noticed if a different clerk deals with each side of the dual postings.

Source documents for control accounts

The source documents you need for posting to control accounts are the books of prime entry. But you only need monthly (or other period) totals, not individual entries as with other postings. Each entry in the sales day book, for example, you post separately to a specific account in the sales ledger, but you only post the total of gross invoice values to the sales ledger control account.

The four day books for sales and purchases are well suited to control accounts; column totals are readily available. It may be a good idea to add a gross invoice total column if control accounts are going to be kept. The other day books are not quite so helpful in this respect, since they do not analyse totals of different classes. Take the cash book, for example. From here you take the total of payments to suppliers, but 'purchases' may be mixed up with 'expenses' such as drawings, wages, transfers to petty cash, and other types of payments, all of which must be totalled up for posting to control accounts. Still, while not being quite so easy as posting from the sales and purchase day books, it is not too difficult to use the cash book for control accounts.

Dr.		Sales Ledger Control						Cr.
200X				200X				
Sep 30	Balance b/d	20,263.60		Oct 31	Sales returns			500.00
Oct 31	Sales	24,630.70		31	Cheques			22,840.90
				31	Discount allowed			250.80
				31	Bad debts			420.50
				31	Balance	c/d		20,882.10
		44,894.30						44,894.30
Nov 1	Balance b/d	20,882.10						

Fig. 48. A. Frazer's sales ledger control account.

1. Suppose:
The balance of A. Frazer's sales ledger control account as at the end of September 200X was £20,263.60 Dr.

   Total sales for the month of October 200X were £24,630.70.
   Total payments received for the month were £22,840.90.
   Total discounts allowed for the month were £250.80.
   Total bad debts written off for the month were £420.50.
   Total sales returns were £500.00.

Write up the sales ledger control account for October 200X.

2. Suppose:
The balance of A. Frazer's purchase ledger control account as at 31 August 200X was £1,293.00 Cr.

   Total purchases during September 200X amounted to £18,950.
   Total payments to creditors were £9,800.00.
   Total discounts received were £250.

Write up the purchase ledger control account for the month of September 200X.

Dr.			Purchase Ledger Control					Cr.
200X				200X				
Sept 30	Cheques		9,800.00	Aug 31	Balance	b/d		1,293.00
30	Discount rec.		250.00	Sept 30	Purchases			18,950.00
30	Balance	c/d	10,193.00					
			20,243.00					20,243.00
				Oct 1	Balance	b/d		10,193.00

Fig. 49. A. Frazer's purchase ledger control account.

28 Preparing control accounts step by step

What you need
- the ledger (or those parts of it for which you want to operate control accounts)

- the relevant day books.

Step by step
1. Unless the control account is a new one, your opening balances will already be there. These are merely the closing balances for the previous month. If the control account is created at the start of a year, you can take your opening balances of assets and liabilities from the trial balance.

2. Take each of the four day books relating to sales and purchases. Post the monthly gross invoice (or credit note) totals to the sales or purchase ledger control account as the case may be. Post the totals to the same side as the individual postings were made, i.e. debit customers accounts for sales, and so on. Annotate each posting accordingly, for example 'sales', 'sales returns' and so on.

3. Take each of the other books of prime entry, and extract from them totals for all the classes of transaction that relate to the ledger divisions concerned. Post each of these in turn to the relevant control acounts. Again, the appropriate side is exactly the same you would use if you were posting the items individually. Annotate each posting accordingly, for example 'cash', 'bank' and so on.

4. Total up and balance each control account as you would any other ledger account.

Note on purchase and sales ledger control accounts
The purchase and sales ledger control accounts can be treated as part of the double entry system, but if they are the individual personal accounts in the purchase and sales ledgers must not be; they must simply be treated as an analysis. One or the other can be included in the double entry system – not both.

ARMSTRONG ENGINEERING
Trial balance as at 31 March 200X

Ledger balances

Sales		100,000
Fixtures and fittings	15,000	
Freehold premises	40,000	
Motor van	8,000	
Debtors	10,000	
Stock (opening)	10,000	
Cash at bank	10,000	
Cash in hand	50	
Capital		63,050
Bad debts	2,000	
Bad debts provision		2,000
Drawings	6,450	
Depreciation	2,350	
Provision for depreciation on motor van		1,600
Provision for depreciation on fixtures and fittings		750
Purchases	60,000	
Motor expenses	750	
Heat and light	800	
Wages	10,000	
Postage and stationery	550	
Repairs and renewals	250	
Creditors		12,000
Interest and banking charges	200	
Carriage	3,000	
Closing stock	9,000	9,000
	188,400	188,400
	(debit balances) =	*(credit balances)*

Fig. 50. A typical trial balance, listing all the debit and credit balances in the ledger.

29 The trial balance

A listing of ledger balances

The trial balance is unlike anything we have seen so far, but it is quite simple to understand and quite simple to do. It is just a listing of all the ledger balances at a particular moment in time. You list the balances in two columns – one for the debit balances and one for the credit balances. If all the ledger divisions have been correctly posted your two columns will balance. Remember, for every transaction there have been two postings, a debit and a credit, so the sum of all the debits should equal the sum of all the credits. See example opposite.

We always talk of 'extracting' a trial balance, or 'constructing' or 'drawing up' a trial balance.

Summary

The trial balance is:

- a way of checking the accuracy of all previous postings

- a source, in a useful summary form, for putting together the firm's final accounts later on.

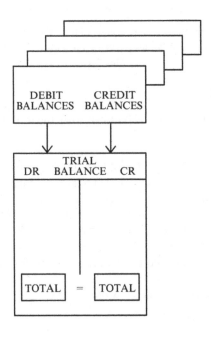

77

TRIAL BALANCE: A. FRAZER & CO

	Dr.	Cr.
Purchases	28,879.00	
Sales		48,133.00
Bank	981.00	
Cash	50.00	
Land and buildings	490,000.00	
Machinery	100,000.00	
Fixtures and fittings	60,000.00	
Motor vehicle	80,000.00	
Stock	3,600.00	
Debtors	2,010.00	
Creditors		3,190.00
Opening capital		178,199.00
Long-term, secured loan creditor		548,031.00
Heat and light	400.00	
Motoring expenses	1,480.00	
Insurance	240.00	
Wages	6,913.00	
Salaries	3,000.00	
	777,553.00	777,553.00

Fig. 51. Worked example of a trial balance. Note: there will be pence as well as pounds in a real life trial balance, but we have omitted them to keep things simple.

Suppose the ledger balances of A. Frazer for the month of August 200X were as follows:

Purchases, £28, 879.00 Dr, Sales £48,133.00 Cr, Bank £981.00 Dr, Cash £50.00 Dr, Land and buildings £490,000.00 Dr, Machinery £100,000 Dr, Motor vehicle £80,000.00 Dr, Fixtures and fittings £60,000 Dr, Stock £3,600.00 Dr, Debtors £2,010.00 Dr, Creditors £3,190.00 Cr, Opening capital £178,199 Cr, Long-term, secured loan creditor £548,031.00 Cr, Heat and light £400.00 Dr, Motoring expenses £1,480.00 Dr, Insurance £240.00 Dr, Wages £6,913.00 Dr, Salaries £3,000.00 Dr.

Construct a trial balance as at 31 August 200X.

30   How to extract a trial balance

What you need
- the ledger (including of course the cash book and petty cash book, which are both part of the ledger)

- a sheet of A4 paper.

Preparation
Make sure that all the folio columns have been entered in all the ledger accounts. Enter them now if necessary.

Extracting a trial balance step by step
1.   Head your blank sheet 'trial balance as at [date]'. Rule two cash columns down the right hand side. Head them, 'debit' and 'credit'.

2.   List the balances of every single ledger account, including the cash book and petty cash book. Put each one in the correct column of your trial balance (debit, or credit).

3.   Total up the two columns. If they balance, the job is done! If not, proceed as follows.

4.   Look for an error of complete omission of an account balance in the trial balance, or of one side of a posting in the ledger. You should spot this if you look for a figure equal to the error.

5.   If this fails, look for an error due to something being entered on the wrong side of the trial balance, or to both sides of a transaction being posted to the same side in the ledger. Divide the discrepancy in your trial balance by two, and look for a figure which matches this.

6.   If this fails, look for an error of transposition. Is the discrepancy divisible by nine? If so, there could well be such an error. If these methods all fail, the error could be in the totalling up, or in under- or overstating one side of a transaction, or a mixture of errors.

7.   Check through the ledger again to look for any folio column omissions.

8.   Check off each ledger balance against the trial balance. Have you recorded it on the correct side? Tick each in pencil as you go. If this does not solve the problem, proceed to step 9.

	Ledger balances		Adjustments		Trading profit and loss account		Balance Sheet	
	Dr	Cr	Dr	Cr	Dr	Cr	Dr	Cr
Purchases	32,087				32,087			
Sales		48,133				48,133		
Heat and light	400				400			
Motor expenses	1,480				1,480			
Insurance	240				240			
Wages	6,913				6,913			
Salaries	3,000				3,000			
Stock	3,600				3,600			
Closing stock P & L				4,000		4,000		
Closing stock B/S			4,000				4,000	
Cash	50						50	
Bank	981						981	
Land and buildings	490,000						490,000	
Machinery	96,000						96,000	
Fixtures and fittings	60,000						60,000	
Motor vehicles	80,000						80,000	
Debtors	2,010						2,010	
Creditors		3,190						3,190
Capital		178,199						178,199
Long-term creditor		547,239						547,239
	776,761	776,761	4,000	4,000	47,720	52,133	733,041	728,628
						47,720	728,628	
					4,413		4,413	

Fig. 52. Example of an extended trial balance

TRIAL BALANCE

trading, profit & loss account items			balance sheet items		
	Dr.	Cr.		Dr.	Cr.
Purchases	28,879.00		Cash	50.00	
Sales		48,133.00	Bank	981.00	
Heat and light	400.00		Land and buildings	490,000.00	
Motor expenses	1,480.00		Machinery	100,000.00	
Insurance	240.00		Fixtures and		
			fittings	60,000.00	
Wages	6,913.00		Motor vehicles	80,000.00	
Salaries	3,000.00		Debtors	2,010.00	
Stock	3,600.00		Creditors		3,190.00
			Capital		178,199.00
			Long-term		
			creditor		548,031.00
	44,512.00	48,133.00		733,041.00	729,420.00
				44,512.00	48,133.00
				777,553.00	777,553.00

Fig. 53. Example of a four column trial balance using the same figures as on page 78.

9. Re-check the addition of all your ledger columns, and balance each account. If this still doesn't solve the problem proceed to step 10.

10. Check that the values in the posting of both sides of each transaction are equal. Start at the first page of the ledger and work through to the end. Tick each in pencil as you go.

If you have carried out all the steps accurately, the trial balance will now balance. Note: a small error need not hold up the preparation of final accounts; you can post the error to a 'suspense account' to save time. When eventually the error is tracked down a 'statement of amended profit or loss' can be drawn up.

The four column trial balance
A variation of the trial balance described above is the four column version. This is simply one with two debit columns and two credit columns. In fact the page is most usefully split down the middle so that each side can have its own debit and credit columns. On one side you enter all the balances relating to the revenue accounts. On the other side you enter those which relate to the balance sheet. On

each side you total up the debit and credit columns separately to give either a debit or credit balance. If things are right the debit balance on one side will equal the credit balance on the other.

Sometimes these two types of trial balance are combined, side by side, with a balance of adjustments to make what is called an extended trial balance.

We could, if we wished, also show profit (or loss) on this too, since we debit profit and loss account, to close it, and credit capital account, to transfer the balance, at the end of the year.

31　The trial balance: errors

Errors revealed and errors not revealed
The trial balance will immediately show that there is an error if it does not balance. However, it will not guarantee that the posting is error free if it does. In other words, things cannot be right if it does not balance, but can still be wrong if it does! Furthermore, a failure to balance does not tell us where in the posting the error or errors exist. So while the trial balance performs something of an error-checking role, it is not a foolproof one.

Errors not revealed
1.　Errors of complete omission, where neither debit nor credit has been entered.

2.　Compensating errors, where errors of equal value cancel each other out.

3.　Errors of commision – posting to the wrong accounts, though to the correct sides of the correct ledger division.

4.　Errors of reverse posting: the debit entry of a transaction has been wrongly posted to the credit side, and vice versa. (See also page 171.)

5.　Errors of principle, for example posting of an asset to an expenses account.

Errors which will be revealed by a trial balance
1.　Errors arising from both parts of the double entry (debit/credit) being posted to the same side (e.g. debit).

2.　Errors of partial omission, for example, where only one side of a transaction was posted, such as the credit side but not the debit side, or vice versa.

3.　Errors in adding up.

4.　Errors of transposition, where digits have been accidentally reversed, for example 54 has been written as 45. See page 168 for how to identify this error.

5.　Errors due to under- or overstating one side of the transaction.

6.　Errors of original entry, for example when making a mistake while entering a sales invoice into the sales day book.

Electricity								
200X					200X			
Mar	1	Balance	b/d	2,100	Mar 31	Profit and loss		2,520
	31	Balance	c/d	420				
				2,520				2,520
					Apr 1	Balance	b/d	420

Fig. 54. Example of an accrual for electricity charges.

Insurance								
200X					200X			
Mar	31	Balance	b/d	230	Mar 31	Profit and loss		120
					31	Balance	c/d	110
				230				230
Apr	1	Balance	b/d	110				

Fig. 55. Example of prepayment of insurance.

1. Suppose A. Frazer's insurance premium of £1,200 is payable yearly in advance from 1 June, but its accounting year runs from 1 May. By the end of the accounting year only 11 months of the premium will have been used up, there will still be an asset of 1 month's prepaid premium to carry forward to the next year. This is how it will appear in the ledger:

Insurance							
200X				200X			
June 1	Bank		1,200	Apr 31	Profit and loss		1,100
					Prepayment	c/d	100
			1,200				1,200
Prepayment		b/d	100				

Fig. 56. Worked example of the posting of a prepayment.

2. Suppose that aggregate weekly wages of £1,500 are payable on a Friday and the end of the firm's acounting year falls on a Tuesday. There will be a liability for 3 days aggregated, unpaid wages to account for in the end of year accounts. This is how it will appear:

Wages A/C								
200X					200X			
Aug	31	Balance	b/d	77,100	Aug 31	Profit and loss a/c		78,000
	31	Accruals	c/d	900				
				78,000				78,000
					Sep 1	Accruals	b/d	900

Fig. 57. Worked example of the posting of an accrual.

Adjustments to accounts

Accruals and prepayments are adjustments we need to make to the accounts at the end of the year (or other management accounting period).

- Accruals are sometimes called accrued expenses, expense creditors or expenses owing. Accruals are a liability for expenses for goods or services already consumed, but not yet billed (invoiced).

- Prepayments are an asset of goods or services already paid for, but not yet completely used. Prepayments are, therefore, in a sense the opposite of accruals.

Example of accrued expenses

Suppose we are drawing up accounts for the year ended 31 March. We know there will be an electricity bill for the three months ended 30 April, a month after the end of our financial year. By 31 March, even though we haven't had the bill, we would already have used two months' worth of it, but as things stand the cost of this won't appear in our accounts because it is too soon to have received a source document (i.e. the invoice) from which to enter it. Still, electricity clearly was an expense during the period, so we have to 'accrue' a sensible proportion. For example:

Electricity account period	1 February to 30 April
Estimated charge	£630.00 (three month period)
Period falling within our accounts	1 February to 31 March (two months)

Charged accrued for period: $\dfrac{£630.00 \times 2 \text{ months}}{3 \text{ months}} = £420.00$

Wages and rent

Other items that often have to be accrued are wages and rent. The firm receives the benefit of work, and of premises, before it pays out wages and rent (assuming rents are payable in arrears; if rent is payable in advance we would need to treat it as a prepayment).

ACCRUALS

The balance c/d will be a debit one, but the ultimate effect on the expense account (the balance b/d) will be a credit entry.

PREPAYMENTS

The balance c/d will be a credit one, but the ultimate effect on the expense account (the balance b/d) will be a debit entry.

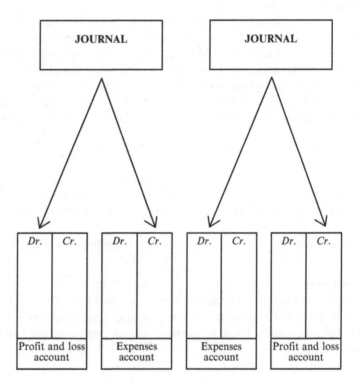

Fig. 58. Accruals and prepayments at a glance.

Example of prepayment

A prepayment arises, for example, where an insurance premium or professional subscription is paid annually in advance but only one or two month's benefit has been used by the end of the year. We must adjust the figures so that we don't charge the whole amount against profits for the year. Clearly, much of the benefit remains as an asset for use in the next year. Example, again assuming that our accounting period ends on 31 March:

Professional subscription for calendar year:	£100.00
Period falling within our accounts:	1 January to 31 March
Period falling into next accounting period	1 April to 31 December (9 months)
Prepaid for next year:	$£100.00 \times \dfrac{9}{12} = £75.00$

Carrying down accruals and prepayments

When these amounts have been calculated or assessed, you place them in the relevant ledger accounts as 'carried down' balances. In this way you increase or decrease the amount to be transferred to the profit and loss account for the year, depending on which side the posting is made. The resulting 'b/d' balances are listed in the balance sheet just like any other balance remaining on the nominal ledger at the end of the year. If they are credit balances (accruals) they are current liabilities. If they are debit balances (prepayments) they are assets.

```
┌─────────────────────────────────────────────────────────────┐
│                                                             │
│                  THE TRADING ACCOUNT                        │
│                                                             │
│   1  Sales                                                  │
│                                                             │
│   2  Purchases                                              │
│                                                             │
│   3  Opening stock                                          │
│                                                             │
│   4  Closing stock                                          │
│                                                             │
│   5  Carriage inwards (and any warehousing and packaging costs) │
│                                                             │
│                                                             │
│                                                             │
└─────────────────────────────────────────────────────────────┘
```

Fig. 59. Items listed in a trading account. Remember the mnemonic SPOCC.

```
┌─────────────────────────────────────────────────────────────┐
│                                                             │
│              TYPICAL PROFIT AND LOSS ACCOUNT ITEMS          │
│                                                             │
│   Wages and salaries                                        │
│                                                             │
│   Heat and light                                            │
│                                                             │
│   Rent and rates                                            │
│                                                             │
│   Motor expenses                                            │
│                                                             │
│   Bank charges                                              │
│                                                             │
│   Bad debts                                                 │
│                                                             │
│   Depreciation                                              │
│                                                             │
│   Insurance                                                 │
│                                                             │
│   Carriage outwards                                         │
│                                                             │
│   There can be many more; it just depends on the type of business. │
│                                                             │
└─────────────────────────────────────────────────────────────┘
```

Fig. 60. Items listed in a profit and loss account.

The trading account and profit and loss account

The revenue accounts are a pair of ledger accounts called the trading account and the profit and loss account. They are much like any other ledger account except that they are not ongoing (except for limited companies, dealt with later). Also, they are needed by more people outside the firm for example:

- HM Revenue and Customs to assess tax liability
- shareholders to see how the business is doing
- prospective purchasers to value the business
- prospective lenders to assess the risk of lending to the business, and its ability to pay interest.

But we adapt these accounts to a more easy-to-read version. Instead of two main columns we have only one (though we also use subsidiary columns for calculations). The two sides of the accounts are then represented in progressive stages of addition and subtraction. So the revenue accounts forwarded to interested parties don't look like ledger accounts at all.

The trading account

This shows the gross profit, and how it is worked out:
>   sales − cost of goods sold = gross profit

To work out the cost of goods sold (i.e. cost of sales):
>   purchases + opening stock + carriage inwards, packaging and warehouse costs − closing stock = cost of sales

When transferring the balances to the trading acount, deduct sales returns from sales, before posting in the trading account. After all, they are merely 'unsales' so to speak. The same goes for purchase returns: there is no place for any returns in the trading account.

Contribution to overheads

Gross profit is not the same things as net profit. Gross profit is first and foremost a contribution to overheads. It is only when they are paid for that any net profit may, or may not be available for shareholders.

The profit and loss account

The profit and loss account sets out the calculation of net profit like this:

>   gross profit + other income − expenses = net profit

We know that there must be two sides to every ledger posting: as you post each item in the revenue accounts, make an opposite side posting in the original ledger account from where your balance came. Against such postings just write 'trading account' or 'profit and loss' account. You are now closing down the revenue and expense ledger accounts, ready for a fresh start in the next accounting period.

TRADING ACCOUNT

Sales			100,000
Purchases		58,000	
Opening stock	12,000		
Closing stock	10,000	2,000	60,000
Gross profit			40,000

BALANCE SHEET (EXTRACT FROM)

Current assets	
Stock	10,000
Debtors	8,000
Cash at bank	2,000
Cash in hand	50
	20,050

Fig. 61. Stock appears three times in the final accounts. Closing stock appears twice (although it is conventional to only use the adjective 'closing' in the trading account to distinguish it from 'opening stock').

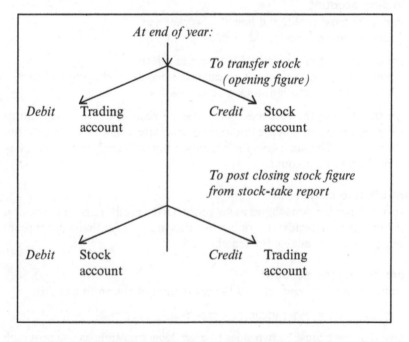

Fig. 62. What to do about stock at the end of the year.

34 Stock in the final accounts

Opening and closing stock

Stock is dealt with three times in the revenue accounts and balance sheet – once as opening stock and twice as closing stock. Suppose we started the year with £1,000 worth of stock; we purchased a further £10,000 of stock during the year, but had none left at the end of it. Altogether, it means that we have sold assets of £11,000 during the year. Purchases and opening stock must be the same kind of asset, since they were both finished goods on the shelf; otherwise we could not have sold them both and had nothing left to sell. Clearly, stock and purchases need to be treated in the same way in the final accounts.

This year's opening stock was, in fact, last year's closing stock. Throughout this year it was an asset, appearing on the debit side of the ledger. So this year's closing stock must also be carried forward to the next year as an asset; it too must stay on the ledger, just like all other assets at the end of the year. The only balances we must transfer out permanently to the revenue accounts are those for expenses and revenues (which of course are not assets).

Physical stocktake

Closing stock will not even be in the ledger until we have done a stocktake (a physical counting and valuation of the stock in hand). We must then post to the debit side of the stock account in the nominal ledger the actual asset value of stock remaining, and being carried forward into next year.

Why we need a counter-entry for stock

The counter-entry must be posted to the credit of the trading account. Why? Let us go back to our basic example. We posted opening stock as a debit in the trading account because we assumed it had all been sold, along with the purchases for that year. But what if we bought £12,000 worth but still had £2,000 worth left? We will need to make an entry to the opposite side for this. Closing stock is a credit posting in the trading account.

Another way to look at it is this: if we purchased £12,000 worth of stock but only sold £10,000, it would be as if we had purchased only £10,000 worth for sale during the year. The other £2,000 worth would be for sale in the next year. So we are right to deduct closing stock from purchases.

Remember, a credit posting in the final accounts can also be done as a subtraction from the debit column. You have to do this when converting the ledger format to vertical format (see page 101).

```
        TRADING ACCOUNT FOR A. FRAZER
           for year ended 31 March 200X
              £           £           £
Sales                                90,000
Less cost of sales:
  Purchases               50,000
  Opening stock  6,000
    Less closing stock  2,000      4,000    54,000
Gross profit                                36,000
```

Fig. 63. Worked example of revenue accounts.

1. From the following ledger balances draw up the trading account of A. Frazer for the year ended 31 March 200X.

Sales £90,000
Purchases £50,000
Stock (from ledger) £6,000
Stock (from final stock-take) £2,000

2. From the following ledger balances draw up the revenue accounts of A. T. Office Supplies for year ended 30 April 200X.

Sales   180,000
Purchases   100,000
Ledger balance for stock   6,000
Stock as per final stocktake   14,000
Heat and light   1,000
Motor expenses   1,500
Bank charges   500
Rent   3,000
Wages   37,000
Insurance   2,000

```
TRADING, PROFIT AND LOSS ACCOUNT FOR A.T. OFFICE SUPPLIES
              for the year ended 30 April 200X
                £           £           £
Sales                                180,000
Less cost of sales:
  Purchases              100,000
  Opening stock  6,000
    Less closing stock 14,000    (8,000)    92,000
Gross profit                                88,000

Wages                     37,000
Heat and light             1,000
Rent                       3,000
Motor expenses             1,500
Bank charges                 500
Insurance                  2,000            45,000
Net profit                                  43,000
```

Fig. 64. Further worked example of revenue accounts.

35 How to compile revenue accounts

What you will need
- the trial balance

- the ledger (all divisions)

- details of end of year adjustments to the accounts, such as depreciation, bad debts, closing stock

- the journal.

Adjustments before you start
You will need to adjust the trial balance for various end of year adjustments. Remember to enter all your adjustments into the trial balance twice, once on the debit side and once on the credit side. You can achieve the same effect by adding to and subtracting from the same side as, indeed, you would need to with accruals and prepayments. For a prepayment for example, you would debit 'prepayments' in the trial balance, and subtract the same amount from the debit balance of the expense account concerned, e.g. 'insurance'. Check that the trial balance still balances after you have adjusted it: there is no point in starting to put together your final accounts until it is correct.

Getting the right balance into the right accounts
It is a good idea to label each balance, to show where it will go in your final accounts. For example against 'sales' write 'T' 'for trading acccount'. Write 'P & L' beside 'rent & rates' to show that it is going into the profit and loss account. Write 'B' beside each asset account, to show you will be taking it into your balance sheet.

Items on the debit side of the trial balance are expenses or assets; those on the credit side are revenues or liabilities. In the revenue accounts we are only interested in revenues and expenses. How do we recognise them?

A revenue is an income; an expense is an outgoing. Neither has to be in cash. If you have more stock left at the end than you had at the beginning of the accounting period, that is just as much a revenue as a sales figure. Another way of putting it is to say that excesses of expenses over revenues are called losses. Expenses represent an outflow of funds within the period. They include such things as electricity, motor expenses, rents paid or payable, and discounts allowed. Items classed as revenues represent incomes within the same period. They include things like commissions, rents receivable, and discounts received.

A. FRAZER
TRADING PROFIT AND LOSS ACCOUNT
for year ended 31 March 200X

Stock as at 1 April 200X	10,000	Sales	100,000
Purchases	60,000	Stock as at	
Carriage inwards	3,000	31 March 200X	9,000
Gross profit c/d	36,000		
	109,000		109,000
		Gross profit b/d	36,000

Profit and loss account

Wages	6,000		
Motor expenses	2,000		
Heat and light	450		
Cleaning	· 1,500		
Depreciation	2,550		
Net profit c/d	23,500		
	36,000		36,000
		Net profit b/d to	
		capital account	23,500

Fig. 65. Trading profit and loss account in horizontal format in the ledger. This can now easily be transformed into the more useful vertical format shown below.

A. FRAZER
TRADING PROFIT AND LOSS ACCOUNT
for year ended 31 March 200X

Sales			100,000
Less purchases		60,000	
Carriage inwards		3,000	
Opening stock	10,000		
Less closing stock	9,000	1,000	64,000
Gross profit b/d			36,000
Less expenses			
Wages	6,000		
Motor expenses	2,000		
Heat and light	450		
Cleaning	1,500		
Depreciation	2,550		12,500
Net profit b/d to capital account			23,500

Fig. 66. Trading profit and loss account in vertical format.

36   Compiling revenue accounts step by step

Once you have labelled each item in the trial balance according to where it will go in the final accounts you can put together your revenue accounts as follows.

1. Write in the next available space in the 'particulars' column of the journal: 'sales'.

2. In the debit column, enter the balance of your sales account.

3. Beneath the last entry in the 'particulars' column, write: 'trading account' (indenting it slightly).

4. Enter the same figure in the credit cash column.

5. In the next space in the 'particulars' column, write: 'trading account'.

6. Enter in the debit/cash column the balance of your purchases account.

7. Write in the next space in the 'particulars' column (indenting slightly) the name of the account from which you are transferring (in this case 'purchases') and enter the value of purchases in the credit cash columns.

8. Repeat steps 5 to 8 for each of the other categories in the 'cost of sales' equation (see page 89).

9. When you have made all the entries relating to the trading account, write beneath them: 'To close revenue and expense accounts and transfer the balances to the trading account'.

10. Now do the same for any other income accounts (items other than 'trading income', e.g. rents). Debit the accounts concerned. Credit your profit and loss account.

11. Now do the same for each of the overhead expense accounts. Debit your profit and loss account and credit each account concerned.

12. When you have made all the entries for your profit and loss account, write underneath: 'To close expense accounts and transfer balances to profit and loss account.'

13. Now post to the ledger, including a trading, profit and loss account, exactly following the instructions you have just written in your journal. The trading, profit and loss account can be seen as two divisions of the same account, since they are written on the same page. The balance of the fomer is brought down to the latter, and marked: 'Gross profit b/d' (see opposite page, top).

14. Total up and balance all the ledger accounts concerned. This will mean closing all but the trading profit and loss account (except where an accrual or prepayment is present).

15. Mark the balance of profit and loss account: 'Net profit c/d to capital account'.

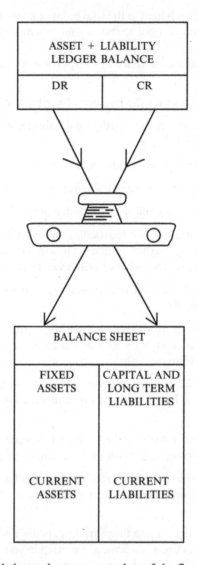

Fig. 67. The balance sheet as a snapshot of the financial affairs.

37   The balance sheet

A financial snapshot

We have already seen standard sorts of statement summarising particular aspects of the business. The bank reconciliation was an example. The balance sheet is another – but a much more important one. Unlike the trading, profit and loss account, the balance sheet is not an 'account' as such. Rather, it is a useful snapshot of the firm's financial situation at a fixed point in time. It sets out clearly all the firm's assets and liabilities, and shows how the resulting net assets are matched by the capital account.

The balance sheet always goes hand-in-hand with the trading, profit and loss account. We need it to show:

- where the net profit has gone (or how the net loss has been paid for)

- how any net profit has been added to the capital account

- how much has been taken out as 'drawings' and whether any of it has been used to buy new assets (stating what those assets are).

Management data

Accounting ratios can be worked out to help decision-making. For example the ratio of current assets/current liabilities shows how easily a firm can pay its debts as they become due (a ratio of 2/1 is often seen as acceptable in this respect). More will be said about these ratios later.

Five main components of the balance sheet

The balance sheet tells us about five main categories:

1. Fixed assets. These are assets the business intends to keep for a long time (at least for the year in question). They include things like premises, fixtures and fittings, machinery and motor vehicles. Fixed assets are not for using up in day to day production or trading (though a small part of their value is used up in wear and tear, and that is treated as an expense – 'depreciation'). Property should be valued at net realisable value or cost whichever is the lower.

2. Current assets. These are assets used up in day to day trading or production. They include such things as stock, debtors, cash at bank and cash in hand.

3. Current liabilities. These are amounts the business owes to creditors, and which usually have to be paid within the next accounting year. They include trade creditors, and bank overdraft.

A. FRAZER
BALANCE SHEET
as at 31 December 200X

	Cost	Less provision for depreciation	Net book value
Fixed assets			
Premises	40,000		40,000
Fixtures and fittings	15,000	750	14,250
Motor van	8,000	1,600	6,400
	63,000	2,350	60,650
Current assets			
Stock		9,000	
Debtors	10,000		
Less provision for doubtful debts	2,000	8,000	
Cash at bank		10,000	
Cash in hand		50	
		27,050	
Current liabilities			
Creditors		12,000	
Total net assets (or working capital)			
			15,050
			75,700
Financed by			
Capital as at 1 January 200X			63,150
Add profit for period			19,100
			82,250
Less drawings			6,550
			75,700

Fig. 68. Example of a balance sheet in vertical format.

A. FRAZER
BALANCE SHEET
as at 31 December 200X

Fixed assets			Capital	
Premises		40,000	Balance as at	
Fixture and fittings	15,000		1 January 200X	63,150
Less provision for depreciation	750	14,250	Add profit for year	19,100
				82,250
			Less drawings	6,550
				75,700
Motor van	8,000			
Less provision for depreciation	1,600	6,400		
		60,650		
Current assets				
Stock		9,000	Current liabilities	12,000
Debtors	10,000			
Less provision for bad debts	2,000	8,000		
Cash at bank		10,000		
Cash in hand		50		
		87,700		87,700

Fig. 69. Example of a balance sheet in horizontal format.

4.   Long-term liabilities. A business may also have financial obligations which do not have to be settled within the next accounting year. These include such things as long term loans, for example to buy plant, equipment, vehicles or property.

5.   Capital. This means the property of the owner of the business. He has invested his personal property in the business – cash, any other assets, and profits ploughed back. The business holds the value of all this for him in safe-keeping; it must deliver it up to him on cessation of the business, or earlier if he requires. Capital is, in a way, a liability to the business; but it's a rather different one from the other liabilities, which is why we don't include it with them.

Postings to capital account
There are four types of posting we may need to make to capital account in the ledger: opening capital, extra capital injections, drawings, and the addition of profit.

Terminology
'Capital' should not be confused with 'working capital', which is a very different thing (current assets − current liabilities). And do not confuse capital with capital expenditure, which just means expenditure on fixed assets rather than on expenses.

If the books have been written up correctly, the assets and liabilities must balance against capital in the balance sheet, to embody the equation we first saw on page 13:

$$\text{assets} - \text{liabilities} = \text{capital}$$

What you need
• The trial balance 'adjusted' or 'redrafted' after compilation of the trading, profit and loss account to show the stock figure and the profit or loss.

Preparation
Make sure that the balances listed on the trial balance that have already been used in the trading, profit and loss account are clearly ticked off. The remaining balances can then easily be spotted for use in compiling the balance sheet.

BALANCE SHEET OF A. FRAZER
as at 30 June 200X

Fixed assets			
Land and buildings			200,000
Fixtures and fittings		50,000	
Less provision for depreciation		12,000	38,000
Office machinery		100,000	
Less provisions for depreciation		15,000	85,000
Motor van		50,000	
Less provision for depreciation		30,000	20,000
			343,000
CURRENT ASSETS			
Stock		40,000	
Debtors	33,000		
Less provision for bad debts	1,000	32,000	
Cash at bank		3,950	
Cash in hand		50	
		76,000	
Less CURRENT LIABILITIES			
Creditors		35,000	
Working capital			41,000
			384,000
Represented by			
Opening capital			347,777
Less drawings			9,950
			337,827
Add profit			46,173
Closing capital			384,000

Fig. 70. Balance sheet of A. Frazer in vertical format.

From the following details construct a balance sheet as at 30 June 200X in vertical format for A. Frazer (answer above).

Land and buildings	200,000
Office machinery	100,000
Motor van	50,000
Fixture and fittings	50,000
Provision for depreciation on machinery	15,000
Provision for depreciation on motor van	30,000
Provision for depreciation on fixtures and fittings	12,000
Closing stock	40,000
Cash at bank	3,950
Cash in hand	50
Drawings	9,950
Debtors	33,000
Creditors	35,000
Bad debts provision	1,000
Capital	347,777
Net profit	46,173

38   Compiling a balance sheet step by step

1. Make a heading 'Balance Sheet of [firm] as at [date].

2. Make a sub-heading on the left, 'Fixed assets'.

3. Beneath this, in column three, write the value of any premises. Annotate it; on the left 'Land and buildings'.

4. In column two, list the balance of other fixed assets, in order of permanence. Annotate each one on the far left. Beneath each one record the provision for depreciation, annotating 'Less provision for depreciation'.

5. Subtract the depreciation from each asset and place the difference in column three.

6. Total up column three.

7. Now make a second sub-heading, 'Current assets'.

8. Beneath this, in the second cash column, write the balances of the short-life assets, in the order of permanence, annotating accordingly.

9. Total up these balances.

10. Make a third sub-heading on the left, 'Less current liabilities'.

11. Below that, list, in the first cash column, the creditors figure and the bank overdraft figure, if there is one.

12. Total up this column. Place the total in the second column beneath that for current assets. If there is only one item you can place it directly into the second column.

13. Now rule off this column and subtract the latter total from the former. Place the difference in the third column below the total for fixed assets, annotating it 'Working capital'. Add these two totals and rule off with a double line, annotating it 'Total net assets'.

14. Make a sub-heading below this, 'Represented by'.

15. Enter the opening capital in the third column, annotating it 'Opening capital'.

16. Enter the drawings balance, annotating it 'Less drawings'.

17. Rule off and deduct.

18. Enter the profit in column three, annotating it 'Add profit'.

19. Rule off and add. Underline the answer with double line and annotate it 'Closing capital'.

Horizontal and vertical formats
A balance sheet may be shown in horizontal or vertical format. Unless told otherwise, use the vertical format in exams and in practice.

```
                    ARMSTRONG ENGINEERING
                    MANUFACTURING ACCOUNT
                     as at 31 December 200X


Raw materials
  Opening stock                                      10,000
  Add purchases                                     102,000
                                                    112,000
  Less closing stock                                 12,000
Cost of raw materials consumed                      100,000
Manufacturing wages                                 200,000
Prime cost                                          300,000



Overhead costs

  Rent (½)                         10,000
  Rates (½)                         2,000
  Heat, light and power (³/₄)       8,000            20,000
                                                    320,000



Adjustment for work in progress

  Opening stock                    12,000
  Less closing stock               15,000          (3,000)
Cost of finished goods
Transferred to trading account                     317,000
```

Fig. 71. Simple example of a manufacturing account.

Part of the revenue accounts

Like the trading account, the manufacturing account is part of the revenue accounts. Its format is similar, but it has quite different components. It is used when we want to show the manufacturing costs involved in the production of goods. This final cost of production is transferred from the manufacturing account to the trading account. For a manufacturing firm this figure is the equivalent of purchases for a purely trading firm.

39 Manufacturing accounts

We need to show two important cost figures in the manufacturing account:

- **prime cost** – the sum of the costs of direct labour, direct materials and direct expenses; and

- **overheads** – the sum of all costs which cannot be directly related to output (e.g. factory rent).

Three stages of the production process are shown in a manufacturing account:

1. Raw materials consumed.

2. Adjustment for stocks of partly finished goods (work in progress).

3. Finished goods transferred to trading account.

The cost of raw material consumed is arrived at like this:

Opening stocks	600
Add purchases	200
	800
Less closing stocks	150
Cost of raw material consumed	650

The prime cost is found by adding the direct wages and direct expenses to cost of raw materials consumed.
Work in progress is calculated similarly:

Opening stocks	600
Less closing stocks	150
Work in progress adj.	450

Purchases do not come into this equation.
The end product of the manufacturing account is the value of the stock of finished goods (just as the gross profit is the end product of the trading account). This value is then transferred to the trading account, just as the trading account transfers its gross profit to the profit and loss account.

MANUFACTURING ACCOUNT OF ARMSTRONG ENGINEERING
for the year ended 31 October 200X

Stock of raw materials as at 1.11.200X		4,000
Add Purchases		40,000
		44,000
Less Stock of raw materials as at 31.10.200X		5,500
Cost of raw materials consumed		38,500
Add Direct labour		4,500
Prime cost		43,000
Factory overheads		1,600
		44,600
Add Work in progress as at 1.11.200X	8,000	
Less Work in progress as at 31.10.200X	9,500	(1,500)
Cost of finished goods transferred		
to trading account		43,100

Fig. 72. Worked example of a manufacturing account.

Suppose Armstrong Engineering is a manufacturer who at the end of the year to 31 October 200X has a stock of raw materials valued at £5,500 and work in progress valued at £9,500. The firm started the year with a stock of raw materials worth £4,000 and work in progress valued at £8,000. During the year it purchased a further £40,000's worth. The factory wages bill was £4,500 and the cost of power used solely in the factory was £1,600.

Figure 72 shows how you would write up its manufacturing account.

40 Compiling a manufacturing account step by step

1. Calculate the cost of raw materials consumed. Write the correct heading against each line of your calculation.

2. Add the figures for direct wages and direct expenses, annotating accordingly.

3. Annotate the total 'prime cost'.

4. In a subsidiary column, itemise the various overhead expenses. Note: it may be that only part (e.g. half) of a cost (e.g. rent) can be fairly attributed to the manufacturing process, the other part being more fairly attributed for example to sales. In such a case, only the first part should be itemised. Just mark it like this: 'Rent (½)'.

5. Total up this column. Place the total in the main cash column and total that column.

6. In the subsidiary column write your work in progress adjustment. Write the correct heading against each line of your calculation. Place the resultant figure in your main cash column and add or deduct it from your subtotal according to whether it is a positive or negative figure.

7. Write against the difference: 'Cost of finished goods transferred to trading account'.

	£	£
Cost		100,000
Less Estimated residual value		3,000
Amount to be depreciated over 5 years		
Provision for depreciation		
Yr 1 97,000 × 0.2 =	19,400	
Yr 2 97,000 × 0.2 =	19,400	
Yr 3 97,000 × 0.2 =	19,400	
Yr 4 97,000 × 0.2 =	19,400	
Yr 5 97,000 × 0.2 =	19,400	
	97,000	97,000

Fig. 73. Worked example of depreciation using the straight line method.

1. Suppose a lorry costing £100,000 had an estimated lifespan within the company of 5 years and an estimated residual value at the end of that period of £3,000.

Using the straight line method and a rate of 20% the effect would be as shown in Figure 73.

41 Depreciation: the straight line method

When assets drop in value

So far we have recorded figures, analysed them, summed and balanced them, and learned the standard ways of doing so. Now, with depreciation, we will also need to make calculations involving percentages.

Depreciation is the drop in value of an asset due to age, wear and tear. This drop in value is a drain on the firm's resources, and so we must put it in the accounts as an expense. We will need to write down the value of the asset in the books, to reflect its value more realistically. A company car, for example, loses value over time. So do plant, equipment and other assets. All have to be written down each year.

Methods of calculating depreciation

- straight line method

- diminishing (or reducing) balance method

- sum of the digits method

- machine hours method

- revaluation method

- depletion method

- sinking fund method

- sinking fund with endowment method.

Even this list is not exhaustive. But the first two are the most common.

The straight line method

This involves deducting a fixed percentage of the asset's initial book value, minus the estimated residual value, each year. The estimated residual value means the value at the end of its useful life within the business (which may be scrap value). The percentage deducted each year is usually 20% or $33^1/_3$% and reflects the estimated annual fall in the asset's value. Suppose the firm buys a motor van for £12,100; it expects it to get very heavy use during the first three years, after which it would only be worth £100 for scrap. Each year we would write it down by one third of its initial value minus the estimated residual value, i.e. £4,000 per year. On the other hand, suppose we buy a company car for £12,300; we expect it to get only average use and to be regularly serviced. We expect to sell it after five years for £4,800. In that case we would write down the difference of £7,500 by one fifth (20%) each year, i.e. £1,500 per year.

This method is useful where value falls more or less uniformly over the years of the asset's lifetime.

2. Suppose a machine cost £100,000 and it is estimated that at the end of 5 years it will be sold for £3,125. Suppose also that the greatest usage of the machine will be in the early years as will also the greatest costs, for since it is tailor-made for the firm's requirements its resale value is drastically reduced the moment it is installed. The appropriate rate of depreciation on the diminishing balance method will be between 2 and 3 times that for the straight line method, so an acceptable rate will be 50%. (See Figure 74.)

		£	£
Cost			100,000
Depreciation provision year	1	50,000	
	2	25,000	
	3	12,500	
	4	6,250	
	5	3,125	96,875
Residual value after 5 years			3,125

Fig. 74. Example of depreciation by the diminishing balance method.

42　Depreciation: the diminishing balance method

Diminishing balance method (or reducing balance method)

This method also applies a fixed percentage, but it applies it to the diminishing value of the asset each year – not to the initial value. It is used for assets which have a long life within the firm, and where the biggest drop in value comes in the early years, getting less as time goes on.

Suppose a lathe in an engineering workshop cost £40,000 to buy. In the first year it will fall in value much more than it ever will in later years. The guarantee may expire at the end of the first year. The bright smooth paint on the surface will be scratched and scarred; the difference between its appearance when new and its appearance a year later will be quite obvious. But the next year the change will seem less; who will notice a few more scratches on an already scarred surface? Nor will there be a great drop due to the guarantee expiring, for it will not have started out with one at the beginning of the second year. And so it will go on; the value of the asset will depreciate by smaller and smaller amounts throughout its life. Most people would agree that a three-year-old machine has less value than an otherwise identical two-year-old one, but who could say that a 16-year-old machine really has any less value than a 15-year-old one? Since the value of these assets erodes in smaller and smaller amounts as the years go by, we use the diminishing balance method of calculation.

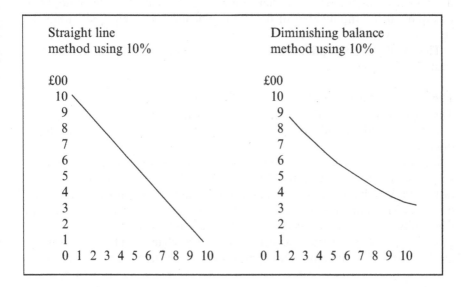

Fig. 75. Common methods of depreciation. The figure of 10% is used in both cases to illustrate the comparison (it is not necessarily the most common percentage to be used).

43 Other methods of depreciation

The sum of the digits method

This method is more common in the USA than in Britain. It works in the opposite way to the diminishing balance method. The latter applies a constant percentage but to a progressively reducing balance, but the sum of the digits method applies a progressively small percentage to a constant figure (the initial cost figure). It is called the sum of the digits method because it involves summing the individual year numbers in the expected life span of the asset to arrive at the denominator of a fraction to be applied in calculating depreciation each year. The numerator is the year number concerned, in a reverse order.

For example if an asset had an expected useful life of 5 years then in year 1 the numerator would be 5, and in year 2 it would be 4 and so on, until year 5 when the numerator would be 1. Supposing an asset was expected to last 10 years before becoming worthless: we would add $1 + 2 + 3 + 4 + 5 + 6 + 7 + 8 + 9 + 10 = 55$. In year one, we would depreciate by multiplying the original value by 10/55, in year 2 by 9/55 and so on until year 10 when we would write it down by only 1/55 of its initial value.

The machine hours method

We divide the initial cost value of a machine by the estimated number of machine hours in its useful life. The depreciation charge is then calculated by multiplying this quotient by the number of hours the machine has been used within the accounting year.

This method is appropriate wherever the erosion of value of an asset is directly related to its usage.

The revaluation method

This method means revaluing the asset each year. It may involve observation, and item counting, and taking into account factors such as current market prices.

It is useful in respect of small tools, for example, for which it would be silly to keep a separate asset account and provision for depreciation account for each little item. Revaluing is also useful in dealing with livestock, for their values go up and down; a dairy cow for example will be less valuable when very young than when fully grown, but then its value will decline as it gets old. Throughout its life this rise and fall in value may be further affected by changes in food prices in the market place. If revaluation is used, no provision for depreciation is needed.

The depletion method

This is used in the adjusting of values of ore bodies, mines, quarries and oil wells. The initial value of the mine, etc is divided by the quantity of ore or mineral that it contained at the beginning; the quotient is then multiplied by the quantity *actually* mined in the accounting year to give the amount of depletion in value.

The sinking fund method

This method, as well as depreciating an asset's value in the books, builds up a fund for replacing it at the end of its useful life. A compound interest formula is applied to the estimated cost of replacement at the end of the asset's life; it shows how much money must be invested each year (outside the firm) to provide the replacement fund when the time comes. This amount is then charged annually to the profit and loss account as depreciation. The credit entry is posted to a depreciation fund account. The amount is then suitably invested and the asset which thereby comes into existence is debited to a depreciation fund investment account, the credit entry obviously going to bank. This method is not popular now because there is so much uncertainty about inflation and interest rates.

The sinking fund with endowment policy method

This is similar but uses an endowment policy to generate the replacement fund on maturity. The premium is payable annually in advance.

JOURNAL

200X	Particulars	Fo.	Debit	Credit
June 30	Profit and loss provision for	NL30	50,000	
	depreciation on machines	NL8		50,000
	Profit and loss provision for	NL30	19,400	
	depreciation on lorry	NL9		19,400

LEDGER

NL8 *Provision for depreciation on machine*
Dr. Cr.
200X 200X
    June 30 Profit and loss 50,000

NL9 *Provision for depreciation on motor lorry*
Dr. Cr.
200X 200X
    June 30 Profit and loss 19,400

NL30 *Profit and loss account*
Dr. Cr.
200X 200X
June 30   Depreciation 69,400

Fig. 76. Worked example of depreciation accounting. This is how the depreciation in the worked examples on pages 106–108 would be written at the end of the year. The same would be the case for the subsequent years, except, of course, that the values would be different in respect of the machine depreciation.

44 Depreciation step by step

What you need
- the nominal ledger
- scrap paper for your calculations
- the journal.

Step by step
1. Decide what kind of asset is concerned, what pattern of erosion applies to it and so which method of depreciation is best.

2. Calculate the annual depreciation figure for the asset.

3. In the next available space in the journal, write the date in the date column, and 'profit and loss' in the 'particulars' column. Remember, never post directly to the ledger – only via a book of prime entry (in this case the journal, a useful book for miscellaneous recordings like depreciation).

4. Enter the amount of depreciation in the debit cash column.

5. Underneath the last entry in the 'particulars' column, indenting slightly, write: 'provision for depreciation on [name of asset]'.

6. Enter the same value in the credit cash column.

7. Repeat for any other assets you need to depreciate in the accounts.

8. Open a 'provision for depreciation' account for each asset concerned. Record the page numbers in the index.

9. Make postings to each of these ledger accounts, following the instructions you have just written in the journal.

Note
A Statement of Standard Accounting Practice (SSAP) was issued in December 1977 and revised in 1981 for the treatment of depreciation in accounts (SSAP12). The student can refer to this for further information if desired.

SALES LEDGER

p2   p2

H. Baker

Date 200X	Particulars	Fo.	Totals	Date 200X	Particulars	Fo.	Totals
Jun 30	Sales	NL6	200.00	Mar 31	Bad debts	NL20	200.00

NOMINAL LEDGER

p20   p20

Bad Debts Account

Date 200X	Particulars	Fo.	Totals	Date 200X	Particulars	Fo.	Totals
Mar 31	H. Baker	SL2	200.00	Mar 31	Profit and loss	NL27	200.00

p19   p19

Provision for Doubtful Debts Account

Date	Particulars	Fo.	Totals	Date 200X	Particulars	Fo.	Totals
				Mar 31	Profit and loss	NL27	600.00

p27   p27

Profit and Loss Account

Date 200X	Particulars	Fo.	Totals	Date 200X	Particulars	Fo.	Totals
Mar 31	Provision for Doubtful debts	NL19	600.00				
31	Bad debts	NL20	200.00				

Fig. 77. Accounting for bad and doubtful debts in the ledger.

Not every credit customer (or other debtor) will pay what he/she owes. They may dispute the amounts; some may disappear or go out of business. The debts they owe to the business may be bad, or of doubtful value. If so, our accounts must reflect the fact.

Accounting for bad and doubtful debts, like depreciation, means estimating an erosion of value. But it differs from depreciation because there it is time that erodes the value. Here it is more a product of fate. We can predict what effect age will have on physical assets like motor cars, but we cannot very easily predict which, and how many, debtors won't pay their bills. If we could, we should never have given them credit in the first place! There are no special calculation techniques for bad and doubtful debts as there are in depreciation. You just need to choose a suitable overall percentage, and make specific adjustments from time to time in the light of experience.

When a·company becomes aware that a debt is uncollectable, because, for example, the customer has been declared bankrupt, or the company has gone into liquidation, the debt is written off by crediting the relevant sales ledger account and debiting bad debts account. Figure 77 provides an example.

Postings

We may know a debt has become worthless because the individual has gone bankrupt, or a company has gone into liquidation. Such a debt must then be posted to a 'bad debts account'. This is an account for specific debts we know to be bad. This is quite aside from our provision for a percentage of debtors control account going bad. If bad debts are recovered later on, we will treat them as credits to bad debts account, and a debit to cash account. We do not need to reopen the individual debtor account, since the posting would result in its immediate closure anyway.

Only if a firm is in liquidation, or if an individual has too few assets to be worth suing, do we need to write off the debt to bad debts account. If the non-payer does have sufficient funds, the firm may be able to sue them successfully for the debt.

Saving tax and being realistic

The reason we need to write down bad or doubtful debts is twofold. First, the firm will be charged income tax on its profits; if the profit figure is shown without allowing for the cost of bad and doubtful debts it will be higher than it should rightly be, and the firm will end up paying more tax than it needs to.

Secondly, the balance sheet should show as realistically as possible the value of the assets of the business. After all, interested parties such as bankers, investors and suppliers will rely on it when making decisions about the firm. Failure to write off bad debts, and too little provision for doubtful debts, will mean an unrealistically high current asset of debtors being shown. Accountants are guided by the principle of *prudence*. This provides that (a) losses should be provided for as soon as anticipated and (b) it is preferable to understate profit than overstate it.

JOURNAL

Date 200X	Particulars	Fo.	Debit	Credit
Aug 30	Bad debts	NL9	200.00	
	VAT	NL8	40.00	
	H. Baker	SL5		240.00
To write off bad debt.				

NOMINAL LEDGER

p9
Bad debts

Dr   Cr

Date 200X				Date 200X	
Aug 30	H. Baker	SL5	200.00		

NOMINAL LEDGER

p8
VAT

Dr   Cr

Date 200X				Date 200X	
Aug 30	Bad debts	SL5	40.00		

SALES LEDGER

p5
H. Baker

Dr   Cr

Date 2000X		Date 200X			
Aug 1		Aug 30	Bad debts	NL9	200.00
			VAT	NL8	40.00

Fig. 78. Worked example of bad debt accounting taking VAT into account.

1. Suppose A. Frazer received information on 30 August that H. Baker, a customer who owed the firm £200, had been declared bankrupt; the appropriate entries in the books would be as shown in Fig. 78.

JOURNAL

200X	Particulars	Fo.	Debit	Credit
Mar 31	Profit and loss	NL30	600.00	
	Provision for doubtful debts	NL20		600.00
	To provide for doubtful debts			

LEDGER

NL20
Provision for doubtful debts

Dr.   Cr.

200X		200X		
		Mar 31	Profit and Loss	600.00

NL30
Profit and loss

Dr.   Cr.

200X			200X	
Mar 31	Provision for Doubtful debts	600.00		

Fig. 79. Worked example of provision for doubtful debts (2).

2. Suppose that A. Frazer estimates his necessary bad debts provision for the year ending 31 March as £600; the bookkeeping entries would be as shown in Fig. 79.

Posting to 'provision for doubtful debts account' and 'bad debts account'

You will need:
- the journal
- the nominal ledger
- the sales ledger.

Step by step

1. Decide the percentage figure and from that the actual amount you will use as a provision for doubtful debts (e.g. 1% or 2%).

2. Write in the next available space in the journal the date (in the date column) and the words 'profit and loss account' in the particulars column.

3. Enter the value of your provision in the debit cash column.

4. Beneath the last entry in the particulars column, indenting slightly, write: 'provision for doubtful debts'.

5. Enter the same value in the credit cash column.

6. Repeat the process when writing off any actual bad debts, but in this case you need to debit the bad debts account and credit the individual debtor accounts.

7. Now post to the nominal and sales ledger, exactly following the instructions you have just written in the journal.

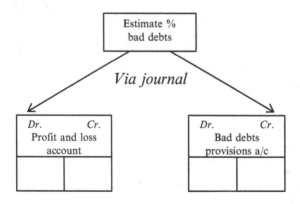

47 Partnership accounts

It is now time to change perspective. We are no longer dealing with pieces of the accounting system, but with different types of accounts for different purposes, beginning with accounts for partnerships. Partnership accounts differ from sole proprietor accounts in two ways:

- a profit and loss appropriation account is needed and
- separate capital accounts are needed for each partner.

In every other way, they are the same.

What is a partnership?

Partnerships are business units owned jointly by more than one person. Such people may have joined in partnership for all kinds of reasons. Perhaps neither had enough capital on their own; perhaps they wished to obtain economies of scale by combining their capitals; perhaps they had matching skills or matching control of the factors of production (e.g. one owned land and buildings while the other had special skills). There are partnerships of solicitors, accountants, building contractors, agencies – in fact of almost any kind of business activity.

Each partner is responsible 'jointly and severally' for all the debts of the partnership. This means that if the business cannot pay its debts, the creditors can hold each and every partner personally responsible. More than that, if one partner has personal assets such as a house and savings, while the other partners have none, creditors can sue the partner who does have assets for all the debts of the partnership – not just for their 'share' of the debts.

There are endless types of financial arrangement in partnerships. For example profits may be shared in proportion to capital invested; or interest may be paid on capital before any residual net profit is shared equally, regardless of capital. Similarly, the partners may agree that interest will be charged on all individual drawings against capital. At the onset, they may decide that each working partner will receive a fixed salary. It is to take care of all such points that partnership accounts have these extra facilities.

Where there is no written partnership agreement, the Partnership Act 1890 (section 24) states that no interest is to be allowed on capital except where provided in excess of any agreement (in which case 5% would be allowed). No interest is to be charged on drawings; no partner will be entitled to a salary, and each will share the profits equally.

Advantages of partnerships over sole proprietorships:

- increased capital
- increased range of expertise
- sharing of responsibilities
- sharing of work
- sharing of risk.

Disadvantages are:

- loss of independent control
- profits have to be shared
- debts, or even insolvency of one partner can negatively affect the other partners.

48 Partnerships: appropriation accounts

The appropriation account is just an extension of the trading, profit and loss account. In it, we post the appropriation (i.e. sharing out) of net profit between the partners. We do not need an appropriation account in the accounts of a sole proprietor, because all the net profit goes to the one proprietor's capital account. In a partnership or limited company, things are a little more complicated.

- In a partnership some of the profit may be owed to the partners for interest on capitals they have invested.

- If a partner has drawn money from the business (other than salary) he/she may have to pay interest on it, according to arrangements between the parties. Any such interest payment will have to be deducted from any interest due to them on their capital. We show such transactions in the appropriation account.

- If a partner has lent money to the partnership, however, that is a very different thing. Any interest payable to that partner would be an expense to the business, not an appropriation of profit. Its proper place would be in the profit and loss account.

After deducting these items from the net profit (brought down from the profit and loss account) we have to show how the rest of the profit will be shared out. We will show an equal split, or an unequal one, depending on the profit-sharing arrangements between the partners.

What you need
- the ledger

- details of interest rate on capital due to partners

- details of interest rate payable by partners on drawings

- details of partners' capitals

- details of partners' drawings

- details of partners' salaries and/or fees

- details of profit-sharing arrangements.

Preparation
Work out the interest on capital due to each partner. Remember to apply the correct percentage interest rate. Work out the interest payable by each partner on their drawings, again applying the correct percentage interest rate.

Horizontal format

FRAZER AND BAINES
PROFIT AND LOSS APPROPRIATION ACCOUNT
for year ended 31 December 200X

Net profit b/d				21,000
Interest on capital (10%)		Interest on drawings (12%)		
Frazer	2,000	Frazer	240	
Baines	5,000	Baines	300	540
Salary: Frazer	8,000	15,000		
Share of Residual profits				
Frazer (67%)		2,180		
Baines (33%)		4,360		
		21,540		21,540

Vertical format

PROFIT AND LOSS APPROPRIATION ACCOUNT
OF FRAZER AND BAINES

Net profit b/d			21,000
Frazer			
Interest on capital (10%)	2,000		
Less interest on drawings (12%)	240		
	1,760		
Salary	8,000	9,760	
Baines			
Interest on capital (10%)	5,000		
Less interest on drawings (12%)	300	4,700	
Share of profits in ratio 2:1			
Frazer	2,180		
Baines	4,360	6,540	21,000
			00,000

Fig. 80. Worked examples of partnership accounts.

49 Partnership accounts step by step

Step by step

1. Make another heading under the completed profit and loss account in the ledger: 'Profit and loss appropriation account'.

2. Bring down the net profit from the profit and loss account.

3. In the credit column record: 'Interest payable on drawings' for each partner, marking it accordingly.

4. In the debit column enter: 'Interest on capitals' for each partner, marking each entry accordingly.

5. In the debit column record the value of individual partners' salaries, marking each one accordingly.

6. Again in the debit column, record the individual profit shares of each partner, marking each one accordingly. Show the proportion, e.g. ½ or a percentage e.g. 50%.

7. Total up and balance this 'account' (the balance c/d will be zero).

Converting final accounts into vertical format

You can now rewrite your final accounts in a more useful vertical format. If you do, change the appropriation account in the same way. The figure opposite (bottom) shows how this is done.

The figure opposite (top) shows an alternative, horizontal layout, but remember that vertical formats are much more popular in Britain and you should use them in exams and in business unless told otherwise.

Example: Frazer and Baines

Frazer and Baines are partners. Frazer initially invested £20,000 in the business and Baines £50,000. Frazer took drawings of £2,000 during the year and Baines £2,500. It had been agreed at the onset that 10% interest would be paid on capitals, interest of 12% would be payable on drawings and that Frazer, because he, alone, would be working full-time in the business, would receive a salary of £8,000. Suppose, also, that the net profit shown in the profit and loss account at the end of the current year is £21,000. Following the step-by-step instruction given here, the examples opposite show what the appropriation account might look like.

A. FRAZER
BALANCE SHEET
as at 28 February 200X

FIXED ASSETS

Workshop and yard			45,000
Machinery	4,000		
Less provision for depreciation	200	3,800	
Motor van	6,000		
Less provision for depreciation	2,000	4,000	7,800
Goodwill			5,800
			58,600

CURRENT ASSETS

Stock of materials	4,500	
Debtors	1,200	
Cash at bank	150	
	5,850	
Less CURRENT LIABILITIES		
Creditors	5,100	
Working capital		750
TOTAL ASSETS		59,350
Financed by:		
CAPITAL as at 1 March 200X		57,050
Add profit		11,300
		68,350
Less drawings		9,000
TOTAL LIABILITIES		59,350

E. BAINES
BALANCE SHEET
as at 28 February 200X

FIXED ASSETS

Machinery	3,000	
Less provision for depreciation	150	2,850
Motor lorry	5,000	
Less provision for depreciation	1,000	4,000
Goodwill		2,000
		8,850

CURRENT ASSETS

Stock of materials	900	
Debtors	4,000	
Cash at bank	41,000	
Cash in hand	500	
	46,400	
Less CURRENT LIABILITIES		
Creditors	2,600	
Working capital		43,800
TOTAL ASSETS		52,650
Financed by:		
CAPITAL as at 1 March 200X		42,450
Add profit		10,200
TOTAL LIABILITIES		52,650

Fig. 81. Two balance sheets before amalgamation into a partnership.

Consolidation

Now we come to a new accounting technique, **consolidation**. The idea is to consolidate or amalgamate the accounts of two separate businesses into those of a single partnership. The method is very simple:

- we just add each of the individual balance sheet items together, after making adjustments in each for any changes in asset values agreed by the parties.

Making the adjustments

Such adjustments may arise for example because A thinks their 'provision for bad debts' of 5% is reasonable, while B feels it should be 7½%; or B might feel that one of A's machines is not worth what A's balance sheet says it is; and so on. If the amalgamation is to go ahead, the parties will have to settle all such disagreements first.

When we make such adjustments, it is bound to affect the capital figure. So we also need to make the adjustment to the capital accounts, before consolidating the balance sheets by adding all their components together. Indeed, if we didn't adjust the capital accounts, the individual balance sheets would cease to balance, and then the consolidated one would not balance either.

The 'goodwill' value of each business

The parties may agree that different values of **goodwill** existed in their businesses before amalgamation. Perhaps one business was long-established, while the other one was rather new and had not yet built such a good reputation. In such a case, each business would write an agreed figure for goodwill into its balance sheet before amalgamation. It would post the other side of the dual posting to the credit of its capital account. On amalgamation we then add the two goodwill amounts together, just like all the other assets.

Writing off goodwill after amalgamation

If it is decided later on to write it off, the one aggregated goodwill figure in the post-amalgamation accounts will be credited to goodwill account; the debit entry to complete the dual posting will be posted to the partners' current accounts, in proportion to their profit-sharing arrangements (unless a different agreement exists between them).

FRAZER AND BAINES
BALANCE SHEET
as at 1 March 200X

FIXED ASSETS

Yard and workshop		45,000
Machinery		6,650
Motor van		4,000
Motor lorry		4,000
Goodwill		7,800
		67,450

CURRENT ASSETS		
Stock of materials	5,400	
Debtors	5,200	
Cash at bank	41,150	
Cash in hand	500	
	52,250	
Less CURRENT LIABILITIES		
Creditors	7,700	
Working capital		
		44,550
TOTAL ASSETS		112,000

Financed by:		
CAPITAL ACCOUNTS		
Frazer		59,350
Baines		52,650
		112,000

Fig. 82. Opening balance sheet of the new partnership.

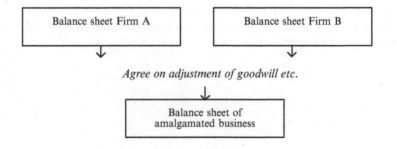

On the previous pages we saw that, to amalgamate two businesses into one, we have to consolidate (add together) their two balance sheets. It is quite a simple procedure.

What you need
- the two balance sheets
- details of any changes (adjustments) to the item values, as agreed between the owners of the two businesses.

Step by step
1. Adjust any item values as appropriate, in other words correct the amounts from their original values to the new agreed values.
2. Take care to amend the capital values, too, so that the individual balance sheets do, in fact, still 'balance'.
3. Add together the values of each item (other than depreciation). Then write out a consolidated balance sheet for the new partnership.

Note on depreciation
Provision for depreciation is not carried over into the new partnership, because the business unit has in effect purchased the assets at their already written down value.

Example
On the facing page we can see the consolidated balance sheet of the businesses of Frazer and Baines (their separate balance sheets were shown on page 122). Notice how the newly amalgamated partnership treats the machinery, motor van and motor lorry. The consolidated value of the machinery is £6,650, representing £3,800 (its written down value in Frazer's balance sheet) plus £2,850 (its written down value in Baines' balance sheet).

New partner joining
When a new partner is admitted to a partnership their acquisition of a share in the existing value of goodwill means that other partners will lose. Those partners who gain should be charged the amount of their gain and those who lose should be compensated for their loss. Figure 83 shows the four stages in the process.

Paying for the goodwill acquired
The new partner can pay for their share of goodwill in one of four ways. He/she can pay each partner for the amount of goodwill they have lost in allowing him/her to take a proportion of the total, e.g. in the example most recently used, Able, Bryce and Collins each gave up £3,750 of goodwill to the new partner, so a simple way would be for Dean to pay each of them a cheque for £3,750 which they can bank in their private accounts and no goodwill account needs to be opened.

Alternatively, a sum equal to the combined loss of goodwill (£11,250) can be paid into the partnership's account and this sum credited proportionally to the

Stage 1 Partners	Old profit sharing ratios %	Share of goodwill	Stage 2 New profit sharing ratios %	Share of goodwill	Stage 3 Gain/loss		Stage 4 Adjustment required
Able	33	15,000	25	11,250	3,750	Loss	Pay Able or credit his/her capital account
Bryce	33	15,000	25	11,250	3,750	Loss	Pay Bryce or credit his/her capital account
Collins	33	15,000	25	11,250	3,750	Loss	Pay Collins or credit his/her capital account
			25	11,250	11,250	Gain	Charge Dean or debit his/her capital account
		45,000		45,000			

Fig. 83. The four stages of adjustment of the profit-sharing ratios and shares of goodwill on the admission of new partner.

Goodwill

Able	Capital	15,000	Balance c/d	45,000
Bryce	Capital	15,000		
Collins	Capital	15,000		
		45,000		45,000

Fig. 84. An illustration of recording the capital changes resulting from the admission of a new partner.

capital accounts of Able, Bryce and Collins, i.e. £3,750 to each. Again, there would be no need to open a goodwill account in this case.

A third method would be to debit the new partner's capital account with the goodwill share they have acquired and credit the same to the capital accounts of the existing partners in accordance with their profit-sharing ratios. Again, there would be no need to open a goodwill account in this case.

A fourth method is to open a goodwill account and capitalise the existing goodwill shares, i.e. debit the goodwill account with the total value of the goodwill and post the equivalent value to the credit of the existing partners' capital accounts in the proportions of their profit-sharing ratios.

Example
Suppose Dean joins the partnership of Able, Bryce and Collins. Goodwill is valued at £45,000 and the partners will share profits equally as has always been the case in the past. Their capitals are different, as you will see, but this does not affect the profit-sharing ratios as their capitals are remunerated by interest paid on them. Figure 84 shows the entries that will be made in the ledger to record the changes.

Writing off the goodwill
After the adjustment has been made the goodwill can be written off by crediting the goodwill account with the full amount to close it down and debiting the partners' capital accounts in the proportions of their new profit-sharing ratios. Figure 85 provides an illustration of this.

Changes in profit-sharing ratios for other reasons
The admission of a new partner is not the only circumstance in which profit-sharing ratios may change. They may change because a partner ceases to work full-time or his/her skills cease to be as important as those of the other partners. If a partner agrees to take a smaller percentage of profits he/she deserves to be compensated for what they have given up. The financial adjustments can be made by the same methods as for changes in profit sharing as a result of a new partner joining. See Figure 86.

Death or retirement of a partner
If a partner dies or retires from the partnership goodwill has to be accounted for so that the retiring partner, or their estate if deceased, can be paid a fair value for their share in the business. The process is essentially the same as for a joining partner and once the adjustments to the capitals have been made the goodwill can be written off if desired and the account closed down.

Example
Suppose Bryce is retiring from the partnership of Able, Bryce, Collins and Dean The value of goodwill has been agreed as £48,000. Their capitals are £50,000,

£30,000, £20,000 and £50,000 respectively, but they share profits equally. Figure 87 shows how this would be dealt with in the accounts.

Bryce's capital account stands at £42,000 now that his share of goodwill has been capitalised, so on retiring from the partnership he will receive this amount.

If a goodwill account had already existed it may have needed updating. It may have been undervalued or overvalued. If a goodwill account is undervalued debit it with the amount by which it should be increased and credit the partners' capital accounts in the proportions of their profit-sharing ratios. If goodwill is overvalued in the accounts then do the exact opposite.

Again, once the adjustments have been made the goodwill can be written off by crediting the account with the full value of goodwill and debiting the partners' capital accounts in the proportions of their post-adjustment, profit-sharing ratios.

Capital accounts

	Able	Bryce	Collins	Dean		Able	Bryce	Collins	Dean
Balances c/d	65,000	45,000	35,000	50,000	Balances b/d	50,000	30,000	20,000	
					Cash for capital				50,000
					Goodwill	15,000	15,000	15,000	
	65,000	45,000	35,000	50,000		65,000	45,000	35,000	50,000

Goodwill

			Able	Bryce	Collins	Dean
Balance b/d	45,000	Able Capital	11,250			
		Bryce Capital		11,250		
		Collins Capital			11,250	
		Dean Capital				11,250
	45,000					45,000

Fig. 85. An illustration of writing off goodwill after the admission of a new partner.

Capital accounts

	Able	Bryce	Collins	Dean		Able	Bryce	Collins	Dean
Goodwill	11,250	11,250	11,250	11,250	Balances b/d	65,000	45,000	35,000	50,000
Balances c/d	53,750	33,750	23,750	38,750					
	65,000	45,000	35,000	50,000		65,000	45,000	35,000	50,000

Fig. 86. An illustration of accounting for a change in the profit-sharing ratios in a partnership.

Goodwill

			Balance c/d	48,000
Able	Capital	12,000		
Bryce	Capital	12,000		
Collins	Capital	12,000		
Dean	Capital	12,000		
		48,000		48,000

Capital accounts

	Able	Bryce	Collins	Dean
Balances c/d	62,000	42,000	32,000	62,000
	62,000	42,000	32,000	62,000

	Able	Bryce	Collins	Dean
Balances c/d	50,000	30,000	20,000	50,000
Shares of goodwill	12,000	12,000	12,000	12,000
	62,000	42,000	32,000	62,000

Fig. 87. An illustration of using the goodwill account to adjust the capital accounts on the retirement of a partner.

CERTIFICATE OF INCORPORATION
OF A PRIVATE LIMITED COMPANY

Company No.

The Registrar of Companies for England and Wales hereby certifies that

is this day incorporated under the Companies Act 1985 as a private company and that the company is limited.

Given at Companies House, Cardiff, the

THE OFFICIAL SEAL OF THE
REGISTRAR OF COMPANIES

Companies House
—— *for the record* ——

Fig. 88. Certificate of Incorporation of a Limited Company.

Public and private companies

The form and extent of the accounts of limited companies are governed by the Companies Act 1985.

There are two main types of limited company:

- **public** limited companies, which have Plc after their name; and

- **private** limited companies, which have Ltd after their name.

Public companies have to disclose more information than private companies.

The company as a 'person'

The main difference between the company and other business entities is that it is a legal entity or 'person' quite separate from the shareholders. The partnership and the sole proprietorship on the other hand are inseparable from the people involved: if these two businesses cannot pay their debts then the partners or proprietors may be called upon to settle them personally, because 'the business's debts' are in reality 'their debts'. On the other hand a company's debts are its debts alone. The shareholders cannot be called upon to settle the company's debts: their liability is limited to the original value of their shares. In law, a company is a separate legal 'person' (though obviously not a human one), and so has its own rights and obligations under the law.

Share capital

The capital account has its own special treatment in limited company accounts. The capital of limited companies is divided into shares, which people can buy and sell. A share in the capital of the company entitles the shareholder to a share of the profits of the company – just as a partner owning capital in a firm is entitled to profits.

Authorised share capital

Authorised share capital is just a statement of the share capital a company is authorised to issue, not what it has issued. The issued share capital is the amount of that limit that it actually has issued, i.e. the shares it has sold. It is only this latter amount that actually represents the company's capital.

The authorised share capital shows the nominal value of the company's shares. That is a rather arbitrarily chosen rounded-figure value at incorporation of the business selected for the purpose of making it easy to divide up the equity of the firm. Suppose a sole proprietor, whose total net assets are £360,000 is incorporating his/her business in order to take in two other investors, but wishes to retain the controlling share of 51%. Allocation of shares representing the net assets would be a messy business unless an easily divisible figure was used to represent the £360,000 net asset value. A figure of £100,000 can be registered as its authorised share capital, divided into 100,000 ordinary shares of £1, each of which represents £3.60 of the actual share capital.

Even if the authorised share capital did reflect exactly the net assets of the business, as might be the case where a new business is incorporated from scratch, five years later the company may be worth twice as much as when it started because of reinvested profits. Therefore any shares still to be issued will be worth probably twice as much as they were when the company started even though their nominal value will still be listed as the same figure as when the company was formed. It is necessary to keep them listed at their nominal value because that reflects the nominal proportion of the share capital that they represent. The difference between the nominal value and the market value is know as **share premium.** The excess over nominal value that is charged for the shares is posted to **share premium account** and shows up in the balance sheet as such.

Ordinary and preference shares

There is, however, a difference, because limited companies can have different kinds of shares with different kinds of entitlements attached to them, e.g. **ordinary shares**, and **preference** shares.

- Preference shares receive a fixed rate of dividend (profit share), provided sufficient profit has been made. For example it might be 10% of the original value of the preference shares.

- Ordinary shares have no such limit on their dividend, which can be as high as the profits allow. However, they come second in the queue, so to speak, if the profit is too little to pay dividends to both the preference and ordinary shareholders.

Furthermore, a company is allowed to retain part of the profits to finance growth. How much, is up to the directors. Unless otherwise stated in the company's memorandum of association, preference shares are cumulative, in other words any arrears of dividend can be carried forward to future years until profits are available to pay them. Since the Companies Act 1985, a company is allowed to issue redeemable shares, preference and ordinary. These are shares that the company can redeem (buy back) from the shareholder at their request.

Debentures

Some of the net assets of a company may be financed by debentures. These are loans, and interest has to be paid on them. Since debentures have to be repaid, we have to show them as liabilities in the balance sheet.

Format 1

1. Turnover
2. Cost of sales
3. Gross profit or loss
4. Distribution costs
5. Administrative expenses
6. Other operating income
7. Income from shares in group companies
8. Income from shares in related companies
9. Income from other fixed asset investments
10. Other interest receivable and similar income
11. Amounts written off investments
12. Interest payable and similar charges
13. Tax on profit or loss on ordinary activities
14. Profit or loss on ordinary activities after taxation
15. Extraordinary income
16. Extraordinary charges
17. Extraordinary profit or loss
18 Tax on extraordinary profit or loss
19. Other taxes not shown under the above items
20. Profit or loss for the financial year

Format 2

1. Turnover
2. Change in stocks of finished goods and in work in progress
3. Own work capitalised
4. Other operating income
5. (a) Raw materials and consumables
   (b) Other external charges
6. Staff costs:
   (a) wages and salaries
   (b) social security costs
   (c) other pension costs
7. (a) Depreciation and other amounts written off tangible and intangible fixed assets
   (b) Exceptional amounts written off current assets
8. Other operating charges
9. Income from shares in group companies
10. Income from shares in related companies
11. Income from other fixed asset investments
12. Other interest receivable and similar income
13 Amounts written off investments
14. Interest payable and similar charges
15. Tax on profit or loss on ordinary activities
16. Profit or loss on ordinary activities after taxation
17. Extraordinary income
18. Extraordinary charges
19. Extraordinary profit or loss
20. Tax on extraordinary profit or loss
21. Other taxes not shown under the above items
22. Profit or loss for the financial year

Fig. 89. Profit and loss account formats under the 1985 Companies Act.

The profit and loss appropriation account

The appropriation of net profit has to be shown in company accounts, so we need to draw up a **profit and loss appropriation account**. This shows how much of the profit is being set aside for taxation, how much is being distributed in dividends on shares, and how much is being retained in the company for future growth.

A limited company's statutory 'books'

The law requires a company to keep the following books, as well as its books of account:

- a register of members (shareholders)

- a register of charges (liabilities such as mortgages and debentures)

- a register of directors and managers

- a minutes book.

Annual audit

It also requires it to appoint an external **auditor**. This person is an accountant, not employed by the company, who checks that the entries in the accounts are all correct, and that the accounts give a 'true and fair view' of the company.

Special points on company accounts

Limited company accounts differ from those of other business units in several other ways. For sole proprietors and partners, the profit and loss account is closed each year by transferring any balance to capital account. In the case of limited companies, any undistributed profits stay on the profit and loss account as **reserves** along with undistributed profits for all previous periods. However, to avoid showing a high profit and loss account balance, a company will often transfer some of it to a **general reserve account**, when compiling the profit and loss account. These reserves, along with paid up shares, are called **shareholders' funds** because they are owned by the shareholders.

In the balance sheet of a limited company creditors have to be analysed into those falling due for payment within a year, and those falling due in more than a year (e.g. long term loans).

ARMSTRONG ENGINEERING
TRIAL BALANCE
as at 31 December 200X

	£	£
Sales		308,000
Opening stock	15,000	
Purchases	180,000	
Closing stock	18,000	18,000
Wages	22,000	
Auditors' fees	5,000	
Motor expenses	6,700	
Insurance	2,000	
Heat and light	5,000	
Postage	1,500	
Stationery	4,000	
Interest on debenture	600	
Depreciation	4,500	
Bad debts	2,500	
Provision for doubtful debts		6,160
Freehold premises	98,240	
Fixtures and fittings	10,000	
Provision for depreciation on fixtures and fittings		500
Motor lorry	10,000	
Provision for depreciation on motor lorry		2,000
Machinery	40,000	
Provision for depreciation on machinery		2,000
Debtors and creditors	48,700	22,500
Cash at bank	16,450	
Cash in hand	50	
Opening balance of profit and loss account		23,400
Share capital: Ordinary shares		77,680
Preference shares		30,000
	490,240	490,240

Fig. 90. A simple example of a trial balance of a limited company.

Directors duties regarding accounts

The directors and auditors of companies are responsible by law for compiling an annual report in a form governed by law. This is for shareholders, the public and HM Revenue and Customs (HMRC).

The annual report must include a trading, profit and loss account and balance sheet, showing fixed and current assets, all costs of current and long-term liabilities, share capital and reserves, provision for taxation and loan repayments. The report must also include any unusual financial facts, e.g. effects of any changes in accounting procedures. It must also disclose things like values of exports, donations to political parties and directors salaries, where they exceed £60,000 per annum.

The auditors report must also state the methods of depreciation used.

The combined document must give a *true and fair view* of the financial affairs of the company.

Reasons companies must publish their accounts are:

- to provide information to enable shareholders to make informed decisions on whether to invest
- to help prevent fraud and corruption.

The Companies Act 1985 gives four alternative layouts for the profit and loss account (two horizontal and two vertical) and two for the balance sheet (one horizontal and one vertical). The choice is up to the directors, but must not then be changed without good and stated reasons. Vertical layouts are the most popular in the UK, so it is those we will deal with here. Remember, though, that the trading, profit and loss account is first of all a ledger account, so it inevitably starts out in horizontal format. When we are ready to distribute it, inside or outside the firm, we can rewrite it in the more popular vertical format. The two alternative vertical formats laid down by the Companies Act 1985 are shown opposite.

Turnover and cost of sales

Turnover means sales. Cost of sales is found by adding purchases and opening stock, plus carriage inwards costs, and deducting the value of closing stock.

Distribution costs

Includes costs directly incurred in delivering the goods to customers.

Administration expenses

Includes such things as wages, directors' remuneration, motor expenses (other than those included in distribution costs), auditor's fees, and so on.

Other operating income

This means all income other than from the firm's trading activities, e.g. income from rents on property or interest on loans.

Directors' report

A Directors' report must accompany all published accounts. 'Small' companies, however, are exempt from filing one with the Registrar of Companies; also they only have to file a modified version of their balance sheet, and do not have to file a profit and loss account at all. Medium-sized companies also have some concessions, in that a modified form of profit and loss account and accompanying notes is allowed.

Limitations of published accounts

- Creative accounting can hide negative information.
- Not all the relevant facts have to be disclosed.

Internal accounts

Internal accounts or management accounts are those prepared only for use within the company. Unlike published accounts, they are not required by law to be set out in a certain way. However, it pays to keep them as consistent as possible with the published accounts, so that the latter can be drawn up just by adapting the internal accounts slightly.

55 Revenue accounts of limited companies

A ledger account
Remember, the trading, profit and loss account is first and foremost a ledger account, so we should begin by treating it as such. Suppose we have all the accounting information ready in the trial balance: this is how we would go about preparing the final accounts.

What you need
- the ledger (all divisions)
- the journal
- the trial balance
- details of end of year adjustments.

Compiling company final accounts step by step
Turn back to page 95 and see the tips for preparatory work before you put together the final accounts. Remember to alter your trial balance to take account of adjustments, and to label each item in it according to where it will end up in the trading (T), profit and loss (P) account, or balance sheet (B).

1. Journalise the ledger postings exactly according to the labelling you have just written on the trial balance. In other words, post each item labelled 'T' to the trading account and each item labelled 'P' to the profit and loss account. Post them all to the same side of such accounts (debit or credit) as those on which they appear in the trial balance. The other side of the posting, of course, goes to the account from which they are being transferred. (If you are in doubt about how to journalise, see page 51.)

2. When you have entered all the ledger postings, write beneath them: 'To close revenue and expense accounts and transfer balances to the trading, profit and loss account'.

3. Now post to the trading account, following exactly the instructions you have just written in the journal.

4. Total up and balance the trading account. Bring the balance down to the profit and loss account, as 'gross profit b/d'.

5. Now post to the profit and loss account, following exactly the instructions you have just written in the journal.

DEBENTURE INTEREST

Dr						Cr
200X			**200X**			
Aug 31	Bank	600				
Dec 31	Accrued c/d	450	Dec 31	Profit and loss	1,050	
		1,050			1,050	

ELECTRICITY

Dr						Cr
200X			**200X**			
Apr 30	EDA	300	Dec 31	Profit and loss	1,100	
Jul 31	EDA	300				
Oct 31	EDA	300				
Dec 31	Accrued c/d	200				
		1,100			1,100	

INSURANCE

Dr						Cr
200X			**200X**			
Jul 31	Bettercover	2,000	Dec 31	Profit and loss	1,000	
			Dec 31	Prepayment c/d	1,000	
		2,000			2,000	

PROVISION FOR DOUBTFUL DEBTS

Dr						Cr
200X			**200X**			
Jul 31			Jan 1	Balance b/d	6,160	
			Jul 31	Profit and loss	1,540	
Dec 31	Balance c/d	7,700				
		7,700			7,700	

Fig. 91. An illustration of accounting for various end of year adjustments.

End of year adjustments

Now things are never quite that tidy at the end of the year as to allow for merely transferring all the relevant ledger balances to the trading, profit and loss account and listing those remaining in the balance sheet. The ultimate source documents for sales and purchase records are the invoices and they do not tell the complete story.

Accrued expenses

The company will have had bills for its electricity and gas usage but the meter reading dates are unlikely to coincide exactly with the end of the company's financial year. There will, therefore, have been some power usage that has not yet been billed. If we are going to show a true and fair view of the profit or loss, as is always the aim, we have to make adjustments in the final accounts to reflect these items of expenditure that have not yet been billed.

A similar situation may exist with loans. Supposing a firm has debenture loans payable annually but the date of the interest payment is a month after the end of the financial year. There will be a figure of $^{11}/_{12}$ of the annual interest payment to be accounted for in the final statements because that has been an expense to the firm over the past year but one which does not appear in the books to date. These items are called accrued expenses or accruals.

Other expenses which can accrue are rent, business rates, employees' wages and indeed, any service that is supplied over a period of time is likely to leave the firm some accrued expense to deal with at the end of the financial year.

An assessment needs to be made of their value. For example, if quarterly electricity usage is £1,200 and the last meter reading was a month ago then it would be reasonable to estimate that usage of £400 worth of electricity has accrued since the last bill was entered into the accounts. An adjustment has to be made in the final accounts for this. The simplest way of doing it is by entering the accrual as a c/d figure on the debit side of the ledger account for Electricity. This will increase the figure posted to the profit and loss account to the extent that it will now reflect the real usage of electricity – that which has been billed for plus that which has not. At the commencement of the next accounting year this c/d balance will be brought down to the opposite side, which will have the opposite effect, deducting that amount from the value showing for that year, thus ensuring that the amount will not be claimed twice

Prepayments

On the other hand, there are some accounts that are paid in advance. Insurance premiums are an example. Suppose a firm pays the insurance on its premises annually and six months have elapsed since the last renewal date. It would be wrong for the firm to claim the expense of 12 months insurance against its profits if it has only used six months of the cover. It still has the other six months left so it cannot claim the cost of that six months against tax. A similar but opposite adjustment has to be made here. A carried down balance is used but on the

ARMSTRONG ENGINEERING
TRIAL BALANCE
as at 31 December 200X

	£	£
Sales		308,000
Opening stock	15,000	
Purchases	180,000	
Closing stock	18,000	18,000
Wages	22,000	
Auditors' fees	5,000	
Motor expenses	6,700	
Insurance	1,000 ~~2,000~~	
Heat and light	5,200 ~~5,000~~	
Postage	1,500	
Stationery	4,000	
Interest on debenture	1,050 ~~600~~	
Depreciation	4,500	
Bad debts	2,500	
Provision for doubtful debts		6,160
Freehold premises	98,240	
Fixtures and fittings	10,000	
Provision for depreciation on fixtures and fittings		500
Motor lorry	10,000	
Provision for depreciation on motor lorry		2,000
Machinery	40,000	
Provision for depreciation on machinery		2,000
Debtors and creditors	48,700	22,500
Cash at bank	16,450	
Cash in hand	50	
Opening balance of profit and loss account		23,400
Share capital: Ordinary shares		77,680
Preference shares		30,000
Prepayments	1,000	
accruals		650
Increase in provision for doubtful debts		1,540
Profit and loss	1,540	
	~~490,240~~	~~490,240~~
	492,430	492,430

Fig. 92. A trial balance adjusted to take account of accruals and prepayments.

opposite side of the ledger account for insurance. At the beginning of the new accounting year these accruals are reversed in the ledgers.

Figures 91 and 92 provide illustrations of accounting for an accrual and a prepayment in the ledger accounts.

Making things easy for yourself

There is no harm in making longhand adjustments in the trial balance to crystallise your thinking and relieve the demands on your memory; it is, after all, a working document rather than a document for publication. If there are many adjustments, however, it will be better to use an extended trial balance format to avoid clutter and maintain clarity. You can find an example of this in the chapter on trial balances. See Figure 52 on page 80.

Using accruals and prepayments accounts in the ledger

Instead of simply treating accruals and prepayments as carried down balances on the relevant expense accounts some people prefer to open ledger accounts specifically for accruals and prepayments.

Accruals

Any additional amount of an expense debited to the profit and loss account over and above that which appeared in the ledger account for that expense, i.e. accrued usage not yet billed for, would have the counter-entry posted in the credit side of the accruals account. At the commencement of the new financial year that posting to the credit of accruals account would be reversed by debiting the account and the counter-entry posted to the credit side of the relevant expense account, so that once the next bill arrives and the amount is posted to the ledger, the balance will be reduced by the amount accounted for in last year's figures.

Prepayments

Any part of the balance on an expense account which is not posted to the profit and loss account, representing part of the expense paid for but not yet used would be posted to the debit side of the prepayments account, thus allowing both sides of the expense account to balance and close.

At the start of the new financial year the prepayments account would be credited and the debit entry would be posted to the relevant expense with the effect that the unused part of the prepaid expense would then appear as an expense in the period in which it would be used.

Dealing with corporation tax in the final accounts

It is current orthodox practice to account for corporation tax in the profit and loss account, or income statement as it is increasingly being called. When all the expenses have been deducted from the gross profit you arrive at a figure of profit before taxation. The computed figure for taxation is then deducted from this to

TRADING PROFIT AND LOSS ACCOUNT
for the year ended 31 December 200X

Opening stock	15,000	Turnover	308,000
Purchases	180,000	Closing stock	18,000
Balance c/d	131,000		
	326,000		326,000
		Gross profit b/d	131,000
Wages	22,000		
Auditor's fees	5,000		
Motor expenses	6,700		
Insurance	1,000		
Heat and light	5,200		
Postage	1,500		
Stationery	4,000		
Depreciation	4,500		
Bad debts	2,500		
Increase in provision for bad debts	1,540		
Loan note (debenture) interest	1,050		
Balance c/d	76,010		
	131,000		131,000

Fig. 93. The trading, profit and loss account after end of year adjustments.

ARMSTRONG ENGINEERING
Trading profit and loss account
for year ended 31 December 200X

Turnover		308,000
Less cost of sales		
Stock as at 1 January 200X	15,000	
Add purchases	180,000	
	195,000	
Less stock as at 31 December 200X	18,000	
		177,000
Gross profit b/d		131,000
Less administration expenses		
Wages	22,000	
Auditor's fees	5,000	
Motor expenses	6,700	
Insurance	1,000	
Heat and light	5,200	
Postage	1,500	
Stationery	4,000	
Depreciation	4,500	
Bad debts	2,500	
Increase in provision for bad debts	1,540	53,940
		77,060
Loan note interest		1,050
Profit for year before taxation		76,010
Corporation tax		32,000
Retained profits		44,010

Note: Share dividends paid			
Preference	5%	1,500	
Ordinary	12%	9,322	

Fig. 94. Trading, profit and loss account in vertical format.

```
┌─────────────────────────────────────────────────────────────┐
│                   ARMSTRONG ENGINEERING                     │
│                Trading profit and loss account             │
│                 for year ended 31 December 200X             │
│                                                             │
│ Turnover                                          308,000   │
│ Less cost of sales                                177,000   │
│ Gross profit                                      131,000   │
│ Less administration expenses                       53,940   │
│                                                    77,060   │
│ Less loan note interest                             1,050   │
│ Profit on ordinary activities before taxation      76,010   │
│ Less tax on profit from ordinary activities        32,000   │
│ Retained profit on ordinary activities after taxation 44,010│
│                                                             │
│ Proposed share dividends:                                   │
│ Preference (5%)              1,500                           │
│ Ordinary (12%)               9,322                           │
└─────────────────────────────────────────────────────────────┘
```

Fig. 95. The same trading, profit and loss account simplified and converted for use within the company.

```
┌─────────────────────────────────────────────────────────────┐
│                   ARMSTRONG ENGINEERING                     │
│                Statement of changes in equity              │
│                for the year ending 31 December 200X         │
│                                                             │
│ Retained profits                                   44,010   │
│                                                             │
│ Less transfer to non-current assets replacement reserve  10,000 │
│                                                             │
│ Share dividends paid:                                       │
│      Preference   5%              1,500                      │
│      Ordinary    12%              9,322        10,822  20,822│
│                                                       23,188 │
└─────────────────────────────────────────────────────────────┘
```

Fig. 96. Example of accounting for a transfer to a reserve account and payment of dividends in a statement of changes in equity.

give a figure for profit for the year after taxation (or retained profits as it is called in the new international terminology).

Dealing with dividends

Dividends on preference shares and ordinary shares should be shown only as a note on the profit and loss account, as it is not actually an expense but rather a distribution of profit. The place where its effect on the finances of the company is shown is in the statement of changes in equity, as it represents some equity leaving the company. However, even there it is important to only show those dividends that have actually been paid and which, therefore, represent funds that have actually left the company.

Worked example

Let's take the trial balance extracted from the books of Armstrong Engineering Ltd shown on page 142. Suppose we have to make the following adjustments before drawing up the final accounts. Debenture interest of £1,200 per annum is payable by the firm at half yearly intervals on 14 August and 14 February so there is an accrual of four and a half months' debenture interest that has to be accounted for.

Electricity usage is billed quarterly at the end of April, July, October and January. It averages out at £300 per quarter, so there is an accrual of $2/3$ of a quarter since the last meter reading which has not been billed and so won't be reflected in the accounts. We would be understating the expenses if we did not account for it in the final figures.

Suppose an annual insurance premium of £2,000 is paid each year on the renewal date of 1 July. Only half of this will have been used up as at the date of the final accounts so we would be overstating the expenses if we did not account for a prepayment of £1,000.

Suppose we have found that the bad debts provision we had made of £6,160, based on 2% of turnover, was insufficient to cover the value of debts that actually became uncollectable during the past year and, in view of the worsening of the economic climate that is being predicted, we have decided it would be prudent to increase the bad debts provision by a further ½% of turnover. The extra provision must be debited to the profit and loss account and credited to the provision for bad debts account. We can only charge the increase. The balance carried over from the previous year has already been charged against tax. The full amount of the debts which actually were written off in the past year have been charged against tax as bad debts so the provision that was set up and charged against tax remained intact. It can't be charged for twice. We can charge the increase, though, as that has not been claimed against tax yet.

Let's suppose corporation tax payable is computed to be £32,000 and the firm proposes to pay dividends of 5% on the preference shares and 12% on the ordinary shares.

Figures 91 to 96 provide an illustration of the accounting for all these items in the final accounts.

No ledger posting needed

The balance sheet is not a ledger account, so there is no ledger posting to do. We simply draw up a statement showing the balances left on the ledger after we have compiled the trading, profit and loss account. Using the trial balance on page 142 we will compile a balance sheet for internal use, that also meets the requirements of the Companies Act 1985 (Format 1).

Compiling a company balance sheet step by step

1. Make a heading: 'Fixed assets'. Allocate three cash columns on the right of a sheet of paper, and head them 'Cost', 'Less provision for depreciation', and 'Net book value'. Underneath, record the values for each fixed asset. Net book value means value after depreciation. On the left write against each the name of the asset concerned. Total up each column and cross cast (cross check).

2. Make a heading: 'Current assets'. Enter in the second column the value of stock then write against it on the left: 'Stock'. Beneath the figure enter the value of debtors, and write against it on the left: 'Debtors'. In the second column list the values of the other current assets. On the left write against each the name of the current asset concerned. Total up this column.

3. Make a heading: 'Less creditors'. In the first column list the values of creditors and accruals relating to this category. On the left, against each, write the names of each class, (i) 'Amounts falling due within one year' and (ii) 'Accruals'. Total up this column. Place the total in the second column below the total for current assets.

4. Subtract the total current liabilities (creditors) from the total current assets. Place the total in the third column below the total net book value for fixed assets. You need to place it below the level of the last total because there is an important phrase to be written against this subtotal: 'Net current assets' (in other words 'Working capital'). Add the two totals in the third column and write against that sum: 'Total net assets'. If there were any long term creditors (falling due after one year), e.g debentures, we would now list them,

    e.g. total net assets   100,000
    Less × % debentures   20,000
                              80,000

    but in our data there are none.

BALANCE SHEET
as at 31 December 200X

	Cost	Less provision for depreciation	Net book value
Fixed assets			
Premises	103,400		103,400
Fixtures and fittings	10,000	500	9,500
Machinery	40,000	2,000	38,000
Motor lorry	10,000	2,000	8,000
	163,400	4,500	158,900
Current assets			
Stock		18,000	
Debtors		48,700	
Cash at bank		19,850	
Cash in hand		50	
		86,600	
Less creditors			
Amounts falling due within			
1 year	22,500		
Accruals	4,000		
Proposed dividends	34,500	61,000	
Net current assets			25,600
Total net assets			184,500
Provision for liabilities			
and charges			
Taxation			32,000
Shareholders' funds			
Authorised share capital			
100,000 Preference shares of £1	100,000		
100,000 Ordinary shares of £1	100,000		
	200,000		
Issued share capital			
30,000 Preference shares of £1		30,000	
90,000 Ordinary shares of £1		90,000	
		120,000	
Capital and reserves			
Profit and loss account balance		32,500	152,500
			184,500

Fig. 97. An example of a limited company's balance sheet suitable for publication.

5. Make a heading: 'Provision for liabilities and charges'. Beneath it make a sub-heading 'Taxation'. In the third column record the value of the provision for taxation and write against it: 'Taxation'.

6. Make a subheading: 'Shareholders' funds'.

7. Underneath that make a subordinate sub-heading, 'Authorised share capital'.

8. In the first cash column list the total authorised value of each class of share, annotating accordingly, e.g. 'Preference shares of £1', 'Ordinary shares of £1'.

9. Total up this column and rule it off with a double line.

10. Make a sub-heading: 'Issued share capital'. In the second column enter the total value of shares issued in each class of share capital, annotating each, e.g. 'Preference shares of £1', 'Ordinary shares of £1'.

11. Total up this column.

12. Make a heading: 'Capital and reserves'. In the second column, list the profit and loss account balance. Add the last two figures in the second column, i.e. total issued share capital and profit and loss account balance, and place the total in the third column. Add the last two figures in the third column to arrive at the second major total, which must balance with the first (total net assets). There is room for variation in the use of columns. It depends on how many items you need to deal with in each group. But the objectives are clarity and simplicity.

Note on terminology
Accounting in the UK is in a period of transition towards the adoption of international terminology. Public companies listed on UK or other European stock exchanges already use the international terms such as:

UK term	International term
Profit and loss account	Income statement
Debenture	Loan note
Turnover	Revenue
Stock	Inventory
Debtors	Accounts receivable
Creditors	Accounts payable
Profit and loss account b/d	Retained profits
Provision for doubtful debts	Allowance for doubtful debts
Long-term liabilities	Non-current liabilities

ARMSTRONG ENGINEERING
BALANCE SHEET
as at 31 Mar 200X

INTANGIBLE ASSETS

Goodwill   5,000

FIXED ASSETS

Freehold premises		35,000	
Plant and machinery	15,000		
Less depreciation	750	14,250	
Motor van	8,000		
Less depreciation	1,600	6,400	55,650
Total fixed assets			60,650

CURRENT ASSETS

Stock		9,000	
Debtors	10,000		
Less provision for doubtful debts	2,000	8,000	
Cash at bank		10,000	
Cash in hand		50	
	27,050		

Less CURRENT LIABILITIES

Creditors		12,000	
Working capital			15,050
TOTAL ASSETS			75,700

Financed by
CAPITAL

Opening balance		63,050
Add profit for period		19,100
	82,150	
Less drawings		6,450
TOTAL LIABILITIES		75,700

Fig. 98. The balance sheet of Armstrong Engineering before it became a limited company.

57 Going limited

Three methods of 'going limited'

A sole proprietor or partnership may wish to change the status of its business entity to that of a limited company. If so, it must draw up a balance sheet for the existing business and form a new company to purchase it at an appropriate price. The new company can pay the seller (sole proprietor or partnership) in any of three ways:

1. Buying paid up shares. If the value of the business is say £100,000, then the share capital of the new company will be registered at at least that figure. The seller will transfer the business to the company in exchange for an equal value, not in cash, but in shares.

2. Mixture of shares and debenture. The seller may, on the other hand, wish to accept only part of the payment in shares, and the other part in the form of a debenture. In other words, he/she would be selling the second part for money – but giving the company time to pay (debentures are a type of secured and usually long-term loan).

3. Selling shares to other parties. Some of the extra cash raised by this means can then be used to buy some of the assets from the former owner (sole proprietor or partnership).

Adjustments to the balance sheet

If outside parties are becoming involved, they may not agree with the various asset values shown in the business's balance sheet. They may for example disagree with the figures for bad debts provision, or with the listed value of stock or goodwill. Adjustments then need to be made to these values to satisfy everyone concerned.

You would need to make a corresponding adjustment to the capital account on the balance sheet of the business before it was bought by the limited company. When all has been agreed, we simply need to record the opening figures in the books of the new company.

There will be two fundamental differences between those entries and the details of the closing balance sheet of the business purchased:

• The capital in the opening balance sheet of the limited company will be analysed into shares (rather than into proprietor's or partners' capital). It will not show the profit or the proprietor's drawings for the period up to the takeover.

• Provision for depreciation will not feature in the opening balance sheet of the new company since it will have purchased the assets at their 'written down value'.

Armstrong, a sole proprietor, traded as Armstrong Engineering. He decided to form a limited company and transfer the assets and liabilities to it in return for ordinary shares. Assuming that the creditors had agreed to his transferring to the limited company the responsibility for the debts he had, as a sole proprietor, personally owed to them (by no means always the case), the opening balance sheet of the new company would be as shown below.

ARMSTRONG ENGINEERING LTD
BALANCE SHEET
as at 31 Mar 200X

INTANGIBLE ASSETS		
Goodwill		5,000
FIXED ASSETS		
Freehold premises	35,000	
Plant and machinery	14,250	
Motor van	6,400	55,650
Total fixed assets		60,650
CURRENT ASSETS		
Stock	9,000	
Debtors	8,000	
Cash at bank	10,000	
Cash in hand	50	
	27,050	
Less CURRENT LIABILITIES		
Creditors	12,000	
Working capital		15,050
		75,700
Financed by		
Authorised share capital		
100,000 Ordinary shares		
@ £1.00 each	100,000	
Issued Share Capital		
75,700 Ordinary shares		
@ £1.00 each		75,700

Fig. 99. The balance sheet of Armstrong Engineering after it became a limited company.

Here is another variation in format of final accounts. By clubs, we mean here clubs owned by their members, for example political clubs, social clubs and sports clubs. These organisations do not exist to make a 'profit'. All the revenue comes from the shareholders themselves (e.g. as members' subscriptions) and just reflects the cost of the goods and services they consume at the club. Their accounts are a matter of housekeeping, rather than 'trading'; the members contribute to an **accumulated common fund** for the common good.

Surpluses and accumulated funds

Of course, all housekeepers like to 'put a bit by'. Committees of clubs are in effect housekeepers, too, and often develop a small excess of revenue over expenses. But this is not profit: it is merely shareholders' contributions (in various ways) left over after all expenses have been paid. In the accounts it is termed a **surplus**. It is added to the accumulated common fund to be used for the future benefit of members. It is just as an individual may save surplus income to buy things tomorrow which they could not afford today, or to make ends meet if they fall on hard times.

Format of club accounts

Club accounts differ in format from commercial accounts, in just three ways:

- The money we call profit or loss in a partnership, sole proprietorship or limited company, we call a surplus or deficit in a club.

- Instead of a profit and loss account, clubs have an income and expenditure account.

- Instead of a capital account, clubs have an accumulated fund.

- The receipts and payments account is in effect a summary of cash and banking transactions, much like the cash book of a business.

The income and expenditure account is the equivalent of the profit and loss account of a commercial business. On the income side it shows the various sources of revenue, e.g. donations, and surpluses from activities like dances, or bingo while on the other side it analyses costs into those which can be set against income, such as bank interest, depreciation and wages (revenue expenditure) and spending on assets that will last a long time, such as buildings and equipment (capital expenditure).

Receipts and payments accounts are usually kept on a single entry basis (memorandum form) but the income and expenditure account is usually kept in double entry format.

That is not to say that no profit-making activities go on in clubs. A club may well run a bar, for example, on commercial lines. If so, a bar trading account is kept, to calculate and record gross profit; bar staff wages appear in the account along with cost of goods sold, as we dealt with on page 89. Any profit is then brought down to the club's income and expenditure account (rather than to a profit and loss account as it would be in a truly commercial business).

You can show other income-generating activities in separate trading accounts (e.g. club shop trading account), but for things like raffle and dance proceeds which do not really involve trading goods, you usually just 'net' the incomes concerned in the income and expenditure account. In other words you set against the income from the sale of tickets the cost of prizes, band hire, and so on.

SUBSCRIPTIONS ACCOUNT

200X				200X			
Mar 31 Balance	b/d	100	Mar 31 Balance	b/d		50
31 Income and expenditure account		10,100		Bank		10,100
31 Balance	c/d	150		Balance	c/d	200
		10,350				10,350

Fig. 100. Subscription fees paid by members are usually one of a club's main sources of income. This income is transferred to an 'income and expenditure account'.

Raffle proceeds	40.00	
Less expenses	10.00	
Net proceeds		30.00
Dance tickets	200.00	
Less expenses	90.00	
Net proceeds		110.00
To income and expenditure account		140.00

Fig. 101. A club may also raise income by commercial activities such as raffles and dances. The income from this is also transferred to the income and expenditure account.

60 Club accounts: income and expenditure

Preparing final accounts

So far we have considered how to write the final accounts of profit-making organisations including sole-proprietors, partnerships and limited companies. We will now see how to write the final accounts of a non profit-making organisation, such as a club, or society.

What you need

- receipts and payments account
- details of end of year adjustments.

Statement of affairs

Start by drawing up a statement of affairs as at the end of the last financial year. We call it a statement of affairs rather than a balance sheet because we don't have the full records to work from and when we are working from incomplete records it is conventional to say we are drawing up a statement of affairs.

You will need details of all the fixed assets and their depreciated values, all the current assets and all the liabilities as at the end of the last financial year. The only ones of these you will get from the receipts and payments account are the cash (at bank and in hand) at the start of the period, as that account only deals with cash and what it was used to buy. It doesn't deal with any records of what is still physically present in the club's possession at any moment in time – except the cash, that is. All the other details will have to be supplied by the treasurer and/or the secretary of the club.

1. List the fixed assets in order of their permanence, e.g.
   - land
   - buildings
   - other structures
   - equipment.
2. Add them and place the sub-total in a column to the right.
3. List all the current assets in reverse order of their liquidity.
4. Add them and place the sub-total beneath the other sub-total.
5. Add both sub-totals and this will give you the total assets.
6. Now list the current liabilities and other values.
7. Add them up and place the total (total liablilites) beneath the total assets.
8. Deduct the latter from the former and you have the accumulated fund figure as at the start of the financial year.

Figure 104 provides an illustration.

Bar trading account

The next thing to do is the bar trading account. Most of the material for this will come from the receipts and payments account, but any transactions that have not yet involved actual cash, e.g. purchases that have not yet been paid for, will have to be gleaned from the notes you have been supplied with. Draw up the bar

TRIAL BALANCE
of George Street Social Club
as at 31 March 200X

Opening stock	1,000	
Purchases	30,000	
Bar staff wages	4,500	
Bar sales		50,000
Staff wages (non-bar)	30,300	
Rent and rates	5,000	
Postage	58	
Telephone	300	
Cleaning	500	
Bank charges	150	
Donations received		2,500
Net dance and concert proceeds		10,000
Subscriptions		5,000
Net raffle and bingo ticket proceeds		500
Commission on fruit machine		4,000
Club premises	62,000	
Fixtures and fittings	10,000	
Provision for depreciation on fixtures and fittings		500
Depreciation	500	
Bar stocks	900	900
Subscriptions in arrear	250	
Cash at bank	2,200	
Cash in hand	50	
Creditors		1,100
Accumulated fund balance as at 1 April 200X		73,208
	147,708	147,708

Fig. 102. Typical trial balance used to prepare a bar trading account and income and expenditure account of a social club.

trading account just as you would any trading, profit and loss account, ticking the items off in the source documents as you go to make it easy for yourself to see which items are left to deal with.

1. Deal with sales and then the cost of sales equation to find the gross profit.
2. Total up the administration costs.
3. Enter the sub-total beneath the gross profit in the right hand column.
4. Deduct the total bar administration costs from the gross profit.
5. Bring down the total to the income and expenditure account.

Income and expenditure

Next draw up an income and expenditure account. If you are using a vertical format, you'll probably need two sub-total columns to the left of the main column for the kind of sums you will be doing.

Start with the income section and enter the subscriptions for the current year. You arrive at this by taking the subscription income for the current year from the receipts and payments account and adding the subscriptions in arrear for the current year as communicated to you by the treasurer. You then have the total value of subscription income for the current year. Just because some of it hasn't arrived in cash doesn't necessarily change the subscription income. Unless we have a sound reason to think otherwise we must assume it will be in due course. If we do have sound reason to doubt this we can write it off as a loss, in which case that member would probably be expelled. Bring down the bar profits and add in any other income, e.g. donations, legacies, etc., as listed in the receipts and payments account. Add them up to arrive at the total income.

Next list the various expense payments, those paid for, as listed in the receipts and payments account, ticking them off as you go, and any not yet paid for, as indicated in the notes you have been supplied with, e.g. bar expenses still owing.

Some expenses will not be reflected in the income and expenditure account because they are paper transactions only. Depreciation, for example, is an expense, but it won't show up in the receipts and payments account because nothing has actually been paid out in money – the expense has occurred in the form of an erosion of value. This will come from the notes you have been supplied with. Debts to write off are another example. There may be subscriptions in arrear for members who have since left the club and the committee may feel it is unlikely they will ever be paid. This writing off is also an expense that will not be reflected in the receipts and payments account.

When all the expenses have been listed and ticked off in the source documents add them up and enter the total expenses figure in the right hand column. Then deduct that from the gross profit brought down from the bar trading account and you have the *surplus income over expenditure*, which is the not-for-profit organisation equivalent of the *net profit* in a commercial firm.

You will need to write up the subscriptions account. This is drawn up in T-account or ledger format. All subscription revenue is entered on the credit side, analysed separately for the years to which each component of the total relates,

Tanner Street Bowls Club
Receipts and payments account for year ended 31 December 2008

Receipts		Payments	
Balance at bank 01/01/08	440	Bar supplies	29,100
Subscriptions received		Groundsman's wages	15,000
For 2006	760	Bar staff wages	6,500
For 2007	19,100	Bar steward's salary	20,000
Advance payments for 2008	800	Bar expenses	300
		Repairs to fencing	400
Bar takings	75,000	Security expenses	740
Donations	500	Transport costs	2,500
Legacies	5,000	Cash at bank 21/12/07	27,060
	101,600		101,600

Notes

	31/12/06	31/12/07
Bar stocks (inventory)	4,250	5,100
Creditors	3,900	4,850
Bar expenses	185	210
Transport costs	110	290
Value of land	110,100	
Buildings	27,225	
Equipment	4,900	
Subscriptions in arrear as at 31/12/06	760	
Subscriptions in arrear as at 31/12/07	1,510	

Fig. 103. An example of a receipts and payments account for a club.

Tanner Street Bowls Club
Statement of affairs as at 31 December 2008

Non-current assets		
Land		110,100
Buildings		27,225
Equipment		4,900
Current assets		
Bar inventory	4,250	
Subscriptions receivable	760	
Cash at bank	440	5,450
Total assets		147,675
Current liabilities		
Accounts payable	3,900	
Bar expenses payable	185	
Transport costs payable	110	
Total liabilities		4,195
Net assets		143,480
Accumulated fund		143,480

Fig. 104. An example of a statement of affairs for a club.

e.g. membership subscriptions for 2005, 2006 and 2007. Now if the counter-posting on the debit side were taken as the total of the subscriptions the figure would be wrong. We have to add in the figure for those subscriptions for the current year that haven't yet been paid, because these members are obliged to pay them and unless we have a good reason to think they won't we must regard them as revenue even if it is not in hard cash. We enter them as a carried down figure 'Accounts receivable c/d'. Those parts of the total that are for previous years and those that are advance payments for future years must be posted on the debit side as balances c/d, which reduces the difference between the two sides to be carried down to the income and expenditure account.

A similar process is used where the amount paid for goods and services only tells part of the story. The amount paid for, as taken from the receipts and payments account, is posted to the debit side of the purchase control account and the amount purchased but still to be paid for is posted to the same side in order to increase the amount c/d to the income and expenditure account to reflect the full value of the goods and services purchased or consumed.

To allow for the fact that some of the payments for goods and services in the receipts and payments account were for bills outstanding at the end of the previous year (and the treasurer or secretary will, hopefully, have given you the details in the adjustment notes) the figure that represents payment for last year's bills is posted on the credit side of the purchases control account to reduce the amount that will be carried down to the income and expenditure account for purchases in the current year. If you add up the two sides the difference represents the figure to carry down to the income and expenditure account for the year for which you are accounting.

All other expenses and revenues picked up from the receipts and payments account which are complicated by the fact that part of them is for settling bills from previous years and part is perhaps advance payments for future years are unravelled in the same way – by setting up ledger type accounts for each such expense, debiting them with the cash paid, adding to the debit side the amount of any accounts or bills still to be paid to increase the figure c/d to the income and expenditure account and crediting the account with any part of the total payments that were for the previous year's bills, thus reducing the amount to be c/d to the income and expenditure account. Figure 107 gives an illustration of the subscriptions account and Figure 108 gives an illustration of the purchases control account.

If the club offers life memberships the committee may wish the fee income for this to be spread over the natural life expectancy of the member in the accounts. For example, a person joining at the age of 50 may be expected to have 30 years of life expectancy during which they will use the facilities of the club and the membership fee income should be spread over this time, bringing down decreasing portions of it each year. This is, perhaps, an unnecessarily onerous requirement though, as the fee could be much less troublesomely regarded as the fee for the privilege of joining rather than a charge for the expected number of years the facilities will be used.

```
┌─────────────────────────────────────────────────────────────┐
│                   Tanner Street Bowls Club                    │
│       Bar trading account for the year ending 31 December 2008│
│                                                               │
│  Sales                                             75,000     │
│                                                               │
│    Opening inventory   01/01/2008    4,250                    │
│    Add purchases                     30,050                   │
│                                      34,300                   │
│    Closing inventory                  5,100        29,200     │
│    Gross profit                                    45,800     │
│                                                               │
│  Less expenses                                                │
│    Bar steward's wages              20,000                    │
│    Bar expenses                        325                    │
│    Bar staff wages                   6,500         26,825     │
│  Net profit b/d to income and                                 │
│    expenditure account                             18,975     │
└─────────────────────────────────────────────────────────────┘
```

Fig. 105. An example of a bar trading account for a club.

```
┌─────────────────────────────────────────────────────────────┐
│                   Tanner Street Bowls Club                    │
│  Income and expenditure account for the year ending 31 December 2008│
│                                                               │
│  Income                                                       │
│  Subscription for 2008                             20,610     │
│  Bar profits                                       18,975     │
│  Donations received                                   500     │
│  Legacies                                           5,000     │
│                                                    45,085     │
│                                                               │
│  Less expenditure                                             │
│    Groundsman's wages                    15,000               │
│    Repairs to fencing                       400               │
│    Security expenses                        740               │
│    Transport costs                        2,680               │
│    Depreciation                                               │
│      Buildings               2,722                            │
│      Equipment                 980        3,702    22,522     │
│  Surplus of income over expenditure                22,563     │
└─────────────────────────────────────────────────────────────┘
```

Fig. 106. An example of an income and expediture account for a club.

Subscriptions received			
Balance c/d from previous year	760	Cash for 2006	760
Income and expenditure a/c	20,610	2007	19,100
		c/d 2008	800
Balance c/d (advance payments)	800	Balance c/d	1,510
	22,170		22,170

Fig. 107. An example of a subscriptions account.

Purchases control			
Cash	29,100	Balance b/d (from previous year)	3,900
Balance c/d	4,850	Trading account	30,050
	33,950		33,950

Fig. 108. An example of a purchase control account for a club.

Bar expenses			
Cash	300	Balance b/d (from previous year)	185
Balance c/d	210	Trading account	325
	510		510

Transport costs			
Cash	2,500	Income and expenditure account	
Balance c/d	290	b/d (from previous year)	110
		Income and expenditure a/c	2,680
	2,790		2,790

Fig. 109. Examples of accounting for expenditure where part is for settling previous year's bills.

Tanner Street Bowls Club
Balance sheet as at 31 December 2008

Non-current assets			
Land at valuation		110,100	
Buildings at valuation	27,225		
Less depreciation	2,722	24,503	
Equipment at valuation	4,900		
Less depreciation	980	3,920	
Total net non-current assets			138,523
Current assets			
Inventory of bar stocks	5,100		
Accounts receivable: subscriptions	1,510		
Cash at bank	27,060		
Total current assets			33,670
Total assets			172,193
Current liabilities			
Accounts payable (bar supplies)	4,850		
Bar expenses	210		
Transport costs outstanding	290		
Subscriptions paid in advance	800		
Total liabilities			6,150
Net assets			166,043
Accumulated fund			
Balance as at 01/01/2008			143,480
Add surplus income over expenditure			22,563
			166,043

Fig. 110. An example of a balance sheet of a club.

Fixed asset register

A fixed asset register is for logging the details of each fixed asset. They include:

- the identification/serial number
- description of the asset
- date of acquisition
- cost
- how it was financed
- rate of depreciation and the method for calculating this
- annual depreciation for each year of its life
- current net book value
- date of disposal
- proceeds from disposal.

The reasons why it is important to keep a fixed asset register include:

- It details how the fixed asset figure on the balance sheet is made up.
- The business can check the presence and condition of fixed assets against their record in the register from time to time.
- It shows the current net book values, so that accurate posting can be made in the ledger at the time of disposal.
- It shows whether there is any finance on the assets, which is important at the time of disposal.

FIXED ASSET REGISTER	
Identification/serial number	FM2736
Description of asset	Harvey XI sheet cutter
Date of acquisition	2/2/2003
Cost	£6,000
How financed	Cash
Rate and method of depreciation	Machine hours method. £1.04 per hour used
Annual depreciation for each year of asset's life	£1,820.00
Current net book value	£2,360
Date of disposal	
Proceeds of disposal	

Fig. 111. Example of a fixed asset register.

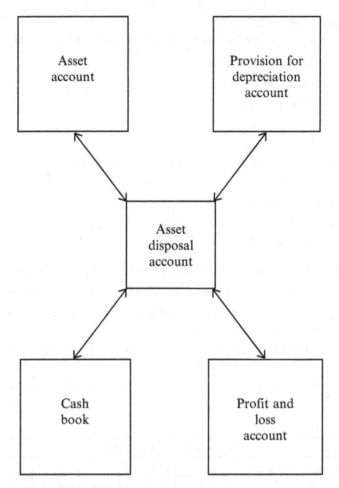

Fig. 112. A schematic illustration of asset disposal. The dual postings with the particular asset account, the account for provision for depreciation on that asset and the cash book take place when the asset is sold. The fourth does not take place until the final accounts are compiled.

62 Asset disposals

A form of final account
Asset disposal accounts are like miniature trading, profit and loss accounts: they are final accounts, and not going on any further. Once written up, with their one and only set of entries, they are balanced and carried down to show the profit or loss on the asset disposal concerned. The account will then remain untouched until such figure is transferred to the profit and loss account. The trading, profit and loss account reports all the revenues and expenses of a business at once. In contrast, asset disposal accounts only report particular transactions, in other words the disposal of individual assets. You write up a separate asset disposal account for each asset disposed of, such as a motor van or machine.

Closing down two related accounts
The idea is not only to record the disposal of the asset, but at the same time to close down the two other accounts which relate to the asset in the books – the 'asset account' itself, and the 'provision for depreciation on asset account'. It both co-ordinates and combines the closing down of these accounts in the way it follows the double entry principle. Otherwise, recording asset disposals would be a messy business, and mistakes would be easily made.

Three pairs of postings
With the asset disposal account you will need to make three pairs of postings:

- transfer the asset concerned from its asset account to your new asset disposal account

- transfer the provision for depreciation from its own account to your asset disposal account

- post the sale proceeds to your asset disposal account, with the counterpart posting to cash, bank, or a personal ledger account if sold on credit.

The resulting profit or loss
The balance c/d on the asset disposal account will then represent a profit (if credit) or loss (if debit) on sale of asset. In the end, along with all the other revenue and expense account balances, it will go to the trading, profit and loss account.

JOURNAL

Date	Particulars	Fo.	Dr.	Cr.
200X				
Feb 22	Sundries			
	Asset disposal	NL40	10,000	
	Motor van	NL20		10,000
	Provision for depreciation	NL30	6,000	
	Asset disposal	NL40		6,000
	Bank	CB25	3,000	
	Asset disposal	NL40		3,000
	To record the disposal of a motor van			

---

p40 **NOMINAL LEDGER**

Asset disposal account

200X		Fo.		200X		Fo.	
Feb 22	Motor van	NL20	10,000	Feb 22	Provision for depreciation	NL30	6,000
					Bank	CB25	3,000
					Balance c/d		1,000
			10,000				10,000
Feb 23	Balance b/d		1,000				

---

p20 *Motor van account*

200X		Fo.		200X		Fo.	
Jan 1	Balance	b/d	10,000	Feb 22	Asset disposal	NL40	10,000

---

p30 *Provision for depreciation account*

200X		Fo.		200X		Fo.	
Feb 22	Asset disposal	NL40	6,000	Jan 1	Balance	b/d	6,000

---

p25 **CASH BOOK**

200X				200X
Feb 22	Asset disposal	NL40	3,000	

Fig. 113. An example of journalising and ledger posting for an asset disposal
(a motor van originally bought for £10,000 and now sold for £3,000).

63   Asset disposals step by step

What you will need
- the nominal ledger
- the journal
- the cash book.

Step by step

1. In the next available space in the journal, write the date in the appropriate column, and the word 'Sundries' to indicate a combination posting. Below that write 'Asset disposal [name of asset]', as in the example opposite.

2. Enter the original value of the asset, i.e. the value actually recorded in the asset account, in the debit cash column (in the example, £10,000).

3. Beneath your heading, indenting slightly, write the name of the asset concerned: 'Motor van'.

4. Enter the same book value (£10,000) in the credit cash column.

5. Beneath your last entry in the particulars column, write: 'Provision for depreciation on [name of asset]'.

6. In the debit cash column, enter the balance showing on provision for depreciation account, e.g. £6,000.

7. Beneath your last entry in the particulars column, indenting slightly, write the name of the asset disposal account concerned.

8. In the credit cash column, enter the balance of the provision for depreciation account, e.g. £6,000.

9. In the particulars column write 'Cash' or 'Bank' as appropriate (or the name of a personal account if the van was sold on credit).

10. Enter sales proceeds in the debit cash column (e.g. £3,000).

11. Beneath the last entry in the particulars column, indenting slightly, write the name of the asset disposal account concerned.

12. Enter the value of sales proceeds in the credit cash column, e.g. £3,000.

13. Beneath this set of entries write: 'To record disposal of [asset concerned]'.

14. Make postings to the ledger following the instructions you have just recorded in the journal. Open new accounts where necessary.

15. Total up and balance the asset account, the provision for depreciation account and the asset disposal acount, the last of which will be the only one which may have a balance remaining. Remember, you need a separate asset disposal account for each asset disposed of.

16. Remember to complete the folio columns.

ERRORS IN ACCOUNTS

1. *Errors of omission*
    A transaction has been missed out altogether.

2. *Errors of commission*
    A transaction has been posted to the wrong account, though to the right side. For example, posted to 'John Smith A/c' instead of 'Colin Smith A/c'.

3. *Compensation errors*
    Different errors of the same value, occurring on the opposite sides of the ledger divisions. The effect of one is obscured by the equal effect of the other, so that the trial balance still balances. There could, in fact, be more than two errors involved, the total debit errors matching the total credit errors.

4. *Errors of principle*
    Where an expense item has been posted to an asset account. Example, a 'Motor expense' has been posted to 'Motor car account'.

5. *Errors of original entry*
    The original entry was wrong. Perhaps the source document, such as an invoice, has been added up incorrectly by a sales office clerk, or misread by the bookkeeper.

6. *Errors of reversal*
    Both aspects have been posted to the wrong sides: the debit aspect to the credit side, and vice versa.

7. *Posting to the wrong side of the ledger*
    Errors due to the transaction being posted to the wrong side of the ledger.

8. *Omitting one side of dual posting*
    Errors due to complete omission of one side of the dual posting.

9. *Under or overstatement*
    Errors due to under- or overstating one side of the transaction. Example: a gross invoice value, inclusive of VAT, has been posted to an asset or expense account in the ledger.

10. *Errors of summation*
    Sometimes known as 'casting errors'. Columns have been added up incorrectly, and the wrong balance carried down.

11. *Errors of transposition*
    A figure has been accidentally reversed. For example 32 has been written as 23, or 414 as 441. This error is always a multiple of 9, and if the error is one of transposition it can be spotted fairly easily.

Fig. 114. Errors in accounts.

The right way to correct errors

No figure should ever be crossed out anywhere in the accounts. If allowed it could hide embezzlement. Of course, genuine mistakes are made, but there is a special way of putting them right. If an error is found it must be recorded in the journal, together with whatever additions or subtractions are needed to the accounts to put matters right.

Types of error

There are 11 types of error, which we can summarise as follows:

Errors of omission

Errors of commission

Compensating errors

Errors of principle

Errors of original entry

Errors of reversal

Errors of posting to the wrong side of ledger

Errors of omitting one side of dual posting

Errors of over/understating one side

Errors of summation ('casting errors')

Errors of transposition.

On the opposite page each one is explained in more detail.

Only the last five of these will be shown up by the trial balance failing to balance.

An error of commission, original entry or reversal will become apparent when a customer or supplier, whose account has been wrongly affected, informs you. They will certainly be quick to let you know if the error is to their disadvantage.

JOURNAL

Date	Particulars	Dr.	Cr.
200X			
April 30	K. Gange	2,000.00	
	Sales		2,000.00
	To correct error of omission		
30	Heat and light	400.00	
	Purchases		400.00
	To correct error of principle		
30	S. Jones	90.00	
	Motor expenses	10.00	
	Cash sales		100.00
	To correct compensating errors due to motor expenses and cash sales both being undercast and S. Jones (debit) being omitted		
30	A. Singer	50.00	
	A. Singh		50.00
	To correct error of commission		
30	Motor expenses	15.00	
	Edwards Garage		15.00
	To correct error of original entry		
30	Depreciation	80.00	
	Provision for depreciation		80.00
	To correct error of reversal affecting both accounts in the sum of £40.00*		

Fig. 115. Accounting for errors: entries in the journal. Note: if depreciation account has been credited with £40.00, instead of debited, we must debit it with £80.00 and vice versa for provision of depreciation account.

170

65 Correcting errors step by step

Identifying errors
As we saw on page 83, only the following errors will be shown up by the trial balance failing to balance:

- errors of posting one aspect of the transaction to the wrong side of the ledger
- errors of omission of one side of the dual posting
- errors of under- or overstating one side of the transaction
- errors of summation ('casting errors')
- errors of transposition of digits (e.g. 32 written as 23).

Looking for errors in the trial balance step by step
1. If the trial balance fails, look for a figure equal to the error amongst all the balances. If such a figure appears once only, its dual posting may have been omitted from the trial balance (though it may also be included in a larger posting), or that figure may have been missed out when summing the column.

2. Next, divide the discrepancy by 2. Look for a figure equal to the quotient of the calculation in the trial balance. If the error is due to something being posted on the wrong side, this will show it up.

3. Check whether the discrepancy is divisible by 9. If it is, it may be due to an error of transposition.

4. Check your addition of the columns.

5. Check that each of the balances in turn have been correctly copied from the ledger accounts.

6. Check the balances of the ledger accounts.

Treatment of minor errors
If an error reflected in the trial balance is small (e.g. £30) and it is hard to trace, it is permissible to add it to current liabilities or current assets under the heading **suspense account** just so that compilation of final accounts can go ahead. But you should never do this when the error is large. When you find the error, correct it in the journal as described (see example on opposite page).

Of course, the true profit or loss figure may be distorted as a result of this error. That is why it is only permissible to handle small errors in this way. When the error is later discovered and corrected, a statement of corrected net profit can be written up to supplement the year's final accounts.

Correcting errors and closing the suspenses account
Before the error is corrected

NOMINAL LEDGER

Suspense account

Current assets   30.00

Current assets

Suspense account   30.00

When the error is corrected

JOURNAL

Current assets	30.00	
Suspense account		30.00
Name of 1st correct account	30.00	
Name of 2nd correct account		30.00
Correcting ledger accounts		

NOMINAL LEDGER

Current assets

Suspense account   30.00

Suspense account

Current assets   30.00

Name of 1st correct account

Name of 2nd correct account   30.00

Name of 2nd correct account

Name of 1st correct account   30.00

Fig. 116. Correcting error and closing the suspense account.

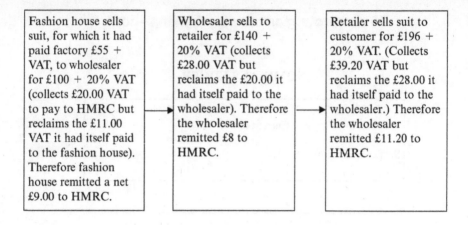

Fashion house sells suit, for which it had paid factory £55 + VAT, to wholesaler for £100 + 20% VAT (collects £20.00 VAT to pay to HMRC but reclaims the £11.00 VAT it had itself paid to the fashion house). Therefore fashion house remitted a net £9.00 to HMRC.

Wholesaler sells to retailer for £140 + 20% VAT (collects £28.00 VAT but reclaims the £20.00 it had itself paid to the wholesaler). Therefore the wholesaler remitted £8 to HMRC.

Retailer sells suit to customer for £196 + 20% VAT. (Collects £39.20 VAT but reclaims the £28.00 it had itself paid to the wholesaler.) Therefore the wholesaler remitted £11.20 to HMRC.

So in the chain from fashion house to consumer the VAT content has grown at an increasing rate and the total amount of VAT that has gone to the HMRC is £28.20 (£9 + £8 + £11.20 = £28.20).

Fig. 117. VAT is collected at various stages in the chain of transactions from manufacturer to end-user.

A tax on purchases

Value Added Tax (or VAT) is very different from income tax and corporation tax. The last two are claimed at the point of income – VAT is claimed at the point of purchase. Also, a business is a source of taxation for income tax and corporation tax, but for VAT it is simply a kind of collector. A **taxable** firm has to collect VAT on the sale price of all its goods and services from its customers, and pay it over to HM Revenue and Customs (HMRC) as **output tax**. Of course, the firm is also a customer of other firms, because it needs to buy goods and services itself. But the VAT it pays on these purchases (**input tax**) can be set against the VAT it has collected from its customers; it only has to pay the balance (difference) to HMRC. (If the balance is a negative one, then HMRC refund the balance to the firm.) So in the end, it is only private individuals who actually pay VAT – plus firms too small to have to register for VAT (though they can still register if they wish).

Which businesses need to register for VAT?

The answer is any business whose turnover in the past year was at least £83,000 unless it reasonably expects that by end of the next month the annual turnover to date will fall below that threshold figure. If a firm's sales in the next month alone are likely to be at least £83,000 it must register for VAT. If its annual turnover subsequently falls below £81,000 it can deregister if it wishes.

Registration is also compulsory without any threshold level if:

- it sells excise goods such as tobacco or alcohol;
- it makes any sales of assets on which a VAT refund has been claimed by a predecessor in the chain. These are known as Relevant Goods in VAT terminology.

Which businesses have to keep VAT accounts?

All registered business must keep full VAT accounts. Firms that are not registered do not need to account for VAT and will ignore the fact that part of the invoice totals they enter in their purchase day books and petty cash books represent VAT. They cannot reclaim VAT they have paid to suppliers nor charge VAT on their invoices to customers. VAT does not appear anywhere in their accounts.

VAT periods

VAT periods are normally quarterly, but a business can elect to account to HMRC on a monthly basis instead. If the business supplies mainly or exclusively exempt and /or zero-rated goods and services it will usually receive a VAT refund. In such cases it is better if the business elects to account on a monthly basis so that the refunds arrive sooner and start earning interest in the bank sooner. The managers will have to decide whether the refunds are of a significant size to warrant the extra work involved in tripling the number of VAT returns that have to be completed and filed (monthly instead of quarterly).

VAT rates

There are a number of VAT statuses falling into two main categories:

- exempt
- taxable.

In the second category there can be an infinite number of different tax rates applying to different kinds of goods or services. The rate can be zero per cent, or any number of positive rates. 'Zero rated' does not mean 'exempt'. They are two different things.

The standard rate of VAT in the UK is currently 20%. There is also currently a reduced rate of 5% which applies to children's car seats and domestic fuel and power. Things like food and children's clothing are currently zero rated. VAT rates in existence at the time of writing are as follows:

	Examples of goods and services
Standard rate	Most goods and services
Reduced rate	Children's car seats, domestic fuel and power and mobility aid for people over 60
Zero rate	Most foods, children's clothing, books, newspapers and motorcycle helmets

Exempt goods and services include such things as postal and banking services and any goods supplied by an exempt business.

Keeping up to date

VAT rules and rates change from time to time and up-to-date information can be obtained from notices published on HMRC's website www.hmrc.gov.uk.

Notice no. 700 is the general VAT guide and there is a comprehensive range of booklets to cover a multitude of different subjects.

Other terms you need to know and understand

- Inputs
- Input tax
- Outputs
- Output tax
- VAT on acquisitions from other EU states.

Inputs are the taxable goods and services the business has purchased. Outputs are the taxable goods and services it has supplied to customers. Output tax is the tax it has added to its invoices to customers and for which it must remit to HMRC. Input tax is the VAT it has been charged by its suppliers and which it can deduct from the figure it has to remit to HMRC. VAT is not charged by suppliers of goods from other EU states but such a figure has to be remitted to HMRC directly by the purchaser rather than indirectly via the supplier. There is a special box on the VAT return form for such figure.

Up until recently VAT was not charged to customers in the UK by suppliers of services from other EU member states. However, the customers, themselves, had to pay such a figure to HMRC on the services they received. This was because they were deemed to have been supplied in the country of origin rather than the country of receipt, where the customers would be liable for VAT. From January 2010, the VAT rules have changed so that those provided by suppliers in another EU member state are deemed to be supplied in the country of the customer rather than the country of origin and services relating to land or property are deemed to be supplied where the land or property is located. VAT has, therefore, to be charged on them by the suppliers. Financially, it hasn't really made any difference to VAT registered customers; it has just made things simpler at the VAT return stage.

There are exceptions to this *place of supply* rule and in that respect it is complicated. Precise treatment is outside the scope of this book and readers should refer to the HMRC website for further details when required.

Invoicing and VAT

VAT has to be calculated on the net amount of the income after deduction of any trade discount. Do not confuse this with early settlement discount (see page 67). That is a different issue and does not affect the VAT calculation on the invoice.

When making out the invoice:

1.   Add up all the goods and/or services being charged for.
2.   Deduct trade discount if any.
3.   Calculate VAT.

If there is a mixture of different rated goods and perhaps also some exempt goods then:

1.   List them in separate batches.
2.   Add up each batch and calculate the VAT on each total.

The calculation is easy.

Calculating the VAT figure

There is more than one way to work out the VAT to be applied to a price. They are just looking at the same thing from different angles. The more ways you think about the same thing the more it should become understood and the more it will stick in your memory.

Here's one way:

$$\text{Net price} \times \frac{\text{VAT percentage}}{100}$$

This merely turns the VAT percentage into a decimal. When you realise this you will find it easier just to remember to multiply the net price by the VAT percentage expressed as a decimal and this means just moving the decimal point two places to the left. For example, if the VAT rate is 20% then the VAT rate expressed as a decimal is 0.20. So just think '× 0.20'.

As mentioned earlier this is exactly the same thing as multiplying the net amount by the VAT rate/100 because dividing anything by 100 simply moves the decimal point two places to the left. This technique just cuts out the first stage of the calculation. It's easier to remember, it takes less time and uses up less paper.

Many pocket calculators have a percentage key and providing they use '*as you say it*' logic it takes the same number of steps to calculate the VAT figure:

$$\boxed{\times} \quad \boxed{\text{VAT rate}} \quad \boxed{\%} \quad \boxed{=}$$

It's just as quick and simple to multiply by the VAT rate expressed as a decimal, although you may wish to use the calculator for this simple multiplication, depending on how arithmetically skilled you are:

$$\boxed{\times} \quad \boxed{.} \quad \boxed{\text{VAT rate}} \quad \text{i.e.} \quad \boxed{\times} \quad \boxed{.} \quad \boxed{20} \quad \text{for a rate of 20\%}$$

You then just add this figure to the net figure to arrive at the gross figure which you are asking the customer to pay.

Cash discount or early settlement discount

Where a cash discount or early settlement discount (e.g. for settlement within 14 days) is offered VAT is calculated on the discounted figure. The VAT does not change even if settlement is not made within the stated period.

You will often see an annotation on invoices saying *deduct x% if paid within 7 days*, or words to that effect. Such discounts offered are typically figures like 2%, 2½%, 5%, etc. This discount is not deducted in the cash column of the invoice but stated as an addendum. The VAT figure shown in the cash column, however, takes into account this discount and so may at first sight appear to be an error. Take the following invoice for goods VAT rated at 20%, for example:

Goods total net of VAT	100.00
VAT	19.00
Total including VAT	119.00

It would be tempting to jump to the conclusion that the VAT figure is wrong and that it should be £20.00. But if there is an addendum on the invoice offering a 5% discount for early settlement then the 20% VAT has been calculated on £95, not £100.

Where invoices only show the VAT-inclusive figure

Sometimes invoices for goods and services purchased will not show VAT separately from the gross total. In such cases the bookkeeper must calculate the VAT content. This is an easy process – the opposite of finding the VAT inclusive, or gross figure from the net and the VAT rate.

To find the gross figure you can do one of two things.

1. Calculate the VAT and add it to the starting figure, e.g.

$$£200 \times 0.20 = 40 + 200 = £240$$

2. Or you can multiply the original figure by '1 . rate', e.g.

$$£200 \times 1.20 = £240$$

These are not fundamentally different ways, for when we multiplied £200 by 0.20 in the first example '200 × 1'was added at the end:

$$\boxed{200 \times 1}$$

$$200 \times .20 = 40 + 200 = 240$$

> It could just as easily have been added in here to make this 1.20 instead of .20

The second version is quicker, easier to remember and takes up less space on paper.

Suppose you have the gross figure and you wish to find the net figure. Well, if you found the gross figure from the net by multiplying by:

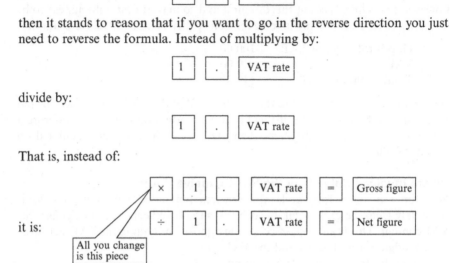

then it stands to reason that if you want to go in the reverse direction you just need to reverse the formula. Instead of multiplying by:

divide by:

That is, instead of:

it is:

When you have the net content the difference between that and the gross is the VAT.

	VAT summary				
200X			**200X**		
Input tax	Jan	950.50	Output tax	Jan	1,410.32
	Feb	1,140.25		Feb	2,015.35
	Mar	1,209.20		Mar	2,200.95
		3,299.95			5,626.62
Add VAT allowable on acquisitions from other EU states		65.60	VAT due on acquisitions from other EU states		65.60
Deduct net input tax overclaim from previous returns		(115.00)	Add net output tax understatement on previous returns		210.08
Bad debt relief		195.75	Annual adjustment for special retailer scheme		75.45
Sub-total		3,446.30	Sub-total		5,977.75
Less VAT on credit notes inwards		(35.53)	Less VAT on credit notes outwards		(52.56)
Total VAT deductable		3,410.77	Total VAT payable		5,925.19
			Less total VAT deductable		(3,410.77)
			VAT payable to HMRC		2,514.42

Fig. 118. A typical VAT summary.

Requirement to keep VAT records

Registered businesses have to keep records of VAT paid and received at the various rates – including zero – and also a record of all exempt supplies it makes. Different kinds of businesses record VAT differently.

Partly exempt businesses

Where a firm sells both exempt, zero and positive-rated goods the accounting gets a bit complex. It becomes necessary to apportion their turnover. There are special schemes for retailers to make it easier to make the apportionments. However, as there are a number of such schemes they are outside the scope of this book. Here we can only focus on the mainstream VAT requirements and methods of accounting.

VAT records

There are several ways of keeping VAT records – a basic one used by most types of business, and various special schemes for particular kinds of business.

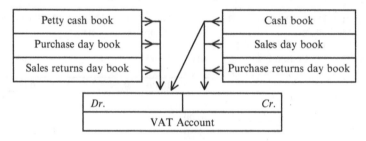

Fig. 119. Sources for the VAT account.

The prime entries for VAT

If a business is registered for VAT it needs a place to make the prime entries for VAT. This can simply be an extra column or so in the day books (see examples on page 182). In the extra column you separately record the VAT content of purchase invoices (**inputs**) and of sales invoices (**outputs**). The petty cash book, too, can be used to record VAT in the same way; in a special column you can enter the VAT charged on petrol and other small items.

We have already come across this extra column in the day books and the petty cash book earlier on (page 46). From there it is just a matter of posting the extra column to the ledger (i.e. a 'VAT account' in the ledger) along with others, i.e. the individual, analysed 'Net amount' columns:

- you post the VAT on purchases to the debit of the VAT account
- you post the VAT on sales to the credit of the VAT account.

SALES DAY BOOK

Date 200X	Customer	Inv no	Gross value	Net zero R (0%)	Net rate A (20%)	Net rate B (5%)	VAT	Analysis columns
Jan 1	S. Jones	59	150.00	150.00				
4	A. Singh	60	540.00	192.75	208.00	93.00	46.25	
			690.00	350.36	208.00	93.00	46.25	

PURCHASE DAY BOOK

Date 200X	Supplier	Inv no	Gross value	Net zero R (0%)	Net rate A (20%)	Net rate B (5%)	VAT	Analysis columns
Jan 4	Entwhistle	1/01	460.00		383.33		76.66	

PETTY CASH BOOK

p50

Dr.   Cr.

← Analysis columns →

Amount	Fo.	Date 200X	Particulars	Rcp. no.	Gross value	Net exempt	Net rate A	Net rate B	VAT	Postg.	Stnry
40.00		Jan 1	Balance b/d								
		28	Stamps	1/1	10.00	10.00				10.00	
			Envelopes	1/2	11.50			9.58	1.91		9.58
					21.50	10.00	9.58		1.50	10.00	9.58
21.50	CB8	31	Cash						NL30	NL15	NLl17
			Balance c/d		40.00						
61.50					61.50						
40.00		Feb 1	Balance b/d								

LEDGER

p30

NL50   VAT
Dr.   Cr.
200X   1991

Jan 31	Bought ledger Control	BL60	60.00	Jan 1	Balance	b/d	30.00
	Petty cash	PCB50	1.50	31	Sales ledger Control	SL61	38.64
31	Bank	CB47	7.14				
			68.64				68.64

Note: The entry annotated 'Bank' represents a cheque paid to HM Revenue and Customs for the balance payable for the quarter.

Fig. 120. Accounting for VAT: worked example of VAT recordings in daybook, petty cash book and ledger.

You then total up and balance the VAT account, just like any other account in the ledger. The balance represents the tax payable or repayable, depending on whether the firm has collected in more than it has paid out.

Registered businesses are also required to keep a VAT summary. This is not a ledger account but a summary or memorandum as such things are called in accounting terms. It is not part of the double entry system. Figure 118 provides an illustration.

VAT relief on bad debts
If a debt owing to the business is more than six months old the output tax paid on the invoice can be reclaimed from HMRC. If it is in the end paid, the output tax reclaimed must be repaid to HMRC.

VAT that cannot be reclaimed
- *VAT on cars used by the business.* Businesses cannot usually reclaim VAT on cars purchased for use in the business.
- *Goods taken from the business for private use.* If the owner of a business takes goods from the business for his or her own private use their drawings account must be debited with the full amount which the business paid for the goods, including the VAT, while, on the other hand, the purchases account must be credited with the net amount and the VAT account credited with the VAT content.

VAT and the final accounts
The collection of VAT is not part of the essence of business transactions; it is just a duty that is imposed upon businesses by HMRC that has to be carried out alongside them. Consequently it does not figure in the profits or losses of the firm and so will not appear anywhere in the profit and loss account. It will show in the balance sheet, however, as the business, if it is registered for VAT, will almost certainly hold funds that are owed to VAT or have money owed to it in the form of a repayment of VAT at the date of the balance sheet. The latter will, therefore, be likely to contain a figure for VAT in either its current assets or its current liabilities.

At the end of the VAT period a business has to complete and send in a VAT return to HMRC (see Fig. 121). Accuracy in accounting and prompt filing of returns is required by HMRC. Penalties apply for late filing. In Figure 121:

- Boxes 1–5 are for computation of tax payable or reclaimable.
- Boxes 6–9 are for statistical purposes.

Completing the VAT return
At the end of each of the three months, prior to the end of the current VAT period:

- The total net sales should have been posted from the sales day book to the credit side of the Sales account in the nominal ledger and the total VAT to the credit side of the VAT account in the same ledger.
- The total net sales returns should have been posted from the sales returns day book to the debit side of the Sales account in the nominal ledger and the total VAT to the debit side of the VAT account in the same ledger.
- The total net purchases should have been posted from the purchases day book to the debit side of the Purchases account in the nominal ledger and the total VAT to the debit side of the VAT account in the same ledger.
- The total net purchase returns should have been posted from the purchase returns day book to the credit side of the Purchases account in the nominal ledger and the total VAT to the credit side of the VAT account in the same ledger.
- The total net purchases should have been posted from the petty cash book to the debit side of the Purchases account in the nominal ledger and the total VAT to the debit side of the VAT account in the same ledger.

If VAT was overpaid or underpaid at the end of the last VAT period it will show in the ledger as a balance b/d at the start of the period with which you are now dealing.

If any debts have been written off during the period they will have been debited to the Sales account and the VAT content which applied debited to the VAT account, both in the nominal ledger.

The first thing to do is the VAT summary. Simply follow the format of Figure 120 on page 182 taking the figures from the Purchases, Sales and VAT accounts in the nominal ledger. The figures in the summary go on the same side as they are found in the ledger, e.g. monthly purchase totals will have been posted to the debit (left-hand) side of the Purchases account. Just copy them to the left-hand side of the VAT summary and vice versa for the monthly sales figures.

If you have any VAT due on acquisitions from other EU states it will show on the credit side of the VAT account. Copy the figure to the credit (right-hand) side of the VAT summary. If you can claim this back, as may be the case, the reclaim will appear on the debit side of the VAT account reflecting a seemingly peculiar state of affairs where you are both paying it and reclaiming it. Copy the figure to the same side of the VAT summary as it appears in the ledger.

Copy to the VAT summary any VAT underclaim or overclaim that has been carried down to the period for which you are accounting.

Copy over details of any bad debt relief you are claiming as it shows on the debit side of the VAT account.

Annual adjustments may have to be made in special retailers' schemes and if such a case applies the adjustment figure will have been posted to whatever side of the VAT account it applies. Copy it over to the VAT summary

Now you do the arithmetic. Add in the input and output tax columns. (If you are using a spreadsheet just draw a line and enter below it the formula $= sum$ and the cells concerned in brackets, e.g. = *sum(b3:b5)*.) Add all the other inputs on each side to give a sub-total and then deduct the value of credit note VAT on each side. Deduct the smaller from the larger of the two totals and you arrive at a figure for VAT payable or reclaimable.

You can now use this as the source document for completing the VAT return. The figure for box 1 is the total VAT deductible less the VAT allowable on acquisitions from other EU states if any such figure appears in the VAT summary. The latter figure goes in box 2 and box 3 is the total of these two boxes, which should be the total of the VAT deductible in the VAT summary. The figure to enter in box 4 is the total VAT payable figure from the VAT summary. Here there is no need to separate the VAT due on acquisitions figure from the rest. Box 5 is simply the difference between box 3 and box 4. Box 6 is the total value of all other outputs including any VAT. This is the total of the three months of credit postings in the Sales account of the nominal ledger, whether sold in the UK or abroad, minus any sales returns. Box 7 is same for the inputs and is the total of the three months' postings to the Purchases account, whether sold in the UK or abroad, minus any purchase returns. Box 8 requires you to provide the total value of goods net of VAT, together with any related costs, supplied to other EU countries and box 9 requires the same for acquisitions.

Computerisation

Automatic systems and specialised tools now deal with VAT easily. For example, Sage line 50 will automatically calculate the VAT and complete a VAT return which is acceptable to HMRC as long as you simply enter the date parameters of the period for which it is to account.

There are certain differences in the format used when filing a return online to those that apply for paper returns. For example, if there is nothing to enter in a box in an online form you enter 0.00 while in a paper form you are required to write NONE. A negative value (a figure to be subtracted) must be written with a minus sign before it while a negative value on a paper form must be represented by bracketing the figure. No minus signs must appear on a paper VAT return.

After thoroughly checking the accuracy of the form write your name if you are the authorised person and sign and date it. If a payment is being sent with the form tick the box on the left of the signature. Write, or procure from the cashier, the cheque and send the form off to HMRC.

Special arrangements for retailers

It would be a virtually impossible task for some shops to record every individual sale. Take a sweet shop, for example. It may well sell hundreds of packets of sweets or bars of chocolate a day. The proprietor simply wouldn't be able to record each item individually, so special schemes have been devised for retailers, which excuse them from having to keep itemised VAT records on sales. There are several such schemes, each with their own special return forms, and the retailer chooses one most suited to his or her kind of business.

Online filing is becoming compulsory

New HMRC rules require that all businesses with an annual turnover of £100,000 or more and all newly registered businesses must file their VAT return and settle their VAT account online for VAT Periods that commence on or after 1 April 2010.

For those who are not yet compelled by this rule to pay online, HMRC has also changed the way payments by cheque are treated. It previously treated the receipt of the cheque as the date payment was received, but now it will regard the date the funds go into the account as the payment date. Therefore, payments may have to be sent earlier.

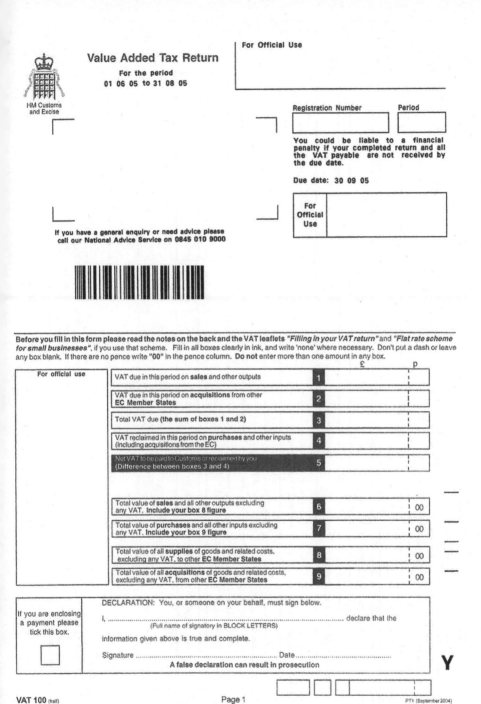

Fig. 121. Sample VAT Form (VAT 100): Courtesy Controller of
HMSO (Crown Copyright).

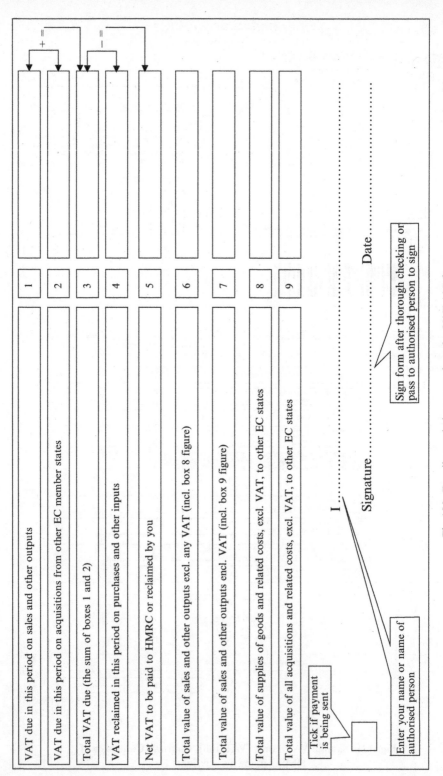

VAT due in this period on sales and other outputs	1
VAT due in this period on acquisitions from other EC member states	2
Total VAT due (the sum of boxes 1 and 2)	3
VAT reclaimed in this period on purchases and other inputs	4
Net VAT to be paid to HMRC or reclaimed by you	5
Total value of sales and other outputs excl. any VAT (incl. box 8 figure)	6
Total value of sales and other outputs encl. VAT (incl. box 9 figure)	7
Total value of supplies of goods and related costs, excl. VAT, to other EC states	8
Total value of all acquisitions and related costs, excl. VAT, to other EC states	9

+ =
- =

I ....
Signature..........
Date..........

Tick if payment is being sent

Enter your name or name of authorised person

Sign form after thorough checking or pass to authorised person to sign

Fig.122. Details needed to complete the VAT 100 form.

188

68   Incomplete records

'Shoebox jobs'

Sometimes, small businesses neglect their bookkeeping in the first year or two. They find other day-to-day business operations too demanding. The administrative side of the business seems non-productive. 'Let's make hay while the sun shines, 'they say: 'we'll catch up with the bookkeeping when business is slack'. But often the accounts are put off, until suddenly the proprietor receives a high income tax assessment and demand. This comes because HMRC has not received his final accounts on which to charge the correct tax. He is given 30 days to appeal against the assessment; the appeal will probably be granted, but he will only have a short time to get his records up to date and produce final accounts.

When he begins the task, he finds sales and purchase invoices all over the place, in no particular date order. Cheque book stubs have not all been filled in; he cannot find all his old bank statements; there are screwed up petrol receipts in every pocket of his working clothes and all corners of his lorry or van. He becomes bewildered, dumps everything he can find in a box and takes them along to an accountant. Little wonder accountants call these 'shoebox jobs'. Invariably some documents have been lost, so normal double entry bookkeeping is impossible. A way has to be found to fill in all the gaps.

The capital comparison method

One method is to draw up an opening and a closing statement of affairs, and deduct the opening capital from the closing capital. This is called the capital comparison method. The idea is to add together the fixed assets, the merchandise (stock), the accounts receivable (money owed to the proprietor after bad debt provision), cash in hand and cash at bank at the date in question. Deduct from that the accounts payable (money owed by the proprietor) and the difference will be capital. These statements are in effect the balance sheet, though the term balance sheet should really only be used when it has actually been drawn up from the proper ledger 'balances'.

- The difference between the capital at the end of the year, and that at the start of the year, is the net profit.

There is one big flaw in using this method alone. Some of the profit – we do not know how much – may have been taken out by the proprietor in drawings during the year; so the difference between opening and closing capitals will not itself necessarily tell us the profit. Example: suppose the opening capital was £10,000 and the closing capital £11,000. Deducting opening from closing capital suggests a net profit of £1,000. But what if the proprietor had drawn £5,000 during the year? The profit would then really have been £6,000 (£1,000 plus £5,000).

If we have accounts for drawings, however, this problem is resolved. We just add the drawings to the difference between opening and closing capitals to measure the profit.

Capital comparison method step by step

Let us see how we might put these statements together. Remember the formula:

$$\text{Total assets} - \text{Current liabilities} = \text{Total net assets}$$

Capital plus long-term liabilities (not payable within the next year) must equal that.

1. The first part of our closing statement of affairs will give us total net assets. We can complete it from current information, e.g. value of premises, fixtures and fittings, machinery and motor vehicles, stock (counted and valued), debtors, bank balance, cash in hand, and creditors.

2. The first section of the second half can also be filled in from current information, i.e. the details of any longterm liabilities such as bank loans. We will have to assemble both these sections from whatever evidence is available to us, where the opening statement of affairs is concerned.

3. We can also fill in the total for the second half of the statement. It will essentially be the same as the total net assets. Provided there are no long-term loans this figure will represent the capital. In our closing statement of affairs we will need to analyse this capital figure to show the net profit. This is found by addition and deduction, filling in the gaps as required. We will know the total: what we need are the figures to get us there. These are the steps in the calculation:

Example	
Opening capital (from opening statement of affairs)	1,000
Add capital injections	Nil
Add profit	(?)
Less drawings	4,000
Equals closing capital	2,000

If the opening capital was £1,000, closing capital £2,000, no additional capital injections, and drawings of £4,000, then profit must be £5,000 (£1,000 + £0 + £5,000 − £4,000 = £2,000).

ARMSTRONG ENGINEERING
STATEMENT OF AFFAIRS
as at 1 July 200X

FIXED ASSETS			
Leasehold premises			40,000
Fixtures and fittings			5,000
Motor vehicle			3,000
			48,000
CURRENT ASSETS			
Stock	2,500		
Debtors	1,900	4,400	
Less CURRENT LIABILITIES			
Creditors	2,200		
Bank overdraft	1,200	3,400	1,000
Total net assets			
Represented by capital			49,000

ARMSTRONG ENGINEERING
STATEMENT OF AFFAIRS
as at 30 June 200X

FIXED ASSETS			
Leasehold premises	40,000		
Less depreciation	2,000		38,000
Fixtures and fittings	5,000		
Less depreciation	250		4,750
Motor vehicle	3,000		
Less depreciation	1,000		2,000
			44,750
CURRENT ASSETS			
Stock	3,600		
Debtors	2,900	6,500	
Less CURRENT LIABILITIES			
Creditors	1,800		
Bank overdraft	100	1,900	
Net current assets			4,600
TOTAL NET ASSETS			49,350
Financed by:			
Opening capital			49,000
Add profit			*8,550*
Less drawings			(8,200)
			49,350

Fig. 123. Using the capital comparison method to complete. The profit figure, given in italics, is the only figure which could fulfil the requirements of the sum.

69 Capital comparison method step by step

What you need
- Records of assets and liabilities at the start of the accounting period.
- Records of assets and liabilities at the end of the period.
- As many other records as possible for the period in question.

Step by step
To draw up the statement of affairs at the start of the accounting period:

1. List the fixed assets in order of permanence, and total.
2. List and total up the current assets (in order of permanence).
3. List and total up the current liabilities.
4. Deduct from last total.
5. Add to the total fixed assets.
6. List any long-term liabilities (other than proprietor's capital) e.g. bank loans, mortgages and leases of more than a year.
7. Enter as capital whatever figure you need to make this column exactly equal the total net assets figure.

Construct, in exactly the same way, a statement of affairs as at the end of the accounting period. Deduct the opening capital from the closing capital. Add any drawings, and deduct any capital injections by the proprietor throughout the year to arrive at the net profit for the year.

The last two steps are usually built into the format of the closing statement of affairs. In the capital section you deduct the opening capital from the closing capital, and record drawings and capital injections when arriving at and displaying the net profit. You construct the statement as far as possible in standard balance sheet format, and then fill in the missing figures by simple arithmetic.

Example
Suppose Armstrong has failed to keep proper accounts during the last year. Faced with a tax demand, he asks us to calculate his profit for the year to 30 June 200X but he can only provide us with the following information: his leasehold premises were worth £40,000 at the start of the year, but have gone down in value by £2,000 since then. He had plant and machinery worth £5,000 which he has not added to; depreciation of £250 is assumed since then. A motor vehicle valued at £3,000 at the start of the year is now worth only £2,000. The stock level has risen from £2,500 to a present level of £3,600, the debtors figure has gone from

Dr.		TOTAL DEBTORS ACCOUNT		Cr.
Balance b/d	200.00	Cheques	150.00	
Sales	300.00	Balance c/d	350.00	
	500.00		500.00	

	TOTAL CREDITORS ACCOUNT		
Cash paid to		Balance b/d	2,000.00
Suppliers	1,200.00	Purchases	2,200.00
Balance c/d	3,000.00		
	4,200.00		4,200.00

BANK RECONCILIATION
as at 31 December 200X

Balance as per bank statement (overdrawn)		7,010.00
Add cheques drawn but not as yet presented for payment:		
S. Jones	90.00	
Frazer & Baines	100.00	190.00
Corrected balance as per bank statement (overdrawn)		7,200.00

BANK RECONCILIATION
as at 31 December 200X

Balance as per bank statement (overdrawn)		6,247.00
Add cheques drawn but not as yet presented for payment:		
A. Singh	45.00	
Inko	145.00	190.00
Corrected balance as per bank statement (overdrawn)		6,437.00

Fig. 124. Opening and closing bank reconciliations.

£1,900 to £2,900. The bank overdraft has gone down from £1,200 to £100 and creditors have gone down from £2,200 to £1,800. Furthermore, we know he has taken drawings of £8,200 to live on during the year. Page 193 shows how we would calculate his profit using the capital comparison method.

Additional proof for the taxman

While the calculation of profit based on this method alone may satisfy the proprietor of a small business, the staff at HM Revenue and Customs are, understandably, likely to require additional proof that the profit figure claimed is accurate. After all, it is asking them to rely 100% on the honesty of the proprietor, not to mention the quality of his memory, in respect of the drawings he has taken.

If we have details of cash and banking transactions, plus accrued debtors and creditors for trading transactions and expenses, we can put together a trading, profit and loss account for the period, and we can use it to prove the figures in the closing statement of affairs. In fact, we could even compile the closing statement of affairs directly from those same sources, with the addition of information from the opening statement of affairs and details of any capital changes and changes in long term liabilities.

This is how to compile final accounts where many – but not all – the records are available. It involves drawing up:

- opening and closing statements of affairs
- cash and bank account analyses, which itself requires opening and closing bank reconciliations
- total debtors account
- total creditors account
- trial balance
- revenue accounts.

Dr.	200X	Particulars	Motor	Wages	Rent	Heat/light	Post/tel	Drwgs	Spec items	Cr. Totals
		A. FRAZER **BANK ACCOUNT ANALYSIS** for year ended 31 December 200X								
1,200.00	Jan 1	Balance b/d								
	1	Edwards Garage	40.00							40.00
	3	S. Wilson		250.20						250.20
	5	Edwards Garage	310.10							310.10
1,520.00	15	Debtors								
	18	Razi & Thaung			20.70					20.70
	20	A. Morris		31.50						31.50
220.40	27	Entwhistle								
	27	Northern Elec				100.00				100.00
	28	L. Cleaves		30.00						30.00
	31	Cash						400.00		400.00
	31	Brit. Telecom					50.00			50.00
	31	Keele Engineering							4,100.00	4,100.00
	Feb 6	S. Wilson		200.00						200.00
	22	A. Morris		70.00						70.00
3,800.00	23	Morgan & Baldwyn								
	28	Northern Elec.				50.00				50.00
	28	Cash						400.00		400.00
	28	Balance c/d								714.90
6,740.40		Totals	350.10	581.70	20.70	150.00	50.00	800.00	4,100.00	6,767.40
714.90	Mar 1	Balance b/d								

Fig. 125. Part of a typical bank account analysis. There would probably be many of such sheets required. This simple worked example assumes all income was banked and all expenditure was by cheque (which is highly unlikely but convenient for our purposes). If there was income and expediture in cash then a cash analysis would be desirable, but not always possible due to lack of records.

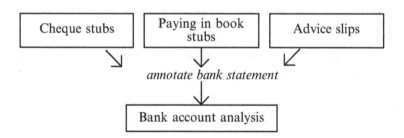

Fig. 126. Annotating the bank statements and then working from them has practical advantages.

70 Bank account analysis step by step

What you need

- Cheque book stubs, paying-in book stubs, bank statements, and any advice slips from the bank explaining entries on the bank statements. The proprietor may have to obtain duplicates of lost bank statements, and his bank will charge for these. He may also have to obtain paid (cancelled) cheques from the bank, where the counterfoils of such cheques have not been filled in.

- Several sheets of wide analysis paper with plenty of columns (e.g. up to 20), including a boldly ruled cash column on each side.

Sort the source documents into date order. Fill in any uncompleted cheque stubs after obtaining the information from cleared cheques or the proprietor's knowledge. Rule off the first bank statement at the date just before the start of the accounting period and do a bank reconciliation as at that date.

Step by step

1. Head an analysis sheet: 'Bank account analysis for... [business name]... for period... [dates concerned]'.

2. Enter the opening balance from your reconciliation as at the last date of the previous accounting period – not the balance as per the bank statement. (Remember, if the balance is 'in favour' it will go on the left, and vice versa.)

3. Head the first column on the left 'Dr.' and the last column on the right 'Cr.'.

4. List the values of each of the lodgements in the far left hand cash column (Dr.) and the values of each of the cheques in the far right hand column (Cr.). Do this for the whole period covered by the first bank statement. You can take them directly from the bank statements to save time. If most lodgements represent sales revenue you can annotate the exceptions on the bank statement and use it also as a source for analysis later.

5. Add and balance the two columns. Bring forward your balance, just as you would any ledger account.

6. Repeat the process for the period covered by the next bank statement, and so on to the end of the accounting period.

7. Prepare a bank reconciliation statement for the final date of the accounting period.

```
ANYBANK Plc.                    Sheet Number 14

                         BANK STATEMENT




Statement as at 31 December 200X


                                                              03542256

Date     Particulars        Payments          Receipts              Balance

200X     Opening balance                                            350.55
12 Dec   sundry credit                        400.00 sales          750.55
15 Dec               543255  25.00 motor exp                        725.55
18 Dec               543256  105.10 telephone                       620.45
20 Dec   sundry credit                        350.50 rent received  970.95
28 Dec               543257  10.85 stationery                       960.10
```

Fig. 127. Example of an annotated bank statement.

Sales	Particulars	Motor exp	Wages	Rent	Heat/ light	Post/ tel	Drawgs	Bldg reprs
3,800.00	Sheet 1	350.20	511.50	20.70	150.00	50.00	800.00	4,100.00
2,000.00	2	50.80	500.00	20.70	100.00	50.00	300.00	
1,200.00	3	19.00	800.00	20.70	110.00	10.00	400.00	
7,000.00	Totals	420.00	1,811.50	62.10	360.00	110.00	1,500.00	4,100.00

Fig. 128. Example of a summary of bank account analysis columns.
Note: it does not include the totals columns.

8. Extend your bank account analysis to show any extra details (leading to a different balance) shown in your bank reconciliation as at the end of the period (if, of course, the balance is different).

9. Now go back to your first analysis sheet and work your way through analysing each payment and each lodgement into an analysis column, as if it were a day book. The analysis columns for the payments will be credit columns, and those for lodgements will be debit columns: you are analysing the total credit entry to bank account that results from paying all the cheques involved. The double entry principle is not directly involved here; if it were, anlaysis of expenses would not be credit entries. The dividing line between the debit and credit columns will depend on how much of the categories apply to lodgements and payments respectively. Your list of headings, which refer to imaginary ledger accounts, will develop as you go along. You can't decide them all in advance, since you won't know the nature of each transaction until you get to it. You may well run out of analysis columns for payments. Keep one column aside as a 'miscellaneous one'; then you can record any odd bits and pieces there, and analyse them separately on another sheet. To do this, set up a supplementary sheet with the headings you need. Transfer each item by analysing it in the appropriate columns on the supplementary sheet. When all the items have been dealt with enter on the original sheet, in brackets or in red ink, in the miscellaneous column, a figure equal to the column total, to complete the transfer. In the unlikely event that you need a *misc* column on the debit side too, just follow the same procedure.

10. Sum the analysis columns for each sheet.

11. Prepare a summary of analysis column totals for each sheet.

12. Total up the summary columns.

Finishing the job: drawing up final accounts
1. Prepare total debtors and creditors accounts.

2. Extract a trial balance.

3. Adjust for depreciation, bad and doubtful debts, accruals, prepayments, asset disposals and closing stock, obtaining details from the proprietor.

4. Draw up final accounts. Refer to appropriate chapters.

KEY RATIOS AND WHAT THEY MEAN

	Concept	Equation	Optimum value	Diagnostic value
1.	Current ratio	$\dfrac{\text{Current assets}}{\text{Current liabilities}}$	2:1	Test of solvency: i.e. a firm's ability to pay its debts
2.	Acid test ratio	$\dfrac{\text{Current assets} - \text{stock}}{\text{Current liabilities}}$	1:1	A refinement of the above
3.	Asset turnover	$\dfrac{\text{Sales}}{\text{Net assets}}$	*	Reveals efficiency of asset usage in terms of sales
4.	Mark up	Gross profit as a percentage of cost of goods sold	*	A test of profitability. It reveals whether wholesale prices and other costs of sales are low enough to allow a good level of profit
5.	Gross profit margin	Gross profit as a percentage of sales	*	As above
6.	Net profit margin	Net profit as a percentage of sales	*	Shows whether overheads are too high to allow a suitable profit
7.	RoCE (return on capital employed)	Net profit margin × asset turnover × 100	*	Of special interest to investors: shows the return on investment in the company
8.	Stock turnover	$\dfrac{\text{Cost of goods sold}}{\text{Average stock}}$	*	Shows how efficiently the firm is using its asset of stock

If average stock level throughout the year is not known it may be estimated from the average of opening and closing stocks: using closing stock alone is not satisfactory, since it may be unusually high or low depending on when the last deliveries were made in relation to the Balance Sheet date.

	Concept	Equation	Optimum value	Diagnostic value
9.	Debt collection period	$\dfrac{\text{Debtors} \times 365}{\text{Sales}}$		Shows how well or badly the firm controls the amount of credit it gives. The lower the better

Note *The higher the better. These optimum values are a rule of thumb only; some firms maintain very different ones without any implication of financial instability or inefficiency. It depends, in the end, on the firm and its aims.

Fig. 129. Key ratios and what they mean.

A variety of needs

Different people want to examine a firm's final accounts for different reasons. Final accounts are a means of proving the profits of a business to HM Revenue and Customs; but to other users they will mean much more. A purchaser of a business, an investor, a bank or other lender, or a major supplier will study them in detail to discover more information than profit alone. In fact, banks, other lenders and trade creditors will be far more interested in liquidity than profitability. Firms with high profits are not necessarily the most stable ones: often the opposite is true.

Don't confuse capital with cash either. They are different things. Capital is assets minus liabilities and even though a firm may have made high profits it could still be short of cash, because the profit simply means its net assets have increased and these may contain little or no cash.

The accounts also help the management team. Managers will study interim accounts (accounts produced more than once in the accounting year) as well as the final accounts. They need to compare actual performance and spending figures against budgeted figures, figures of previous periods, figures of competitors and average figures for the size and type of business. They, like other interested parties, will want to check the ratios between different balance sheet items because they can warn of weaknesses in the financial structure of the firm.

Criticism of accounts

An interested party will compare this year's figures with last year's, for example sales and purchases, closing stocks and gross profit as a percentage of sales. How have the key ratios changed from one year to the next? Were changes in the first three of these due to changes in market prices or valuation changes? Or were they due to improved market share or efficiency of operation? Has gross profit as a percentage of sales remained constant in spite of increased turnover? A change in gross profit margin could be due to retail price cutting, wholesale price increase absorption (not passing it all on to customers), increases in delivery charges or reduced efficiency of the sales forces.

A change in the net profit to sales ratio will be due to increased overheads, but the firm will need to investigate which ones are to blame.

A high RoCE (return on capital employed) should be investigated: is it realistic? Profits may be inflated by simply over-valuing stocks, through poor estimating of quantities and/or values. There is more than one way of defining RoCE, but the formula shown is a common one. What matters is that the same formula is used consistently when comparing figures, from one period to the next, or one firm to another.

Different ways of valuing assets	
Asset category	**Method**
Fixed assets	Net realisable value Revenue generating capacity

	Historical cost less depreciation calculated by:
	        Straight line method
	        Diminishing balance method
	        Machine hours method

Current assets *Stock* *Debtors*	LIFO Average cost method
Provision for bad and doubtful debts	The percentage allowed for bad and doubtful debts should only change for good reason and clear notification and explanation to interested parties

Fig. 130. Different ways of valuing assets.

Failure to write down assets properly (vehicles, machinery, etc) or to make enough provision for bad debts (page 117) will also inflate the profits.

A favourable current ratio could also be due to overvaluing stocks or underassessing doubtful debts. The latter would also affect the acid test ratio.

Consistency

It is important to people reading the accounts of a company that they are comparing like with like, e.g. that the company has not used different methods of measurement for different costs, revenues, assets or liabilities. It is also important that the same practices are used from year to year and if changed that all interested parties are clearly informed of the change. This is known as the principle of *consistency* and applies to all aspects of the accounts.

ARMSTRONG ENGINEERING LTD
TRADING, PROFIT & LOSS ACCOUNT
for year ended 31 December 200X

Turnover	308,000
Cost of sales	177,000
Gross profit	131,000
Administration expenses	54,500
	76,500
Interest payable	900
Profit on ordinary activities before taxation	75,600
Tax on profit from ordinary activities	32,000
Profit on ordinary activities after taxation	43,600
Profit and loss account balance	
Undistributed profits b/f from last year	23,400
	67,000
Proposed dividends	34,500
Undistributed profits c/f to next year	32,500

BALANCE SHEET
as at 31 December 200X

	Cost	Less provision for depreciation	Net book
Fixed assets			
Premises	103,400		103,400
Fixtures and fittings	10,000	500	9,500
Machinery	40,000	2,000	38,000
Motor van	10,000	2,000	8,000
	163,400	4,500	158,900
Current assets			
Stock	18,000		
Debtors	48,700		
Cash at bank	19,850		
Cash in hand	50		
		86,600	
Less creditors			
Amounts falling due within 1 year	22,500		
Accruals	4,000		
Proposed dividends	34,500	61,000	25,600
Total net assets			184,500
Provision for liabilities and charges			
Taxation			32,000
Shareholders funds			
Authorised share capital			
100,000 Preference shares of £1	100,000		
100,000 Ordinary shares of £1	100,000		
	200,000		
Issued share capital			
30,000 Preference shares of £1		30,000	
90,000 Ordinary shares of £1		90,000	
		120,000	
Capital and reserves			
Proft and loss account balance		32,500	152,500
			184,500

Fig. 131. Final accounts ready for interpretation.

Example of interpretation of accounts in Fig. 131 opposite.

Information	Worked	Example	Comment
Current ratio	$\frac{86{,}600}{61{,}000}$	$= 1.42/1$	Rather low
Acid test ratio	$\frac{68{,}600}{61{,}000}$	$= 1.12/1$	Acceptable
Asset turnover	$\frac{308{,}000}{184{,}500}$	$= 1.67/1$	
Mark-up	$\frac{131{,}000}{177{,}000}$	$\times 100 = 74\%$	Very high
Gross profit margin	$\frac{131{,}000}{308{,}000}$	$\times 100 = 43\%$	Acceptable
Net profit margin	$\frac{75{,}600}{308{,}000}$	$\times 100 = 25\%$	Acceptable
RoCE	$0.25 \times 1.67 \times 100 = 41.75\%$		
Stock turnover	$\frac{177{,}000}{16{,}500}$	$* = 11$ times	Depends on type of business
Debt collection period	$\frac{48{,}700}{308{,}000}$	$\times 365 = 58$ days	

* This average stock figure is not actually shown in the accounts, because they are *published* ones and it is not required by law to be shown. However, it can be calculated from opening stock and closing stock, both of which will appear in internal accounts. These figures have been taken from the worked example on page 142.

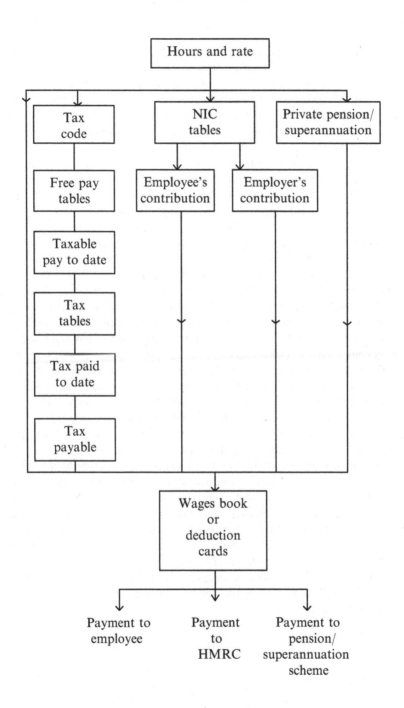

Fig. 132. Wages and salaries at a glance.

Wages and salaries are payments for people's labour. They are called **wages** when paid weekly and calculated from the number of hours worked (hourly rates) or units of production finished (piece rates). When payments are made monthly, and there is no direct relationship between them and the hours worked or units produced, they are called **salaries**. Manual and unskilled workers are paid wages; clerical workers, managers and professional people are paid monthly salaries.

Often wage earners are paid a higher hourly rate if they work after the scheduled finishing time; they may be paid an even higher one if they work very unsociable hours. For example, working after 5pm may entitle them to 50% more pay per hour, and they may receive twice the normal rate for work done on a Sunday. These rates are popularly known as 'time and a half' and 'double time'. To find a wage earner's gross pay entitlement the wages clerk multiplies the hours worked by the rate concerned (e.g. 1, 1½ or 2) and then multiplies the product by the hourly pay rate, e.g. £10.50.

Workers usually have to pay income tax on the money they earn. Everyone is entitled to some pay free from tax; the amount of exemption depends on their circumstances. For example people with dependent children have a higher level of tax exemption than those without. This level is called **free pay** and is identified by a **tax code** number. The wages clerk can simply look up the employee's code number and read off against it the cumulative free pay to date (for that tax year) to which that employee is entitled. He/she then adds this week's pay to total pay to date in the tax year, and deducts from that the free pay to date. He/she thus arrives at the taxable pay to date. He/she then calculates, by referring to a table, the cumulative tax payable on this; he/she deducts from it the tax *actually* paid to date to find out how much tax he/she must deduct this pay day.

Everyone earning more than a certain level of income (**threshold** level) must also pay regular National Insurance Contributions (NIC), to entitle them to free medical treatment and other state benefits. The wages clerk must also deduct NIC from the wages or salaries paid. The firm itself *also* has to make a contribution to each employee's NIC cover; the amount is related to level of pay.

When an employee earns above a certain figure they are charged a higher tax rate for the amount over that figure. Employee's wages are taxed at source. The company acts as a sort of sub-tax collector for HM Revenue and Customs, just as it does for collection of VAT. Income tax collected at source is called **Pay As You Earn** (PAYE).

WAGES

Suppose Mr Jones works 50 hours, the first 40 of which are at his standard rate of £10.50 p/h, the next 5 of which amount to overtime at 'time and a half' and the next 5 after that represent Sunday work at 'double time'. Suppose also, he pays to a company pension scheme at the rate of 7% of his gross earnings. His wage slip may look something like this.

Hours worked	Standard rate	= 40 =	420.00
	Standard rate × 1½	= 5 =	78.75
	Standard rate × 2	= 5 =	105.00
			603.75
Gross pay			
	Less income tax	100.75	
	NIC contribution	66.41	167.16
			436.58
	Less pension scheme contribution		42.26
	Net pay		394.31

Fig. 133. Worked example of the completion of a wage slip.

Wages	£20	£10	£5	£1	50p	20p	10p	5p	2p	1p
125.39	120		5			20	10	5	4	
73.40	60	10		3		40				
101.21	100			1		20				1
300.00	280	10	5	4		80	10	5	4	1

Fig. 134. A coin analysis for three wage packets.

Making up the wage packets

When all the wages have been calculated the wages clerk prepares a **coin analysis**, this is a list of all the coins needed to make up the wage packets (see opposite). Otherwise, how could he/she make them up? Let's take a simple example. Suppose there are three employees and their wages for a week are £125.39, £73.40, £101.21, a total of £300.00. If the wages clerk merely collected £300 in, say, ten pound notes from the bank he/she would not be able to make up the wages; he/she wouldn't have sufficient coins to pay out the amounts; £10s, £5s, 20ps, 10ps, 5ps, and 1ps are all needed in our example.

Wages book/deduction cards

The wages and salaries records of the firm are kept in a **wages book** and/or on **deduction cards** supplied by the HMRC. The records show such details as gross pay to date, free pay to date, taxable pay to date, tax paid to date, and NIC contributions paid to date by employee and employer.

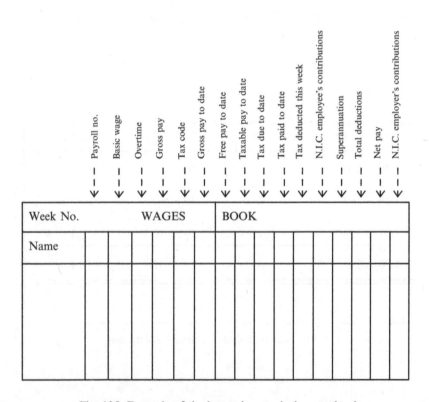

Fig. 135. Example of the layout in a typical wages book.

£	£	£	
1st purchase	10 @ 50		500
2nd purchase	10 @ 55		550
			1,050
1st withdrawal	2 @ 50		100
Balance	8 @ 50	400	
	10 @ 55	550	950
2nd withdrawal	8 @ 50	400	
	1 @ 55	55	455
Balance	9 @ 55		495

Fig. 136. Illustration of stock valuation using FIFO.

	£	£
1st purchase	10 @ 50 =	500
2nd "	10 @ 55 =	550
		1,050

1st withdrawal from warehouse, so average
out the item costs to date, i.e. $\dfrac{1,050}{20}$ = £52.50 each,

Withdrawn 2 @ £52.50
Balance 18 @ £52.50   945

3rd purchase	10 @ 60 =	600
		1,545

2nd withdrawal from warehouse, so average
out the item costs to date taking the previous
average as the cost of each and every one of the
items purchased before that date, i.e. $\dfrac{1,545}{28}$ = £55.18

Withdrawn 10 @ £55.18
Balance 18 @ £55.18 =   993.24
and so it would go on.

Fig. 137. Stock valuation using 'average cost' method.

75 Stock records and valuation

Basic records

Individual stock items can be quite valuable, e.g. household appliances like washing machines or tools like electric drills. In such cases the firm may well want to have a system for booking them in and out of the warehouse whenever they are bought or sold. The supplier's delivery note will be the source document for the booking in; a requisition docket of some kind will be the source document for booking out. So there will always be a record of the stock that should be in hand; periodical physical stock checks (actually going round and counting the stock) will show up any discrepancies arising from errors or pilferage.

Stock valuation methods

At the end of the accounting period stocks have to be valued for the balance sheet. Such value is based on the cost price or replacement price, whichever is the *lower*. The idea is that the asset figures in the accounts should reflect the true values as closely as possible. Each item (or at least each group of items) should be treated separately in this valuation process.

If we are valuing the stock at cost price there may have been a number of price changes throughout the year, and if the goods are identical we may not be able to tell which ones cost which amounts. There are three main ways of dealing with this:

- FIFO (first in first out)

- LIFO (last in first out)

- average cost method.

First in first out

FIFO assumes that the remaining stock is the subject of the most recent prices. Suppose a firm had purchased 30 televisions, the first 10 at £50, another 10 some months later at £55, and near the end of the year another 10 at £60.00. Let's suppose, also, that it sold 15 to one customer, a hotelier perhaps, just before the end of the accounting year. Since 30 had been purchased and only 15 sold there should be 15 left in stock. These 15 would be valued at the prices of the most recently purchased 15; that means all 10 of the most recent purchase at £60 each and 5 of the previous order at £55 each.

Last in first out

LIFO does the opposite. It says that *all* remaining stock on hand is valued at the *earliest* purchase price. To value stock according to LIFO you do the same as for FIFO, using the earliest invoices, instead of the most recent.

Average cost method

The average cost method (sometimes referred to as AVCO) requires you to divide the remaining stock (numbers of items) into the total cost of all that stock, each time an item is withdrawn from stock. You then apply the cost figure to the withdrawn stock, and to the stock remaining afterwards. When another withdrawal is made you add the last valuation to the cost of all purchases since; you then divide the total by the actual number of items in stock. Again you apply this value to the goods withdrawn *and* to the balance remaining. So the average value of remaining stock may change continuously.

Example

Let's suppose a shop made purchases as in the example; it sells two televisions immediately after the second wholesale purchase and 10 more close to the end of the year. You would then value the stock as shown in the example in Figure 130.

FIFO is the most commonly used method. It also seems the most realistic, because businesses usually try to sell their oldest stock first.

Advantages of FIFO method

- Unrealised profits or losses will not occur, i.e. increases in stock values due to inflation.

- Issuing the oldest items first reduces likelihood of stock perishing.

- Stock valuation will be closer to current prices than with other methods.

- This method is acceptable to HM Revenue and Customs.

- This method complies with SSAP9. This statement of standard accounting practice prescribes that stock should be valued at the lower of cost or net realisable value.

Disadvantages

- In inflationary times costs are understated and profits overstated. This is because the cost of replacing the stock is higher than the cost of the stock used and accounted for. The reverse is true in deflationary times.

- Material issue prices vary so that it is difficult to compare prices over a range of jobs.

Advantages of LIFO method

- It keeps stock values to a minimum.

- It causes the firm's product prices to reflect the most recent component prices.

- It could, theoretically, enable the firm to weather the storm better in times of rising component costs, because it could produce goods more cheaply than other firms when the stock in its storeroom is valued at old prices.

Disadvantages

This method is not acceptable to HM Revenue and Customs and does not comply with SSAP9, so all consideration of its advantages is purely academic.

Stock reorder levels

The stock levels that trigger reordering are calculated as follows:

$$\text{buffer stock} + (\text{budgeted usage} \times \text{maximum lead time})$$

i.e. the level of stock the firm keeps as a margin of safety plus (an order figure equal to the budgeted usage per day, or week multiplied by the number of days, or weeks it takes to receive the stock after ordering).

Computerising the stock control system

Computerised stock control systems offer many advantages over manual systems:

- Faster data processing.

- Increased accuracy.

- Savings in wages costs.

- Continuous analysis to establish economic order quantities.

- Automatic reordering made possible.

- *Just in time* stock ordering is made feasible, reducing stock holding costs to a minimum.

- More effective control of minimum and maximum levels.

- Point of sale stock control facilitated.

- Immediate and up to date reports on performance of particular stock lines made possible and easy to obtain.

- Stock keeping software can be integrated into the firm's general accounting software.

This book seeks to teach the principles of double entry bookkeeping. However, readers may, in the course of their careers, come across small businesses which use single entry methods.

The Simplex system

The most common single entry method is the **Simplex system**. This is an integrated system involving two books. One is designed for recording daily takings, daily payments and a weekly cash and bank account. All are dealt with on the same page and one page is used per week. The balances of the cash and bank accounts are carried forward to the next week, as the opening figures.

There are special VAT recording arrangements for small businesses. In corner shops for example, it would be burdensome to record each individual item of sale separately – a bar of chocolate to one customer, a newspaper to another and a ballpen to another, for example. In such cases therefore, there are special formulae for computing the VAT payable or repayable. There are a number of different schemes to suit the particular problems of different types of business. In recognition of this the Simplex range contains different versions of the daily takings and purchases book for each scheme.

The second of the two books is a sales and purchases record.

At the end of the daily takings and purchases book there is an analysis section. By following guidance notes printed on the page, owners of businesses can compile their draft profit and loss accounts and balance sheets.

The slip system

As was pointed out on page 15, in double entry bookkeeping the sources of information for posting to the ledger are the books of **prime entry**. Nothing should be posted directly from, for example, an invoice, or credit note.

However, this rule is sometimes broken. Occasionally, you'll find this stage bypassed and entries made directly into the ledger. This is called the **slip system**. It is used where accounts have to be kept very up to date, such as in banking and wherever automated systems are used. Where postings are made directly to the ledger, from invoice copies, those copies are filed to form the equivalent of the day book. This I call the **slip + 1 system**, because an extra invoice copy is needed.

In the accounts of some very small firms, the ledgers, too, are sometimes dispensed with. Instead, the invoices (or copies in the case of invoices sent out) are merely filed together with other unpaid ones, in date order. This takes the place of the personal ledger (sales and purchase). When each is paid it is stamped and removed to be filed with all the paid ones. This version I call the **slip + 2 system**, because two additional copies of each invoice are needed.

For the 'slip + 1' version a firm's invoices really need to be printed in triplicate. For the 'slip + 2' version they need to be in quadruplicate.

A	B	C	D	E	F
Date	Particulars	Fo.	Details	Amount	
200X					
	=IF(F7<M7,"Balance c/d"," ")			=IF(F7<M7,M7-F7," ")	=SUM(E3:E6)
					=SUM(E3:E7)
	=IF(F7<M7,"Balance b/d"," ")				=IF(M7<F7,F7-M7," ")

G	H	I	J	K	L	M
Date	Particulars		Fo.	Details	Amount	
200X						
	=IF(F7>M7,"Balance c/d"," ")				=IF(M7<F7,F7-M7)	=SUM(L3:L6)
						=SUM(L3:L7)
	=IF(F7>M7, "Balance b/d"," ")					=IF(F7<M7,M7-F7," ")

Fig. 138. This is what your sheet will look like if you command your program to show the formulae you have entered. To do this, click on the Tools menu and select *Options*. Then click on *Formulae* and, finally, click the *OK* button. Don't forget to remove the tick from the *formulas* option after you are satisfied that you have entered the formulae correctly, otherwise your formulae will show instead of your figures.

Date	Particulars	Fo.	Details	Amount
200X				
Jan-10	Wood			20.00
Jan-15	Nails			2.00
				22.00
Feb-01	Balance b/d			2.00

Date	Particulars	Fo.	Details	Amount
200X				
Jan-31	Cheque			20.00
31	Balance c/d			2.00
				22.00

Fig. 139. This is what your sheet will look like when you have entered figures onto it. You will see that the formulae do not show.

How it works

Nowadays we can use the electronic pages of a spreadsheet program if we have access to a computer. As long as you know how to write on them you can simply follow the instruction in the chapters of this book in the same way as you would for paper pages.

There are various spreadsheet packages on the market, but the differences in the way they work are not great. If you can use one you will be able to grapple with another. The examples used here relate to Microsoft Excel.

Writing on spreadsheet pages

Just as you move to the appropriate spot on a paper page and write on it with a pen, with a spreadsheet page you move to the spot with the direction keys ⬅ ⬆ ⬇ ➡ or a mouse and type the information through the keyboard. It's as simple as that.

Adding them up

You will need your standard and formatting toolbars showing. If they are not, click on the view menu and choose the toolbars option. Next, click in the *standard* and *formatting* boxes and then click 'OK'.

When you come to adding the columns up draw the lines of the answer boxes, using the ⊞ ⬇ buttons on the formatting toolbar. Use the arrow key to select a single line for the top and a double line for the bottom. The column will add itself up if you click on the answer box and then click the Σ button on the standard toolbar.

Calculating the c/d balance

Where you have both debit and credit columns you will need to calculate c/d balance. To do this you have to add both sides and take the smaller figure from the larger. Then you enter the difference in the smaller column. That means you've got to jot the two totals down somewhere. Here's how you do that. First make room for a c/d balance by inserting a row if necessary above the answer boxes.

Next insert a column next to the debit column being added, by clicking on the insert menu and choosing the *columns* option while the cursor is to the right of the column. Enter in it the instruction to sum the column immediately above and to its left. To do this click on the Σ button. ' = SUM ( )' will appear in the box. Enter in the brackets the pair of cell references which bound the column you wish to add. Separate them with a colon. Example: E3:E6.

Do the same with the credit column. Example: L3:L6. Here you will find you have to replace a cell reference already showing.

Instructions don't show up on the page – they're invisible – but the answers which they make do. This one is just a jotting though; you don't want it to show, so you must deliberately hide it. You can do this by clicking on the format menu and selecting the *columns* option, then clicking on *hide*, while the cursor is in the column concerned.

Next, enter the '*If*' command. To do this click on the *f** button on the toolbar and choose the '*If*' button while the cursor is in the last space above the total box in the debit column. Click the button labelled *Next*.

Type the first of the two cell references in which you put the column addition formula (i.e. the first of the hidden cells), followed by a < sign, and this is followed by the second of those cell references. Example F7 < M7. In the second box down, marked '*value if true*' type the reverse of this. This time the two cell references should be separated by a minus sign instead of a < symbol. In the third box down simply type a space (press the space bar once). Click the button labelled *Finish*.

Now repeat this on the credit side in the cell above the answer box, reversing the formula.

There is no point in showing zeros in these cells, so if they do appear click on the tools menu and select *options*. Make sure *Zero values* is not ticked and then press the key labelled *OK*.

Next, click in the first of the actual answer boxes and then click on the Σ button twice. Do the same in the right hand answer box.

The balance c/d is then transferred to the opposite side after the total box, as the opening figure (Balance b/d) for the next month. To do this on the spreadsheets just type in the space below the total box on each side the formula which has been entered in the c/d balance box on the opposite side.

Click in the last available space in the particulars column (above the answer box line) and then click the *function* key. Select the *If* option and then, in the dialogue space, type the co-ordinates in which the subtotals are stored in the hidden columns, separated by a ' < ' symbol, (e.g. F7 < M7). In the second dialogue space type 'Balance c/d'. In the third dialogue box type a space (just press the space below once). Click on finish. Now do the same in the space adjacent to this one on the credit side of the sheet, reversing the formula. Lastly, enter the b/d balance narratives. Using the function key, simply enter in the particulars column, below the totals boxes on each side, the exact formula you entered in the diametrically opposite position (i.e. the space above the total box in the opposite column), but substitute the term c/d with the term b/d.

As you type in the formulae they will appear temporarily in the boxes, but will disappear as soon as you press *finish* in each case.

Configuring a spreadsheet page for day books

It is easy to configure pages which will add themselves up and cross balance for day books. All you have to do is draw in the answer boxes, as you did for the ledger pages. Click on each answer box to highlight it and then click on the Σ button on the toolbar.

Making things easy for yourself
Now you don't have to go through this each month. You can keep this specimen page without any actual monthly figures in it as a template.

Four steps for creating a template
1. Create a single sheet workbook.
2. Format it with the titles and formulae.
3. Save as a template.
4. Enter the folder in which you wish to store it.

Speeding up ledger posting
You can keep all accounts of a single ledger division (e.g. all customer accounts) on the same sheet, one after the other, as the placing of automated summing and balancing instructions will ensure that the accounts do not get mixed up. Each ledger division becomes a different sheet (e.g. sheet 1 = Sales daybook, sheet 2 = Nominal ledger and sheet 3 = Sales ledger, and so on.) A big advantage of doing this is that you can make posting from daybooks to ledger sheets easy, by putting all the sheets involved on the screen at once. The larger your screen the easier this will be. For example:

• Sales daybook. • Nominal ledger. • Sales ledger.

Then you can simply use copy and paste across the boundaries of the sheets to do your positing. For example, to post a transaction from the Sales daybook to the relevant ledger sheets, just follow these steps:

1. Call up all the relevant sheets on the screen at once.
2. Click on the gross invoice value for each entry on the Sales daybook sheet.
3. Press 'Alt' 'E' 'C'.
4. Scroll down the Sales ledger sheet to the personal account of the customer concerned.
5. Click on the next available space in the debit column.
6. Press 'Alt' 'E' 'P'.
7. Enter the date in the date column.
8. When all the entries have been posted to the Sales ledger accounts, proceed as follows.
9. Click on the net total in the Sales daybook.
10. Press on 'Alt' 'E' and 'C'.
11. Scroll to the next available space in the credit column of the Sales account in the Nominal ledger.
12. Press 'Alt' 'E' 'P'.
13. Click on the VAT total in the Sales daybook and press 'Alt' 'E' 'C'.

14. Scroll to the next available space in the credit column of the VAT account in the Nominal ledger and press '**Alt**' '**E**' '**P**'.

Automating depreciation calculations

Asset depreciation calculations can be done swiftly and simply, using Excel's built in functions.

Straight line method

Click on the '***f***' tab on the menu bar (this is the toolbar which always shows at the top of the screen).

1. Select the '**Financial**' option.
2. Click, then, on the '**SLN**' option.
3. The following dialogue boxes will appear on the screen:
   asset value; estimated salvage (scrap) value; estimated useful life.
4. Enter the relevant figures and click '**OK**' to find the annual depreciation figure.

Diminishing balance method of depreciation

1. Click on the '**Insert**' tab on the menu bar.
2. Select the '**f***' option.
3. Then select the '**DDB**' option.
4. The following five dialogue boxes will appear.
   cost; estimated salvage value; estimated useful life; start of the period; end of the period.
5. Enter the relevant figures and click on '**OK**' to find the depreciation for the asset.

Sum of the years (or sum of the digits) method of depreciation

Follow the same procedure as for the diminishing balance method, selecting the '**SYD**' instead of the '**DDB**' option.

For a fuller treatment of bookkeeping using spreadsheets, refer to my other book *Mastering Spreadsheet Bookkeeping*. There I show you how to easily build an integrated bookkeeping system that will do most of the work for you automatically.

In previous editions of this book I have showed readers how to make use of the electronic pages of spreadsheets. I have, however, tended to stop short of dealing with computerised bookkeeping packages, as they were, hitherto, rather too complicated for many people. Things have changed though; there are now various packages on the market to suit all needs and various ability and skill levels. A comprehensive bookkeeping course book must now give some attention to these too.

Their use is not a substitute for a thorough knowledge of bookkeeping however. It is not much use having accounts if you don't know what they mean and how to use them to control your business. Their use will merely speeds things up and take the donkeywork out of the job.

The types of software available

The software packages that are available fall into two categories:

- computer-based
- web-based.

Systems can also be categorised as form-based or transaction-based.

Form-based systems

Sage is an example of a form-based system. It is a comprehensive system that has been around for some time and has enjoyed the status of industry standard. It requires some degree of bookkeeping knowledge and skill to use and quite a bit of setting up is required. To learn how to use *Sage*, refer to my book *Computerised Book-keeping*.

Another form-based system is *Simply Accounts*. This requires less setting up, less knowledge and skill to use and is less expensive than *Sage*.

Transaction-based systems

Contrasting with form-based systems are transaction-based systems. *Accountz* is such a system. It minimises the need to get to grips with input forms by recognising that all transactions fall into one of three kinds:

- sales
- purchases
- transfers.

Only three very simple tables are used and all the transactions you have to enter can be put into one or other of these. You simply take your batch of invoices, or cheque stubs, enter them into the relevant table in any order and then move them around as required afterwards, before locking their positions.

De-jargonated

The data input is simplified by the fact that rather than debit and credit fields, the relevant fields are labelled 'from' and 'to' – where the value is coming from and where it is going to. This further simplication will, of course, only help the novice. Each transaction is entered on a single line.

Example

If you have settled your credit card account you enter the value as taken from your bank account and as going to your *credit card account*. If you are recording the cash sales you enter the value as taken from your *daily takings* and as going into your *bank* account. If you are recording credit sales you enter the value as coming from *credit sales account* and as going to *unpaid invoices account*. When you settle a bill you record the value as going from the bank account and as going to the *unpaid invoices outwards account*. If VAT is applicable at standard rate you just select 'standard rate' and it will work it out for you.

The producers have done their utmost to minimise the number of key and mouse operations that you have to make.

VAT returns are quick and easy to product and this software caters for VAT accounting and production of returns for all EEC countries. All major global currencies are also provided for.

This system can cater for any kind of business unit, e.g.:

- sole trader
- partnerships
- limited company.

Report formats are infinitely changeable so that even club accounts can be produced.

It is a multiplatform product, which can be run on PCs, Applemacs or Net books.

Web-based systems

Contrasting with computer-based systems are web-based systems. An example is a system called Fusion.

Instead of the software and the data being stored on your computer, web-based systems work from programs accessed through the internet. The user's data is also stored on the web.

There are some advantages to using this type of system. One is that as it web-based, a user can access and work on their accounts from any computer that has internet access; it doesn't have to be their own computer.

No backing up of data is required.

Upgrades are automatic and in the case of Fusion they are free, so a user will always have the latest version. Payment is by monthly subscription and the licence includes 10 users.

Access on a need to know basis

Access can be set to restrict access by staff to only those parts of the accounting information that they need in order to perform their role in the organisation. This improves data security.

Advantages of computerised bookkeeping systems

- Some types of error will be eliminated.

- Casting (summation) is automatic.

- Posting is automatic.

- Ledger balancing is automatic.

- Extraction of trial balance can be done at any time automatically at the touch of a few keys.

- There are also many stock control advantages.

- Reduced skilled labour costs, as large amounts of data are processed by computer rather than manually.

- Easier communication of accounts, as authorised people can access them by computer.

- Live, centralised accounting is made feasible for many remote branches of firms, as happens in some pub chains, where data from tills is processed live at head office.

Computerisation of the accounts will prevent some errors, but not all types. The error types it will prevent are:

- errors of omission
- commission
- compensatory errors
- errors of original entry
- errors of principle.

The types it will not prevent are:

- errors of reversal
- posting one side to wrong side of ledger
- omission of one side only

- under/overstatement of one side
- errors of summation
- casting errors
- transposition errors.

See page 168 for an explanation of what these error terms mean.

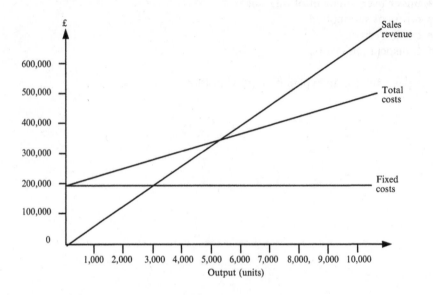

Fig. 140. Example of a break-even chart.

You may be learning bookkeeping for any of the following reasons:

- to practise as a professional bookkeeper;
- to run your own business in any field;
- as the initial stage of a career in accountancy.

Whichever of these is the case, when you have reached this stage of the course and mastered all that lies before it, you may wish to have a peep at where you can go from here. This chapter is designed to give you a taste of the theory and techniques that lie beyond bookkeeping and within the fields of accounting and financial control.

Control accounting

There's little point in planning, investing and organising resources in the pursuit of any goal if things are not properly controlled. Things will not automatically follow the best path to success. We can plan to the utmost degree, invest in the best resources and organise them in the best possible way, but they won't achieve the goal on their own without fine-tuning the system from time to time. Life is far too unpredictable for that. Control is as necessary as planning. So many factors in the economy can depress sales or increase costs, and we can never be sure who else is going to enter the market and depress prices as a consequence. All the following need controlling:

- cash
- capital gearing
- credit
- costs
- working capital
- liquidity
- stock levels
- share prices.

Break-even analysis

Before a company decides to embark on a particular project break-even analysis will be carried out to predict the point below which it will cease to make a gross profit on sales – its **break-even point**.

The difference between a projected level of sales and break-even point is known as the **margin of safety**. It represents how much sales can fall short of the target before a loss is made. It therefore gives an indication of how much the project could withstand adverse trading conditions. Margin of safety can be expressed either as a percentage of sales or as units of product sold.

To construct a break-even chart step by step

Add up all the costs that you'll incur even if you don't sell any of your products or services, e.g. rent, administrative wages, etc. These are your **fixed costs**. Draw an *x* (horizontal) and a *y* (vertical) axis to meet each other at the bottom left hand corner. Label this point 0 (zero), because it represents no unit sales and no costs or revenues. Calibrate the *x* axis in whatever units of hypothetical sales seems appropriate, i.e. plot marks on the line representing hundreds, thousands, or any other scale of unit sales that seems appropriate.

Calibrate the *y* axis with monetary levels, i.e. mark it off in units of hundreds or thousands of pounds sterling, or whatever other scale you regard as appropriate.

Plot the total fixed costs on the *y* axis and draw a horizontal line. Label this 'Fixed costs'.

Next, add up all the costs that can be directly attributed to a single unit, or particular quantity of units sold, e.g. saleperson's commission, purchases and cost of production. Plot this figure multiplied by each quantity marked on the *x* axis vertically above that quantity and horizontally against the appropriate height on the *y* axis, after first adding the fixed cost value (which is the same regardless of how many are sold). In other words, start counting up the *y* axis, not from zero, but from the level at which fixed costs are plotted. Draw a line through the plotting. The line will be sloping and will meet the *y* axis at the point where the *fixed costs* line starts. Next plot the revenues for each volume of sales in the same way, escept that here you start from the zero level. See Figure 140 for an example.

The principle advantage of break-even analysis is that because the break-even point is presented graphically:

- The information is externalised so that it can be communicated and shared.

- The project can be handled more objectively.

Month number

Income (£)	1	2	3	4	5	6	7	8	9	10	11	12
Sales	9,000	9,500	10,000	10,500	11,000	11,500	12,000	12,500	13,000	13,500	14,000	14,500
Income from other sources	500	500	500	500	500	500	500	500	500	500	500	500
(A) Total income	9,500	10,000	10,500	11,000	11,500	12,000	12,500	13,000	13,500	14,000	14,500	15,000
Outgoings (£)												
Purchases	3,000	3,200	3,300	3,500	3,700	3,800	4,000	4,200	4,300	4,500	4,700	4,900
Overheads	8,000	7,000	7,000	7,000	8,500	7,000	7,000	7,000	8,000	7,000	7,000	7,000
Other outgoings	0	0	0	0	0	2,000	0	0	0	2,600	0	0
(B) Total outgoings	11,000	10,200	10,300	10,500	12,200	12,800	11,000	11,200	123,00	14,100	11,700	11,900
(A–B) Net income/outgoings	(1,500)	(200)	200	500	(700)	(800)	2,500	1,800	1,200	(100)	2,800	3,100
Add opening bank balances	3,000	1,500	1,300	1,500	2,000	1,300	500	3,000	4,800	6,000	5,900	8,700
Closing bank balance	1,500	1,300	1,500	2,000	1,300	500	3,000	4,800	6,000	5,900	8,700	11,800

Fig. 141. Example of a simple cash flow projection.

There are some disadvantages, though

- Costs many not be linear, or only linear within a particular range. In fact economies and diseconomies of scale will, to some degree, prevent costs and revenues being linear.

- It is sometimes difficult to distinguish between fixed and variable costs.

- The use of break-even analysis assumes a single product. Most companies have a mixture of products and services for sale, so you would either need several break-even charts, or plot sales in purely monetary units, rather than units of any particular product. Then it may be difficult to accurately plot direct costs since there may be different direct costs for each sales product.

Cash flow projection

No matter how much profit a firm is making it can still run out of cash. This can happen if, for example, it allows its customers eight weeks to pay their debts while it pays its own in four, or if it channels a lot of its sales revenues into purchasing fixed assets, leaving insufficient amounts to pay its trade creditors on time. If this happens the company may miss out on early settlement discounts or, worse still, suppliers might withdraw credit terms. Other cash commitments may be affected too – for example, the firm may be unable to pay wages on time. To avoid this happening a cash flow projection is drawn up, comparing planned inflows and outflows month by month over the period of the trading year.

CONTROLLING THE CASH

Many people find it hard to see how a firm making high profits can be short of cash, but it can. Just as the purpose of an aeroplane is to deliver you to a destination and an unbroken supply of aviation fuel is its means of getting you there, profit is the purpose of an enterprise and an unbroken cash flow is its means of achieving it. Cash flow is far more critical than profitability. An aeroplane that has lost its way but has enough fuel to find it again will arrive; one that is on course and ahead of time but short of fuel will not. In the same way, a company enduring a rough ride can buy time with cash, while a firm enjoying high sales figures but is short of cash may fail to reap the rewards. If you've got fuel (cash), you can keep the vehicle going and eventually get there; if you're short of fuel, you can't.

Cash received

When we talk about cash, we mean money in the bank and in the cash box (although in modern firms, the latter will be just a small amount to pay various expenses). The income that a firm receives from its trading activities can be in cash (which includes cheques) or credit, i.e. customers will not have to pay for the goods or services they have purchased straightaway. They are typically given thirty days' credit, but very often take more. If a firm has a sudden profit bonanza but all the business is on thirty-day credit terms, the extra profit produces no cash at all – *at the time.*

Furthermore, suppose the firm was only able to generate that profit bonanza by selling goods cheaply, having purchased them from wholesalers at reduced prices on the basis that it paid 'cash on the nail'. The firm's cash resources may well have been drained in the process. If it runs out of stock before its own customers pay their bills, it will have no cash funds to replenish it.

This, of course, is an oversimplification – things are rarely this straightforward – but it does show generally how profitable firms can easily run out of cash. It's more usual that a firm's own customers are simply slower in paying their bills than the firm's suppliers allow them to be, but the effect is the same.

Running out of cash is a result of a lack of synchrony between costs and revenues. It can also happen if a firm uses its cash resources to pay for fixed assets that will not generate their own value in revenue very quickly.

As a rule, fixed assets (e.g. plant, premises, equipment, vehicles, etc.) should not be purchased with cash. They should be funded by loan or credit over a period equal to the assets' projected lifespan. That way, at least the annual total of payments will be almost matched by what is, in effect, an income in the form of depreciation allowance against tax. The remainder not covered in this way (i.e. the interest) will be offset as an overhead expense. Even here, though, there will be an imbalance between what is coming in and what is going out, for the loan or credit will probably have to be paid quarterly or even monthly, while the effective income mentioned will only be received at the end of the year.

What a cash shortage means

The consequence of cash shortages can be:

- Unwillingness of suppliers to supply goods until the firm's accounts are settled. This prevents the firm from generating cash to 'trade its way out' of the problem. It's a vicious circle.
- Inability to pay wages.
- Inability to make repayments to financiers, e.g. banks.
- Use of bank overdraft will result in high-interest charges.
- Expensive machinery may have to lie idle because of lack of cash for raw materials, power or fuel, and production workers' wages.
- There may well be interest to pay on the loans that have financed their purchase.
- Maintenance contracts may be put at risk.
- Some depreciation cost will arise even though the machines are not being used.
- Insurance premiums will still have to be paid.
- Factory rent still has to be paid.
- Office staff's salaries still have to be paid.

The instrument for controlling the cash flow is the **cash flow forecast**, or **cash budget** as it is sometimes called. This is a table which sets out the forecasted cash requirements at particular times and matches them with the projected cash incomes, revealing any shortfalls and stating how that shortfall will be financed. A simple example is given in Figure 141.

Cash flow shortages happen suddenly. By forecasting and budgeting in advance, supplies of cash can be arranged in good time to make up the shortfall, achieved, for example, by arranging bank overdrafts, factoring or offering *new share issues*.

First aid for cash flow problems
These are some of the remedial steps which can be taken:

- Delaying payment of bills;
- Reducing stock levels (selling off stock, purchasing less new stock);
- Reducing payments to any reserve fund;
- Using factoring facilities (borrowing money on the strength of customers' accounts).

When too much cash can be a bad thing
It's not only shortage of cash that can be harmful to a firm – too much cash is a drain on its productivity, because it represents the underemployment of an asset. All a firm's resources should be devoted to earning a return and money left lying in a bank is not doing so. Furthermore, its value will be eroded by inflation. Even if interest is paid, if bank interest would satisfy the investors' demands for a return, they might as well have placed the cash straight in the bank themselves. The amount of cash maintained in a business should be enough but not excessive.

Compiling a cash flow projection step by step
Prepare a table with 13 columns and 11 rows. Use the first column to label the meaning of the values in each row and the first row to label the months 1–12 in the trading year. This will leave 12 columns and 10 rows for data. These will, from here on, be referred to as columns 1–12 and rows 1–10 respectively. The first three labels down the left hand side are income categories: *Sales revenue, Income from other sources and Total income.* The next four (rows 4–7 inclusive) are outgoings: *Purchase, Overheads, Other outgoings* and *Total outgoings.* The next row (row 8) is for *Net income/outgoings,* i.e. the surplus of one or the other. Row 9 is for *Opening bank balance* (predicted at start of that month). The final row is for *Closing bank balance* calculated for that month, which will be the sum of rows 8 and 9.

Then you plot the figures you calculate it will be reasonable to expect. Sum rows 1 and 2 and put the answers in the total boxes in row 3. Sum rows 4–6 and enter the answers in the total boxes in row 7. Deduct row 7 from row 3 and put the differences in the answer boxes in row 8. Sum rows 8 and 9 and put the answers in the total boxes in row 10. Figure 141 is an example.

This is a general guide. In particular situations there may be more income and expenditure categories than those used here.

CONTROLLING CREDIT

This is necessary for two reasons:

- If customers take longer to pay their bills than the firm's suppliers allow them to pay theirs, the firm will run out of cash eventually, no matter how high its paper profits are.
- The older a debt becomes, the greater the likelihood of it becoming a bad (uncollectable) debt.

One way of controlling this is by working out a regular **debtor turnover ratio** (sales volume divided by debtors' volume) and **purchases to creditors ratio** and trying to keep the two in rough balance. This is only a partial answer, though, because if not enough control is effected on the debtor end, suppliers (creditors) will become impatient and refuse to supply goods until their bills are paid. Delay may sour the firm's relationship with them altogether, resulting in their total unwillingness to continue supplying the firm on credit. It's crucial, therefore, to keep firm control on the debtor end in order to get the cash in as quickly as possible.

The debtor turnover ratio can be converted into a debtor turnover period by dividing it into 52 (to give it in weeks) or 365 (to give it in days).

Example

$$\frac{52 \text{ weeks}}{\text{Debtor turnover ratio: } 8} = \text{Debtor turnover period} = 6.5 \text{ weeks}$$

$$\frac{365 \text{ days}}{\text{Debtor turnover period: } 8} = \text{Debtor turnover period} = 46 \text{ days}$$

WATCHING COSTS

Whether you're running a private firm or a government department, you'll have to control costs all the time. There's no point in planning and organising your resources to produce the best return if you're not going to put the plan into action – costs won't control themselves. They can rise subtly without you realising, because few of them are as simple as they seem. Take wage costs, for example. There's not just the actual gross pay involved, there are employers' NI contributions, welfare benefits and, perhaps, the cost of providing an inflation-proof pension scheme. What if the government suddenly increases NI contributions? What if inflation starts rising again? It's necessary to continuously monitor costs of producing each good or service and 'tweak' them wherever necessary. This is done by standard costing and variance analysis.

Standard costs

The standard cost comprises materials, labour and a proportion of overheads. It is calculated for each unit of production, whether goods or services are being produced. Each of these component costs is worked out as follows:

Materials costs = usage × price;
Labour costs   = hours per unit × wage rate per hour;
Overheads   = total budgeted cost for this production run ÷ the number of units to be produced.

Efficiency is governed by costs and output. It will increase when costs remain constant and output goes up, or when output stays the same but costs fall.

Adjusting standard cost

It's sometimes necessary to adjust standard costs because of rising prices or errors of judgment in forecasts of the efficiency levels. Actual production costs are compared regularly with the standard costs and the variance (adverse or favourable) noted. If an adverse variance is found, it has to be analysed into its constituent parts: materials, labour and overheads. Each of these, in turn, is broken down into its elements to see whether it is usage or price which has run to excess. This is called **management by exception**, because the focus is on correcting exceptions or deviations from the planned course.

To find the value of usage variants, if any, you multiply the usage deviation by the price. To find the value of price variants, you multiply the usage by the price deviation. The problem can lie in one or more of the following:

● material usage;
● material prices;
● labour usage;
● labour wage rates;
● number of units produced;
● overhead costs.

A simple example of the variance analysis used in budgetary control is shown in Figure 142.

(F) indicates the variance is favourable and (A) indicates that it is adverse.

Item	Budgeted costs £	Actual costs £	Variance £	
Materials (1)	500,000	489,600	10,400	(F)
Labour (2)	300,000	332,500	32,500	(A)
Overheads	60,000	61,980	1,980	(A)
Total	860,000	884,080	24,080	(A)

Fig. 142. Example of variance analysis in budgeting.

Analysed further:

(1) *Materials variance*

		£
Usage =	standard price x (standard quantity – actual quantity)	
=	£5 × (100,000 – 102,000)	= 10,000 (A)
Price =	actual quantity × (standard price – actual price)	
=	102,000 × (£5 – £4.80)	= 20,400 (F)

(2) *Labour efficiency variance*   10,400 (F)
(Usage per unit)

	£
Standard rate × (standard hours – actual hours)	
= £3 × (60,000 – 63,000)	= 15,000 (A)

Labour price variance
Actual hours × (standard rate – actual rate)
=   63,000 × (£5 – £5.27777778)   = 17,500 (A)
                                                     32,500 (A)

Overhead cost variance   = 1,980 (A)

The right attitude to budgetary control

Some people resent their performance being monitored closely in this way and see it as a conspiracy. But hopefully this chapter will show you why it is so necessary.

Successful budgetary control owes as much to a common, fostered attitude as to a skill or technique. It means the willingness of all employees to be accountable for their performance.

Government departments will set budgets annually, known as PPBS (Planning, Programming and Budgetary Systems), in consultation with the Treasury. They will then compare their actual with budgeted performance every three or six months. Retail firms may have major reviews of actual performance against budgeted performance every six months.

The budgetary process

The budgetary process is as follows:

1. Define the project;
2. Set realistic standards of efficiency of resource usage (materials, labour and overheads);
3. Collect data on actual performance systematically;
4. Compare budgeted with actual performance at regular intervals;
5. Take remedial action when and where necessary.

Keeping the right stock levels

All the factors of production (land, labour, capital and enterprise) must earn a return. Together, they enable a firm to keep its prices to a minimum and so compete with other efficient firms. Capital tied up in stock earns nothing while it's sitting in the stock room. There are exceptions, though, such as in times of high, general inflation, or when there's a scarcity of a commodity the firm deals in (e.g. valuable antiques). On the other hand, the firm will lose revenue if it doesn't have stock available when customers want it and it will incur a manufacturing loss if materials are not available as and when its factory needs them. The right balance has to be struck between over- and understocking.

Other disadvantages of overstocking are as follows:

- Some stocks are perishable and overstocking will cause losses, as goods have to be thrown away.
- Some goods (especially high-tech ones) quickly become obsolete when new developments come onto the market.
- Stocks of clothes go out of fashion.
- High-tech goods tend to fall in price, so stocks would eventually be rendered unsaleable at the original prices and, in fact, may have to be sold below cost price.

In times of high inflation, stock-holding can, theoretically, be advantageous, because stock values will increase. But firms often continue to sell at the listed retail prices at the time they, themselves, purchased the goods. Indeed, this policy may be required by the manufacturers. Petrol companies, however, are frequently accused of exploiting oil scarcities by setting pump prices higher, not only on the new stocks they have had to pay more for, but also on the stocks they already had before the oil prices went up.

But we must not forget that the direct purpose of revenue from sales is to buy more stock to keep the money circulating. You will, therefore, need more funds to do so than if prices had not gone up as a result of a scarcity.

But stock-holding is expensive. Not only is the working capital tied up in the stock, but the land and buildings required for storage also cost money in rent (or rent foregone if let to another firm). In addition, there is the heating, lighting and store-keeping labour to take into account. Furthermore, any increase in value of stock as a result of inflation will not necessarily compensate for the loss of the multiplying effect of rapid turnover and will certainly do nothing for cash flow.

Analysing stock levels

The main instrument for stock control is the **stock turnover ratio** and its derivation, the **stock turnover period**. Stock turnover is calculated by the formula:

$$\frac{\text{Cost of goods sold}}{\text{Average stock}} \qquad \text{e.g.} \qquad \frac{£480,000}{£80,000} = 6$$

This is turned into the stock turnover period by dividing it into 52 to find the stock turnover period in weeks, or into 365 to find it in days, e.g.:

$$\frac{52}{6} = 8.67 \text{ weeks}; \qquad \frac{365}{6} = 60.83 \text{ days}.$$

Stock turnover means the number of times during a year that the entire average stock value has been sold and replaced. The stock turnover period is the average time it has taken to sell and replace the average stock.

A reasonable figure for the stock turnover period has to be worked out based on customer or factory demand patterns on the one hand, and suppliers' delivery patterns on the other. Once decided, the stock levels are planned. Of course, this measure requires the values of 'cost of goods sold' (opening stock at cost + additions to stock at cost – closing stock at cost) and 'average stock':

$$\text{Average stock} = \frac{\text{opening} + \text{closing stock}}{2}$$

It therefore requires the production of the annual, or interim, accounts. The stocks can then be controlled by a booking in and out system. Periodic stock checks (biannually or annually, for example) can be used to discover discrepancies and adjust the stock figures. In many firms, such as supermarkets, a real-time computer system adjusts stock records the moment any goods are sold by taking electronic data direct from the cash tills.

Stock valuation methods
As explained in Chapter 75 (pages 210–13), the actual values of the stocks are calculated in one of three ways, known as:

- FIFO (first in first out);
- LIFO (last in first out);
- Average cost method.

The most common method is FIFO, which assumes firms will seek to sell their oldest stock first.

FIFO values stock at its cost price, assuming always that what remains in stock represents the most recent purchases. The cost prices are, therefore, those on the most recent invoices. LIFO does the opposite. The average cost method averages out the cost of all the stocks present every time a withdrawal is made.

Stock control
The crucial part stock control plays in the success of an enterprise is often not fully appreciated. Efficient control of the asset turnover ratio has a direct bearing on the return on capital employed. Stock is invariably the largest single asset group after debtors. Careful control of stock can save money, release cash funds, reduce losses from pilfering and smooth the production flow by improving the effectiveness of the firm's stores.

A powerful tool for stock control is Pareto Analysis. It involves plotting values and annual usage for all the items in the range. This permits identification of the most fast-moving ones. It is common to find that about 80% of annual materials usage is accounted for by around 20% of items (referred to as the 80:20 law) and, furthermore, that about 10% of the item range accounts for about 70% of annual usage. By controlling that 10% you are actually controlling around two thirds of the stock.

It is not unusual to find that as much as 50% of stock accounts for less than 5% of annual usage. These items would not, therefore, warrant the same level of scrutiny. Analysis of sales income related to item often shows that a high proportion of total income is accounted for by a small proportion of the product range. Analysis of contribution related to item reveals which products are associated with the major part of the profit.

Stock recording
In order to make such analysis possible, effective stock recording is essential. Unique stock codes should be given to each item, using numbers rather than names, and running totals should be kept of value and usage in the year to date.

There are a number of methods of valuing stock, and the reader should refer to pages 210–11 for guidance on this.

Stock cards should be marked:
A – if they are in the top 10% for annual usage.
B – if they are in the bottom 50%.
C – if they fall between the two.

This assumes that the usage pattern described above is found to be present. Treat these categories as illustrated in Figure 143.

Item code	Purchase authorisation required	Stocktake interval	Checking & amending of re-order quantity (ROQ) and re-order levels (ROL)
A	Chief Buyer	Quarterly	Every time
B	Asst. Buyer	Biannually	When necessary
C	Clerks	Random checks by Asst. Buyer	Annually

Fig. 143. Example of analysis of re-order authorisation, stocktake intervals and management of ROQ and ROL for different classes of stock.

$$\frac{\text{No. of items in random sample}}{\text{No. of items in stock}} \times \frac{\text{Stock figure from current balance sheet}}{} = \frac{\text{Total value of stock on the sample of cards}}{}$$

$$\frac{\text{No. of items in random sample}}{\text{No. of items in stock}} \times \frac{\text{Materials usage figure from the current manufacturing a/c}}{} = \frac{\text{Total usage figure for the items on the sample of cards}}{}$$

Fig. 144. Example of stock audit calculations.

Stock audits enable assessments to be made of the accuracy of the stock records. These involve taking a random sample of stock cards (say one hundred) and performing the equations given in Figure 144. Some degree of error is inevitable, as there is likely to have been some stock usage since the accounts were last updated, but by reference to the time interval involved, the degree of acceptable error can be estimated.

There are two basic approaches to stocktaking: annual and perpetual. Annual stocktaking is a task constrained rigorously, e.g. carried out at 8 a.m. when the store will again be active thus undermining the count. Perpetual stocktaking focuses on a small group of items at a time and goes on throughout the year. Thus, it is easier to manage.

Forecasting

How can you assess how much stock the firm will need? Where demand varies with some regularity throughout the year, the corresponding period in the previous year can be used as a guide. However, the unexpected keeps cropping up to complicate the picture, so this method is not very accurate. A better method is to use moving averages. For example, you would add the values for the previous three months and divide by three to predict the next month's level.

There are even more accurate methods, but they are beyond the scope of this book and the reader should refer to my other works on finance for such information.

Weathering storms in advance

Businesses exist in an uncertain environment. We never know for certain what conditions will be thrust upon us tomorrow. All sorts of things can affect the environment, from competitor action on the one hand, to political or economic changes on the other. It is wise to be prepared for rough seas in the business environment.

The trading figures of some firms are easier to predict than others. Food retailing, for example, is a safer bet than high-tech, innovative, product manufacturing. The lower profit margins in food retailing reflect the lesser degree of risk. If expected sales don't materialise, insufficient funds will be generated to pay interest on permanent loan capital (preference shares and debentures), if much of the firm's capital is financed in this way. Debenture holders must be paid whether the firm makes a profit or not; failure to pay could result in enforced cessation of business and subsequent liquidation.

If, on the other hand, most of the capital is from the proprietor's own funds, or made up of ordinary share capital, it's more likely to be able to keep going.

If your trading figures are highly predictable, you can benefit by financing the firm with a lot of permanent loan capital (preference shares and debentures). If, on the other hand, they are highly unpredictable, it's better to finance the firm largely by the proprietor's own, or ordinary shareholders', funds. The higher the risk, the greater should be the ratio of own, or shareholders', funds to permanent loan capital. The lower the risk, the greater may be the ratio of permanent loan capital to owners', or shareholders', funds. This is called the **capital gearing ratio**.

Keeping the liquidator at bay

When things get tight – for example when interest rates rise, making overdrafts increasingly expensive, suppliers begin to enforce their credit limits more severely. Bank managers or bank policies can change overnight, with sudden demands on firms to clear their overdrafts. The firm may respond by pressing all its customers to settle their accounts, but there's no guarantee they will; some may even fold under the pressure of the new economic conditions. In the meantime, your bank won't wait. If you haven't left yourself a margin for error, your firm could be in trouble. The rule of thumb to use here is keep your current assets (cash, stock and debtors) equal to twice your current liabilities (creditors and bank overdraft, if any).

Ratios to look out for

The surplus of current assets over current liabilities is called the **working capital**. It's the fund used for buying goods and raw materials for production, and for paying overhead expenses. If working capital runs out, the firm can't 'work'. The proportion of current assets to current liabilities is known as the **current ratio**; providing this is kept at an acceptable level, then if some of your customers don't pay up quickly there may be enough others who do. Similarly, if some of your stock doesn't sell quickly, there may be enough other lines which do. Overall, your effort to turn your current assets into cash to pay your bills may only have worked by half, but half was enough.

If, coupled with these economic conditions, there is also a slowdown in trading figures, you will not be able to rely on selling stocks to settle the sudden demands upon your firm from creditors. For this reason, it's a good rule of thumb to keep your liquid assets (cash and debtors) equal to your current liabilities in the ratio of 1:1. This is because you can't force people to buy your goods, but you can, in theory, force them to pay their debts (if they have sufficiently good credit statuses, and if they don't, you shouldn't have given them credit in the first place).

$$\frac{\text{Current assets}}{\text{Current liabilities}} = \text{ratio} \qquad \frac{£2.4 \text{ million}}{£1.2 \text{ million}} = 2$$

Current ratio — *Example*

$$\frac{\text{Stocks and debtors}}{\text{Current liabilities}} = \text{ratio} \qquad \frac{£1.2 \text{ million}}{£1.2 \text{ million}} = 1$$

Acid test ratio — *Example*

If a firm becomes insolvent, the managers will have to account to shareholders as to why the working capital dried up. The instrument for this is the **working capital flow analysis**. This analyses the inflow and outflow of funds and shows the difference as an increase or decrease of working capital.

Keeping the vultures away

Many people wonder why business directors are so concerned about the prices of their firm's shares on the stock market. After all, they are only second-hand shares changing hands. The firm doesn't get any of the profit when share prices rise, nor suffer any direct loss when they fall. Once the firm has issued and been paid for them, they are out of their hands for the holders to do what they wish with them.

Low share prices attract asset strippers

But there's a very good reason for directors' concerns. Normally the share prices of companies closely reflect the asset values that they represent, but even on the stock exchange, prices are determined by the forces of supply and demand. If nobody wants the shares, the price drops; if everyone is rushing to buy them, the price rises. If the price drops below the underlying asset values, a predatory firm can make a quick profit by buying them up, dismantling the firm and selling off its assets piecemeal. This is known as 'asset stripping'. The predator may also be getting rid of a competitor into the bargain – quite a smart move when you're even getting a profit for your efforts. That's why directors are so concerned about share prices. Takeovers can be highly detrimental to the interests of a company and its personnel; they can lead to thwarted prospects and wholesale job losses.

So how can directors keep share prices up and buoyant? Well, prices will fall if nobody wants them. People buy and keep shares because they out-perform others in terms of dividends and share-price increases (dividends are share-outs of profit). They are less concerned that such companies spread their risk by diversification, because they, themselves, will do that, but they do evaluate the stability of the firm and the predictability of its performance. The return they will expect will be based on that.

This explains why firms sometimes have to make the unpopular decision to reduce manning levels. Unions argue that there is no justification for sacking people if a firm is making a profit at all, but it's not just *any* level of profit that will do. If its profits are not high enough to enable it to pay dividends equal to those of other firms, shareholders will sell their shares, prices will fall and the firm will become vulnerable to takeover – then everyone could lose their jobs. Three ratios used for assessing share performance are given on page 242.

Investment appraisal

Before assessing what there is to gain by investing in a project a firm needs to take the opportunity cost into account. That is the return it could expect if it placed its funds in a safe investment, like a building society account, or UK treasury bonds, instead. The difference is what there is to gain from taking the risk. However, entrepreneurs need to make some other checks too. Here are four well-used strategies for investment appraisal.

- Pay back period.
- Average rate of return (ARR).
- Internal rate of return (IRR).
- Net present value.

Pay back period

The pay back period is the first test that is usually made. It tells you how long it will take to get your money back if things go to plan. This, in turn, says something about the risk, for the further into the future we have to extend our exposure to risk the more uncertain things become. It is often used as an initial screening strategy for investment proposals using a set maximum pay back period above which rejection is automatic.

Average rate of return

The average rate of return is a measure of the average annual profit the firm will receive from the averaged out value the assets in the project will have over the project's lifespan. The latter is found by deducting projected residual value from initial cost to allow for depreciation. However, many firms often dispense with this deduction and just keep the assets figure at cost. This is not a bad idea, since that more accurately reflects their investment than does a depreciated figure. This, too, is often used as a screening method with a set minimum ARR below which rejection is automatic.

The weakness of this method is that it assumes that returns will not vary across the years. This might not be the case. The highest returns might not come until the later years. If an average rate of return of 30% annually actually reflects 10% in year 1, 20% in year 2 and 60% in year 3 (which still produces an average of 30% annually) then only a small portion of the total return will earn interest in the bank over the long period, but the large proportion of it will earn little or none, since it will not be earned until year 3.

It would be quite the reverse if the 60% return was expected in the first year and the 10% in the last year.

Internal rate of return

A method that takes this into account is the internal rate of return method. This converts the expected returns to compound interest equivalents.

The internal rate of return method considers that rate of discount which when applied to the returns of the proposed investment would result in a zero level *net present value*. (i.e. the reverse of compound interest which starts with no interest and ends with the accumulated returns). This percentage is often used as an accept or reject screening process with a minimum rate of discount being required (say, for example 18%) to avoid automatic rejection.

To find the projected internal rate of return on a project, list and sum the expected annual returns over the projected lifespan of the investment. Deduct the initial investment figure and divide the difference by the number of years. Then divide that figure by half of the initial investment figure and multiply by 100 to give an approximation to begin a trial and error process towards finding the internal rate of return.

Using a discount table select the column which most closely matches the approximation and select the figures by which to multiply each year's return to find the discounted return for that year. Then sum the products for all the years and check how close it is to the initial investment. If it is substantially more then reduce the approximation and try again; if substantially less then increase the approximation. Keep doing this until the sum of the products is more or less equal to your initial investment figure (say within 0.1%). The discounted rate of return (column heading) you last used is the internal rate of return the investment can be expected to produce.

Investing in company shares

Before investing in a company's shares investors compare their value with that of other similar companies and with various yardsticks. Here are the three most basic and commonly used key ratios.

Earnings per share =

$$\frac{\text{Net profit (after tax and dividend on preference shares)} \times 100}{\text{Number of ordinary shares}}$$

Price earnings ratio = $\dfrac{\text{Market price}}{\text{Earnings per share}}$

Dividend yield = $\dfrac{\text{Dividend per share} \times 100}{\text{Market price}}$

A fall in earnings per share may not in itself be sufficient reason to avoid investment, as it may mean the company has simply kept more on general reserve. However, in reality any announcements that suggest reductions on distributed profits usually have a negative effect on demand for shares, sending prices lower.

Type of overhead £000	Total cost £000	Criteria for apportionment	Cost centre	Criterion values for cost centre	Workings	Overheads absorbed £000
Factory rent and rates	150	Per cent of floor space used	Assembly line	70%	150 × 0.7 =	105
			Spray shop	20%	150 × 0.2 =	30
			Finishing	10%	150 × 0.1 =	25
				100%		150
Maintenance	200	Maintenance staff time used	Assembly line	75%	220 × 0.75 =	150
			Spray shop	20%	200 × 0.2 =	40
			Finishing	5%	200 × 0.05 =	10
				100%		200
Canteen	80	Number of employees	Assembly line	30	80 × 30/45 =	53
			Spray shop	10	20 × 10/45 =	18
			Finishing	5	80 × 5/45 =	9
				45		80

Fig. 145.

243

Price/earnings ratio is commonly used as a measure of value in investment decisions. Different sectors of the stock market have different average price/earnings ratios, reflecting the different levels of risk. Both the level of risk and a share's PER is compared with others in the sector.

Overhead absorption

A product's contribution to overheads is the net sales revenue from that product less the direct costs of production (materials and labour). See Figure 146.

Product	Product A £	Product B £	Product C £	Total £
Sales revenue	100,000	150,000	200,000	450,000
Direct materials	20,000	32,000	45,000	97,000
Direct labour	20,000	30,000	60,000	110,000
Contribution to overheads	60,000	88,000	95,000	243,000
Total of overhead costs				150,000
Profit				93,000

Fig. 146. The relationship between sales, direct costs, contribution to overheads and profit.

Overhead apportionment refers to dividing the total overhead costs in a production run by the number of units produced, but this is done in a weighted way. For example if the production of **Product A** uses a machine twice as much as **Product B** then the overhead cost of that machine will be apportioned to **Products A** and **B** in the ratio of 2:1. Similarly, if the production of **Product B** requires 30% more factory space than **Product A** then the factory overhead will be apportioned to **A** and **B** in the ratio 1:1.3.

Often overheads are apportioned to cost centres and products then absorb them in the same proportions as they use those cost centres' time.

As long as you know:

- the total costs of each type of overhead
- the criteria for apportionment
- the criterion values for each cost centre

the rest is just a matter of simple ratio analysis. Figure 146 gives an example.

Your double-entry bookkeeping skills will enable you to work in most countries in the developed world, as the double-entry system, after all, did not originate here in the UK but in Genoa, Italy. At least, that's where the earliest evidence of the practice exists dating back to AD 1304. From there it has spread throughout the world.

What you will find different, though, are the final reporting practices. In the USA, for example, the assets are listed on the balance sheet in order of liquidity, whereas bookkeepers in the UK will be used to listing them in order of permanence – the exact opposite. Furthermore, in the USA, assets on the balance sheet tend to start with goodwill, whereas in the UK it is usual for this to be written off immediately.

Valuation of assets may also be different. UK bookkeepers may be used to valuing assets at cost, but in countries with high inflation such as Brazil, that would not provide a very useful picture, as their value would increase rapidly and the depreciation allowance would not be sufficient to replace an asset when it came to the end of its useful life. A revaluation method is more useful in such countries. That is not to say that revaluation is not used in countries with low inflation; in the EU, firms can use it by choice. If the revaluation method is chosen in EU countries, then firms are obliged to keep the valuations up to date.

In the USA, assets have to be valued on a fair value basis so that they are never reported as having a value exceeding what they can realistically be expected to fetch if sold. Nor is it permitted for the fair values to be quoted as greater than the historical cost of assets. In Europe, however, the requirement is that firms cannot report a fair value greater than the market value of the asset, i.e. what it can realistically be expected to fetch if sold.

In the USA, different depreciation methods can be used for taxation and published financial statements for investors.

Other differences between countries include the fact that research and development costs are regarded as expenses in Japan but are capitalised as assets in other countries, such as Canada and France.

Accountancy standards and practice are related to the kind of legal system a country has. Broadly speaking, the legal systems of countries fall into two categories. Either they are based on codified Roman law or they are based on common law. In the former case, accountancy practices tend to be dictated by government, while in the latter they tend to be fashioned by the accountancy profession. In the former, there will tend to be less detail required, while in the latter the reverse is true.

Where a country's legal system derives from codified Roman law, accounting practices tend to be determined by the state, primarily for taxation purposes. In those which have a legal system based on common law, such as the UK, such practices tend to be fashioned by the accountancy profession and are focused primarily towards providing information for investors. In the former case, disclosure requirements tend to be less detailed but more rigorous than the latter case.

Bookkeepers from the UK will find the accounting systems of Commonwealth countries most familiar to them.

The kind of business ethos and where the funding comes from are factors, too. In countries like France, funding normally comes from banks and they are more interested in the accounts revealing the liquidity of a business, whereas when the funding comes largely from the capital markets, profit is more important.

Accounting practices in some countries allow more transparency than others. Accounting values can be contrasted on four axes:

- professionalism v. statutory control
- uniformity v. flexibility
- conservativism v. optimism
- secrecy v. transparency.

Inevitably, those countries that hold values of optimism and transparency in business affairs will require the greatest degree of disclosure in accounts.

UK bookkeepers will also find differences in practice in Islamic countries. Such countries cannot, for example, charge interest on loans, and traditional accounting rules do not cover some of their requirements. Some of these countries have their own accounting standards laid down by such bodies as the Accounting and Auditing Organization for Islamic Financial Institutions (AAOIFI) and the Malaysian Accounting Standards Board (MASB).

Accounting practices in different countries will also depend on such factors as the state and quality of accounting education, the stage of economic development of the country and the nature of the political system.

In countries where most of the financing of businesses comes from families, such as in Italy, there will be fewer requirements for disclosure in the published statements of accounts, because the families will have other means of obtaining this information. In contrast, when most of the financing come from banks or capital markets, a much greater degree of disclosure will be required.

In some countries, there is a difference between the accounts for the purposes of investors and those for the purposes of taxation. The UK is an example. In contrast, taxation in Germany is based on the same published statements that are used by investors, financiers and creditors.

The general state of accounting across the world can be summarised under four models:

- The fair presentation/full disclosure model. This is an Anglo-Saxon/Anglo-American model orientated towards the decision needs of investors and creditors;
- The legal compliance model (sometimes referred to as the continental European model). This is found in Europe and Japan, among other countries. Under such systems, banks are usually the primary financiers and accounts are orientated towards the needs of taxation authorities and government planning;
- The third model is the inflation-adjusted model, which is found in countries with high inflation such as those in South America.

These differences in accounting standards and practice, of course, cause problems in the increasingly global transactions of businesses. Firstly there is the difficulty for investors in interpreting accounts and evaluating risk in relation to companies that operate under a different system than that with which they are familiar. There are also similar problems for international financiers. For accountants, the differences in reporting practices cause very significant difficulties in consolidation accounting, because it is not a simple matter of amalgamating like with like.

Because of this, attempts have been made to establish common international accounting standards and practices, known as International Financial Reporting Standards (IFRS).

The Institute of Certified Bookkeepers

Level II Certificate in Bookkeeping
Sample Paper 1

This Paper forms one section of the ICB Level II Certificate in Bookkeeping. The paper is taken online, at home or in the place of work. You have two hours to complete the questions and submit your answers. All questions are compulsory.

The paper is a combination of multi-choice answers (which you answer by selecting one of the options from a given menu or by ticking either a single button or multiple buttons to identify your choice) and data entry answers where you will need to enter a numeric amount into a box.

Numeric answers should generally be entered correct to two decimal places in the format ####.## unless either the answer is obviously a whole number when numbers may be entered as integers, or, entered correct to the stated number of decimal places (####.# if correct to 1 decimal place).

As a general rule, all figures should be entered as positive numbers, regardless of whether they are to be added or deducted, unless a) the answer is one where the final result is negative, or b) a question provides specific instructions that override it.

For the purposes of this paper please note that VAT should always be rounded down, even if you are calculating a VAT inclusive amount.

Note: to complete the Level II Certificate in Bookkeeping and Accounts, you will take a total of three papers. All are taken at home and include sample papers 1 and 2. Paper 3 is a computerised paper which requires the use of a computerised accounts package. Marks for all three papers will be aggregated to complete the grading of the final qualification.

Assessment Criteria

This piece of work will be graded at Distinction, Merit, Pass or Fail.

Pass	To gain a Pass, candidates must achieve between 85–89%
Merit	To gain a Merit, candidates must achieve between 90–94%
Distinction	To gain a Distinction, candidates must achieve between 95–100%
Fail	Candidates who achieve less than 85% of the total marks will be failed.

Level II Certificate in Bookkeeping
Sample Paper 1 2014

Underpinning knowledge

1. A person operating as a self-employed person working by himself is normally termed:

   a. A limited company
   b. A sole trader
   c. A partnership
   d. A charity

2. The identifying number for a UK bank branch is called the:

   a. Account number
   b. Sort code
   c. IBAN
   d. Swift Code

3. Paying for goods purchased for resale on credit via the business bank account online is normally carried out by which of the following methods:

   a. Cheque
   b. Debit Card
   c. BACS
   d. CHAPS

4. When purchasing goods by debit card the code normally entered into the payment point terminal is called a:

   a. Password
   b. Payment number
   c. PayPal number
   d. PIN number

5. The current standard rate of VAT is:

   a. 0%
   b. 5%
   c. 20%
   d. 21%

6. A sole trader business making and selling garden furniture **must** register for VAT:

    a. On the first day of trading
    b. If they reach the VAT threshold within a twelve month trading period
    c. As a sole trader business they will never have to register for VAT
    d. At the end of their first year of trading regardless of income

7. Original money used to open a business by a sole trader is termed:

    a. Bank balance
    b. Assets
    c. Liabilities
    d. Capital

8. Items that a business owns are termed:

    a. Assets
    b. Liabilities
    c. Capital
    d. Balances

9. Items that a business owes are termed:
    a. Assets
    b. Liabilities
    c. Capital
    d. Balances

10. A business's credit suppliers are termed its:

    a. Debtors
    b. Creditors
    c. Bank
    d. Capital

Business documents including calculation of VAT

1. An invoice is issued for the following items:

   15 sets garden tools @ £8.00 each
   25 wheelbarrows @ £35 each
   10 bags garden compost @ £3.50 each

   i) What is the total net figure that appears on the invoice?

   ii) If trade discount of 5% is offered, what amount of VAT at 20% must be added to the invoice?

2. The document that would be sent from the supplier to request payment for goods or services supplied is termed:

   a. Invoice
   b. Credit note
   c. Remittance
   d. Statement

3. A business sends back goods that have been received in error. The document to confirm that the invoice will be cancelled is termed:

   a. a return invoice
   b. a statement
   c. a remittance slip
   d. a credit note

4. At the end of the month the documents sent from a supplier to a customer to detail the final balance owed is termed a:

   a. Invoice
   b. Credit Note
   c. Returns Note
   d. Statement

5. Why is obtaining a source document so important?

   a. Because it is needed to claim the expense as a business item
   b. It provides evidence of the financial transaction
   c. It allows you to reclaim any VAT
   d. All of the above

Accounts and the division of the ledger plus accounting for VAT

Peter opens a business and brings in the following personal items: a computer worth £350, a motor van worth £800 and furniture worth £175. He also opens a business bank account and transfers in £1000 from his personal account.

1. What will be the total amount of capital that he is using to start the business?

 a. £1150
 b. £1000
 c. £1325
 d. £2325

2. What will be the opening entries to the ledger accounts to record the start-up?

 a. Debit capital, Credit office equipment, Credit motor vehicles, Credit furniture, Credit bank
 b. Debit office equipment, Debit motor vehicles, Debit furniture, Debit bank, Credit capital
 c. Debit bank, Credit capital, Credit office equipment, Credit motor vehicles, Credit furniture
 d. Debit office equipment, Debit motor vehicles, Debit furniture, Credit bank, Credit capital

3. Peter takes out a loan from the bank for £3500. How will this be entered into the ledger accounts?

 a. Credit bank, Debit, loan
 b. Debit bank, Credit loan
 c. Debit bank, Credit capital
 d. Credit bank, Debit capital

4. Sylthan Soft Furnishings buys and sells materials and associated items. The business maintains a full double entry ledger system with customer and supplier invoices being kept in their own ledger.

 In which ledger would the accounts for customers be kept?

 a. General Ledger
 b. Nominal Ledger
 c. Purchases Ledger
 d. Sales Ledger

5. Sylthan raises a sales invoice to a customer, Shaun David. The net value of the goods was £360.00 to which £72.00 is added for VAT. Entries in the ledger should be:

    a. Debit Shaun David £432.00, Credit Sales £360.00, Credit VAT £72.00

    b. Debit Shaun David £360.00, Credit Sales £288.00, Credit VAT £72.00

    c. Debit Shaun David £360.00, Debit VAT £ 72.00, Credit Sales £432.00

    d. Debit Sales £360.00, Debit VAT 72.00, Credit Shaun David £432.00

6. An invoice is received from Howsend Ltd for the purchase of some cutting equipment to the value of £500 plus VAT. The account entries would be:

    a. Dr Stock £500, Dr VAT Input £100, Cr Bank £600

    b. Dr Equipment £600, Cr Howsend Ltd £600

    c. Dr Equipment £500, Dr VAT Input £100, Cr Howsend £600

    d. Dr Equipment £500, Dr VAT Input £100, Cr Bank £600

7. Some stock was purchased for resale for £240 including VAT, paid directly from the bank account by debit card. The account entries would be:

    a. Dr Stock £200, Dr VAT Input £40, Cr Bank £240

    b. Dr Purchases £240, Cr VAT Input £40, Cr Bank £200

    c. Dr Stock £200, Dr VAT output £40, Dr Bank £240

    d. Dr Purchases £200, Dr VAT Input £40, Cr Bank £240

8. Peter issues an invoice to Marks and Co for £300 plus VAT. He also offers a 5% discount for prompt payment. What will be the entries:

    a. Dr Marks & Co £342.00, Cr Sales £285, Cr VAT Input £57.00

    b. Dr Marks & Co 360.00, Cr Sales £285.00, Cr VAT Input 75.00

    c. Dr Marks & Co £342, Cr Sales £300, Cr VAT Output £42.00

    d. Dr Marks & Co £357.00, Cr Sales £300, Cr VAT Output £57.00

9. Purchase returns from a creditor of £120.00 (inc VAT) need posting to the accounts. The business is VAT registered. The entries would be:

    a. Cr Purchase Returns £100, Cr VAT £20, Dr Creditor Account £120

    b. Dr Purchase Returns £100, Dr VAT £20, Cr Creditor Account £120

    c. Dr Purchase Returns £120, Cr Creditor Account £120

    d. None of these

10. A sales invoice had been issued to a customer for £150 plus VAT and entered into the accounts. The customer sends the payment in full. The entries would be:

    a. Debit customer £150, Credit VAT £30, Credit bank £180
    b. Debit bank £180, Credit customer £150, Credit VAT £30
    c. Debit bank £180, Credit customer £180
    d. Credit bank £180, Debit customer £180

11. A non-VAT registered sole trader buys a second hand motor vehicle for business use and pays by cheque. He should record this by:

    a. Debiting bank account, crediting motor vehicles account
    b. Crediting bank, debiting motor vehicles account
    c. Debiting cash account, crediting motor vehicles account
    d. Crediting cash account, debiting motor vehicles account

12. Peter withdraws £300 from the business bank account for his personal expenditure. The debit entry for this transaction will be posted to the:

    a. Bank account
    b. Capital account
    c. Drawings account
    d. Cash account

13. Rent received (exempt of VAT) from a tenant in cash should be recorded by:

    a. Debiting the cash account, crediting the rent received account
    b. Crediting the cash account, debiting the rent received account
    c. Debiting the bank account, crediting the rent received account
    d. Crediting the bank account, debiting the rent received account

14. Which of the following accounts is correctly balanced?

a.

Date	Details	£	Date	Details	£
201X Jan			201X Jan		
1	Capital	5,000.00	2	Equipment	300.00
4	Sales	175.00	3	Purchases	100.00
			6	Drawings	100.00
				Balance c/f	2,675.00
		5,175.00			5,175.00

b.

Date	Details	£	Date	Details	£
201X Jan			201X Jan		
1	Capital	5,000.00	2	Eqsuipment	300.00
4	Sales	175.00	3	Purchases	100.00
	Balance c/f	2,675.00	6	Drawings	100.00
				Balance c/f	7,350.00
		7,850.00			7,850.00
6	Balance b/f	7350.00	6	Balance b/f	2675.00

c.

Date	Details	£	Date	Details	£
201X Jan			201X Jan		
1	Capital	5,000.00	2	Equipment	300.00
4	Sales	175.00	3	Purchases	100.00
			6	Drawings	100.00
				Balance c/f	4,675.00
		5,175.00			5,175.00
6	Balance b/f	4,675.00			

d.

Date	Details	£	Date	Details	£
201X Jan			201X Jan		
1	Capital	5,000.00	2	Equipment	300.00
4	Sales	175.00	3	Purchases	100.00
			6	Drawings	100.00
		5,175.00		Balance	2,676.00
6	Balance b/f	2,675.00			

15. Consider the following bank account:

Bank Account					
Date	Details	£	Date	Details	£
Jan 1	Bank	400.00	Jan 1	Purchases	300.00
2	Sales	250.00	2	Travel	12.00
3	Sales	110.00	3	Balance c/f	448.00
		760.00			760.00
Jan 3	Balance b/f	448.00			

The totals of £760 mean that:

    a. £760 has been paid out
    b. There is £760 in hand
    c. That both sides are equal
    d. The account is overdrawn by £760

16. What will be the brought down balance on the following account:

Bank Account					
Date	Details	£	Date	Details	£
Jan 1	Capital	1000.00	Jan 1	Purchases	250.00
2	Loan	500.00	2	Travel	56.00
3	Sales	110.00	15	Rent	850.00
			20	Business rates	500.00

    a. £46 Dr
    b. £46 Cr
    c. £1610 Dr
    d. £1656 Cr

17. What will be the brought down balance on the following account:

Sales Account					
Date	Details	£	Date	Details	£
			Jan 1	Bank	450.00
			20	Cash	101.00
			25	Bank	300.00
			30	Cash	250.00

    a. £1101 Cr
    b. £1101 Dr
    c. There is a zero balance
    d. £2202 Cr

18. A debit balance of £1250 in P Samuels' account in the books of P Saul means that:

    a. P Samuels owes P Saul £1250
    b. P Saul owes P Samuels £1250
    c. P Samuels has paid P Saul £1250
    d. P Saul has paid P Samuels £1250

19. The entries for interest paid on a loan would be:

    a. Debit bank account, Credit loan account
    b. Debit bank account, Credit loan interest account
    c. Credit bank account, Debit loan interest account
    d. Credit bank account, Debit loan account

20. Trade discount is:

    a. Recorded in the discount allowed account
    b. Only allowed when bills are paid within the allowable term
    c. Recorded in the discount received account
    d. Not shown in any ledger account

21. An electricity bill for £67.20 including VAT at 20%, paid by direct debit from the business bank account will be entered into the ledgers as follows:

   a. Debit Electricity £67.20, Credit Bank £67.20
   b. Credit Electricity £56, Credit VAT Output £11.20, Debit Bank £67.20
   c. Debit Electricity £56, Debit VAT Input £11.20, Credit Drawings £67.20
   d. Debit Electricity £56, Debit VAT Input £11.20, Credit Bank £67.20

22. A business buys a new machine from a supplier for £15,000 plus VAT. A deposit of £5000 plus VAT is paid immediately with the remainder being paid in two equal instalments. How would you enter the original invoice?

   a. Debit machinery £5000, Debit VAT Input £1000, Credit Supplier £6000
   b. Debit machinery £15000, Debit VAT Input £3000, Credit Supplier £18,000
   c. Debit machinery £5000, Debit VAT Input £1000, Credit Bank £6000
   d. Debit machinery £15000, Debit VAT Input £3000, Credit Bank £18000

23. A sole trader draws £500 out of the business bank account. He decides to leave half in a petty cash account and keep the rest for personal use. How will you enter this into the accounts?

   a. Debit petty cash £500, Credit bank £500
   b. Debit drawings £500, Credit bank £500
   c. Debit bank £500, Credit drawings £250, Credit petty cash £250
   d. Debit petty cash £250, Debit drawings £250, Credit bank £500

24. In a cash book a payment for expenses would be entered into:

   a. The credit side
   b. The debit side
   c. Both sides
   d. Would not be entered at all

25. The drawings of a proprietor count as which of the following for VAT purposes?

   a. Standard rate
   b. Zero rate
   c. Exempt of VAT
   d. Outside the scope of VAT

26. VAT on sales is posted to which VAT account:

    a. VAT Input Account
    b. VAT Output Account

27. The gross amount shown on an invoice is £432.00. What would the net amount have been before VAT was added at standard rate?

28. A business pays £35.00 for fuel. If the business is registered for VAT How much of this amount represents the VAT? (Note – it is ICB policy to round the net amount up and the VAT down in all cases)

29. If the business had been non-VAT registered how much would have been posted to the motor expenses account?

30. What is the net amount on an electricity invoice, total value £163.80 where VAT has been charged at 5% for domestic fuel?

31. A debit balance on a single VAT account in the ledgers means:

    a. The business owes the balance to HMRC
    b. HMRC owes the balance to the business

32. VAT on a credit note issued for a sales return would be posted to:

    a. Credit side of the VAT Output Account
    b. Debit side of the VAT Output Account
    c. Credit side of the VAT Input Account
    d. Debit side of the VAT Input Account

33. Which of the following counts as revenue expenditure (tick all that apply)?

    a. Capital
    b. Motor Vehicles
    c. Wages
    d. Rent
    e. Premises
    f. Advertising
    g. Purchases
    h. Drawings
    i. Electricity
    j. Sales

Making and receiving payments

1. Peter is a VAT registered business operating a standard VAT scheme. A bank transfer of £120 including VAT is received from David, a credit customer, on 15 January to clear his account.

   What would be the account entries to record this?

   a. Dr Bank £100, Cr David £100
   b. Dr David £120, Cr Bank £100, Cr VAT Output £20
   c. Dr Bank £120, Cr David £120
   d. Dr Bank £120, Cr Sales £100, Cr VAT Output £20

Martin operates a two-column cash book and a petty cash book. The balance on his bank account on 31 December is £56.00 debit and his cash account £50 debit. He transfers £100 from his bank account to his cash account and £75 from his cash account to the petty cash book.

2. In book keeping terms these transfers would be called:

   a. Payments
   b. Receipts
   c. Contras
   d. Duplicates

   1 mark

3. What would be the balance on the bank and cash accounts after the transfers are made and would it be a debit or a credit balance?

4. When a columnar petty cash book is used, what action should normally be taken with the totals of each analysis column?

   a. They are transferred to a general expense account in ledger.
   b. They are transferred to the ledger accounts that exist for the expense concerned.
   c. They are entered into the trial balance as a petty cash total.
   d. They are entered into the purchases account in the ledger

5. The petty cash imprest amount is £160.00 The following are transactions through the account for the first week in April:

   Fuel £60 including VAT
   Postage £15
   Office sundries £10.50 including VAT

   How much will be the needed to restore the imprest amount?

6. The following two column cash book contains details from the books of Carlo Ceron for the month of September.

Date	Details	Bank £	Cash £	Date	Details	Bank £	Cash £
Sept 1	Capital	5000.00		Sept 4	Equip-ment	500.00	
10	Sales		1200.00	6	Rent	650.00	
12	Sales		850.00	7	P Rose (creditor)	1000.00	
25	R Farmer (debtor)	300.00		21	Drawings	400.00	
				25	Wages		600.00

On 30th Carlo retained a cash balance of £450 and banked the remainder.

i. How much would he have banked?
ii. How would this banking be recorded in the two column cash book?
   a) Dr Bank, Cr Cash
   b) Dr Cash, Cr Bank
iii. What is the final balance on the bank account?
iv. To which side of R Farmer's account will the receipt dated 25 September be entered?
   Dr / Cr

Production of a trial balance

The following balances have been taken from the accounts of Peter on 1 January 201X:

	£
Capital	43,613.70
Motor Vehicles and equipment	33,432.00
Stocks	1,356.50
Cash in the bank	4,650.75
Debtor (David)	9,850.70
Creditor (Susan)	125.60
HMRC balance owing for VAT	550.65
A bank loan	5,000.00

1. State whether each of the following balances would be a debit or a credit balance in the ledger:

Capital	Dr / Cr
Motor Vehicles and equipment	Dr / Cr
Stocks	Dr / Cr
Cash in the bank	Dr / Cr
Debtor	Dr / Cr
Creditor	Dr / Cr
HMRC Balance owing for VAT	Dr / Cr
Bank loan	Dr / Cr

2. Ignoring the Capital account, what is the total of Peter's liabilities?

   a. 37700.00
   b. 5676.25
   c. 5930.70
   d. 676.25

3. What would be the total of the trial balance columns?

Level II Certificate in Bookkeeping Sample Paper 1 2014

Answers (all questions are worth 1 mark unless otherwise indicated)

Underpinning Knowledge

1. b
2. b
3. c
4. d
5. c
6. b
7. d
8. a
9. b
10. b

Business documents including calculation of VAT

1. i) 1030.00   2 marks
   ii) 195.70   2 marks
2. d
3. d
4. d
5. b

Accounts and the division of the ledger plus Accounting for VAT

1. b
2. b
3. d
4. a
5. c
6. d
7. d
8. a
9. c
10. b
11. c
12. a
13. c   (2 marks)
14. c
15. b
16. a
17. a
18. c

19. d
20. d
21. b
22. d
23. a
24. d
25. b
26. £360.00
27. £5.83   (2 marks)
28. £35
29. £156.00   (2 marks)
30. b
31. b
32. Wages, rent, advertising, purchases, electricity (1 mark each)

Making and receiving payments

1. c
2. c
3. Bank - £44.00 Cr, Cash £75.00 Dr   (4 marks in total)
4. b
5. £85.50 (2 marks)
6. Invalid, Valid, Invalid, Valid, Invalid   (1 marks each)
7. i)   £1000   (2 marks)
   ii) a
   iii) £3750   (2 marks)
   iv) Cr

Production of a trial balance

1. Capital   Cr
   Motor Vehicles and equipment   Dr
   Stocks   Dr
   Cash in the bank   Dr
   Debtor   Dr
   Creditor   Cr
   HMRC Balance owing for VAT   Cr
   Bank loan   Cr (1 mark each)

2. b
3. 49,289.95

The Institute of Certified Bookkeepers

Level II Certificate in Bookkeeping
Sample Paper 2

This Paper forms one section of the ICB Level II Certificate in Bookkeeping. The paper is taken online, at home or in the place of work. You have two hours to complete the questions and submit your answers. All questions are compulsory.

The paper is a combination of multi-choice answers (which you answer by selecting one of the options from a given menu or by ticking either a single button or multiple buttons to identify your choice) and data entry answers where you will need to enter a numeric amount into a box.

Numeric answers should generally be entered correct to two decimal places in the format ####.## unless either the answer is obviously a whole number when numbers may be entered as integers, or, entered correct to the stated number of decimal places (####.# if correct to 1 decimal place).

As a general rule, all figures should be entered as positive numbers, regardless of whether they are to be added or deducted, unless a) the answer is one where the final result is negative, or b) a question provides specific instructions that override it.

For the purposes of this paper please note that VAT should always be rounded down, even if you are calculating a VAT inclusive amount.

Note: to complete the Level II Certificate in Bookkeeping and Accounts, you will take a total of three papers. All are taken at home and include sample papers 1 and 2. Paper 3 is a computerised paper which requires the use of a computerised accounts package. Marks for all three papers will be aggregated to complete the grading of the final qualification.

Assessment Criteria

This piece of work will be graded at Distinction, Merit, Pass or Fail.

Pass   To gain a Pass, candidates must achieve between 85-89%
Merit   To gain a Merit, candidates must achieve between 90-94%
Distinction To gain a Distinction, candidates must achieve between 95-100%
Fail   Candidates who achieve less than 85% of the total marks will be
            failed.

Level II Certificate in Bookkeeping
Sample Paper 2 2014

Underpinning knowledge

1. Amounts that are owed by the business to its creditors are termed:

   a) Assets
   b) Liabilities
   c) Capital
   d) Loans

2. A business purchases a large photocopier for use in the business. This purchase is classified as:

   a) A fixed asset
   b) A current asset
   c) Capital
   d) Loan

3. The start-up funds put into a sole trader business by the owner are termed:

   a) Assets
   b) Liabilities
   c) Capital
   d) Loans

4. What is the accounting equation?

   a) Assets plus Liabilities = Capital
   b) Assets less Liabilities = Capital
   c) Assets = Capital less Liabilities
   d) Liabilities = Capital plus Assets

5. The separation of the financial affairs of a sole trader's business from his or her personal affairs is covered by the concept of:

   a) Duality
   b) Historic cost
   c) Equity
   d) Business Entity

6. Entering invoices at the price paid for the goods or services is covered by the concept of:

   a) Duality
   b) Historic cost
   c) Equity
   d) Business entity

7. The Cash VAT scheme means that VAT is declared in a VAT return

   a) at the point of the issue of an invoice
   b) at the point of payment of an invoice

8. Which if the following reasons for keeping clients' documents locked away in a fire proof safe would ensure that you keep to an acceptable code of ethics?

   a) Confidentiality
   b) Security
   c) Availability
   d) Openness

   Tick all that apply

9. Which of the following business types would be most suitable for a group of people who wish to protect their liability for debts whilst running a business?

   a) Sole Trader
   b) Partnership
   c) Not-for-profit organisation
   d) Limited company

Ledger accounts and divisions of the ledger, Books of Prime entry and Accounting for VAT

When posting the figures to the ledgers using the Sales Ledger and Purchases Ledger Control Accounts as part of the double entry system, where would the following figures be posted?

1. Net total of the Purchases Day Book:

   a) Debit side of the purchases account
   b) Debit side of the purchases ledger control account
   c) Credit side of the purchases ledger control account
   d) Debit side of the personal accounts in the Purchases Ledger

2. Gross total of the Sales Day Book:

   a) Credit side of the sales account
   b) Debit side of the sales ledger control account
   c) Credit side of the sales ledger control account
   d) Debit side of the personal accounts in the Sales Ledger

3. Gross amount of a single purchases returns invoice:

   a) Debit side of the purchases returns account
   b) Credit side of the purchases ledger control account
   c) Debit side of the purchases ledger control account
   d) Debit side of the personal account in the Purchases Ledger

Questions 4 – 12 refer to the sales day books and the sales ledger control account for Highfield.

4. At 1 April, Highfield had the following outstanding debtor balances on his ledgers:

   Meantime Processing £120.00 debit balance
   Super Supplies £360.00 debit balance

   What is the opening balance on the sales ledger control account? State if this is a debit or a credit balance

5. The following entries were made in the day books of Highfield for the month of April:

Sales Day Book				
Date	Details	Net	VAT	Gross
4	Meantime Processing	350.00		
15	Super Supplies	220.00		

Sales Returns Day Book				
Date	Details	Net	VAT	Gross
12	Meantime Processing	50.00		

Complete the entries in the day books

6. What is the figure from the sales day book that would be posted to the sales ledger control account at the end of the month?

7. If a 5% cash discount had been offered to all customers, what would be the amount of VAT in the Sales Day Book?

8. Cash discount is given:

   a) Only when goods are bought for cash
   b) When accounts are paid according to the terms of payment
   c) When dealing with other traders only
   d) Only when the goods are paid for by cash or cheque

9. To which side of the control account will the gross total from the sales returns day book be posted?

   Dr / Cr

10. The following cheques were received during April:

    April 28 from Meantime Processing £120.00
    April 30 from Super Supplies £300

    To which side of the sales ledger control account will these receipts be posted?
    Dr / Cr

11. What is the balance on the sales ledger control account after all postings have been made?

12. If a bad debt is written off during the month to which side of the control account will this be posted?

    Dr/Cr

Questions 13 – 15 refer to the purchases day books and the purchases ledger control account for Mitchell Ltd.

13. The following entries were made in the day books of Mitchell Ltd for the month of June:

Purchases Day Book				
Date	Details	Net	VAT	Gross
18	Future Developments	160.00		
25	JR Trading & Co	1520.00		
30	Petersham Ltd	680.00		

    Complete the entries in the day books

14. To where will the gross amount for the invoice issued on 25 October be posted in the ledgers of Mitchell Ltd?

    a) Debit side of J R Trading's Account
    b) Credit side of JR Trading's account
    c) Debit side of the purchases account
    d) Debit side of the VAT Input account

15. The total of the balances on the creditors' accounts should be checked monthly with the balance on the:

    a) Cash book (bank column) payments
    b) Purchases Ledger Control Account
    c) Sales Ledger Control Account
    d) VAT Control Account

16. When using a set of control accounts as part of the double entry process, the customer and supplier accounts are stored in their respective ledgers and are called:

    a) Miscellaneous accounts
    b) Memorandum accounts
    c) General accounts
    d) Individual Accounts

17. A customer pays an invoice and takes off an agreed £10 cash discount for prompt payment. What would the entries be in the nominal ledger to record this:

    a) Credit discount received, Debit sales ledger control account
    b) Debit discount received, Credit sales ledger control account
    c) Debit discount allowed, Credit sales ledger control account
    d) Credit discount allowed, Debit sales ledger control account

18. In a business's ledger B Mann's account shows a debit balance of £200 on 1 January. During the month of January the business (who has not registered for VAT) sold him goods invoiced at £250 less 20% trade discount. B Mann returns goods to the value of £50 before trade discount is calculated. The business received a cheque from Mann for £260 on account. What will be the closing balance on his account?

19. Philip stops at a fuel station and fills his van with diesel. The final bill comes to £94.50. If he has also bought a sandwich and drink to the value of £4.50 as part of the bill for lunch, how much VAT will he be able to reclaim on his business?

20. When is a set-off used in the control accounts?

    a) when a customer defaults on payment
    b) when the bank total of receipts from customers is posted
    c) when a customer and supplier are the same business and there are two balances in the respective ledgers
    d) when a business owner takes goods out of the business for his or her own use

21. Samir is a self-employed electrician, operating under the Construction Industry Scheme. He sends Thames Side Building, the main contractor, an invoice for labour £300 plus VAT at 20%. How would Thames Side enter the invoice into their system?

    a) Debit Direct Labour £240, Debit VAT Input £60, Credit Samir £300
    b) Debit Direct Labour £300, Debit VAT Input £60, Credit Samir £360
    c) Debit Direct Labour £360, Credit Samir £360
    d) Debit Direct Labour £420, Credit VAT Input £60, Credit Samir £360

22. Samir has not yet been verified and tax will be deducted under the CIS scheme at 30%. How would Thame Side record the deduction of tax?

    a) Debit CIS tax deducted, Credit Samir
    b) Credit CIS Tax deducted, Debit Samir

23. How much will Thames Side actually send Samir for the net payment?

    a) £200
    b) £270
    c) £300
    d) £360

24. A debt of £240 including VAT has been outstanding for 8 months and the customer has gone into liquidation. How will the debt be written off in the books?

    a) Dr Bad debts £240, Cr Customer £240
    b) Dr Bad debts £200, Dr VAT Input £40, Cr Customer £240
    c) Dr Bad debts £200, Dr VAT Output £40, Cr Customer £240
    d) Dr Bad debts £200, Cr Customer £200

25. If the above debt was only 4 months old and the company has not gone into liquidation, what would be the entries for writing off the bad debt?

    a) Dr Bad debts £240, Cr Customer £240
    b) Dr Bad debts £200, Dr VAT Input £40, Cr Customer £240
    c) Dr Bad debts £200, Dr VAT Output £40, Cr Customer £240
    d) Dr Bad debts £200, Cr Customer £200

26. A VAT registered business sell a piece of machinery that has been used within the business and is paid a total of £636 by the buyer. What would the entries be to record the sale?

    a) Debit bank account £636, Credit sale of asset account £636

b) Debit bank account £636, Credit sale of asset account £530, Credit VAT Output Account £106

c) Debit bank account £636, Credit sale of asset account £530, Credit VAT Input Account £106

d) Credit bank account £636, Debit sale of asset account £530, Debit VAT Input account £106

27. If a proprietor of a business uses goods purchased for resale for his own use the amount would be posted to:

a) Wages
b) Stock
c) Purchases
d) Drawings

28. If you saw an income item for subscriptions received, which type of organisation would this indicate?

a) Not-for-profit
b) Sole trader
c) Partnership
d) Limited company

29. The director of a limited company withdraws £2000 from the bank. To which account should you post the debit entry for this amount?

a) Share capital account
b) Directors' salaries account
c) Bank account
d) Directors Loan account

30. You are given the following list of amounts for the month end salary for a company:

Gross salary   £2000
PAYE Deducted   £300
Employees NICs deducted   £320
Net salary due   £1380
Employers NICs   £360

How would the information above be posted to the accounts?

a) Debit salaries £2000, Debit employer's NICs £360, Credit HMRC 980, Credit net salaries due £1380

b) Debit salaries £2000, Credit Employer's NICs £360, Credit HMRC £260, Credit net salaries due £1380

c) Debit salaries £1380, Debit Employers' NICs £360, Credit bank £2000, Debit HMRC £260

d) Debit salaries £2000, Credit HMRC £620, Credit net wages due £1380

31. At the start of the year, James Mason has the following balances in his ledger:

Motor Vehicle	28500
Tools and Equipment	26100
Office Equipment	2900
Stocks of Material	3100
Bank (overdraft)	3600
Debtors	6350
Creditors	3600
VAT (Cr)	1450

What is the value of the capital worth of his business?

32. Peter purchases a motor van on credit for his business. The van cost £16500 plus VAT. How would you enter this into the accounts:

a) Dr Motor vehicles £16500, Dr VAT Input £3300, Cr Creditor £19800
b) Dr Motor vehicles £16500, Dr VAT Output £3300, Cr Creditor £19800
c) Dr Motor vehicles £16500, Dr VAT Input £3300, Cr Bank £19800
d) Dr Motor vehicles £16500, Cr VAT Output £3300, Cr Bank £19800

33. You receive an invoice for goods that are imported from the USA. Local sales tax is shown on the invoice but how should you code the invoice for VAT purposes in your UK accounts?

a) Standard rate
b) Exempt
c) Zero rate
d) Out of scope for VAT

34. When posting a journal for wages and salaries, which of the following does not count as a business expense?

a) Gross wage
b) Employer's National Insurance Contributions
c) Employee's National Insurance Contributions
d) Employer's pension contributions

Making and receiving payments

1. On 25 January Sian (a credit customer) sends funds to clear her account balance of £125.60. She pays by bank transfer and takes a previously offered cash discount of £5.60. How would this be entered:

   a) Dr Bank £125.60, Cr discount allowed £5.60, Cr Susan £120.00
   b) Dr Bank £120.00, Dr discount allowed £5.60, Cr Susan £125.60
   c) Dr Bank £120.00, Cr discount received £5.60, Cr Susan £125.60
   d) Dr Bank £125.60, Cr discount allowed £5.60, Cr Susan £120.00

2. The following is an extract from a three column cash book:

THREE COLUMN CASH BOOK									
Date June	Details	Disc	Cash £	Bank £	Date June	Details	Disc	Cash £	Bank £
1	Balance b/d		800	1200	2	Stationery			120
3	Sales		822	766		X Creditor	10		200
8	Cash			1000	4	Wages		320	
10	A Debtor	12	522		5	Purchases			1280
11	Sales			268	7	Fuel		44	
14	B Debtor	15		125	8	Bank		1000	
					9	Drawings			100
					12	Y Creditor	20		540
					14	Wages		320	
					14	Balance c/d		460	1119
		27	2144	3359			30	2144	3359
14	Balance b/d		460	1119					

To which account would the £30 shown in the total of the discount column in the above cash book be posted:

a) To the debit side of the discounts allowed account
b) To the credit side of the discounts allowed account
c) To the debit side of the discounts received account
d) To the credit side of the discounts received account

3. To which account would the £27 shown in the total of the discount column in the above cash book be posted:

a) To the debit side of the discounts allowed account
b) To the credit side of the discounts allowed account
c) To the debit side of the discounts received account
d) To the credit side of the discounts received account

4. How would the receipts from A Debtor and B Debtor be posted to the relevant control account?

a) Debit sales ledger control account £647
b) Credit sales ledger control account £647
c) Debit purchases ledger control account £647
d) Credit purchases ledger control account £647

5. A brought down credit balance on a bank current account means:

a) The account is overdrawn
b) The account is a loan account
c) The bank owes the business the balance
d) There must be an error in the account

6. The transaction on 8 June means:

a) Cash has been banked
b) The owner withdrew cash from the business for personal reasons
c) The owner transferred the money from the bank to the cash tin
d) Cash sales were paid directly into the bank

7. What document does a business receive from the bank detailing a list of transactions that have gone through the account?

a) remittance note
b) statement
c) bank giro
d) paying in book

Trial Balance

The following balances are taken from the ledgers at the end of the year (note: the balances are not necessarily correct).

	£
Capital	49950
Bank Loan	8700
Motor Vehicle	25500
Tools and Equipment	24100
Office Furniture	3200
Stocks of Material	2200
Bank Overdraft	2670
Cash in hand	80
Debtors	5100
Creditors	2850
VAT owed to HMRC	1250

1. What will be the total of the fixed assets?
2. What will be the total of the debit balances?
3. What will be the total of the credit balances?
4. What is the discrepancy between the two total amounts?
5. What is the account that you would open to record this difference?

   a) Drawings
   b) Profit and Loss
   c) Suspense
   d) Petty Cash

6. Would the amount be entered as a debit or a credit balance?

   Dr / Cr

7. Which of the above balances are fixed assets (tick all that apply)

   Motor Vehicles
   Tools and Equipment
   Office Furniture
   Stocks of Materials

8. Which of the following is not a current liability?

   a) Bank Loan
   b) Bank current account
   c) Creditors
   d) VAT owed to HMRC

Level II Certificate in Bookkeeping
Sample Paper 2 2014

Answers – each question is worth 1 mark unless otherwise advised

Underpinning knowledge

1. b
2. a
3. c
4. b
5. d
6. b
7. b
8. a and b (1 mark for each)
9. d

Ledger accounts and divisions of the ledger,
Books of Prime entry and Accounting for VAT

1. a
2. b
3. d
4. £480 Dr
5. 1 mark for each entry

Sales Day Book					
Date	Details		Net	VAT	Gross
4	Meantime Processing		350.00	70.00	420.00
15	Super Supplies		220.00	44.00	264.00
			570.00	114.00	684.00
Sales Returns Day Book					
Date	Details		Net	VAT	Gross
12	Meantime Processing		50.00	10.00	60.00

6. £684.00   (2 marks)
7. £108.20   (2 marks)
8. b   (2 marks)
9. Cr   (2 marks)
10. Cr   (2 marks)
11. £264.00   (2 marks)
12. Cr   (2 marks)
13. 1 mark for each entry

Purchases Day Book				
Date	Details	Net	VAT	Gross
18	Future Developments	160.00	32.00	192.00
25	JR Trading & Co	1520.00	304.00	1824.00
30	Petersham Ltd	680.00	136.00	816.00
		2360.00	472.00	2832.00

14. b   (2 marks)
15. b   (2 marks)
16. b   (2 marks)
17. c
18. £100 Dr   (2 marks)
19. £15   (2 marks)
20. c
21. b
22. b
23. b   (2 marks)
24. b   (2 marks)
25. a   (2 marks)
26. b   (2 marks)
27. d
28. a
29. d
30. a   (2 marks)
31. £58300   (3 marks)
32. a
33. c
34. c

Making and receiving payments

1. b
2. d   (2 marks)
3. a   (2 marks)
4. b   (2 marks)
5. a
6. a
7. b

Trial Balance

1. £52800
2. £60180
3. £65420
4. £5240
5. c
6. Cr
7. Motor Vehicles, Tools and Equipment, Office Furniture (1 marks each)
8. a

**THE INSTITUTE
OF CERTIFIED
BOOKKEEPERS**

The Institute of Certified Bookkeepers

Level III Certificate in Bookkeeping and Accounts
Sample Paper 2014

This Paper forms one section of the ICB Level III Certificate in Bookkeeping and Accounts. The paper is taken online, at home or in the place of work. You have twenty four hour to complete the questions and submit your answers but please note that the live paper will also include a computerised element which requires the use of a computerised accounts package. All questions are compulsory.

The paper is a combination of multi-choice answers (which you answer by selecting one of the options from a given menu or by ticking either a single button or multiple buttons to identify your choice) and data entry answers where you will need to enter a numeric amount into a box.

Numeric answers should generally be entered correct to two decimal places in the format ####.## unless either the answer is obviously a whole number when numbers may be entered as integers, or, entered correct to the stated number of decimal places (####.# if correct to 1 decimal place).

As a general rule, all figures should be entered as positive numbers, regardless of whether they are to be added or deducted, unless a) the answer is one where the final result is negative, or b) a question provides specific instructions that override it.

For the purposes of this paper please note that VAT should always be rounded down, even if you are calculating a VAT inclusive amount.

Note: to complete the Level III Certificate in Bookkeeping and Accounts, you will take a total of four papers. Three of these are taken at home (Sample papers 3, 4 and 5) but it is necessary to sit the fourth paper at an external examination centre. The contents of this external paper will cover all the three sample papers. Marks for all four papers will be aggregated to complete the grading of the final qualification.

Assessment Criteria

This piece of work will be graded at Distinction, Merit, Pass or Fail.

Pass   To gain a Pass, candidates must achieve between 85-89%
Merit   To gain a Merit, candidates must achieve between 90-94%
Distinction To gain a Distinction, candidates must achieve between 95-100%
Fail   Candidates who achieve less than 85% of the total marks will be
             failed.

Level II Certificate in Bookkeeping and Accounts

Sample Paper 2014

Underpinning Knowledge

1. If a client invites you to dinner at a local hotel which legislation do you need to consider

   a) Data Protection
   b) Freedom of Information
   c) Bribery Act
   d) Whistle Blowing

2. Which of the following scenarios should you consider to be possible fraudulent behaviour by a client?

   a) Giving you petrol receipts 3 months after the VAT return has been submitted
   b) Calculating an incorrect VAT amount on a sales invoice
   c) Presenting you with a bill for a weekend break with the family and claiming it as a business expense
   d) Constantly paying creditors late

3. The business concept that covers the recording of purchases at cost price is:

   a) Historical Cost
   b) Business entity
   c) Consistency
   d) Accruals

4. A sole trader can take a salary from his business, and have PAYE and NIC deducted from that salary True/False

   a) True
   b) False

5. Which is the VAT scheme that means the business declares VAT only as a percentage of the profit it makes on a sale?

   a) Second hand VAT Margin Scheme
   b) Flat Rate Scheme
   c) Partial Exemption Scheme
   d) Retail Scheme

Reconciliations and correction of errors

1. Philippa Bevan has the following account for Mutual Designs in her sales ledger:

Date	Details	£	Date	Details	£
Jan 1	Bal b/f	468.50	Jan 3	Bank	300.00
Jan 5	Sales	250.00	Jan 31	Bal c/f	583.50
Jan 15	Sales	165.00			
		883.50			883.50
Jan 31	Bal b/f	583.50			

Philippa send out a statement on 31 January and is contacted by her customer to say that they disagree with the amount due. They maintain that they should have received a credit note for goods returned on 20 January to the value of £50 plus VAT and that they transferred £300.00 by BACS transfer on 31 January to Philippa's account.

How much does Mutual Designs believe the outstanding balance should be on their account?

2. Two Shoes receives the following bank statement on 30 April 201X (note: the balances with the exception of the opening balance have not been shown) and the cash book has been updated to cover missing items.

<table>
<tr><td colspan="5" align="center">Morrison Bank Plc
3 Cheapside
WC1Z 2ZZ
Account 44444444   30 April 201X
Statement of Account</td></tr>
<tr><td>Date</td><td>Details</td><td>Paid Out</td><td>Paid In</td><td>Balance</td></tr>
<tr><td>1 April</td><td>Balance</td><td></td><td></td><td>3648.00</td></tr>
<tr><td>5 April</td><td>5010</td><td></td><td>2500.00</td><td></td></tr>
<tr><td>8 April</td><td>Cheque 1256</td><td>1500.00</td><td></td><td></td></tr>
<tr><td>10 April</td><td>5011</td><td></td><td>568.00</td><td></td></tr>
<tr><td>15 April</td><td>BACS – Southern Electric</td><td>359.75</td><td></td><td></td></tr>
<tr><td>20 April</td><td>DD Higham Insurance</td><td>600.00</td><td></td><td></td></tr>
<tr><td>30 April</td><td>Charges</td><td>50.00</td><td></td><td></td></tr>
<tr><td></td><td>Cheque 1259</td><td>200.00</td><td></td><td></td></tr>
</table>

			Cash Book		
Date	Details	Bank £	Date	Details Cheque No	Bank £
Apr 1	Bal b/d	3648.00	Apr 1	1256 Wages	1500.00
2	Myrton Grange	2500.00	6	1257 Van Repairs	650.00
6	Rushton Manor	568.00	15	1258 Purchases	700.00
29	Combo Ltd	236.00		1259 Fuel	200.00
				Electricity	359.75
			20	Insurance	600.00
			30	Charges	50.00

Starting with the balance in the cash book, enter the total of outstanding lodgements and payments and, either adding or subtracting as appropriate, reconcile to the balance in the statement

Bank Reconciliation Statement as at 31 March 201X
Balance as per cash book
Outstanding lodgements
Un-presented payments
Balance as per bank statement

3. The sales ledger control account for January contained the following information:

Opening debtors £16,580
Sales for the month £356,400
Receipts from customers £285,655
Sales returns £2400
Bad debt written off £600.00
Set off against purchases ledger control account £1000

What was the closing balance on the account at the end of the month?

4. The purchases ledger control account for March contained the following information:

Opening creditors £7,500
Purchases on credit £63,500
Purchases returns £600
Receipts from credit customers £56750

What will be the closing balance on the purchases ledger control account?

5. A BACS payment for £56 for the electricity bill has been credited to the cash account rather than the bank account. Which of the following would correct this?

a) Dr Cash £56 Cr Bank £56
b) Dr Electric £56, Cr Bank £56
c) Dr Cash £56, Cr Electric £56
d) Dr Bank £56, Cr Electric £5

6. A cash sale for £450 for a non-VAT registered business has been entered into the accounts as debit sales, credit cash. What type of error does this represent?

   a) Principal
   b) Commission
   c) Reversal
   d) Original entry

VAT returns

1. The following summary figures have been taken from the books of Carmon Mirna, a self-employed art advisor who uses the standard VAT scheme.

Sales Day Book				
Date	Details	Net	VAT	Gross
Apr - Jun 2014	Sales work done	56,000	11,200	67,200

Purchases Day Book				
Date	Details	Net	VAT	Gross
Apr - Jun 2014	Purchases	6,000.00	1,200.00	7,200.00

Sales Returns Day Book				
Date	Details	Net	VAT	Gross
Apr – Jun 2014	Credit Notes	2,500	500.00	3,000.00

Purchases Returns Day Book				
Date	Details	Net	VAT	Gross
Apr - Jun 2014	Credit Notes	500.00	100.00	600.00

In addition to the above, Carmon paid out £2640 in overheads, all of which were standard rated for VAT, plus the following:

Overheads at zero rate£300.00
Wages and salaries £4,500.00
She also withdrew £9,000 for her own personal expenses.

Calculate the figures that would be input into the following relevant boxes on the VAT Return:

VAT due on sales and other outputs	Box 1	
VAT reclaimable on purchases	Box 4	
Total VAT due	Box 5	
Total sales excluding VAT	Box 6	
Total purchases excluding VAT	Box 7	

2. Carmon sells a piece of art work to a client in the USA. The artwork is exported within 2 months of the sale. How would you classify this sale for VAT purposes?

    a) Zero rated
    b) Standard Rated
    c) As an exempt item
    d) As an EU sale

3. If she also buys £3000 worth of goods from a VAT registered customer in Germany which counts as an EU Acquisition, into which of the following sets of boxes on the VAT return would you expect to make an entry?

    a) Boxes 4 and 7
    b) Boxes 7 and 9
    c) Boxes 1, 4, 7 and 9
    d) Boxes 2, 4, 7 and 9

4. The following are extracts taken from the day books of Glorianus Ltd who uses the cash VAT scheme, with their next quarterly VAT return due for submission at the end of September 201X:

Sales Day Book					
Date	Details	Net	VAT	Gross	Date Paid
May 4	Abbotts & Co	350.00	70.00	420.00	30/05/1X
June 15	Creative Accounting	500.00	100.00	600.00	31/08/1X
July 31	Mentoring Services	1500.00	300.00	1800.00	
Aug 15	Memo Services Ltd	200.00	40.00	240.00	30/09/1X
Aug 31	Jenny Daley	500.00	n/a	500.00	21/09/1X
Sep 30	Benjamin Docherty	55.00	11.00	66.00	

Purchases Day Book					
Date	Details	Net	VAT	Gross	Date Paid
May 1	Genuine Supplies	1500.00	300.00	1800.00	01/07/1X
June 15	Farmingham Ltd	100.00	20.00	120.00	30/06/1X
July 15	Genuine Supplies	400.00	80.00	480.00	
Sept 15	Corporate Commissions	250.00	50.00	300.00	20/09/1X

Calculate the figures that would be input into the following relevant boxes on the VAT Return:

VAT due on sales and other outputs	Box 1	
VAT reclaimable on purchases	Box 4	
Total sales excluding VAT	Box 6	
Total purchases excluding VAT	Box 7	

Adjustments and accounts for a sole trader

1. Sybil purchased an industrial ironing machine for her dry cleaning business which costs £10,000 new before VAT. She decides that it will last her 5 years and have a resale value of £1000. What would be the annual deprecation charge?

2. After three years she pays a further £4000 to improve the machine. This is expected to give the machine a further three year's life after which it will be scrapped. What will the new annual depreciation figure from year 4 onwards?

3. Morris Ltd buys three new motor vehicles for its hire car business at £36,000 each including VAT. The depreciation charge is 20% per year on a reducing balance method. What will be the net book value of all three vehicles after

   a) 1 year
   b) 2 years
   c) 3 years

4. At the end of his last financial year, Quincy Jones was advised by his accountant that the bill for their services for the year would be £800 plus VAT. He entered this as an accrual. He is told at the end of this year that the bill will be an estimated £950 plus VAT. What would be the amount to be shown in the profit and loss account for the current year for accountancy?

5. The annual rates bill amounting to £3500 arrives for the year commencing 1 April 2013. It was paid in advance in two equal instalments on 1 April and 1 October. If the year-end is 31 December, what is the value of the prepaid rates to be shown in the balance sheet as at 31 December?

6. At the end of the financial year the figure for outstanding debtors is £15,000. At the end of the previous year a provision for doubtful debts had been made for £200, which was 3% of the debtors figure. How much would be put through the profit and loss account for the year to maintain this level.

7. Jenny purchased some office furniture on 1 April 2012 for £3600 plus VAT. She sold it on 31 March 2014 for £200 plus VAT at which time it had been depreciated by £1200. The bookkeeping entries for the disposal involve a number of accounts. Taking each section of the double entry in turn, identify the amount to be entered into the disposal account and state whether the entry would be a debit or a credit in that particular account.

a) What will be the final balance on the disposal account?
b) Will this balance be a debit or a credit balance?
c) Does this represent a profit or a loss on disposal?

Final Accounts of a sole trader – 20 marks

The following trial balance has been extracted from the accounts of Longfellow & Co.

	Dr	Cr
	£	£
Capital		36324
Motor vehicles at cost	68596	
Provision for depreciation MV		15296
Tools and equipment	15450	
Provision for depreciation T&E		9560
Stocks of materials	9750	
Bank	15356	
Deposit account	35000	
Debtors	12697	
Creditors		25463

VAT Account		3469
Bank Loan		25000
Sales		356200
Purchases	158976	
Motor vehicle running costs	6800	
Insurances	13587	
Office Expenses	23500	
Wages	48600	
Drawings	63000	
	471312	471312

The following notes apply:	
Closing stock of materials	12350
A bad debt is to be written off	1250
Insurances are pre-paid	500
Office expenses are accrued	650
The fixed assets are to be depreciated by 20% RBM	

Complete the boxes below with the appropriate figures to enable the net profit to be calculated and the balance sheet to be produced. (Note: enter your answers as whole numbers – do NOT enter commas in your answer. Where you need to subtract a figure you can enter it as a positive or a negative number)

Trading and profit and Loss Account for the year ended 31 December 201X		
	£	£
Sales		
Less cost of sales		
Opening Stock		
Purchases		
Closing Stock		
Cost of Sales		
Gross Profit		
Motor vehicle running costs		
Insurances		
Office expenses		
Wages		
Bad debt		
Depreciation Motor Vehicles		
Depreciation Tools and Equipment		
Total Expenses		
Net profit		

Balance Sheet as at 31 December 201X			
	Cost	Dep to date	NBV
Fixed Assets			
Motor vehicles			
Tools and Equipment			
Total Assets			
Current Assets			
Stock			
Debtors			
Bank			
Deposit account			
Prepayments			
Total Current Assets			
Current Liabilities			
Creditors			
VAT			
Accruals			
Total Current Liabilities			
Working Capital			
Long Term Liabilities			
Bank Loan			
Net Assets			
Financed by			
Opening Capital			
Net Profit			
Drawings			
Closing Capital			

Level III Certificate in Bookkeeping and Accounts Sample Paper 2014

Answers – each entry is worth 1 mark unless otherwise identified

Topic 1 – Underpinning Knowledge

1. c
2. b
3. a
4. b
5. a

Topic 2 – Reconciliations and correction of errors

1. £223.50
2. Balance as per cash book   £2892.25 (2 marks)
   Outstanding lodgements   £236.00 (2 marks)
   Un-presented payments   £4242.25 (2 marks)
   Balance as per bank statement   £4006.253 (2 marks)
3. £83,325 (2 marks)
4. £13,650 (2 marks)
5. a
6. b

Topic 3 – VAT returns

1.

Box 1	10,700
Box 4	1,540
Box 5	9,160
Box 6	53,500
Box 7	8,000

2. a
3. d
4.

Box 1	140.00
Box 4	350.00
Box 6	1200.00
Box 7	1750.00

Topic 4 – Adjustments and Accounts for a Sole Trader

1. £1800
2. £1720
3. a) £72000
   b) £57600
   c) £46080
4. £950
5. £875
6. £250
7. a) £2200
   b) Dr
   c) Loss

Topic 5 – Final Accounts of a Sole Trader

Trading and profit and Loss Account for the year ended 31 December 2013			Marks
	£	£	
Sales		356200	1
Less cost of sales			
Opening Stock	9750		1
Purchases	158976		1
Closing Stock	12350		1
Cost of Sales		156376	
Gross Profit		199824	
Motor vehicle running costs	6800		1
Insurances	13087		2
Office expenses	24150		2
Wages	48600		1
Bad debt	1250		1
Depreciation Motor Vehicles	10660		1
Depreciation Tools and Equipment	1178		1
Total Expenses		105725	
Net profit		94099	

Balance Sheet as at 31 December 2013				
	Cost	Dep to date	NBV	Marks
Fixed Assets				
Motor vehicles	68596	25956	42640	1
Tools and Equipment	15450	10738	4712	1
Total Assets	84046	36694	47352	
Current Assets				
Stock		12350		1
Debtors		11447		1
Bank		15356		
Deposit account		35000		
Prepayments		500		1
Total Current Assets		74653		
Current Liabilities				
Creditors	25463			
VAT	3469			
Accruals	650			1
Total Current Liabilities		29582		
Working Capital			45071	
			92423	
Long Term Liabilities				
Bank Loan			25000	
Net Assets			67423	0.5
Financed by				
Opening Capital			36324	
Net Profit			94099	
Drawings			63000	
Closing Capital			67423	0.5

**THE INSTITUTE
OF CERTIFIED
BOOKKEEPERS**

IAB Level I question paper

June 2014 Examination
Question Paper

159 Exam ID
1050 Exam ID

Question Paper for the following Qualifications:

150: Level 1 Award in Bookkeeping QCF: 50090069
160: Level 1 Award in Manual Bookkeeping QCF: 50094063
1000: Level 1 Award in Bookkeeping QCF: 60104703
1020: Level 1 Award in Manual Bookkeeping QCF: 60104739

Units
157: Preparing and processing bookkeeping documents: M6008740
158: Recording Credit transactions: A6008742
156: Making and receiving payments: J6008744
155: Maintaining petty cash records: R6008746
1002: Maintaining petty cash records: R5051120

Time Allowed 2 Hours
Paper No: 0038

General Instructions

1. Enter your IAB Student Number, Candidate Number and Name of Examination Centre in the spaces provided on the front cover of your Answer Booklet
2. All Answers to be written in blue or black ink
3. Cross out errors neatly or use correcting fluid in moderation
4. Calculators are permitted
5. A blank page is provided in the Answer Booklet for workings if required
6. The Question Paper and Answer Booklet have information and data printed on both sides of the pages
7. Mobile phones are not permitted

International Association of Book-keepers, Suite 5, 20 Churchill Square, Kings Hill, West Malling, Kent ME19 4YU
Tel: 01732 897750, Fax: 01732 897751, email:education@iab.org.uk Website: www.iab.org

SECTION A – PREPARING AND PROCESSING BUSINESS DOCUMENTS

THERE ARE **FOUR** TASKS IN THIS SECTION OF THE PAPER

YOU MUST COMPLETE **ALL** TASKS

DATA AND TASKS

You work for Wheelies Ltd who buy and sell car parts and cleaning products on a credit basis. Today's date is 30 June 2014.

You are required to prepare customer invoices and credit notes and also check invoices and credit notes received from suppliers. You are provided with an extract of the customer file and the current price list from Wheelies Ltd, which are shown below:

Wheelies Ltd – Customer Files (Extract)

Customer Account No	Customer Trading Name and Address	Terms of Trade
SL – AG03	Autogeek Ltd 2 King Street Derby DE5 9KT	Payment – Net 30 days
SL – JC12	Jackson Carparts 17 Market Street Nottingham NG2 4FW	Payment – Net 60 days
SL – HS10	Hargreaves & Son 5 Oldham Street Derby DE4 8TE	Payment – Net 14 days

Wheelies Ltd – Price list (Extract)

Product Code	Product Description	Product Price (Exc. VAT)
B001	Brake Disks	49.99
B002	Brake Fluid	4.99
B008	Brake Pads	14.99
C001	Car Shampoo	12.99
C002	Car Wax	8.99
C003	Car Hand Polishing Mitt	5.99
F012	Air Filter	9.99
F014	Fuel Filter	6.99
F017	Oil Filter	4.99
S001	Spark Plugs	7.99
W005	Windscreen Wiper Blades 20"	4.99
W006	Windscreen Wiper Blades 21"	5.99
W009	Windscreen Wiper Blades 24"	6.99

Note: All products listed above are subject to VAT at standard rate (20%)

You have now received two delivery notes and a goods returned note which should be used to prepare two invoices and a credit note to customers today.

Delivery Note 1

DELIVERY NOTE   **No:** DN 643

        Wheelies Ltd   VAT Reg No: 426 3714 02
        10 Whitchurch Street
        Derby
        DE1 3DE

                     Order No: AG 2875
                     Date: 30 June 2014

To: Autogeek Ltd
      2 King Street
      Derby
      DE5 9KT

Quantity	Description	Code
40	Windscreen Wiper Blades 20"	W005
30	Windscreen Wiper Blades 24"	W009

Delivered To: Above address   **Terms:** Net 30 days

VAT: All goods supplied above are subject to VAT at standard rate (20%)

Delivery Note 2

DELIVERY NOTE	**No:** DN 644

Wheelies Ltd
10 Whitchurch Street
Derby
DE1 3DE

VAT Reg No: 426 3714 02

Order No: JC 0943
Date: 30 June 2014

To: Jackson Carparts
17 Market Street
Nottingham
NG2 4FW

Quantity	Description	Code
10	Brake Discs	B001
20	Brake Pads	B008

Delivered To: Above address   **Terms:** Net 60 days

VAT: All goods supplied above are subject to VAT at standard rate (20%)

Goods Returned Note (Goods returned by trade customer)

GOODS RETURNED NOTE **(Goods Inwards)**	**No:** GRN (1) 275 VAT Reg No: 426 3714 02

Wheelies Ltd
10 Whitchurch Street
Derby
DE1 3DE

Goods Returned by: Hargreaves & Son
Date of Return: 30 June 2014

Quantity	Product Description	Product Code
2	Car Hand Polishing Mitt	C003

Reason for Return   Damaged

REQUIRED

Task 1   Prepare the two sales invoices to be issued to Autogeek Ltd and Jackson Carparts.

   NB: The last sales invoice prepared was numbered W 1355   **(10 marks)**

Task 2   Prepare the credit note to be issued to Hargreaves & Son

   NB: The last credit note prepared was numbered CN 84   **(4 marks)**

Note: The following proformas are provided for your use in completing the above tasks:

   • Sales invoices (see **pages 1 and 2** of your **Answer Booklet**). Take care in using these sales invoices as they are already addressed for you to the trade customers to whom they are to be issued.

   • Credit note (see **page 3** of your **Answer Booklet**). The credit note is already addressed for you to the trade customer to whom it is to be issued.

Checking Invoices and Credit Notes Received

When Wheelies Ltd receive invoices from trade suppliers for goods purchased from them on credit, the invoice is checked against the original purchase order and the delivery note before being passed for payment. This includes the arithmetic accuracy of each calculation and quantity ordered.

A slip is attached to each invoice received. Where the invoice details, quantity, price extensions and totals are correct the words **'passed for payment'** are written on the slip in the action required section. The supplier account code and a purchase invoice number are also allocated to the invoice and written on the slip. Where, however, the invoice contains errors the words **'contains errors – return to supplier'** are written on the slip in the action required section together with the errors the document contains and no supplier account code or purchase invoice number are allocated to the invoice.

Credit notes received from suppliers for goods returned to them are also checked against supporting documentation and for arithmetic accuracy.

A slip is attached to each credit note received. Where the credit note details, quantity, price extensions and totals are correct the words **'take credit'** are written on the slip in the action required section. The supplier account code is also written on the slip.

Where, however, the credit note contains errors the words **'contains errors – return to supplier'** are written on the slip in the action required section together with the errors the document contains and no supplier code is allocated. It is not necessary to allocate the credit note a number.

Provided below is an extract from the supplier files kept by Wheelies Ltd:

Wheelies Ltd – Supplier Files (Extract)

Supplier Account Code	Supplier Trading Name and Address	Terms of Trade
PL – CG032	Clarks Garage 11 Oldham Road Stafford ST13 6FW	Trade Discount 10% Payment – Net 30 days
PL – JC021	James & Co 27 Portland Street Derby DE3 4JN	Trade Discount 10% Payment – Net 30 days
PL – TA012	Tyler Autos Ltd 5 Chestnut Road Nottingham NG2 7LT	Trade Discount 5% Payment – Net 60 days

The following purchase orders, delivery notes and goods returned note relate to invoices and a credit note received today, 30 June 2014 and now need to be checked.

Purchase Orders

PURCHASE ORDER　　　　　　　　　　**Order No:** PO 0824

Wheelies Ltd
10 Whitchurch Street　　　　　　　　**VAT Reg No:** 426 3714 02
Derby
DE1 3DE

To:　Clarks Garage　　　　　　　　**Date:** 5 June 2014

Quantity	Description	Code
10	Brake Discs	3165
10	Brake Fluid	3169
5	Brake Pads	3187

Deliver To:　Above address

Signed:　　*J Cooper (Head Buyer)*

PURCHASE ORDER　　　　　　　　　　**Order No:** PO 0825

Wheelies Ltd
10 Whitchurch Street　　　　　　　　VAT Reg No: 426 3714 02
Derby
DE1 3DE

To:　James & Co　　　　　　　　　**Date:** 12 June 2014

Quantity	Description	Code
25	Car Shampoo	S0365
10	Car Wax	S0369
10	Spark Plugs	S0198

Deliver To:　Above address

Signed:　　*J Cooper (Head Buyer)*

PURCHASE ORDER

Order No: PO 0826

Wheelies Ltd
10 Whitchurch Street
Derby
DE1 3DE

VAT Reg No: 426 3714 02

To: Tyler Autos Ltd

Date: 16 June 2014

Quantity	Description	Code
15	Air Filter	01786
15	Fuel Filter	01792
15	Oil Filter	01975

Deliver To: Above address

Signed: *J Cooper (Head Buyer)*

Delivery Notes

DELIVERY NOTE

No: DN 2976

Clarks Garage
11 Oldham Road
Stafford
ST13 6FW

VAT Reg No: 735 1435 26

Order No: PO 0824

To: Wheelies Ltd

Date: 9 June 2014

Quantity	Description	Code
10	Brake Discs	3165
10	Brake Fluid	3169
5	Brake Pads	3187

Deliver To: **Goods Received By:**
Wheelies Ltd   *B Humphries*
10 Whitchurch Street
Derby
DE1 3DE

Terms: Trade discount 10%. Net 30 days Carriage Paid

VAT: All goods supplied above are subject to VAT at standard rate (20%)

DELIVERY NOTE

No: DN 0942

James & Co
27 Portland Street
Derby
DE3 4JN

VAT Reg No: 375 9352 62

Order No: PO 0825

To: Wheelies Ltd

Date: 16 June 2014

Quantity	Description	Code
25	Car Shampoo	S0365
10	Car Wax	S0369
10	Spark Plugs	S0198

Deliver To:
Wheelies Ltd
10 Whitchurch Street
Derby
DE1 3DE

Goods Received By:
B Humphries

Terms: Trade discount 10%. Net 30 days Carriage Paid

VAT: All goods supplied above are subject to VAT at standard rate (20%)

DELIVERY NOTE

No: DN 1976

Tyler Autos Ltd
5 Chestnut Road
Nottingham
NG2 7LT

VAT Reg No: 523 7435 51

Order No: PO 0826

To: Wheelies Ltd

Date: 19 June 2014

Quantity	Description	Code
15	Air Filter	01786
15	Fuel Filter	01792
15	Oil Filter	01975

Deliver To:
Wheelies Ltd
10 Whitchurch Street
Derby
DE5 9KT

Goods Received By:
B Humphries

Terms: Trade discount 5%. Net 60 days Carriage Paid

VAT: All goods supplied above are subject to VAT at standard rate (20%)

On **pages 4, 5 and 6** of your **Answer Booklet** you will find invoices received from Clarks Garage, James & Co and Tyler Autos Ltd, which relate to the purchase orders and delivery notes given on page 6, 7 and 8 of this question paper.

REQUIRED

Task 3 (i) Check the details of each invoice – quantities, descriptions and codes, against the quantities, descriptions and codes on the purchase orders and delivery notes.

(ii) Check the arithmetic accuracy of each invoice. You can assume that the unit prices on each of the invoices have already been checked against supplier list and catalogue prices are correct.

You are required to check:

- all price extensions (quantity x unit price)
- all invoice sub-totals and totals
- that the correct trade discounts have been applied
- that the VAT on each invoice is correct
- that the correct terms of trade have been quoted on each invoice

Where invoices are found to be correct complete the slip shown beneath each invoice in accordance with Wheelies Ltd's policy for passing invoices received from trade suppliers for payment. If the documents contain errors you must state the errors found.

NB: The last supplier invoice received and passed for payment today was numbered P 1743   **(4.5 marks)**

On **page 7** of your **Answer Booklet** you will find the credit note received from Clarks Garage which relates to the goods returned note presented below.

Goods returned to trade supplier

GOODS RETURNED NOTE	**No:** GRN (0) 732
(Goods Outwards)	VAT Reg No: 426 3714 02

Wheelies Ltd
10 Whitchurch Street
Derby
DE1 3DE

Goods Returned To: Clarks Garage
Date of Return: 12 June 2014

Quantity	Description	Product Code
1	Brake Pads	3187

Reason for Return: Damaged Goods

REQUIRED

Task 4 (i) Check the details of the credit note – quantities, descriptions and codes, against the quantities, descriptions and codes on the goods returned note.

(ii) Check the arithmetic accuracy of the credit note. You can assume that the unit prices on the credit note have already been checked against the unit prices on the original invoice and are correct.

You are required to check:

- all price extensions (quantity x unit price)
- all credit note sub-totals and totals
- that the correct trade discount has been applied
- that the VAT on the credit note is correct

If the credit note is found to be correct complete the slip shown beneath the credit note in accordance with Wheelies Ltd's policy for taking credit in respect of goods returned to trade suppliers. If the document contains errors you must state the errors found.

(1.5 marks)

SECTION B – RECORDING CREDIT TRANSACTIONS

THERE ARE **FOUR** TASKS IN THIS SECTION OF THE PAPER

YOU MUST COMPLETE **ALL** TASKS

DATA AND TASKS

Ladybirds Furniture distribute garden furniture to local businesses. You work in the office of Ladybirds Furniture as a bookkeeper. Part of your job is to keep the Day Books up to date using information from invoices and credit notes received and issued. This information is then entered into the Day Books on a daily basis and totalled and cross checked for arithmetic accuracy.

The Day Books are provided on pages 8 and 9 of the answer booklet and you will notice that they have already been partly written up.

You have today received several invoices and credit notes and you will need to calculate the invoice and credit note totals. These should now be entered in the respective Day Books.

Today's date is 30 June 2014.

Sales Invoices Issued

Customer – Katie's Garden Shop (account code SL – K015)

Invoice number L 0643

Goods sub total	£1,000
Trade discount (5%)	£50
Net goods	£950
VAT	£190
Invoice total	£

Customer – Outdoor World (account code SL – O036)

Invoice number L 0644

Goods sub total	£1,400
Trade discount (10%)	£140
Net goods	£1,260
VAT	£252
Invoice total	£

Credit note Issued

Customer – Katie's Garden Shop (account code SL – K015)

Credit note number CN 031

Goods sub total		£100
Trade discount (10%)		£10
Net goods		£90
VAT		£18
Credit note total	£	

Invoices Received

Supplier – Hollybush Ltd (account code PL – H009)

Supplier invoice number HL 6743

Our invoice number P 0521

Goods sub total		£3,200
Trade discount (5%)		£160
Net goods		£3,040
VAT		£608
Invoice total	£	

Supplier – Bradwalls Ltd (account code PL – B013)

Supplier invoice number B 4312

Our invoice number P 0522

Goods sub total		£1,000
Trade discount (10%)		£100
Net goods		£900
VAT		£180
Invoice total	£	

Credit Note Received

Supplier – Westies Gardens (account code PL – W021)

Supplier credit note number CN 321

Goods sub total		£100
Trade discount (5%)		£5
Net goods		£95
VAT		£19
Credit note total	£	

REQUIRED

Task 1   Prepare the invoice totals and enter the sales invoices into the sales day book. Total the day book and cross check the totals for arithmetic accuracy. **(5.5 marks)**

Task 2   Prepare the credit note total and enter the credit note into the sales returns day book. Total the day book and cross check the totals for arithmetic accuracy. **(4.25 marks)**

Task 3   Prepare the invoice totals and enter the purchase invoices into the purchase day book. Total the day book and cross check the totals for arithmetic accuracy. **(6 marks)**

Task 4   Prepare the credit note total and enter the credit note into the purchase returns day book. Total the day book and cross check the totals for arithmetic accuracy. **(4.25 marks)**

Note: The following proformas are provided for your use in completing the above tasks:

- Sales day book (see **page 8** of your **Answer Booklet**)
- Sales returns day book (see **page 8** of your **Answer Booklet**)
- Purchase day book (see **page 9** of your **Answer Booklet**)
- Purchase returns day book (see **page 9** of your **Answer Booklet**)

SECTION C – MAKING AND RECEIVING PAYMENTS

THERE ARE **FIVE** TASKS IN THIS SECTION OF THE PAPER

YOU MUST COMPLETE **ALL** TASKS

DATA AND TASKS

Clara's Printers is run by Clara Jackson. Your job role and daily duties include checking receipts from cash sales, preparing cash/cheques for banking, processing cash payments and making payments to suppliers.

Today's date is 30 June 2014

Paying Suppliers

Trade suppliers are paid by cheque. A remittance advice is issued with each cheque.

You have received the following three invoices which are to be paid taking into account the credit note received.

Supplier	Invoice Number	Invoice Total £	Total Goods Value £	VAT £
Click n Print Ltd	C 01765	720.00	600.00	120.00
J & K Printers	0456	144.00	120.00	24.00
Click n Print Ltd	C 01773	300.00	250.00	50.00

Supplier	Credit Note Number	Credit Note Total £	Total Goods Value £	VAT £
J & K Printers	CN 193	96.00	80.00	16.00

REQUIRED

Task 1   Prepare the remittance advices to be issued to the trade suppliers above in settlement of the three invoices and credit note to be paid today.

(2.25 marks)

Task 2   Prepare the cheques to be issued to each supplier in respect of settlement of the above invoices and credit note. Do not sign the cheques.

(2 marks)

Note: The following proformas are provided for your use in completing the above tasks:

- Remittance advices (see **page 10** of your **Answer Booklet**). Note the remittance advices provided are already addressed for you to each of the trade suppliers to whom they are to be issued.

- Cheques (see **page 10** of your **Answer Booklet**)

CHECKING AND BANKING DAILY TAKINGS

Customers can pay for gifts in cash, by cheque or by debit or credit card (Switch or Visa).

Debit and credit card transactions are processed using the Electronic Funds Transfer at Point of Sale (EFTPOS) system. This system ensures that the payment is transferred automatically to the bank account of Clara's Printers.

Cash and cheque sales are processed through a separate till to card sales. At the end of each day's trading a till reading showing the total cash and cheque takings is produced.

The contents of the till are then counted and the opening cash float is deducted, the balance being the day's cash sales which should agree to the total as shown by the till reading. Cash and cheques are then prepared for banking.

The process of reconciling the daily takings by cash and cheques to the till reading figure, and of preparing notes, coins and cheques for banking, is undertaken by completing a Daily Takings and Cash for Banking Form, from which a Paying-in Slip is then prepared.

You are now presented with the following information in respect of sales on the 30 June 2014:

1 At the close of business 30 June 2014 the till contents were:

Notes and Coins		Cheques	
Number in Hand	Denomination	Drawer	Amount £
10	£20 Notes	C. Timpson	30.00
14	£10 Notes	L. Smith	15.00
8	£5 Notes	G. Ward	15.00
8	£2 Coins	P. Harper	25.00
18	£1 Coins	B. Langford	33.00
18	50p Coins	S. Fox	12.00
16	20p Coins	W. Pipper	17.00
20	10p Coins	**Total**	147.00
20	5p Coins		
20	2p Coins		
20	1p Coins		

2 The till reading taken from the till used for the purpose of processing cash (notes and coins) and cheque sales showed daily takings at close of business on 30 June 2014 to be £476.80

3   The till used for the purpose of cash (notes and coins) and cheque sales contains a
      cash float at the beginning of each day with a cash float of £100 made up as follows:

Cash (Notes and Coins)

Number	Denomination	Amount £
5	£10 Notes	50.00
5	£5 Notes	25.00
13	£1 Coins	13.00
14	50p Coins	7.00
10	20p Coins	2.00
19	10p Coins	1.90
12	5p Coins	.60
15	2p Coins	.30
20	1p Coins	.20
		100.00

REQUIRED

Task 3 Check the daily sales in the form of cash and cheques from the till reading at
point 2, against the notes, coins and cheques in the till at the close of
business on 30 June 2014 as listed in point 1. Complete the Daily Takings
and Cash for Banking Form provided, which has been partly completed for
you. The cash float information is given at point 3.

(9.75 marks)

Task 4 Prepare the Paying-in Slip provided, thereby banking the cash and cheque
takings for 30 June 2014. You should sign the paying-in slip in the name of
A Student.

(4.5 marks)

Task 5 You have received a cheque from a non credit customer which is shown on
page 13 of your Answer Booklet together with the receipt issued for this. If
there are any errors state the error/s and necessary action to be taken.

(0.5 marks)

A Customer has returned a damaged photo frame which they had paid for in cash.

Clara's Printers		
Returns		
Date: 30 June 2014		
	£	p
Photo Frame x 1 (inc. VAT @ 20%)	8	40
Total amount due	8	40
Received with thanks		
VAT Reg No: 534 2715 93		

Task 6   Prepare a refund voucher, showing the net and VAT amount, in respect of the above returns. You can sign the voucher (A Student) as having authorised the refund.

1 mark

Note:

The following proformas are provided for your use in completing the tasks:

- Daily Takings and Cash for Banking Form (see **page 11** of your **Answer Booklet**)

- Paying-in Slip, Cheque received and receipt (see **pages 12 and 13** of your **Answer Booklet**).

- Refund voucher (see **page 14** of your **Answer Booklet**)

SECTION D – MAINTAINING PETTY CASH RECORDS

THERE ARE **SIX** TASKS IN THIS SECTION OF THE PAPER

YOU MUST COMPLETE **ALL** TASKS

DATA AND TASKS

You work for Sophie's Hair Design and one of your responsibilities is that of petty cashier. The business is registered for VAT.

Sophie's Hair Design operate a petty cash imprest system with an imprest balance of £300. The Petty Cash Book is balanced off on a monthly basis. The imprest balance is restored at the end of the month by means of a cheque drawn from the bank account.

The following eight petty cash vouchers were prepared in respect of petty cash expenditure in the month of June 2014:

	No: 051
Petty Cash Voucher	
Date: 02/06/14	

	AMOUNT £	p
Window Cleaners (zero rated for VAT)	15	00
	15	00

Claimant:	C. Brooks
Authorised by:	S. Mitchell

	No: 052
Petty Cash Voucher	
Date: 06/06/14	

	AMOUNT £	p
Posters (advertising) (includes VAT)	36	60
	36	60

Claimant:	T. Campbell
Authorised by:	S. Mitchell

	No: 053
Petty Cash Voucher	
Date: 9/06/14	

	AMOUNT £	p
Till Rolls (stationery) (includes VAT)	7	80
	7	80

Claimant:	T. Campbell
Authorised by:	S. Mitchell

	No: 054
Petty Cash Voucher	
Date: 16/06/14	

	AMOUNT £	p
Window Cleaners (zero rated for VAT)	15	00
	15	00

Claimant:	C. Brooks
Authorised by:	S. Mitchell

No: 055		
Petty Cash Voucher		
Date: 23/06/14		
	AMOUNT	
	£	p
Advertising (includes VAT)	42	00
	42	00
Claimant: C. Brooks		
Authorised by: S. Mitchell		

No: 056		
Petty Cash Voucher		
Date: 25/06/14		
	AMOUNT	
	£	p
Shop Mirror (sundries)	18	50
VAT	3	70
	22	20
Claimant: T. Campbell		
Authorised by: S. Mitchell		

No: 057		
Petty Cash Voucher		
Date: 27/06/14		
	AMOUNT	
	£	p
Shop Cleaning (zero rated for VAT) (sundries)	40	00
	40	00
Claimant: T. Campbell		
Authorised by: S. Mitchell		

No: 058		
Petty Cash Voucher		
Date: 30/06/14		
	AMOUNT	
	£	p
Milkman (zero rated for VAT) (sundries)	7	80
	7	80
Claimant: C. Brooks		
Authorised by: S. Mitchell		

REQUIRED

Task 1 Enter the petty cash vouchers for the month of June 2014 into the petty cash book.

Task 2 Sub-total the petty cash expenditure analysis columns and cross check them for arithmetic accuracy.

Task 3 Balance off the petty cash book as at 30 June 2014 carrying down and bringing down the petty cash balance as at that date. Restore the petty cash balance to the imprest amount and show the balance carried forward as at 30 June 2014.

(12 marks for Tasks 1-3)

Note: The following proforma is provided for your use in completing the above task:

- Petty Cash Book (see **page 15** of your **Answer Booklet**)

Your duties as petty cashier include responsibility for the safe-keeping of the petty cash float. You keep the float in a lockable box which you then lock away each evening in the office safe. At the end of each month, having balanced off the petty cash book but **before** you restore the petty cash imprest balance, you check the contents of the petty cash box against the balance per the petty cash book.

At close of business on Monday 30 June 2014 the petty cash box contained the following notes and coins:

Denominations (Notes and Coins)	Quantity In Box
£10 Notes	8
£5 Notes	2
£2 Coins	5
£1 Coins	9
50p Coins	4
20p Coins	4
10p Coins	10
5p Coins	10
2p Coins	9
1p Coins	12

REQUIRED

Task 4 Prepare the form 'Reconciliation of Petty Cash Book Balance with Contents of Petty Cash Box' as at Monday 30 June 2014, thereby reconciling the balance from the petty cash book with the contents of the petty cash box as at that date. **(5.75 marks)**

Note: The following proforma is provided for your use in completing the above task:

- Form – Reconciliation of Petty Cash Book Balance with Contents of Petty Cash Box (see **page 16** of your **Answer Booklet**)

The petty cash float is restored on the last day of each month by means of a cheque drawn from the business bank account.

As the petty cashier you prepare and sign a cheque requisition which you issue to the main cashier requesting the issue of a cheque made payable to 'cash' for an amount necessary to restore the petty cash imprest balance.

REQUIRED

Task 5 Prepare and sign the cheque requisition (A Student) to be issued to the main cashier on Tuesday 1 July 2014 for the amount necessary to restore the petty cash imprest balance. Show the restored balance in the Petty Cash Book at that date. **(1 mark)**

Note: The following proforma is provided for your use in completing the above task:

- Cheque requisition (see **page 16** of your **Answer Booklet**)

As petty cashier your duties also include the preparation of petty cash vouchers in respect of petty cash claims submitted to you. Petty cash vouchers are written up from receipts provided to you by claimants.

Today's date is Tuesday 1 July 2014 and you have received the following receipt from Cath Brooks in respect of a purchase of spare keys. She is now requesting that you reimburse her for the amount she has spent. She has left the receipt on your desk with a note telling you that she will call back to see you later in the day to sign the petty cash voucher and pick up the monies due to her:

Rob's Village Store. **Receipt**		
Date: 1 July 2014		
	£	p
Spare Keys (includes VAT)	5	40
Total amount due	5	40
Received with thanks		
VAT Reg No: 472 9143 62		

REQUIRED

Task 6 Prepare a petty cash voucher in respect of the above petty cash claim and detail the VAT amount separately. You can sign the voucher (A Student) as having authorised the claim. Cath Brooks will sign the voucher as claimant when she returns to your office.

(1.25 marks)

NB: The last petty cash voucher you authorised was numbered 058

Note: The following proforma is provided for your use in completing the above task:

- Petty cash voucher (see **page 17** of your **Answer Booklet**)

June 2014 Examination
Answer Booklet

159   Exam ID
1050 Exam ID

IAB Student No: ....

IAB Candidate No: ....

Name of Exam Centre:...

Date of Exam:..

Answer Booklet for the following Qualifications:

150:   Level 1 Award in Bookkeeping QCF: 50090069
160:   Level 1 Award in Manual Bookkeeping QCF: 50094063
1000: Level 1 Award in Bookkeeping QCF: 60104703
1020: Level 1 Award in Manual Bookkeeping QCF: 60104739

Time Allowed 2 Hours
Paper No: 0038

FOR USE BY ASSESSOR ONLY:

IAB ID	Units covered	Possible marks	Actual marks	Pass or Fail
157	Preparing and processing bookkeeping documents - M6008740	20		
158	Recording Credit transactions - A6008742	20		
156	Making and receiving payments - J6008744	20		
155	Maintaining petty cash records - R6008746	20		
1002	Maintaining petty cash records: R5051120			

International Association of Book-keepers, Suite 5, 20 Churchill Square, Kings Hill, West Malling, Kent ME19 4YU
Tel: 01732 897750, Fax: 01732 897751, email:education@iab.org.uk Website: www.iab.org

SECTION A – PREPARING AND PROCESSING BUSINESS DOCUMENTS

THERE ARE **FOUR** TASKS IN THIS SECTION OF THE PAPER YOU MUST COMPLETE **ALL** TASKS

FOR USE IN ANSWERING SECTION A TASK 1 – PREPARE A SALES INVOICE

SALES INVOICE   **Invoice No:**

Wheelies Ltd
10 Whitchurch Street
Derby
DE1 3DE

VAT Reg No: 426 3714 02

To: Autogeek Ltd
      2 King Street   **Date/Tax Point:** _____
      Derby
      DE5 9KT   **Your Order No:** _____

                            Customer Account No: _____

Product Code	Quantity	Description	Unit Price £	p	VAT Rate %	Goods Total £	p

Carriage Paid

Terms:

		Goods Total		
		VAT		
		Total Due		

VAT Analysis

VAT Rate	Total Net £	p	Total VAT £	p
20%				
0%				

E & OE

1

FOR USE IN ANSWERING SECTION A TASK 1 – PREPARE A SALES INVOICE

SALES INVOICE **Invoice No:**

Wheelies Ltd
10 Whitchurch Street
Derby
DE1 3DE

VAT Reg No: 426 3714 02

To:
Jackson Carparts
17 Market Street
Nottingham
NG2 4FW

Date/Tax Point: _____

Your Order No: _____

Customer Account No: _____

Product Code	Quantity	Description	Unit Price		VAT Rate	Goods Total	
			£	p	%	£	p

Carriage Paid

Terms:

	Goods Total	
	VAT	
	Total Due	

VAT Analysis				
VAT Rate	**Total Net**		**Total VAT**	
	£	p	£	p
20%				
0%				

E & OE

IAB (QCF) June 2014 v3

FOR USE IN ANSWERING SECTION A TASK 2 – PREPARE A CREDIT NOTE

CREDIT NOTE   No:

Wheelies Ltd
10 Whitchurch Street
Derby
DE1 3DE

VAT Reg No: 426 3714 02

To: Hargreaves & Son
     5 Oldham Street   **Date/Tax Point:** _____
     Derby
     DE4 8TE
                           Customer Account No: _____

Product Code	Quantity	Description	Unit Price £	p	VAT Rate %	Goods Total £	p

VAT Analysis						
VAT Rate	Total Net £	p	Total VAT £	p		
20%					Goods Total	
0%					VAT	
					Total Due	

Reason for Credit:

FOR USE IN ANSWERING SECTION A TASK 3 – CHECK A SUPPLIER INVOICE

SALES INVOICE   **Invoice No:** 5721

Clarks Garage
11 Oldham Road
Stafford
ST13 6FW

To: Wheelies Ltd
10 Whitchurch Street
Derby
DE1 3DE

Date/Tax Point: .... 9 June 2014 ....

Your Order No: .... PO 0824 ....

Product Code	Quantity	Description	Unit Price £	Unit Price p	VAT Rate %	Goods Total £	Goods Total p
3165	10	Brake Discs	32	99	20	329	90
3169	10	Brake Fluid	2	49	20	24	90
3187	5	Brake Pads	9	90	20	49	50

Carriage Paid

Terms: Net 60 days

Goods Total	404	30
Less Trade Discount 10%	40	43
Net Goods	363	87
VAT	72	77
Total Due	291	10

VAT Analysis

VAT Rate	Total Net £	Total Net p	Total VAT £	Total VAT p
20%	363	87	72	77
0%	-	-	-	-

E & OE   **VAT Reg No:** 735 1435 26

Complete this slip and attach to invoice

Action Required:

Purchase Invoice No: .... Supplier Account Code: _____

4

FOR USE IN ANSWERING SECTION A TASK 3 – CHECK A SUPPLIER INVOICE

SALES INVOICE	**Invoice No:** 08535

James & Co
27 Portland Street
Derby
DE3 4JN

VAT Reg No: 375 9352 62

To: Wheelies Ltd
10 Whitchurch Street
Derby
DE1 3DE

Date/Tax Point: 16 June 2014

Your Order No: PO 0825

Product Code	Quantity	Description	Unit Price £	p	VAT Rate %	Goods Total £	p
S0365	25	Car Shampoo	8	90	20	222	50
S0369	10	Car Wax	5	90	20	59	00
S0198	10	Spark Plugs	4	90	20	49	00

Carriage Paid

Terms: Net 30 days

	Goods Total	330	50
	Less Trade Discount 10%	33	05
	Net Goods	297	45
	VAT	59	49
	Total Due	356	94

VAT Analysis

VAT Rate	Total Net £	p	Total VAT £	p
20%	297	45	59	49
0%	-	-	-	-

E & OE

Complete this slip and attach to invoice

Action Required:

Purchase Invoice No: Supplier Account Code:

IAB Level I answer booklet

FOR USE IN ANSWERING SECTION A TASK 3 – CHECK A SUPPLIER INVOICE

SALES INVOICE **Invoice No:** 1329

Tyler Autos Ltd VAT Reg No: 523 7435 51
5 Chestnut Road
Nottingham
NG2 7LT

To: Wheelies Ltd
10 Whitchurch Street **Date/Tax Point:** _____ 19 June 2014 _____
Derby
DE1 3DE **Customer Account No:** PO 0826

Product Code	Quantity	Description	Unit Price £	Unit Price p	VAT Rate %	Goods Total £	Goods Total p
01786	15	Air Filter	6	00	20	90	00
01792	15	Fuel Filter	3	00	20	45	00
01975	15	Oil Filter	2	00	20	30	00

Carriage Paid

Terms: Net 60 days

	Goods Total	165	00
	Less Trade Discount 5%	16	50
	Net Goods	148	50
	VAT	29	70
	Invoice Total	178	20

VAT Analysis

VAT Rate	Total Net £	Total Net p	Total VAT £	Total VAT p
20%	178	20	29	70
0%	-	-	-	-

E & OE

Complete this slip and attach to invoice

Action Required:

_____

_____

_____

Purchase Invoice No: _____ Supplier Account Code: _____

IAB (QCF) June 2014 v3

FOR USE IN ANSWERING SECTION A TASK 4 – CHECK A SUPPLIER CREDIT NOTE

		CREDIT NOTE				**No:** CN 176		

Clarks Garage
11 Oldham Road
Stafford
ST13 6FW

VAT Reg No: 735 1435 26

To: Wheelies Ltd
      10 Whitchurch Street
      Derby
      DE1 3DE

Date/Tax Point: 16 June 2014

Product Code	Quantity	Description	Unit Price		VAT Rate	Goods Total	
			£	p	%	£	p
3187	1	Brake Pads	9	90	20	9	90

VAT Analysis				
VAT Rate	Total Net		Total VAT	
	£	p	£	p
20%	9	41	1	88
0%	-	-	-	-

	£	p
Goods Total	9	90
Less Trade Discount 10%	0	49
Net Goods	9	41
VAT	1	88
Total Credit	11	29

Reason for Credit: Damaged goods

Complete this slip and attach to credit note

Action Required:

_____

_____

_____

Supplier Account Code: _____

SECTION B – RECORDING CREDIT TRANSACTIONS

THERE ARE **FOUR** TASKS IN THIS SECTION OF THE PAPER YOU MUST COMPLETE **ALL** TASKS

FOR USE IN ANSWERING SECTION B TASK 1 – COMPLETE THE SALES DAY BOOK

Sales Day Book

Date 2014	Customer	Customer Account Code	Invoice Number	Total Invoice £	VAT £	Net Goods £
30 June	Katie's Garden Shop	SL – K015	L 0640	720.00	120.00	600.00
30 June	Primrose & Co.	SL – P010	L 0641	360.00	60.00	300.00
30 June	Outdoor World	SL – O036	L 0642	480.60	80.10	400.50
Totals						

FOR USE IN ANSWERING SECTION B TASK 2 – COMPLETE THE SALES RETURNS DAY BOOK

Sales Returns Day Book

Date 2014	Customer	Customer Account Code	Credit Note Number	Total Credit Note £	VAT £	Net Goods £
30 June	Primrose & Co.	SL – P010	CN 029	96.00	16.00	80.00
30 June	Outdoor World	SL – O036	CN 030	120.00	20.00	100.00
Totals						

8

FOR USE IN ANSWERING SECTION B TASK 3 – COMPLETE THE PURCHASE DAY BOOK

Purchase Day Book

Date 2014	Supplier	Supplier Account Code	Supplier Invoice Number	Our Invoice Number	Invoice Total £	VAT £	Net Goods £
30 June	Westies Gardens	PL – W021	WG 02435	P 0519	480.72	80.12	400.60
30 June	Bradwalls Ltd	PL – B013	B 4298	P 0520	420.00	70.00	350.00
Totals							

FOR USE IN ANSWERING SECTION B TASK 4 – COMPLETE THE PURCHASE RETURNS DAY BOOK

Purchase Returns Day Book

Date 2014	Supplier	Supplier Account Code	Supplier Credit Note Number	Total Credit Note £	VAT £	Net Goods £
30 June	Hollybush Ltd	PL – H009	CN 0235	180.60	30.10	150.50
Totals						

9

SECTION C – MAKING AND RECEIVING PAYMENTS

THERE ARE **FIVE** TASKS IN THIS SECTION YOU MUST COMPLETE **ALL** TASKS

FOR USE IN ANSWERING SECTION C TASK 1 – COMPLETE REMITTANCE ADVICE

REMITTANCE ADVICE		
From:	Clara's Printers	
	15 York Road	
	Beaconsfield	
	Slough	
	HP9 2HE	
To:	Click n Print Ltd	
	3 High Street	
	Maidenhead	
	Slough	
	SL60 9NT	
Date:		

Details	Amount £	p
Cheque No: Enclosed		

REMITTANCE ADVICE		
From:	Clara's Printers	
	15 York Road	
	Beaconsfield	
	Slough	
	HP9 2HE	
To:	J & K Printers	
	7 Park Avenue	
	Burnham	
	Slough	
	SL4 3PR	
Date:		

Details	Amount £	p
Cheque No: Enclosed		

FOR USE IN ANSWERING SECTION C TASK 2 – COMPLETE CHEQUES

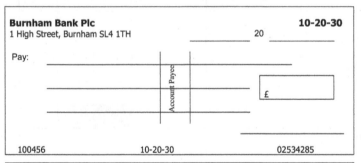

Burnham Bank Plc
1 High Street, Burnham SL4 1TH
10-20-30
_____ 20 _____

Pay:
Account Payee
£

100456   10-20-30   02534285

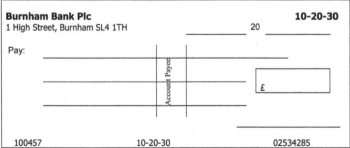

Burnham Bank Plc
1 High Street, Burnham SL4 1TH
10-20-30
_____ 20 _____

Pay:
Account Payee
£

100457   10-20-30   02534285

FOR USE IN ANSWERING SECTION C TASK 3 – COMPLETE A DAILY TAKING AND CASH FOR BANKING FORM

Clara's Printers – Daily Takings and Cash for Banking
Date: _____

Notes and Coins	Till Contents		Less Cash Float		Daily Takings and Cash for Banking	
	£	p	£	p	£	p
£50 Notes	0	00	0	00	0	00
£20 Notes	200	00	0	00	200	00
£10 Notes	140	00	50	00	90	00
£5 Notes	40	00	25	00	15	00
£2 Coins	16	00	0	00	16	00
£1 Coins						
50p Coins						
20p Coins						
10p Coins						
5p Coins						
2p Coins						
1p Coins						
Cash (Total)						
Cheques (Total)			███	███		
TOTAL						

	£	p
Daily Till Reading Total		

	£	p
Difference		

338

IAB Level I answer booklet

FOR USE IN ANSWERING SECTION C TASK 4 – COMPLETE A PAYING-IN SLIP

Paying-in Slip: Front

Paying-In Slip: Reverse

FOR USE IN ANSWERING SECTION C TASK 5 – CONFIRM A CHEQUE RECEIVED IS CORRECT USING THE RECEIPT ISSUED

Bridge Bank Plc   **20-30-40**
High Street, Uxbridge SL5 6FE   30 June   20   14

Pay: Clara's Printers Ltd   only

           Twenty two pounds   and fifty
                                                          £22.50
           pence only

                                                          S. Tiffany

   100287   20-30-40   03726142

                               Receipt No: 82
           Clara's Printers
           15 York Road
           Beaconsfield
           Slough
           HP9 2HE   Date: 30 June 2014

Details	AMOUNT £	p
Printing of Leaflets	22	55
	22	55

State any errors below:

_____
_____
_____
_____
_____
_____

IAB Level I answer booklet

FOR USE IN ANSWERING SECTION C TASK 6 – COMPLETE A REFUND VOUCHER

No: R 27

Refund Voucher – Cash Sales

Date:

Details	AMOUNT £	p

Authorised by:

SECTION D – MAINTAINING PETTY CASH RECORDS

THERE ARE **SIX** TASKS IN THIS SECTION YOU MUST COMPLETE **ALL** TASKS

FOR USE IN ANSWERING SECTION D TASKS 1, 2 AND 3 – COMPLETE A PETTY CASH BOOK

Sophie's Hair Design
Petty Cash Book

Receipts	Date 2014	Details	Voucher No	Total Payment	VAT	Window Cleaners	Advertising	Stationery	Sundries
£				£	£	£	£	£	£
300.00	01 June	Balance b/f							
		Sub Totals							
-	30 June	Balance c/d							
		Totals							
-	30 June	Balance b/d		-					
	1 July	Bank		-					
	1 July	Balance c/f		-					

Expenditure Analysis

IAB Level I answer booklet

FOR USE IN ANSWERING SECTION D TASK 4 – RECONCILE PETTY CASH

<table>
<tr><td colspan="4">Reconciliation of Petty Cash Book Balance
with Contents of Petty Cash Box</td></tr>
<tr><td colspan="4">Date: _____</td></tr>
<tr><td rowspan="2">Denomination (notes and coins)</td><td rowspan="2">Quantity
in Box</td><td colspan="2">Amount</td></tr>
<tr><td>£</td><td>P</td></tr>
<tr><td>Contents of Petty Cash Box</td><td></td><td></td><td></td></tr>
<tr><td>£20 Notes</td><td></td><td></td><td></td></tr>
<tr><td>£10 Notes</td><td></td><td></td><td></td></tr>
<tr><td>£5 Notes</td><td></td><td></td><td></td></tr>
<tr><td>£2 Coins</td><td></td><td></td><td></td></tr>
<tr><td>£1 Coins</td><td></td><td></td><td></td></tr>
<tr><td>50p Coins</td><td></td><td></td><td></td></tr>
<tr><td>20p Coins</td><td></td><td></td><td></td></tr>
<tr><td>10p Coins</td><td></td><td></td><td></td></tr>
<tr><td>5p Coins</td><td></td><td></td><td></td></tr>
<tr><td>2p Coins</td><td></td><td></td><td></td></tr>
<tr><td>1p Coins</td><td></td><td></td><td></td></tr>
<tr><td>Total per Petty Cash Box</td><td></td><td></td><td></td></tr>
<tr><td>Balance per Petty Cash Book</td><td></td><td></td><td></td></tr>
<tr><td>Difference</td><td></td><td></td><td></td></tr>
</table>

FOR USE IN ANSWERING SECTION D TASK 5 – COMPLETE A CHEQUE REQUISITION

<table>
<tr><td colspan="2" align="center">CHEQUE REQUISITION</td></tr>
<tr><td>DATE:</td><td></td></tr>
<tr><td>CHEQUE PAYABLE TO:</td><td></td></tr>
<tr><td>AMOUNT:</td><td></td></tr>
<tr><td>DETAILS:</td><td></td></tr>
<tr><td>SIGNED:</td><td></td></tr>
<tr><td></td><td></td></tr>
</table>

FOR USE IN ANSWERING SECTION D TASK 6 – COMPLETE A PETTY CASH VOUCHER

	No:		
	Petty Cash Voucher		
	Date:		
		AMOUNT	
Details		£	p
Claimant:			
Authorised by:			

IAB Level I answer booklet

This page has been left intentionally blank for your workings

June 2014 Examination
Model Answers

159 Exam ID
1050 Exam ID

Model Answer Booklet for the following Qualifications:

150: Level 1 Award in Bookkeeping QCF: 50090069
160: Level 1 Award in Manual Bookkeeping QCF: 50094063
1000: Level 1 Award in Bookkeeping QCF: 60104703
1020: Level 1 Award in Manual Bookkeeping QCF: 60104739

Time Allowed 2 Hours
Paper No: 0038

FOR USE BY ASSESSOR ONLY:

IAB ID	Units covered	Possible marks
157	Preparing and processing bookkeeping documents - M6008740	20
158	Recording Credit transactions - A6008742	20
156	Making and receiving payments - J6008744	20
155	Maintaining petty cash records - R6008746	20
1002	Maintaining petty cash records: R5051120	20

International Association of Book-keepers, Suite 5, 20 Churchill Square, Kings Hill, West Malling, Kent ME19 4YU
Tel: 01732 897750, Fax: 01732 897751, email:education@iab.org.uk Website: www.iab.org.uk

SECTION A – PREPARING AND PROCESSING BUSINESS DOCUMENTS

THERE ARE **FOUR** TASKS IN THIS SECTION OF THE PAPER YOU MUST COMPLETE **ALL** TASKS

FOR USE IN ANSWERING SECTION A TASK 1 – PREPARE A SALES INVOICE

SALES INVOICE   **Invoice No:** W 1356 ¼

Wheelies Ltd
10 Whitchurch Street
Derby
DE1 3DE

VAT Reg No: 426 3714 02

To: Autogeek Ltd
     2 King Street
     Derby
     DE5 9KT

Date/Tax Point: 30 June 2014 ¼

Your Order No: AG 2875 ¼

Customer Account No: SL – AG03 ¼

Product Code	Quantity	Description	Unit Price £	Unit Price p	VAT Rate %	Goods Total £	Goods Total p	
W005	40	Windscreen Wiper Blades 20"	4	99	20	199	60	1
W009	30	Windscreen Wiper Blades 24"	6	99	20	209	70	1

Carriage Paid

Terms: Net 30 days ¼

Goods Total	409	30 ¼
VAT	81	86 ½
Total Due	491	16 ½

VAT Analysis

VAT Rate	Total Net £	Total Net p	Total VAT £	Total VAT p
20%	409	30 ¼	81	86 ¼
0%	0	00	0	00

E & OE

Marks 5

FOR USE IN ANSWERING SECTION A TASK 1 – PREPARE A SALES INVOICE

SALES INVOICE **Invoice No:** W 1357 ¼

Wheelies Ltd
10 Whitchurch Street
Derby
DE1 3DE

VAT Reg No: 426 3714 02

To:
Jackson Carparts
17 Market Street
Nottingham
NG2 4FW

Date/Tax Point: 30 June 2014 ¼

Your Order No: JC 0943 ¼

Customer Account No: SL – JC12 ¼

Product Code	Quantity	Description	Unit Price £	p	VAT Rate %	Goods Total £	p
B001	10	Brake Discs	49	99	20	499	90 1
B008	20	Brake Pads	14	99	20	299	80 1

Carriage Paid

Terms: Net 60 days ¼

	Goods Total	799	70 ¼
	VAT	159	94 ½
	Total Due	959	64 ½

VAT Analysis

VAT Rate	Total Net £	p	Total VAT £	p
20%	799	70 ¼	159	94 ¼
0%	0	00	0	00

E & OE

Marks 5

FOR USE IN ANSWERING SECTION A TASK 2 – PREPARE A CREDIT NOTE

CREDIT NOTE   **No:** CN 85 ¼

Wheelies Ltd
10 Whitchurch Street
Derby
DE1 3DE

VAT Reg No: 426 3714 02

To: Hargreaves & Son
      5 Oldham Street   **Date/Tax Point:**   30 June 2014 ¼
      Derby
      DE4 8TE   **Customer Account No:**   SL – HS10 ¼

Product Code	Quantity	Description	Unit Price		VAT Rate	Goods Total	
			£	p	%	£	p
C003	2	Car Hand Polishing Mitt	5	99	20	11	98 1

VAT Analysis							
VAT Rate	Total Net		Total VAT			Goods Total	11	98 ¼
	£	p	£	p			

VAT Rate	Total Net		Total VAT		
	£	p	£	p	
20%	11	98 ¼	2	39 ¼	VAT 2 39 ½
0%	0	00	0	00	**Total Due** 14 37 ½

Goods Total   11 98 ¼
VAT   2 39 ½
Total Due   14 37 ½

Reason for Credit: Damaged ½

Marks 4

IAB Level I model answers

FOR USE IN ANSWERING SECTION A TASK 3 – CHECK A SUPPLIER INVOICE

SALES INVOICE   **Invoice No:** 5721

Clarks Garage
11 Oldham Road
Stafford
ST13 6FW

To: Wheelies Ltd
      10 Whitchurch Street   **Date/Tax Point:** _____ 9 June 2014
      Derby
      DE1 3DE

      Your Order No: _____ PO 0824

Product Code	Quantity	Description	Unit Price £	Unit Price p	VAT Rate %	Goods Total £	Goods Total p
3165	10	Brake Disks	32	99	20	329	90
3169	10	Brake Fluid	2	49	20	24	90
3187	5	Brake Pads	9	90	20	49	50

Carriage Paid

Terms: Net 60 days

Goods Total	404	30
Less Trade Discount 5%	40	43
Net Goods	363	87
VAT	72	77
Total Due	291	10

VAT Analysis

VAT Rate	Total Net £	Total Net p	Total VAT £	Total VAT p
20%	363	87	72	77
0%	-	-	-	-

E & OE   **VAT Reg No:** 735 1435 26

Complete this slip and attach to invoice

Action Required:

Contains errors – return to supplier ½

Incorrect terms + incorrect total due ½ + ½

Purchase Invoice No: _____   Supplier Account Code: _____

Marks 1.5

FOR USE IN ANSWERING SECTION A TASK 3 – CHECK A SUPPLIER INVOICE

SALES INVOICE				**Invoice No:** 08535		

James & Co
27 Portland Street
Derby
DE3 4JN

VAT Reg No: 375 9352 62

To: Wheelies Ltd
10 Whitchurch Street
Derby
DE1 3DE

Date/Tax Point: 16 June 2014

Your Order No: PO 0825

Product Code	Quantity	Description	Unit Price £	Unit Price p	VAT Rate %	Goods Total £	Goods Total p
S0365	25	Car Shampoo	8	90	20	222	50
S0369	10	Car Wax	5	90	20	59	00
S0198	10	Spark Plugs	4	90	20	49	00

Carriage Paid

Terms: Net 30 days

	Goods Total	330	50
	Less Trade Discount 10%	33	05
	Net Goods	297	45
	VAT	59	49
	Total Due	356	94

VAT Analysis

VAT Rate	Total Net £	Total Net p	Total VAT £	Total VAT p
20%	297	45	59	49
0%	-	-	-	-

E & OE

Complete this slip and attach to invoice

Action Required:

Passed for payment ½

Purchase Invoice No: P 1744 ½   Supplier Account Code: PL – JC021 ½

Marks 1.5

FOR USE IN ANSWERING SECTION A TASK 3 – CHECK A SUPPLIER INVOICE

	SALES INVOICE			**Invoice No:** 1329				

Tyler Autos Ltd
5 Chestnut Road
Nottingham
NG2 7LT

VAT Reg No: 523 7435 51

To: Wheelies Ltd
      10 Whitchurch Street
      Derby
      DE1 3DE

Date/Tax Point: _____ 19 June 2014 _____

Customer Account No: PO 0826

Product Code	Quantity	Description	Unit Price £	p	VAT Rate %	Goods Total £	p
01786	15	Air Filter	6	00	20	90	00
01792	15	Fuel Filter	3	00	20	45	00
01975	15	Oil Filter	2	00	20	30	00

Carriage Paid

Terms: Net 60 days

	Goods Total	165	00
	Less Trade Discount 5%	16	50
	Net Goods	148	50
	VAT	29	70
	Invoice Total	178	20

VAT Analysis

VAT Rate	Total Net £	p	Total VAT £	p
20%	178	20	29	70
0%	-	-	-	-

E & OE

Complete this slip and attach to invoice

Action Required:

         Contains errors – return to supplier 1

         Incorrect trade discount and incorrect VAT analysis ½

Purchase Invoice No: .... Supplier Account Code: _____

Marks 1.5

FOR USE IN ANSWERING SECTION A TASK 4 – CHECK A SUPPLIER CREDIT NOTE

CREDIT NOTE					**No:** CN 176		

Clarks Garage
11 Oldham Road
Stafford
ST13 6FW

VAT Reg No: 735 1435 26

To: Wheelies Ltd
     10 Whitchurch Street
     Derby
     DE1 3DE

Date/Tax Point: 16 June 2014

Product Code	Quantity	Description	Unit Price		VAT Rate	Goods Total	
			£	p	%	£	p
3187	1	Brake Pads	9	90	20	9	90

VAT Analysis							
VAT Rate	Total Net		Total VAT				
	£	p	£	p			
20%	9	41	1	88			
0%	-	-	-	-			

Goods Total	9	90
Less Trade Discount 5%	0	49
Net Goods	9	41
VAT	1	88
Total Credit	11	29

Reason for Credit: Damaged goods

Complete this slip and attach to credit note

Action Required: Contains errors – return to supplier 1

                   Incorrect trade discount ½

Supplier Account Code: ....

Marks 1.5

NOTE: 2 MARKS TO BE DEDUCTED IN SECTION A FOR UNTIDY WORK IF APPROPRIATE

IAB Level I model answers

SECTION B – RECORDING CREDIT TRANSACTIONS

THERE ARE **FOUR** TASKS IN THIS SECTION OF THE PAPER YOU MUST COMPLETE **ALL** TASKS

FOR USE IN ANSWERING SECTION B TASK 1 – COMPLETE THE SALES DAY BOOK

Sales Day Book

Date 2014	Customer	Customer Account Code	Invoice Number	Total Invoice £	VAT £	Net Goods £
30 June	Katie's Garden Shop	SL – K015	L 0640	720.00	120.00	600.00
30 June	Primrose & Co.	SL – P010	L 0641	360.00	60.00	300.00
30 June	Outdoor World	SL – O036	L 0642	480.60	80.10	400.50
30 June	Katie's Garden Shop	SL – K015 ¼	L 0643 ¼	1,140.00 ¼	190.00 ¼	950.00 ¼
30 June	Outdoor World	SL – O036 ¼	L 0644 ¼	1,512.00 ¼	252.00 ¼	1,260.00 ¼
	Totals			4,212.60 1	702.10 1	3,510.50 1

FOR USE IN ANSWERING SECTION B TASK 2 – COMPLETE THE SALES RETURNS DAY BOOK

Sales Returns Day Book

Date 2014	Customer	Customer Account Code	Credit Note Number	Total Credit Note £	VAT £	Net Goods £
30 June	Primrose & Co.	SL – P010	CN 029	96.00	16.00	80.00
30 June	Outdoor World	SL – O036	CN 030	120.00	20.00	100.00
30 June	Katie's Garden Shop	SL – K015 ¼	CN 031 ¼	108.00 ¼	18.00 ¼	90.00 ¼
	Totals			324.00 1	54.00 1	270.00 1

Marks 9.75

FOR USE IN ANSWERING SECTION B TASK 3 – COMPLETE THE PURCHASE DAY BOOK

Purchase Day Book

Date 2014	Supplier	Supplier Account Code	Supplier Invoice Number	Our Invoice Number	Invoice Total £	VAT £	Net Goods £
30 June	Westies Gardens	PL – W021	WG 02435	P 0519	480.72	80.12	400.60
30 June	Bradwalls Ltd	PL – B013	B 4298	P 0520	420.00	70.00	350.00
30 June	Hollybush Ltd	PL – H009 ¼	HL 6743 ¼	P 0521 ¼	3,648.00 ¼	608.00 ¼	3,040.00 ¼
30 June	Bradwalls Ltd	PL – B013 ¼	B 4312 ¼	P 0522 ¼	1,080.00 ¼	180.00 ¼	900.00 ¼
Totals					5,628.72 1	938.12 1	4,690.60 1

FOR USE IN ANSWERING SECTION B TASK 4 – COMPLETE THE PURCHASE RETURNS DAY BOOK

Purchase Returns Day Book

Date 2014	Supplier	Supplier Account Code	Supplier Credit Note Number	Total Credit Note £	VAT £	Net Goods £
30 June	Hollybush Ltd	PL – H009	CN 0235	180.60	30.10	150.50
30 June	Westies Gardens	PL – W021 ¼	CN 321 ¼	114.00 ¼	19.00 ¼	95.00 ¼
Totals				294.60 1	49.10 1	245.50 1

Marks 10.25

NOTE: 2 MARKS TO BE DEDUCTED IN SECTION B FOR UNTIDY WORK IF APPROPRIATE

9

SECTION C – MAKING AND RECEIVING PAYMENTS   (MARKS 4.5)

THERE ARE **FIVE** TASKS IN THIS SECTION YOU MUST COMPLETE **ALL** TASKS

FOR USE IN ANSWERING SECTION C TASK 1 – COMPLETE REMITTANCE ADVICE

REMITTANCE ADVICE		
From: Clara's Printers		
15 York Road		
Beaconsfield		
Slough		
HP9 2HE		
To: Click n Print Ltd		
3 High Street		
Maidenhead		
Slough		
SL60 9NT		
Date: 30 June 2014 ¼		

Details	Amount £	p
Invoice C 01765 ¼	720	00
Invoice C 01773 ¼	300	00
Cheque No: 100456 ¼ Enclosed	1,020	00
		¼

REMITTANCE ADVICE		
From: Clara's Printers		
15 York Road		
Beaconsfield		
Slough		
HP9 2HE		
To: J & K Printers		
7 Park Avenue		
Burnham		
Slough		
SL4 3PR		
Date: 30 June 2014 ¼		

Details	Amount £	p
Invoice 0456 ¼	144	00
Less Credit Note CN 193 ¼	(96	00)
Cheque No: 100457 ¼ Enclosed	48	00
		¼

FOR USE IN ANSWERING SECTION C TASK 2 – COMPLETE CHEQUES

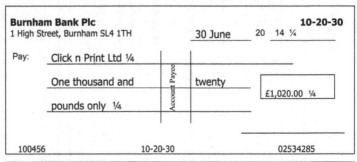

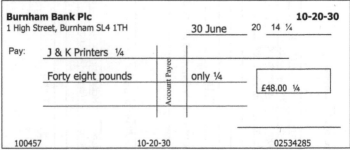

356

FOR USE IN ANSWERING SECTION C TASK 3 – COMPLETE A DAILY TAKING AND CASH FOR BANKING FORM

Clara's Printers – Daily Takings and Cash for Banking
Date: _____30 June 2014 ¼_____

Notes and Coins	Till Contents		Less Cash Float		Daily Takings and Cash for Banking	
	£	p	£	p	£	p
£50 Notes	0	00	0	00	0	00
£20 Notes	200	00	0	00	200	00
£10 Notes	140	00	50	00	90	00
£5 Notes	40	00	25	00	15	00
£2 Coins	16	00	0	00	16	00
£1 Coins	18	00 ¼	13	00 ¼	5	00 ¼
50p Coins	9	00 ¼	7	00 ¼	2	00 ¼
20p Coins	3	20 ¼	2	00 ¼	1	20 ¼
10p Coins	2	00 ¼	1	90 ¼	0	10 ¼
5p Coins	1	00 ¼	0	60 ¼	0	40 ¼
2p Coins	0	40 ¼	0	30 ¼	0	10 ¼
1p Coins	0	20 ¼	0	20 ¼	0	00 ¼
Cash (Total)	429	80 ½	100	00 ½	329	80 ½
Cheques (Total)	147	00 ½			147	00 ¼
TOTAL	576	80 ½	100	00 ¼	476	80 ½

	£	p
Daily Till Reading Total	476	80 ½

	£	p
Difference	0	00 ¼

Marks 9.75

IAB Level I model answers

FOR USE IN ANSWERING SECTION C TASK 4 – COMPLETE A PAYING-IN SLIP

Paying-in Slip: Front

Date: 30 June 2014 ¼			Date: 30 Jun 2014 ¼	**bank giro credit**			
Credit: 02534285 ¼							

Cashier's stamp and initials

	£	p			£	p
£50 notes	0	00	£50 notes		0	00
£20 notes	200	00	£20 notes		200	00
£10 notes	90	00	£10 notes		90	00
£5 notes	15	00	£5 notes		15	00
£2/£1	21	00	£2/£1		21	00
50p	2	00	50p		2	00
20p	1	20	20p		1	20
10p, 5p	0	50	10p, 5p		0	50
Bronze	0	10	Bronze		0	10
Total Cash	329	80	Total Cash		329	80
Total Cheques etc	147	00	Total Cheques etc		147	00
£	476	80 ½	£		476	80
						¼

Code No 10-20-30

Bank: **Burnham Bank Plc**
Branch: Burnham

Credit: Clara's Printers
Account No: 02534285

Number of Cheques
7 ¼

Paid in by: A. Student   ¼

Paying-in Slip: Reverse

Cheques etc	£	p		£	p			£	p
			Brought forward	147	00				
C. Timpson ¼	30	00					C. Timpson	30	00
L. Smith ¼	15	00					L. Smith	15	00
G. Ward ¼	15	00					G. Ward	15	00
P. Harper ¼	25	00					P. Harper	25	00
B. Langford ¼	33	00					B. Langford	33	00
S. Fox ¼	12	00					S. Fox	12	00
W. Pipper ¼	17	00					W. Pipper	17	00
								¼	
Carried forward	147	00 ¼	Carried over	147	00		Carried over	147	00

(counterfoil carried over)

Marks 4.25

FOR USE IN ANSWERING SECTION C TASK 5 – CONFIRM A CHEQUE RECEIVED IS CORRECT USING THE RECEIPT ISSUED

Bridge Bank Plc High Street, Uxbridge SL5 6FE	30 June 20 14	**20-30-40**
Pay: Clara's Printers Ltd		only
Twenty two pounds	and fifty	£22.50
pence only		
		S. Tiffany
100287	20-30-40	03726142

Clara's Printers 15 York Road Beaconsfield Slough HP9 2HE	**Receipt No:** 82	
	Date: 30 June 2014	

Details	AMOUNT	
	£	p
Printing of Leaflets	22	55
	22	55

State any errors below:

The cheque amount and payee name are incorrect ¼ + ¼

Marks ½

FOR USE IN ANSWERING SECTION C TASK 6 – COMPLETE A REFUND VOUCHER

No: R 27

Refund Voucher – Cash Sales

Date: 30 June 14

¼

Details	AMOUNT £	p
Refund – Photo Frame	7	00 ¼
VAT @ 20%	1	40 ¼
	8	40 ¼

Authorised by: *A. Student*

Marks 1

NOTE: 2 MARKS TO BE DEDUCTED IN SECTION C FOR UNTIDY WORK IF APPROPRIATE

IAB Level I model answers

SECTION D – MAINTAINING PETTY CASH RECORDS

THERE ARE **SIX** TASKS IN THIS SECTION YOU MUST COMPLETE **ALL** TASKS

FOR USE IN ANSWERING SECTION D TASKS 1, 2 AND 3 – COMPLETE A PETTY CASH BOOK

Sophie's Hair Design
Petty Cash Book

Receipts £	Date 2014	Details	Voucher No	Total Payment £	VAT £	Window Cleaners £	Advertising £	Stationery £	Sundries £
300.00	01 June	Balance b/f							
	2 June	Window Cleaners ¼	051 ¼	15.00 ¼		15.00 ¼			
	6 June	Posters ¼	052 ¼	36.60 ¼	6.10 ¼		30.50 ¼		
	9 June	Till Rolls ¼	053 ¼	7.80 ¼	1.30 ¼			6.50 ¼	
	16 June	Window Cleaners ¼	054 ¼	15.00 ¼		15.00 ¼			
	23 June	Advertising ¼	055 ¼	42.00 ¼	7.00 ¼		35.00 ¼		
	25 June	Shop Mirror ¼	056 ¼	22.20 ¼	3.70 ¼				18.50 ¼
	27 June	Shop Cleaning ¼	057 ¼	40.00 ¼					40.00 ¼
	30 June	Milkman ¼	058 ¼	7.80 ¼					7.80 ¼
-		Sub Totals		186.40 ¼	18.10 ¼	30.00 ¼	65.50 ¼	6.50 ¼	66.30 ¼
-	30 June	Balance c/d		113.60 ¼					
300.00 ¼		**Totals**		300.00 ¼					
113.60 ¼	30 June	Balance b/d		-					
186.40 ¼	1 July	Bank		-					
300.00 ¼	1 July	Balance c/f		-					

Expenditure Analysis

Marks 12

15

IAB (QCF)/L1 June 2014/Model Answers v3

IAB Level I model answers

FOR USE IN ANSWERING SECTION D TASK 4 – RECONCILE PETTY CASH

Reconciliation of Petty Cash Book Balance with Contents of Petty Cash Box

Date: 30 June 2014

Denomination (notes and coins)	Quantity in Box	Amount £	P
Contents of Petty Cash Box			
£20 Notes	-		-
£10 Notes	8 ¼	80	00 ¼
£5 Notes	2 ¼	10	00 ¼
£2 Coins	5 ¼	10	00 ¼
£1 Coins	9 ¼	9	00 ¼
50p Coins	4 ¼	2	00 ¼
20p Coins	4 ¼	0	80 ¼
10p Coins	10 ¼	1	00 ¼
5p Coins	10 ¼	0	50 ¼
2p Coins	9 ¼	0	18 ¼
1p Coins	12 ¼	0	12 ¼
Total per Petty Cash Box		113	60 ¼
Balance per Petty Cash Book		113	60 ¼
Difference		0	00 ¼

FOR USE IN ANSWERING SECTION D TASK 5 – COMPLETE A CHEQUE REQUISITION

CHEQUE REQUISITION
DATE: 1 July 2014
CHEQUE PAYABLE TO: Cash ¼
AMOUNT: £186.40 ¼
DETAILS: Restore petty cash imprest amount ¼
SIGNED: A. Student ¼

Marks 6.75

FOR USE IN ANSWERING SECTION D TASK 6 – COMPLETE A PETTY CASH VOUCHER

		No: 059 ¼		
		Petty Cash Voucher		
		Date: 1 July 14		

Details	AMOUNT	
	£	p
Spare Keys	4	50 ¼
VAT @ 20%		90 ¼
	5	40 ¼

Claimant: T. Campbell
Authorised by: A. Student ¼

Marks 1.25

NOTE: 2 MARKS TO BE DEDUCTED IN SECTION D FOR UNTIDY WORK IF APPROPRIATE

June 2014 Examination
Question Paper

208 Exam ID
2050 Exam ID

Question Paper for the following Qualifications:

200: Level 2 Certificate in Bookkeeping QCF: 50090537
210: Level 2 Award in Manual Bookkeeping QCF: 50092595
230: Level 2 Certificate in Applied Bookkeeping QCF: 50092625
2000: Level 2 Certificate in Bookkeeping QCF: 60107303
2030: Level 2 Award in Manual Bookkeeping QCF: 60104806

Units
206: Maintaining the Journal: T6008772
205: Maintaining Control Accounts: K6008770
207: Processing Ledger Transactions and Extracting a Trial Balance: F6008760
2005: Maintaining the Journal: H5051123
2004: Maintaining Control Accounts: K5051124
2006: Processing Ledger Transactions and Extracting a Trial Balance: M5051125

Time Allowed 2 Hours 30 Minutes
Paper No: 0039

General Instructions

1. Enter your IAB Student Number, Candidate Number and Name of Examination Centre in
   the spaces provided on the front cover of your Answer Booklet
2. All Answers to be written in blue or black ink
3. Cross out errors neatly or use correcting fluid in moderation
4. Calculators are permitted
5. A blank page is provided in the Answer Booklet for workings if required
6. The Question Paper and Answer Booklet have information and data printed on both
   sides of the pages
7. Mobile phones are not permitted

International Association of Book-keepers, Suite 5, 20 Churchill Square, Kings Hill, West Malling, Kent ME19 4YU
Tel: 01732 897750, Fax: 01732 897751, email:education@iab.org.uk Website: www.iab.org.uk

Maintaining the Journal

Question One – Question One is in three parts (Parts A, B, and C)

Question One (Part A)

Use the Journal to Correct Errors. Eliminate a Suspense Account Balance and Redraft a Trial balance

The following Trial Balance was extracted from the double entry books of Kirkwood Supplies as at the month end 31 July 201Y. On listing the ledger account balances the bookkeeper found that debit balances did not agree with credit balances. The amount necessary to make the Trial Balance totals agree was added to the Trial Balance as a Suspense Account balance:

Kirkwood Supplies
Trial Balance as at 31 July 201Y

Ledger Account	DR £	CR £
Bank	2,500	
Cash	150	
Sales		16,700
Sales Returns	1,200	
Purchases	5,946	
Purchase Returns		877
Sales Ledger Control	20,415	
Purchase Ledger Control		9,827
VAT		1,060
Utilities	821	
Sundry Expenses	3,993	
Wages	3,600	
Capital		10,000
Suspense (Difference in books)		161
Totals	**38,625**	**38,625**

An investigation into the reason for the difference between the debit balances and credit balances as at 31 July 201Y revealed the following bookkeeping errors, and it also revealed a number of other errors not disclosed by the trial balance:

1. It has now been discovered that a purchase invoice for £2,600 plus VAT at the standard rate of 20% received from a credit supplier in July 201Y, has not been entered into the books.

2. A cheque for cash purchases of £980 was posted in the books as follows:

   Debit – Purchases £908
   Credit – Bank £908

3. A payment of £2,400 by cheque in July 201Y in respect of wages was posted in the books as follows:

   Debit – Sundry Expenses £2,400
   Credit – Bank £2,400

4. An error was made in balancing off the Purchases Account in the ledger as at 31 July 201Y, resulting in the balance on the account being understated by £1,000.

5. A payment of £129 by cheque in July 201Y in respect of sundry expenses was posted in the books as follows:

   Debit – Sundry Expenses £1,290
   Credit – Bank Account £129

REQUIRED:

You are required to complete the following tasks:

Task A – Prepare the Journal entries required to correct each of the bookkeeping errors listed above. Please note that some transactions will involve the suspense account and others won't. Date your Journal entries 31 July 201Y and provide a suitable narrative for each entry including the name of the type of error.

Task B – Enter the difference in books balance as at 31 July 201Y into the Suspense Account provided in the Answer Booklet.

Task C – Post the Journal entries above to relevant ledger accounts. Date your postings 31 July 201Y. The following accounts are provided in the Answer Booklet for the purpose of completing this task:

- Suspense
- Purchases
- VAT
- Purchase Ledger Control
- Wages
- Sundry Expenses
- Bank

Note – The Purchases, VAT, Purchase Ledger Control, Wages, Sundry Expenses and Bank accounts provided show the balances (as listed on the Trial Balance) brought forward (b/f) as at 31 July 201Y.

Task D – Close off the Suspense Account Balance as at 31 July 201Y thereby showing the elimination of the account balance. Balance off the Purchases, VAT, Purchase Ledger Control, Wages, Sundry Expenses and Bank Account as at 31 July 201Y bringing down the corrected account balances as at that date.

Task E – Redraft the Trial Balance of Kirkwood Supplies as at 31 July 201Y provided in the Answer Booklet. The redrafted Trial Balance should show the account balances having corrected the bookkeeping errors. Balances on ledger accounts, other than those on the Purchases, VAT, Purchase Ledger Control, Wages, Sundry Expenses and Bank Account, have already been entered on the Trial Balance for you.

Note: The following proformas are provided for your use in completing the above tasks:

- **Journal** (see **page 1** of your **Answer Booklet**)

- **General Leger (extract) – Suspense Account, Purchases, VAT, Purchase Ledger Control, Wages, Sundry Expenses and Bank** (see **page 2 and 3** of your **Answer Booklet**)

- **Trial Balance** (see **page 4** of your **Answer Booklet**)

Question One (Part B)

Use the Journal to Write Off a Bad Debt

You are presented with the Sales Ledger Control Account, Bad Debts Account and VAT Control Account in the General Ledger of Thorpe Supplies on page 5 of the Answer Booklet. The bookkeeper of the business maintains double entry records for the business which is registered for VAT.

Double entry takes place in the General Ledger with the personal accounts of trade debtors and trade creditors being kept in the subsidiary Sales Ledger and Purchase Ledger respectively as memorandum accounts.

As at 30 June 201Y the balance on the Sales Control Account as per the General Ledger of Thorpe Supplies was £13,410. There was a balance of £1,540 on the Bad Debts Account as at 30 June 201Y relating to bad debts already written off in the year, and the VAT Control Account as at 30 June 201Y carried a balance of £3,570 (Credit).

A review of trade debtors as at 30 June 201Y resulted in the credit controller advising that the balance on the account of a trade debtor (ARF Craft Supplies) should be written off as a bad debt. The invoice relates to goods invoiced over nine months ago, but the business had recently gone into liquidation and it was thought very unlikely that any of the balance on their account would be recovered. The balance on the account of ARF Craft Supplies was £780.

REQUIRED:

You are required to complete the following tasks:

Task A – Prepare the Journal entry to write off the balance on the account of ARF Craft Supplies as a bad debt and claim the VAT bad debt relief. Date your Journal entry 30 June 201Y and provide a suitable narrative.

Task B – Post the entry from the Journal prepared in Task A above to the Sales Ledger Control Account, Bad Debts Account and VAT Control Account in the General Ledger and into the account of ARF Craft Supplies in the Sales Ledger. You are not required to balance off any of the ledger accounts having made the postings from the Journal

Note: The following proformas are provided for your use in completing the above tasks:

- **Journal** (see **page 5** of your **Answer Booklet**)

- **General Ledger (extract) – Sales Ledger Control Account , Bad Debts Account and VAT Control Account** (see **page 5** of your **Answer Booklet**)

- **Sales Ledger (extract) – ARF Craft Supplies** (see **page 5** of your **Answer Booklet**)

Question One (Part C)

Use the Journal to Account for Wages, Salaries and Employer On-Costs

All employees of Standford Confectionery are paid monthly. They are paid on the last day of each month via the BACS direct credit system.

The following accounts are kept in the ledger of Standford Confectionery for the purpose of accounting for wages and salaries

- Wages and Salaries Control Account

- PAYE / NIC Creditor Account

- Wages, Salaries and Contributions (Expense) Account

The payroll figures extracted from the Payroll Analysis sheet are as follows:

	£
Net pay	36,700.00
PAYE deductions	8,991.68
NIC deductions (employee)	6,239.24
NIC contributions (employer)	6,862.56

REQUIRED:

You are required to complete the following task:

Task A – Complete the following Journal entries provided on page 6 of the Answer Booklet and account for wages salaries and employment costs on 30 June (month 3) of the current tax year (201Y/201Z). You will need to use the above payroll figures extracted from the Payroll Analysis sheet to prepare journals for the following:

Journal 1) Payment of net pay from the business Bank Account

Journal 2) Employee PAYE income tax deductions

Journal 3) Employee NIC deductions

Journal 4) Employer NIC deductions

Journal 5) Transfer of total employment costs for 30 June 201Y (month 3) from the Wages and Salaries Control Account to the Wages, Salaries and Contributions (Expense) Account.

Please note that for each journal, one entry has the account name already entered into the journal as well as the narrative. You must enter the figures and the opposite general ledger accounts.

Task B – Post the journal entries from Task A into the general ledger accounts on page 7 of your answer booklet.

Task C – Close off the Wages and Salaries Control Account as at 30 June 201Y, and balance off the PAYE /NIC Creditor Account as at 30 June 201Y bringing down the account balance at that date. You are **not** required to balance off and the Wages, Salaries and Contributions (Expense) Account, this account can be left 'open'

Note: The following proforma is provided for your use in completing the above tasks:

- **Journal** (see **page 6** of your **Answer Booklet**)

- **General Ledger Accounts** - (see **page 7** of your **Answer Booklet**)

IAB Level 2 question paper

Maintaining Control Accounts

Question Two

The Vale Car Showroom is registered for VAT, a double entry bookkeeping system is maintained on behalf of the business.

The personal accounts of customers and suppliers are kept as memorandum accounts in the subsidiary Sales Ledger and Purchase Ledger respectively. A Sales Ledger Control Account and Purchase Ledger Control Account are kept in the General Ledger as part of the double entry bookkeeping system. At the end of each week the balances from the two control accounts are reconciled with the balances on the personal accounts of customers and suppliers from the Sales Ledger and Purchase Ledger. A VAT Control Account is also kept in the General Ledger.

Transactions are posted to the Control Accounts from totals extracted from the books of Prime Entry. The books of Prime Entry consist of four Day Books, the Cash Book and the Journal.

Transactions for the week ended 24 August 201Y have been posted to the customer and supplier personal accounts in the subsidiary Sales Ledger and Purchase Ledger and the personal accounts have been balanced off as at 24 August 201Y.

On 31 August 201Y, the total debtors from the Sales Ledger was £61,505 and the total creditors from the Purchase Ledger was £35,300.

Totals from the Cash Book have already been posted to the Sales Ledger Control Account, Purchase Ledger Control Account and VAT Control Account in the General Ledger.

Please find below extracts of information from the accounts of The Vale Car Showroom which relate to the Sales Ledger Control Account and the Purchase Ledger Control Account:

	£
Balance per Purchase Ledger Control Account as at 24 August 201Y	45,124
Balance per Sales Ledger Control Account as at 24 August 201Y	67,895
Sales Day Book – total at 31 August 201Y	28,200
Sales Returns Day Book – total at 31 August 201Y	2,400
Purchase Day Book – total at 31 August 201Y	7,890
Purchase Returns Day Book – total at 31 August 201Y	564

Please find below extracts of information from the accounts of The Vale Car Showroom which relate to the VAT Control Account:

	£
Balance per VAT Control Account as at 1 August 201Y	6,456 (CR)
VAT on Sales - total at 31 August 201Y	4,700
VAT on Sales Returns - total at 31 August 201Y	400
VAT on Purchases – total at 31 August 201Y	1,315
VAT on Purchase Returns – total at 31 August 201Y	94

REQUIRED:

You are required to complete the following tasks:

Task A – Make postings of relevant totals from extracts of information from page 7 of this question paper, as at 31 August 201Y, to the Sales Ledger Control Account and Purchase Ledger Control Account in the General Ledger provided.

Task B - Make postings of relevant totals from extracts of information from page 7 of this question paper, as at 31 August 201Y, to the VAT Control Account in the General Ledger provided.

Task C – Balance off each of the **three** Control Accounts in the General Ledger, as at 31 August 201Y, bringing down the account balances as at 1 September 201Y.

Task D – Prepare a reconciliation of the balances from the Sales Ledger Control Account and Purchase Ledger Control Account as at 31 August 201Y, with the balances from the personal accounts of customers and suppliers from the subsidiary Sales Ledger and Purchase Ledger as at 31 August 201Y.

Note: The following proformas are provided for your use in completing the above tasks:

- **Sales Ledger and Purchase Ledger Control Accounts** (see **page 8** of your **Answer Booklet**)

- **Value Added Tax (VAT) Control Account** (see **page 8** of your **Answer Booklet**)

- **Forms for the reconciliation of the personal account balances to the control account balances** (see **page 9** of your **Answer Booklet**)

Processing Ledger Transactions and Extracting a Trial Balance

Question Three

Rangethorpe Furniture Showroom is a local business owned by Chris Chapman, the business is registered for VAT.

The books of account of the business are kept on a double entry basis. A General Ledger and Cash Book are maintained as part of the double entry bookkeeping system.

The personal accounts of trade debtors and trade creditors are kept as memorandum accounts in the subsidiary Sales Ledger and subsidiary Purchase Ledger respectively. Sales Ledger and Purchase Ledger Control Accounts are kept within the General ledger.

At the end of each week of trading a Trial Balance is prepared for the purpose of checking the arithmetic accuracy of the double entry records. You are presented below with a list of account balances extracted from the General Ledger and the Petty Cash Book as at the week ended 31 July 201Y:

Account Name	Account Balance (£)
Bank (DR balance)	39,160
Cash	250
Sales (balance at 24 July 201Y)	175,918
Sales Returns (balance at 24 July 201Y)	15,161
Sales Ledger Control (balance at 24 July 201Y)	101,946
Purchases (balance at 24 July 201Y)	23,672
Purchase Returns (balance at 24 July 201Y)	4,890
Purchase Ledger Control (balance at 24 July 201Y)	35,607
Wages (balance at 24 July 201Y)	61,770
Capital	62,000
VAT (balance at 24 July 201Y)	13,600
Sundry Expenses (balance at 24 July 201Y)	2,800
Office Equipment	22,626
Rent Received	37,870

You are presented on page 10 of this question booklet with the Cash Book Payments (Summary showing total of Analysis columns) for the week ended 31 July 201Y. The cash book forms part of the double entry book keeping system and therefore there are no transactions required to the bank account or cash account:

Rangethorpe Furniture Showroom – Cash Book Payments (Summary showing total of Analysis columns) for the week ended 31 July 201Y

Date 201Y	Details	Cash	Bank	PL Control	VAT	Purchases	Wages	Sundry Expenses
31 July	Totals	420	61,780	15,900	200	680	45,000	420

Rangethorpe Furniture Showroom – Totals Extracted from the Day Books as at 31 July 201Y

Day Book	Transaction Details	Balance £
Sales Day Book		
	Net Sales	23,560
	VAT on Sales	4,712
	Invoice Totals	**28,272**
Purchase Day Book		
	Net Purchases	10,660
	VAT on Purchases	2,132
	Invoice Totals	**12,792**
Purchase Returns Day Book		
	Net Purchases Returns	4,210
	VAT on Purchases Returns	842
	Credit Note Totals	**5,052**
Sales Returns Day Book		
	Net Sales Returns	1,040
	VAT on Sales Returns	208
	Credit Note Totals	**1,248**

IAB Level 2 question paper

You are presented in the Answer Booklet (pages 10, 11 and 12) with an extract of the General Ledger of the business, showing the following ledger account balances brought forward as at 24 July 201Y:

- Sales
- Sales Returns
- Sales Ledger Control
- Purchases
- Purchase Returns
- Purchase Ledger Control
- Wages
- VAT
- Sundry Expenses

REQUIRED:

You are required to finalise the posting of transactions to the double entry system, and check the arithmetic accuracy of the double entry records, by completing the following tasks:

Task A – Make postings of totals, as at 31 July 201Y, from the Sales Day Book to the following accounts in the General Ledger – Sales Ledger Control Account, Sales Account and VAT Control Account

Task B – Make postings of totals, as at 31 July 201Y, from the Sales Returns Day Book to the following Accounts in the General Ledger – Sales Ledger Control Account, Sales Returns Account and VAT Control Account.

Task C – Make postings of totals, as at 31 July 201Y, from the Purchase Day Book to the following Accounts in the General Ledger – Purchase Ledger Control Account, Purchases Account and VAT Control Account.

Task D – Make postings of totals, as at 31 July 201Y, from the Purchase Returns Day Book to the following accounts in the General Ledger – Purchase Ledger Control Account, Purchase Returns Account and VAT Control Account.

Task E – Make postings of totals, as at 31 July 201Y from the Cash Book Payments side to the following Accounts in the General Ledger – Purchase Ledger Control Account, VAT Account, Purchases Account, Wages Account and Sundry Expenses Account.

Task F – Balance off **all** the accounts within the General Ledger extract to which you have made postings from the Day Books as at 31 July 201Y bringing down the account balances as at that date.

Task G – Prepare the Trial Balance provided on page 13 of the Answer Booklet thereby proving the arithmetic accuracy of the double entry records as at 31 July 201Y. To complete this task you will need to use the account balances from the ledger accounts to which you made postings in Tasks A,B,C,D,E and F above. You will also need to use those balances which were not in need of updating at 31 July 201Y from the list of balances given on page 9 of this Question Booklet.

Note: The following proformas are provided for your use in completing the above tasks:

- **General Ledger Accounts** (see **pages 10, 11** and **12** of your **Answer Booklet**)

- **Trial Balance** (see **page 13** of your **Answer Booklet**)

IAB Level 2 answer booklet

IAB
Qualifications for business

June 2014 Examination
Answer Booklet

208   Exam ID
2050 Exam ID

IAB Student No: ....

IAB Candidate No: ....

Name of Exam Centre:..

Date of Exam:..

Answer Booklet for the following Qualifications:

200:   Level 2 Certificate in Bookkeeping QCF: 50090537
210:   Level 2 Award in Manual Bookkeeping QCF: 50092595
230:   Level 2 Certificate in Applied Bookkeeping QCF: 50092625
2000: Level 2 Certificate in Bookkeeping QCF: 60107303
2030: Level 2 Award in Manual Bookkeeping QCF: 60104806

Time Allowed 2 Hours 30 Minutes
Paper No:0039

International Association of Book-keepers, Suite 5, 20 Churchill Square, Kings Hill, West Malling, Kent ME19 4YU
Tel: 01732 897750, Fax: 01732 897751, email:education@iab.org.uk Website: www.iab.org.uk

Maintaining the Journal

Question One (Part A)

Use the Journal to Correct Errors. Eliminate a Suspense Account Balance and Redraft a Trial balance

For Use in Answering Question One (Part A): Task A

Kirkwood Supplies - Journal

201Y	Details	DR £	CR £
	Correction of error (1)		
	Correction of error (2)		
	Correction of error (3)		
	Correction of error (4)		
	Correction of error (5)		

For Use in Answering Question One (Part A): Tasks B, C and D

Kirkwood Supplies - General Ledger (extract)

Suspense

DR			CR	
201Y	Details	£	201Y	Details	£

Purchases

DR			CR	
201Y	Details	£	201Y	Details	£
31 Jul	Balance b/f	5,946			

VAT

DR			CR	
201Y	Details	£	201Y	Details	£
			31 Jul	Balance b/f	1,060

For Use in Answering Question One (Part A): Tasks B, C and D

Kirkwood Supplies - General Ledger (extract)

DR		Purchase Ledger Control			CR
201Y	**Details**	**£**	**201Y**	**Details**	**£**
			31 Jul	Balance b/f	9,827

DR		Wages			CR
201Y	**Details**	**£**	**201Y**	**Details**	**£**
31 Jul	Balance b/f	3,600			

DR		Sundry Expenses			CR
201Y	**Details**	**£**	**201Y**	**Details**	**£**
31 Jul	Balance b/f	3,993			

DR		Bank			CR
201Y	**Details**	**£**	**201Y**	**Details**	**£**
31 Jul	Balance b/f	2,500			

IAB Level 2 answer booklet

For Use in Answering Question One (Part A): Task E

Kirkwood Supplies
(Redrafted) Trial Balance as at 31 July 201Y

Ledger Account	DR £	CR £
Bank		
Cash	150	
Sales		16,700
Sales Returns	1,200	
Purchases		
Purchase Returns		877
Sales Ledger Control	20,415	
Purchase Ledger Control		
VAT		
Utilities	821	
Sundry Expenses		
Wages		
Capital		10,000
Totals		

IAB Level 2 answer booklet

Use the Journal to Write Off a Bad Debt

For Use in Answering Question One (Part B): Task A

Thorpe Supplies — Journal

201Y	Details	DR £	CR £

For Use in Answering Question One (Part B): Task B

Thorpe Supplies - General Ledger (extract)

DR			Sales Ledger Control		CR
201Y	Details	£	201Y	Details	£
30 Jun	Balance b/f	13,410			

DR			Bad Debts		CR
201Y	Details	£	201Y	Details	£
30 Jun	Balance b/f	1,540			

DR			Value Added Tax (VAT) Control		CR
201Y	Details	£	201Y	Details	£
			30 Jun	Balance b/f	3,570

Thorpe Supplies - Sales Ledger (extract)

DR			ARF Craft Supplies		CR
201Y	Details	£	201Y	Details	£
30 Jun	Balance b/f	780			

Use the Journal to Account for Wages, Salaries and Employer On-Costs

For Use in Answering Question One (Part C): Task A

Standford Confectionery - Journal

201Y	Details	DR £	CR £
30 June	Wages and Salaries Control		
	Net pay in June 201Y		
30 June	Wages and Salaries Control		
	Employee PAYE deductions in June 201Y		
30 June	Wages and Salaries Control		
	Employee NIC deductions in June 201Y		
30 June	Wages and Salaries Control		
	Employer NIC contributions in June 201Y		
30 June	Wages, Salaries and Contribution		
	Transfer of costs of employment June 201Y from Wages and Salaries Control Account to Staff Wages and Contributions Account		

Use the Journal to Account for Wages, Salaries and Employer On-Costs

For Use in Answering Question One (Part C): Task A

General ledger (extract)

DR			Wages and Salaries Control			CR
201Y	Details	£	201Y	Details		£

DR			PAYE/NIC Creditor			CR
201Y	Details	£	201Y	Details		£
			1 June	Balance b/d		44,186.96

DR		Wages, Salaries and Contributions Expense			CR
201Y	Details	£	201Y	Details	£
1 June	Balance b/f	117,586.96			

Maintaining Control Accounts

For Use in Answering Question Two: Tasks A, B and C

The Vale Car Showroom – General Ledger (extract)

DR   **Sales Ledger Control**   **CR**

201Y	Details	£	201Y	Details	£
24 Aug	Balance b/d	67,895	31 Aug	Cash book - receipts	29,740
			31 Aug	Cash book - discounts	2,450

DR   **Purchase Ledger Control**   **CR**

201Y	Details	£	201Y	Details	£
31 Aug	Cash book - payments	15,470	24 Aug	Balance b/d	45,124
31 Aug	Cash book – discounts	1,680			

DR   **Value Added Tax (VAT) Control**   **CR**

201Y	Details	£	201Y	Details	£
31 Aug	Cash book – input tax	3,580	24 Aug	Balance b/d	6,456
			31 Aug	Cash book – output tax	9,450

For Use in Answering Question Two: Task D

The Vale Car Showroom – Reconciliation of Personal Account Balances to Control Account Balances as at 31 August 201Y

Reconciliation of Personal Account Balances per Sales Ledger as at 31 August 201Y to Sales Ledger Control Account Balance as at that Date

	£	DR/CR
Total debtors per Sales Ledger – 31 August 201Y		
Balance per Sales Ledger Control Account – 31 August 201Y		
Difference		

Reconciliation of Personal Account Balances per Purchase Ledger as at 31 August 201Y to Purchase Ledger Control Account Balance as at that Date

	£	DR/CR
Total creditors per Purchase Ledger – 31 August 201Y		
Balance per Purchase Ledger Control Account – 31 August 201Y		
Difference		

Processing Ledger Transactions and Extracting a Trial Balance

For Use in Answering Question 3 – Tasks A,B,C, D, E and F

Rangethorpe Furniture Showroom
General Ledger (extract)

DR				Sales			CR
201Y	**Details**		**£**	**201Y**	**Details**		**£**
				24 Jul	Balance b/f		175,918

DR				Sales Returns			CR
201Y	**Details**		**£**	**201Y**	**Details**		**£**
24 Jul	Balance b/f		15,161				

DR				Sales Ledger Control			CR
201Y	**Details**		**£**	**201Y**	**Details**		**£**
24 Jul	Balance b/f		101,946				

For Use in Answering Question 3 – Tasks A,B,C, D, E and F Continued

Rangethorpe Furniture Showroom
General Ledger (extract)

DR			Purchases			CR
201Y	**Details**	**£**	**201Y**	**Details**		**£**
24 Jul	Balance b/f	23,672				

DR			Purchase Returns			CR
201Y	**Details**	**£**	**201Y**	**Details**		**£**
			24 Jul	Balance b/f		4,890

DR			Purchase Ledger Control			CR
201Y	**Details**	**£**	**201Y**	**Details**		**£**
			24 Jul	Balance b/f		35,607

388

For Use in Answering Question 3 – Tasks A,B,C, D, E and F Continued

Rangethorpe Furniture Showroom
General Ledger (extract)

DR			Wages			CR
201Y	**Details**	**£**	**201Y**	**Details**		**£**
24 Jul	Balance b/f	61,770				

DR			VAT Control			CR
201Y	**Details**	**£**	**201Y**	**Details**		**£**
			24 Jul	Balance b/f		13,600

DR			Sundry Expenses			CR
201Y	**Details**	**£**	**201Y**	**Details**		**£**
24 Jul	Balance b/f	2,800				

389

For Use in Answering Question Three: Task G

Rangethorpe Furniture Showroom
Trial Balance as at 31 July 201Y

Ledger Account	DR £	CR £
Bank		
Cash		
Sales		
Sales Returns		
Sales Ledger Control		
Purchases		
Purchase Returns		
Purchase Ledger Control		
Wages		
Capital		
VAT		
Sundry Expenses		
Office Equipment		
Rent Received		
Totals		

IAB Level 2 answer booklet

THIS PAGE IS INTENTIONALLY LEFT BLANK FOR NOTES/WORKINGS

June 2014 Examination
Model Answers

208 Exam ID
2050 Exam ID

Model Answer Booklet for the following Qualifications:

200: Level 2 Certificate in Bookkeeping QCF: 50090537
210: Level 2 Award in Manual Bookkeeping QCF: 50092595
230: Level 2 Certificate in Applied Bookkeeping QCF: 50092625
2000: Level 2 Certificate in Bookkeeping QCF: 60107303
2030: Level 2 Award in Manual Bookkeeping QCF: 60104806

Time Allowed 2 Hours 30 Minutes
Paper No: 0039

IAB ID	Units covered	Possible marks
206	Maintaining the Journal – T6008772	40
2005	Maintaining the Journal: H5051123	
205	Maintaining Control Accounts – K6008770	20
2004	Maintaining Control Accounts: K5051124	
207	Processing Ledger Transactions and Extracting a Trial Balance – F6008760	40
2006	Processing Ledger Transactions and Extracting a Trial Balance: M5051125	

International Association of Book-keepers, Suite 5, 20 Churchill Square, Kings Hill, West Malling, Kent ME19 4YU
Tel: 01732 897750, Fax: 01732 897751, email:education@iab.org.uk Website: www.iab.org.uk

Answers to Question One (Part A): Task A

Kirkwood Supplies - Journal

201Y	Details	DR £	CR £
	Correction of error (1)		
31 Jul	Purchases ½	2,600	½
	VAT ½	520	½
	Purchase Ledger Control ½	½	3,120
	Correction of error of omission. ¼		
	Purchase Invoice omitted from books. ¼		
	Correction of error (2)		
31 Jul	Bank ¼	908	¼
	Purchases ¼	¼	908
	Purchases ¼	980	¼
	Bank ¼	¼	980
	<u>OR</u>		
	Purchases ½	72	½
	Bank ½	½	72
	Correction of transposition error. A cheque for purchases was posted as the incorrect amount. ½		
	Correction of error (3)		
31 Jul	Wages ½	2,400	½
	Sundry Expenses ½	½	2,400
	Correction of error of commission. ¼		
	Wages incorrectly posted to Sundry Expenses. ¼		
	Correction of error (4)		
31 Jul	Purchases ½	1,000	½
	Suspense ½	½	1,000
	Correction of error. Balance on purchases account understated by £1,000. ½		
	Correction of error (5)		
31 Jul	Suspense ¼	1,290	¼
	Sundry Expenses ¼	¼	1,290
	Sundry Expenses ¼	129	¼
	Suspense ¼	¼	129
	<u>OR</u>		
	Suspense ½	1,161	½
	Sundry Expenses ½	½	1,161
	Correction of error of original entry. ¼ Wrong amount posted to the sundry expenses account. ¼		

13.5 Marks This Page

NB: Also except journal number for the details, I have put these in brackets on pages 2 and 3. Own figure rule - If students have been penalised on page 1 for an incorrect entry into the journal but they account for it correctly in the ledgers then award the marks on page 2 and 3.

IAB Level 2 model answers

Answers to Question One (Part A): Tasks B, C and D

Kirkwood Supplies - General Ledger (extract)

DR			Suspense			CR
201Y	**Details**	**£**	**201Y**	**Details**		**£**
31 Jul	Sundry Expenses (J5) ¼	1,290	31 Jul	Difference in books ¼		161
			31 Jul	Purchases (J4) ¼		1,000
			31 Jul	Sundry Expenses (J5)		129
	¼	**1,290**			¼	**1,290**

Alternative answer for journal 5 in the suspense account

DR			Suspense			CR
201Y	**Details**	**£**	**201Y**	**Details**		**£**
31 Jul	Sundry Expenses (J5) ¼	1,161	31 Jul	Difference in books ¼		161
			31 Jul	Purchases (J4) ¼		1,000
	¼	**1,161**			¼	**1,161**

DR			Purchases			CR
201Y	**Details**	**£**	**201Y**	**Details**		**£**
31 Jul	Balance b/f	5,946	31 Jul	Bank (J2)		908
31 Jul	PLCA (J1) ¼	2,600	31 Jul	Balance c/d ¼		9,618
31 Jul	Bank (J2) ¼	980				
31 Jul	Suspense (J4) ¼	1,000				
	¼	**10,526**			¼	**10,526**
31 Jul	Balance b/d ¼	9,618				

Alternative answer for journal 2 in the purchases account

DR			Purchases			CR
201Y	**Details**	**£**	**201Y**	**Details**		**£**
31 Jul	Balance b/f	5,946	31 Jul	Balance c/d ¼		9,618
31 Jul	PL Control (J1) ¼	2,600				
31 Jul	Bank (J2) ¼	72				
31 Jul	Suspense (J4) ¼	1,000				
	¼	**9,618**			¼	**9,618**
31 Jul	Balance b/d ¼	9,618				

DR			VAT			CR
201Y	**Details**	**£**	**201Y**	**Details**		**£**
31 Jul	PL Control (J1) ¼	520	31 Jul	Balance b/f		1,060
31 Jul	Balance c/d ¼	540				
	¼	**1,060**			¼	**1,060**
			31 Jul	Balance b/d ¼		540

Marks awarded for figures not details but details need to be appropriate

4.25 Marks This Page

For Use in Answering Question One (Part A): Tasks B, C and D

Kirkwood Supplies - General Ledger (extract)

Purchase Ledger Control

DR				CR	
201Y	Details	£	201Y	Details	£
31 Jul	Balance c/d ¼	12,947	31 Jul	Balance b/f	9,827
			31 Jul	Purchases (J1) ¼	3,120
	¼	**12,947**		¼	**12,947**
			31 Jul	Balance b/d ¼	12,947

Wages

DR				CR	
201Y	Details	£	201Y	Details	£
31 Jul	Balance b/f	3,600	31 Jul	Balance c/d ¼	6,000
31 Jul	Sundry Expenses (J3) ¼	2,400			
	¼	**6,000**		¼	**6,000**
31 Jul	Balance b/d ¼	6,000			

Sundry Expenses

DR				CR	
201Y	Details	£	201Y	Details	£
31 Jul	Balance b/f	3,993	31 Jul	Wages (J3) ¼	2,400
31 Jul	Suspense (J5)	129	31 Jul	Suspense (J5) ¼	1,290
			31 Jul	Balance c/d ¼	432
	¼	**4,122**		¼	**4,122**
31 Jul	Balance b/d ¼	432			

Alternative answer for journal 5 in the sundry expense account

Sundry Expenses

DR				CR	
201Y	Details	£	201Y	Details	£
31 Jul	Balance b/f	3,993	31 Jul	Wages (J3) ¼	2,400
			31 Jul	Suspense (J5) ¼	1,161
			31 Jul	Balance c/d ¼	432
	¼	**3,993**		¼	**3,993**
31 Jul	Balance b/d ¼	432			

Bank entry of £72 credit also acceptable

Bank

DR				CR	
201Y	Details	£	201Y	Details	£
31 Jul	Balance b/f	2,500	31 Jul	Purchases (J2) ¼	980
31 Jul	Purchases (J2) ¼	908	31 Jul	Balance c/d ¼	2,428
	¼	**3,408**		¼	**3,408**
31 Jul	Balance b/d ¼	2,428			

5.5 Marks This Page

Answers to Question One (Part A): Task E

Kirkwood Supplies

(Redrafted) Trial Balance as at 31 July 201Y

Ledger Account	DR £		CR £	
Bank	2,428	½		
Cash	150			
Sales			16,700	
Sales Returns	1,200			
Purchases	9,618	½		
Purchase Returns			877	
Sales Ledger Control	20,415			
Purchase Ledger Control		½	12,947	
VAT		½	540	
Utilities	821			
Sundry Expenses	432	½		
Wages	6,000	½		
Capital			10,000	
Totals	**41,064**		**41,064**	
	¾		¾	

NB: Own figure rule - If students have been penalised on page 2 or 3 for an incorrect entry into the journal or ledger but they transfer it correctly to the trial balance then award the mark.

4.5 Marks This Page

Answers to Question One (Part B): Task A

Thorpe Supplies – Journal

201Y	Details	DR £		CR £
30 Jun	Bad Debt ¼	650	¼	
	VAT ¼	130	¼	
	Sales Ledger Control Account ¼		¼	780
	Balance on Customer Account (ARF Craft Supplies) written off as a bad debt as the customer has gone bankrupt. VAT Bad debt relief claimed ¼			

Answers to Question One (Part B): Task B

Thorpe Supplies - General Ledger (extract)

DR			Sales Ledger Control			CR
201Y	**Details**	**£**	**201Y**	**Details**	**£**	
30 Jun	Balance b/f	13,410	30 Jun	Bad Debt ¼	780	

DR			Bad Debts			CR
201Y	**Details**	**£**	**201Y**	**Details**	**£**	
30 Jun	Balance b/f	1,540				
30 Jun	ARF Craft Supplies ¼	650				

DR			Value Added Tax (VAT) Control			CR
201Y	**Details**	**£**	**201Y**	**Details**	**£**	
30 Jun	Bad Debt – ARF Craft Supplies ¼	130	30 Jun	Balance b/f	3,570	

Thorpe Supplies - Sales Ledger (extract)

DR			ARF Craft Supplies			CR
201Y	**Details**	**£**	**201Y**	**Details**	**£**	
30 Jun	Balance b/f	780	30 Jun	Bad Debt ¼	780	

Marks awarded for figures not details but details need to be appropriate

NB: Own figure rule - If students have been penalised for an incorrect entry into the journal but they account for it correctly in the ledgers then award the mark.

2.75 Marks This Page

Answers to Question One (Part C): Task A

Standford Confectionery - Journal

201Y	Details	DR £	CR £
30 June	Wages and Salaries Control Bank ½ Net pay in June 201Y	36,700.00 ¼	36,700.00 ¼
30 June	Wages and Salaries Control PAYE / NIC Creditor ½ Employee PAYE deductions in June 201Y	8,991.68 ¼	8,991.68 ¼
30 June	Wages and Salaries Control PAYE / NIC Creditor ½ Employee NIC deductions in June 201Y	6,239.24 ¼	6,239.24 ¼
30 June	Wages and Salaries Control PAYE / NIC Creditor ½ Employer NIC contributions in June 201Y	6,862.56 ¼	6,862.56 ¼
30 June	Wages, Salaries and Contributions Wages and Salaries Control ½ Transfer of costs of employment June 201Y from Wages and Salaries Control Account to Staff Wages and Contributions Account	58,793.48 ¼	58,793.48 ¼

5 Marks This Page

Answers to Question One (Part C): Task B

General ledger (extract)

DR				Wages and Salaries Control		CR
201Y	**Details**		**£**	**201Y**	**Details**	**£**
30 June	Bank ¼		36,700.00	30 June	Wages, Salaries &	58,793.48
30 June	PAYE ¼		8,991.68		Contributions ½	
30 June	NIC (Employee) ¼		6,239.24			
30 June	NIC (Employer) ¼		6,862.56			
		¼	**58,793.48**			¼ **58,793.48**

DR			PAYE/NIC Creditor			CR
201Y	**Details**		**£**	**201Y**	**Details**	**£**
30 June	Balance c/d ¼		66,280.44	1 June	Balance b/d	44,186.96
				30 June	PAYE ¼	8,991.68
				30 June	NIC (Employee) ¼	6,239.24
				30 June	NIC (Employer) ¼	6,862.56
		¼	**66,280.44**			¼ **66,280.44**
				30 June	Balance b/d ½	66,280.44

DR		Wages, Salaries and Contributions Expense			CR
201Y	**Details**	**£**	**201Y**	**Details**	**£**
30 June	Balance b/d	117,586.96			
30 June	Wages & Salaries Control	58,793.48			
	½				

NB: Do not allow own figure rule here

4.5 Marks This Page

Total Marks this Question = 40

Maintaining Control Accounts

Answers to Question Two: Tasks A, B and C

The Vale Car Showroom – General Ledger (extract)

Sales Ledger Control

DR 201Y	Details		£	CR 201Y	Details		£
24 Aug	Balance b/d		67,895	31 Aug	Cash book - receipts		29,740
31 Aug	Sales Day Book	1	28,200	31 Aug	Cash book - discounts		2,450
				31 Aug	Sales Returns Day Book	1	2,400
				31 Aug	Balance c/d	½	61,505
		½	**96,095**			½	**96,095**
1 Sep	Balance b/d	1	61,505				

Purchase Ledger Control

DR 201Y	Details		£	CR 201Y	Details		£
31 Aug	Cash book - payments		15,470	24 Aug	Balance b/d		45,124
31 Aug	Cash book – discounts		1,680	31 Aug	Purchases Day Book	1	7,890
31 Aug	Purchase Returns Day Book	1	564				
31 Aug	Balance c/d	½	35,300				
		½	**53,014**			½	**53,014**
				1 Sep	Balance b/d	1	35,300

Value Added Tax (VAT) Control

DR 201Y	Details	£	CR 201Y	Details	£
31 Aug	Cash book – input tax	3,580	24 Aug	Balance b/d	6,456
31 Aug	Purchases Day Book ½	1,315	31 Aug	Cash book – output tax	9,450
31 Aug	Sales Returns Day Book ½	400	31 Aug	Sales Day Book ½	4,700
31 Aug	Balance c/d ½	15,405	31 Aug	Purchase Returns Day Book ½	94
	½	**20,700**		½	**20,700**
			1 Sep	Balance b/d 1	15,405

Marks awarded for figures not details but details need to be appropriate

13.5 Marks This Page

Answers to Question Two: Task D

The Vale Car Showroom – Reconciliation of Personal Account Balances to Control Account Balances as at 31 August 201Y

Reconciliation of Personal Account Balances per Sales Ledger as at 31 August 201Y to Sales Ledger Control Account Balance as at that Date

	£	DR/CR
Total debtors per Sales Ledger – 31 August 201Y	61,505 ½	DR ½
Balance per Sales Ledger Control Account – 31 August 201Y	61,505 ½	DR 1
Difference	NIL ½	

Reconciliation of Personal Account Balances per Purchase Ledger as at 31 August 201Y to Purchase Ledger Control Account Balance as at that Date

	£	DR/CR
Total creditors per Purchase Ledger – 31 August 201Y	35,300 ½	CR 1
Balance per Purchase Ledger Control Account – 31 August 201Y	35,300 ½	CR 1
Difference	NIL ½	

NB: Do not allow own figure rule on this question.

6.5 Marks This Page

Total Marks this Question = 20

Processing Ledger Transactions and Extracting a Trial Balance

Answers to Question 3 – Tasks A,B,C, D, E and F

Rangethorpe Furniture Showroom

General Ledger (extract)

DR				Sales					CR
201Y	Details			£	201Y	Details			£
31 Jul	Balance c/d	½		199,478	24 Jul	Balance b/f			175,918
					31 Jul	Sales Day Book	½		23,560
			½	**199,478**				½	**199,478**
					31 Jul	Balance b/d	½		199,478

DR				Sales Returns					CR
201Y	Details			£	201Y	Details			£
24 Jul	Balance b/f			15,161	31 Jul	Balance c/d	½		16,201
31 Jul	Sales Returns Day Book ½			1,040					
			½	**16,201**				½	**16,201**
31 Jul	Balance b/d	1		16,201					

DR				Sales Ledger Control					CR
201Y	Details			£	201Y	Details			£
24 Jul	Balance b/f			101,946	31 Jul	Sales Returns Day Book ½			1,248
31 Jul	Sales Day Book ½			28,272					
					31 Jul	Balance c/d	½		128,970
			½	**130,218**				½	**130,218**
31 Jul	Balance b/d 1			128,970					

Marks awarded for figures not details but details need to be appropriate

NB: Own figure rule - If students have been penalised for an incorrect balance c/d you should still award marks for the balance b/d providing it is on the correct side of the account.

9 Marks This Page

For Use in Answering Question 3 – Tasks A,B,C, D, E and F Continued

Rangethorpe Furniture Showroom
General Ledger (extract)

DR			Purchases				CR
201Y	**Details**		**£**	**201Y**	**Details**		**£**
24 Jul	Balance b/f		23,672	31 Jul	Balance c/d ½		35,012
31 Jul	Purchase Day Book		½ 10,660				
31 Jul	Cash book - payments		½ 680				
		½	**35,012**			½	**35,012**
31 Jul	Balance b/d 1		35,012				

DR			Purchase Returns				CR
201Y	**Details**		**£**	**201Y**	**Details**		**£**
31 Jul	Balance c/d	½	9,100	24 Jul	Balance b/f		4,890
				31 Jul	Purchase Returns Day Book ½		4,210
		½	**9,100**			½	**9,100**
				31 Jul	Balance b/d ½		9,100

DR			Purchase Ledger Control				CR
201Y	**Details**		**£**	**201Y**	**Details**		**£**
31 Jul	Purchase Returns Day Book		½ 5,052	24 Jul	Balance b/f		35,607
31 Jul	Cash Book Payments		15,900	31 Jul	Purchases Day Book ½		12,792
31 Jul	Balance c/d	½	27,447				
		½	**48,399**			½	**48,399**
				31 Jul	Balance b/d 1		27,447

Marks awarded for figures not details but details need to be appropriate

NB: Own figure rule – If students have been penalised for an incorrect balance c/d you should still award marks for the balance b/d providing it is on the correct side of the account.

9.5 Marks This Page

Answers to Question 3 – Tasks A,B,C, D, E and F Continued

Rangethorpe Furniture Showroom
General Ledger (extract)

Wages

DR				CR		
201Y	**Details**		**£**	**201Y**	**Details**	**£**
24 Jul	Balance b/f		61,770	31 Jul	Balance c/d ½	106,770
31 Jul	Cash Book Payments½		45,000			
		½	**106,770**		½	**106,770**
31 Jul	Balance b/d	1	106,770			

VAT Control

DR				CR		
201Y	**Details**		**£**	**201Y**	**Details**	**£**
31 Jul	Sales Returns Day Book	½	208	24 Jul	Balance b/f	13,600
31 Jul	Purchases Day Book ½		2,132	31 Jul	Sales Day Book ½	4,712
31 Jul	Cash Book Payments ½		200	31 Jul	Purchase Returns Day Book	½ 842
31 Jul	Balance c/d	½	16,614			
		½	**19,154**		½	**19,154**
				31 Jul	Balance b/d 1	16,614

Sundry Expenses

DR				CR		
201Y	**Details**		**£**	**201Y**	**Details**	**£**
24 Jul	Balance b /f		2,800	31 Jul	Balance c/d ½	3,220
31 Jul	Cash Book Payments½		420			
		½	**3,220**		½	**3,220**
31 Jul	Balance b/d	½	3,220			

Marks awarded for figures not details but details need to be appropriate

NB: Own figure rule – If students have been penalised for an incorrect balance c/d you should still award marks for the balance b/d providing it is on the correct side of the account.

10.5 Marks This Page

IAB Level 2 model answers

Answers to Question Three: Task G

Rangethorpe Furniture Showroom
Trial Balance as at 31 July 201Y

Ledger Account	DR £		CR £
Bank	39,460	½	
Cash	250	½	
Sales		½	199,478
Sales Returns	16,201	½	
Sales Ledger Control	128,970	½	
Purchases	35,012	½	
Purchase Returns		½	9,100
Purchase Ledger Control		½	27,447
Wages	106,770	½	
Capital		½	62,000
VAT		½	16,614
Sundry Expenses	3,220	½	
Office Equipment	22,626	½	
Rent Received		½	37,870
Totals	2 marks for correct TB total. ½ mark where o/f rule applied **352,509**		2 marks for correct TB total. ½ mark where o/f rule applied **352,509**

NB: Own figure rule - If students have been penalised on page 12, 13 or 14 for an incorrect balance c/d but they transfer the balance b/d correctly in the trial balance then award the mark.

11 Marks This Page

Total Marks this Question = 40

IAB Level 3 question paper I

June 2014 Examination
Question Paper

321 Exam ID

Question Paper for the following Qualifications:

300: Level 3 Certificate in Bookkeeping QCF: 50084793
320: Level 3 Certificate in Manual Bookkeeping QCF: 50092601
340: Level 3 Certificate in Applied Bookkeeping QCF: 50092765
3000: Level 3 Certificate in Bookkeeping QCF: 60107315
3030: Level 3 Diploma in Bookkeeping QCF: 60104843

Units:
309: Record transactions and make accounting adjustments: M6010732
308: Prepare financial statements for a not for profit organisation: D6010757

Time Allowed 3 Hours
Paper No: 0040

General Instructions

1. Enter your IAB Student Number, Candidate Number and Name of Examination Centre in the spaces provided on the front cover of your Answer Booklet
2. All Answers to be written in blue or black ink
3. All Questions and tasks within each section must be answered
4. Cross out errors neatly or use correcting fluid in moderation
5. Calculators are permitted
6. A blank page is provided in the Answer Booklet for workings if required
7. The Question Paper and Answer Booklet have information and data printed on both sides of the pages
8. Mobile phones are not permitted

International Association of Book-keepers, Suite 5, 20 Churchill Square, Kings Hill, West Malling, Kent ME19 4YU
Tel: 01732 897750, Fax: 01732 897751, email:education@iab.org.uk Website: www.iab.org.uk

SECTION A – RECORD TRANSACTIONS AND MAKE ACCOUNTING ADJUSTMENTS

INSTRUCTIONS

There are **THREE** questions in this section of the paper. You must complete **ALL TASKS** within the questions.

QUESTION ONE

RECONCILE TRADE DEBTOR and TRADE CREDITOR BALANCES

Double entry records are kept on behalf of Marton Engineering. Their General Ledger contains Sales Ledger and Purchase Ledger Control Accounts. The control accounts are within the double entry bookkeeping system, the personal accounts of trade debtors and trade creditors are kept in the subsidiary Sales Ledger and Purchase Ledger respectively as memorandum accounts.

As at 1 May 2014 the balance on the Purchase Ledger Control Account of Marton Engineering was £189,240.

You are provided with the following information at 31 May 2014:

	£
Total purchases per Purchase Day Book in May month 2014	99,560
Total purchase returns per Purchase Returns Day Book in May month 2014	4,200
Total payments to trade creditors per Cash Book in May month 2014	104,300
Total cash discounts received per Cash Book in May month 2014	1,540

Personal Account Balances of Trade Creditors in the Purchase Ledger at 31 May 2014
As at 31 May 2014 the personal accounts of trade creditors were balanced off and listed – the list shows that total of trade creditor balances in the Purchase Ledger at that date was £178,760.

1

REQUIRED

TASK A (1 Mark)
Post the balance brought forward at 1 May 2014 to the Purchase Ledger Control Account

TASK B (4 Marks)
Make postings at 31 May 2014 to the Purchase Ledger Control Account from the list of May 2014 month transactions provided above.

TASK C (4 Marks)
Balance off the Purchase Ledger Control Account as at 31 May 2014 bringing down the account balance at that date.

TASK D (2 Marks)
Reconcile the balance on the Purchase Ledger Control Account as at 31 May 2014 with the balance of total trade creditors in the Purchase Ledger at that date.

Note: The following proformas are provided for your use in completing the above tasks:

- General Ledger (Extract): Purchase Ledger Control Account – see **page 1** of your **answer booklet**.

- Schedule reconciling the Purchase Ledger Control Account balance to total trade creditors in the Purchase Ledger at 31 May 2014 – see **page 1** of your **answer booklet**.

2

Part B

One of your colleagues has prepared the Sales Ledger Control Account of Marton Engineering for the month ended 31 May 2014, and has also prepared the following reconciliation of the Sales Ledger Control Account balance to the total of trade debtors in the Sales Ledger at that date:

Schedule Reconciling Sales Ledger Control Account Balance to Total Trade Debtors in the Sales Ledger at 31 May 2014		
	£	
Balance on the Sales Ledger Control Account at 31 May 2014	148,960	(DR)
Total trade debtor balance in the Sales Ledger at 31 May 2014	152,220	(DR)
Difference	3,260	

An investigation into the reason for the difference between the balance on the Sales Ledger Control Account and the total of trade debtors in the Sales Ledger at 31 May 2014 revealed the following:

(i) An invoice for £1,200 issued to a trade debtor in May month 2014 had been posted to the debtor personal account as £2,100.

(ii) A bad debt of £2,400 written off in May month 2014 had not been posted to the debtor personal account in the subsidiary Sales Ledger, as a result the debtor account balance was on the list of balances extracted from the Sales Ledger as at 31 May 2014

(iii) A cheque for £1,800 received from a trade debtor in May month 2014 had been entered in the Cash Book but had not been posted to the debtor personal account in the subsidiary Sales Ledger

(iv) The balance of £1,840 on the personal account of a trade debtor had not been included on the list of trade debtors extracted from the subsidiary Sales Ledger as at 31 May 2014.

3

REQUIRED

TASK E (4 Marks)

Complete the schedule (provided in your **answer booklet**) and amend the trade debtor total of £152,220 in the Sales Ledger at 31 May 2014, thereby bringing the personal account balances of trade debtors in the Sales Ledger into agreement with the balance on the Sales Ledger Control Account at that date.

Note: The following proforma is provided for your use in completing the above task:
- Schedule amending the trade debtors total in the Sales Ledger at 31 May 2014 – see **page 2** of your **answer booklet**.

Total marks question 1 = 15 marks

4

QUESTION TW0

ACCOUNT FOR FIXED ASSETS

The financial year of Alpha-cabs ends on 31 May. The business classifies its fixed assets into several different categories, one of which is vehicles

The business keeps separate accounts to account for the cost and depreciation of fixed assets. To account for the depreciation of fixed assets at each financial year end the business uses a Depreciation Expense account in conjunction with Provision for Depreciation accounts. A Fixed Assets Disposal account is also kept for the purpose of accounting for any fixed assets disposed of in a financial year. As at 31 May 2013 the business had the following two accounts in its ledger:

- Vehicles (Cost) – balance £81,000
- Vehicles (Provision for Depreciation) – balance £26,908

An extract of the General Ledger of Alpha-cabs is provided for your attention, (see **page 4** of your **answer booklet**).

A Fixed Asset Register is kept on behalf of Alpha-cabs in which details of individual fixed assets owned by the business are recorded. You are provided with the vehicles section of the Fixed Asset Register of the business (see **page 6** of your **answer booklet**).

Acquisitions and Disposals of Vehicles in the Year Ended 31 May 2014

In the year ended 31 May 2014 Alpha-cabs acquired and disposed of the following vehicles:

Acquisition of Vehicle – a new vehicle (Vauxhall Movano BD13 ACS) was purchased on 1 November 2013 at a cost of £30,000 (ignore VAT), the vehicle was paid for by cheque.

Disposal of Vehicle – The Vauxhall Vivaro BD08 ACS originally purchased on 1 August 2010 was sold on 31 May 2014. A cheque for £11,500 (ignore VAT) was received on disposal.

Depreciation Policy

Alpha-cabs depreciates its vehicles by 20% each year using the reducing balance method. A full year's depreciation is taken in the year of a vehicles acquisition with no depreciation taken in the year a vehicle is disposed of.

5

REQUIRED

TASK A (2 Marks)
Post the balances provided above, relating to the cost of vehicles and their accumulated depreciation as at 31 May 2013, to appropriate ledger accounts provided in the General Ledger (extract).

Task B (2 Marks)
Enter details of the cost of the Vauxhall Movano BD13 ACS purchased on 1 November 2013 into the Fixed Asset Register (extract) and the Vehicles (Cost) Account in the General Ledger (extract)

TASK C (2 Marks)
Enter details of the vehicle disposed of on 31 May 2014 into the Fixed Asset Register (extract), and post the disposal proceeds of the vehicle disposed of to the Fixed Assets Disposal Account in the General Ledger (extract).

TASK D (6 Marks)
Update the Fixed Asset Register (extract) as at 31 May 2014 by completing the columns 'Annual Depreciation', 'Accumulated Depreciation' and 'Net Book Value' for each vehicle owned by the business as at the year end.

TASK E (2.75 Marks)
Prepare the Journal entry as at 31 May 2014 to account for depreciation of vehicles at the year end. Date your Journal entry 31 May 2014 and provide a suitable narrative

TASK F (2 Marks)
Post the entries from the Journal prepared in Task E above into the relevant ledger accounts in the General Ledger (extract)

TASK G (5.5 Marks)
Prepare the Journal entries required to transfer the cost and accumulated depreciation on the vehicle disposed of on 31 May 2014 to the Fixed Assets Disposal Account. Date your Journal entries 31 May 2014 and provide a suitable narrative

TASK H (3 Marks)
Post the entries from the Journal prepared in Task G above into the relevant ledger accounts in the General Ledger (extract)

TASK I (2.75 Marks)
Prepare the Journal entry as at 31 May 2014 to transfer the profit or loss on disposal of the vehicle disposed of to the Profit and Loss Account. Date your Journal entry 31 May 2014 and provide a suitable narrative

6

TASK J (2 Marks)
Post the Journal entry prepared in Task I above to the Fixed Assets Disposal Account in the General Ledger (extract). (Note that you are not provided with the Profit and Loss Account, therefore you can only post the 'leg' of the Journal entry which relates to the Fixed Assets Disposal Account). Close off the Fixed Assets Disposal Account as at 31 May 2014.

Note: In completing the tasks above, other than closing off the Fixed Assets Disposal Account as required in Task J, you are **not** required to close off or balance off any of the other accounts within the General Ledger (extract).

Total marks question 2 = 30 marks

Note: The following are provided for your use in completing the above tasks:

- General Ledger (extract) – see **page 4** of your **answer booklet**
- Journal – see **page 5 of your answer booklet**
- Fixed Asset Register (extract) see **page 6** of your **answer booklet**

QUESTION THREE

ACCOUNT FOR THE VALUE OF STOCK, PREPAYMENTS AND ACCRUALS AND BAD AND DOUBTFUL DEBTS

The financial year of Sola-Tech ends on 31 May. The following balances appeared in the General Ledger of the business as at the financial year ended 31 May 2014:

	£
Sales Ledger Control	178,500
Provision for Doubtful Debts (as at 31 May 2013)	2,145
Rates	26,400
Power Heat and Light	3,845
Operating Expenses	7,540
Stock (Opening Stock 1 June 2013)	154,500

You are provided with an extract from the General Ledger of Sola-Tech showing the above balances brought forward (see **pages 8 and 9** of your **answer booklet**).

Additional Information

You are provided with the following additional information as at 31 May 2014:

(i)   The balance of £1,500 (ignore VAT) on the personal account of a trade debtor at 31 May 2014 is now to be written off as a bad debt. The balance on the Provision for Doubtful Debts Account is to be adjusted as at 31 May 2014 to represent an amount equivalent to1.5% of total debtors following the bad debt write off.

(ii)   The balance on the Rates Account per the General Ledger as at 31 May 2014 includes a payment of £9,000 in respect of business rates paid for the six months period 1 April 2014 to 30 September 2014.

(iii)   The last payment posted to the Power Heat and Light Account at the year end 31 May 2014 was a cheque for £1,200. The cheque was in respect of power heat and light bills for the three months period ended 31 March 2014. It is expected that power heat and light bills for the three months period ending 30 June 2014 will be 10% lower than bills for the previous quarter.

(iv)   At the year end 31 May 2014 operating expenses of £900 were prepaid, there were also operating expenses of £1,750 accrued at that date.

(v)   Closing stock as at 31 May 2014 had been valued at £164,750. However, since the valuation was carried out the following discrepancy has been discovered.
  -   One end of line item of stock was included in the original valuation at a cost of £1,500 but was now found to have been damaged in storage. Repairs costing £200 would have to be carried out to make the item saleable. The item would then be sold in a clearance sale for £1,000.

Note: The General Ledger of Sola-Tech includes ledger accounts used for the specific purpose of accounting for Prepayments and Accruals.

REQUIRED

TASK A (2 Marks)

Prepare the Journal entry to account for the bad debt write off as at 31 May 2014.

TASK B (2 Marks)

Post the entries from the Journal prepared in Task A above into the relevant accounts in the General Ledger.

TASK C (2 Marks)

Prepare the Journal entry to account for the Provision for Doubtful Debts Account adjustment as at 31 May 2014.

TASK D (2 Marks)

Post the entries from the Journal prepared in Task C above into the relevant accounts in the General Ledger (note that you are not provided with the Profit and Loss Account, therefore you can only post the 'leg' of the Journal entries which relate to the Provision for Doubtful Debts account).

TASK E (8 Marks)

Prepare the Journal entries to account for rates prepaid, power heat and light accrued, and operating expenses prepaid and accrued at 31 May 2014.

TASK F (8 Marks)

Post the entries from the Journal prepared in Task E above into relevant accounts in the General Ledger.

TASK G (2 Marks)

Amend the original closing stock valuation of £164,750 at 31 May 2014 to account for the stock item damaged, by completing the schedule provided on **page 10** of your **answer booklet**

9

TASK H (4 Marks)

Prepare the Journal entries required to transfer the opening stock and closing stock (as amended in Task G above) to the Trading Account as at the year end 31 May 2014.

TASK I (2 Marks)

Post the Journal entries prepared in Task H above to the Stock Account in the General Ledger (note that you are not provided with the Trading Account, therefore you can only post the 'legs' of the Journal entries which relate to the stock account).

TASK J (8 Marks)

Prepare the Journal entries as at 31 May 2014 to transfer the expenses of bad debts, rates, power heat and light and operating expenses to the Profit and Loss Account.

TASK K (7 Marks)

Post the Journal entries prepared in Task J above to the expense accounts of Bad Debts, Rates, Power Heat and Light and Operating Expenses in the General Ledger and close off the accounts. (Note that you are not provided with a Profit and Loss Account, therefore you can only post the 'legs' of the Journal entries which relate to the expense accounts.

TASK L (8 Marks)

Balance off the Provision for Doubtful Debts, Sales Ledger Control, Stock, Prepayments and Accruals accounts in the General Ledger as at 31 May 2014 bringing down the account balances as at that date.

Total marks question 3 = 55

Note: The following proformas are provided for your use in completing the above tasks:

- General Ledger (Extract) – see **pages 8 and 9** of your **answer booklet**

- Schedule amending stock valuation – see **page 10** of your **answer booklet**

- Journal – see **pages 11 and 12** of your **answer booklet**

Total marks this unit = 100

10

SECTION B – PREPARE FINANCIAL STATEMENTS FOR A NOT FOR PROFIT ORGANISATION

INSTRUCTIONS

There is **ONE** question in this section of the paper. You must complete **ALL TASKS** within the question.

QUESTION ONE

The following are the assets and liabilities of the Trent Rowing Club at 31 May 2013:

	£
Clubhouse fixtures and fittings (net book value)	4,800
Clubhouse rent (accrued)	700
Members subscriptions (in arrears)	560
Cash and Bank	3,620
Clubhouse heat and light (accrued)	380
Club boats and boating equipment (net book value)	18,500
Club vehicle (net book value)	10,000

REQUIRED

TASK A (4 Marks)

Calculate the accumulated fund of the members of the Trent Rowing Club at 31 May 2013.

Note: The following proforma is provided for your use in completing the above task:

- Workings – Calculation of Accumulated Fund of Members of the Trent Rowing Club at 31 May 2013 - see **page 14** of your **answer booklet**)

The club treasurer has presented you with the following summary of the club's receipts and payments for the year ended 31 May 2014, together with a list of additional information as at that date.

11

Trent Rowing Club

Receipts and Payments Account for the Year Ended 31 May 2014

(Cash and Bank)

Receipts	£	Payments	£
Balance b/f (31 May 2013)	3,620	Clubhouse rent	5,100
Members subscriptions	12,500	Clubhouse heat and light	1,180
Christmas disco	2,680	New boat and boating equipment	6,000
		Christmas disco expenses	1,150
		Clubhouse maintenance	1,260
		Vehicle expenses	1,650
		Boat repairs	1,250
		Balance c/d (31 May 2014)	1,210
	18,800		18,800
Balance b/d (31 May 2014)	1,210		

Additional Information:

(i)   Members subscriptions of £480 were in arrears at 31 May 2014.

(ii) Clubhouse rent of £800 is accrued at 31 May 2014.

(iii) An accrual of £480 is to be made in respect of clubhouse heat and light bills unpaid as at 31 May 2014.

(iv) Depreciation for the year ended 31 May 2014 is to be charged as follows- Clubhouse fixtures and fittings £480, Boats and boating equipment £1,500 (this includes depreciation on the new boat and boating equipment bought in the year), Club vehicle £1,000.

12

REQUIRED

TASK B (12 Marks)

Prepare the following accounts for the year ended 31 May 2014:

- Members Subscriptions (Income)

- Clubhouse Rent

- Clubhouse Heat and Light

TASK C (12 Marks)

Prepare the Income and Expenditure Account of the club for the year ended 31 May 2014

TASK D (12 Marks)

Prepare the Balance Sheet of the club at 31 May 2014

Total marks question 1 = 40

Note: The following proformas are provided for your use in completing the above tasks:

- Accounts – Members Subscriptions (income), Clubhouse Rent and Clubhouse Heat and Light - see **page 15** of your **answer booklet**

- Income and Expenditure Account - see **page 16** of your **answer booklet**

- Balance Sheet - see **page 17** of your **answer booklet**

Total marks this unit = 40

**June 2014 Examination
Answer Booklet**

321 Exam ID

IAB Student No: ....

IAB Candidate No: ....

Name of Exam Centre:..

Date of Exam:..

Answer Booklet for the following Qualifications:

300:   Level 3 Certificate in Bookkeeping QCF: 50084793
320:   Level 3 Certificate in Manual Bookkeeping QCF: 50092601
340:   Level 3 Certificate in Applied Bookkeeping QCF: 50092765
3000: Level 3 Certificate in Bookkeeping QCF: 60107315
3030: Level 3 Diploma in Bookkeeping QCF: 60104843

Time Allowed 3 Hours
Paper No: 0040

FOR USE BY ASSESSOR ONLY:

IAB ID	Units covered	Possible marks	Actual marks	Pass or Fail
309	Record transactions and make accounting adjustments – M6010732	100		
308	Prepare financial statements for a not for profit organisation – D6010757	40		

International Association of Book-keepers, Suite 5, 20 Churchill Square, Kings Hill, West Malling, Kent ME19 4YU
Tel: 01732 897750, Fax: 01732 897751, email:education@iab.org.uk Website: www.iab.org.uk

SECTION A

INSTRUCTIONS

There are **THREE** questions in this section of the paper. You must complete **ALL TASKS** within the questions

QUESTION ONE

Marton Engineering

General Ledger Extract – Purchase Ledger Control Account for Use in Answering Question One Tasks A, B and C

General Ledger (Extract)

DR			Purchase Ledger Control			CR
2014	Details	£	2014	Details		£

Marton Engineering

Schedule Reconciling the Purchase Ledger Control Account Balance at 31 May 2014, to the Personal Account Balances in the Subsidiary Purchase Ledger at that date - for Use in Answering Question One Task D

Schedule Reconciling Purchase Ledger Control Account Balance to Total Creditors in the Subsidiary Purchase Ledger at 31 May 2014

£

Balance on Purchase Ledger Control at 31 May 2014

Total Creditors in the subsidiary Purchase Ledger at 31 May 2014

Difference

1

421

IAB Level 3 answer booklet I

IAB L3 Cert (June 2014)

Marton Engineering

Schedule Amending Total Trade Debtor Balances at 31 May 2014 - for Use in Answering Question One Task E

Schedule Amending Trade Debtor Balances in the Sales Ledger at 31 May 2014	
	£
Trade debtor balances in the Sales Ledger at 31 May 2014	
Amendments:	
(i) Invoice total transposed when posted to debtor personal account	
(ii) Bad debt not posted to debtor personal account	
(iii) Cheque received not posted to debtor personal account	
(iv) Trade debtor balance not included in list extracted from subsidiary Sales Ledger	
Amended Sales Ledger balances	_____
Balance on Sales Ledger Control Account	_____

IAB Level 3 answer booklet I

IAB L3 Cert (June 2014)

This Page is Intentionally Left Blank for Notes/Workings

IAB Level 3 answer booklet I

IAB L3 Cert (June 2014)

QUESTION TWO

Alpha-cabs

General Ledger (Extract) – For Use in Answering Question Two Tasks A, B, C, F, H, and J

DR			Vehicles (Cost)				CR
Date	Details	£		Date	Details	£	

DR			Vehicles (Provision for Depreciation)				CR
Date	Details	£		Date	Details	£	

DR			Depreciation Expense				CR
Date	Details	£		Date	Details	£	

DR			Fixed Assets Disposal				CR
Date	Details	£		Date	Details	£	

IAB Level 3 answer booklet I

IAB L3 Cert (June 2014)

Alpha-cabs

Journal – For Use in Answering Question Two Tasks E, G and I

Journal

2014	Details	DR £	CR £
	Journal Task E		
	Journal Task G		
	Journal Task I		

Alpha-cabs

Fixed Asset Register – Verhicles Section

For Use in Answering Question Two Tasks B, C and D

Alpha-cabs
Fixed Asset Register (Extract)

Item Description	Date of Acquisition	Capitalised Cost £	Annual Depreciation £	Accumulated Depreciation £	Net Book Value £	Disposal Proceeds £	Disposal Date
Vehicles							
Vauxhall Vivaro BD08 ACS	1/8/10	26,000					
Depreciation – Year ended 31/5/11			5,200	5,200	20,800		
Depreciation – Year ended 31/5/12			4,160	9,360	16,640		
Depreciation – Year ended 31/5/13			3,328	12,688	13,312		
Ford Mondeo BD60 ACS	1/9/11	20,000					
Depreciation – Year ended 31/5/12			4,000	4,000	16,000		
Depreciation – Year ended 31/5/13			3,200	7,200	12,800		
Mercedes BD12 ACS	1/7/12	35,000					
Depreciation – Year ended 31/5/13			7,000	7,000	28,000		

IAB L3 Cert (June 2014)

This Page is Intentionally Left Blank for Notes/Workings

IAB Level 3 answer booklet I

QUESTION THREE

Sola-Tech

General Ledger (Extract) – Ledger Accounts for Use in Answering Question Three Tasks B, D, F, I, K and L

General Ledger (Extract)

DR Date	Details	£	CR Date	Details	£
		Provision for Doubtful Debts	31/5/13	Balance b/f	2,145

DR Date	Details	£	CR Date	Details	£
31/5/14	Balance b/f	178,500	Sales Ledger Control		

DR Date	Details	£	CR Date	Details	£
31/5/14	Balance b/f	26,400	Rates		

DR Date	Details	£	CR Date	Details	£
31/5/14	Balance b/f	3,845	Power Heat and Light		

DR Date	Details	£	CR Date	Details	£
31/5/14	Balance b/f	7,540	Operating Expenses		

IAB Level 3 answer booklet I

IAB L3 Cert (June 2014)

General Ledger (Extract) Continued

DR			Stock		CR
Date	**Details**	**£**	**Date**	**Details**	**£**
1/6/13	Balance b/f	154,500			

DR			Bad Debts		CR
Date	**Details**	**£**	**Date**	**Details**	**£**

DR			Prepayments		CR
Date	**Details**	**£**	**Date**	**Details**	**£**

DR			Accruals		CR
Date	**Details**	**£**	**Date**	**Details**	**£**

IAB Level 3 answer booklet I

IAB L3 Cert (June 2014)

Sola-Tech

Schedule Amending Closing Stock Valuation – For Use in Answering Question Three Task G

Schedule Amending Closing Stock Valuation

Details	£	
Original closing stock valuation	164,750	
Amendment:		
Stock item damaged		
Amended Stock Valuation at 31 May 2014		

IAB Level 3 answer booklet I

Sola-Tech

Journal – For Use in Answering Question Three Tasks A, C, E, H and J

Journal

2014	Details	DR £	CR £
	Journal Task A		
31 May	Bad Debts Sales Ledger Control		
	Balance on debtor account written off as bad debt		
	Journal Task C		
31 May	Profit and Loss Provision for Doubtful Debts		
	Adjustment to increase the provision for doubtful debts at the year end		
	Journal Task E		
31 May	Prepayments Rates		
	Power Heat and Light Accruals		
	Prepayments Operating Expenses		
	Operating Expenses Accruals		
	Adjustments to account for rates prepaid, power heat and light accrued and operating expenses prepaid and accrued at the year end		
	Journal Task H		
31 May	Trading Stock (opening)		
	Stock (closing) Trading		
	Transfer of opening and closing stock to Trading Account at the year end		

IAB Level 3 answer booklet I

IAB L3 Cert (June 2014)

Sola-Tech

Journal (continued)

Journal

2014	Details	DR £	CR £
	Journal Task J		
31 May	Profit and Loss Bad Debts		
	Profit and Loss Rates		
	Profit and Loss Power Heat and Light		
	Profit and Loss Operating Expenses		
	Transfer of expenses to Profit and Loss Account at the year end 31 May 2014		

IAB L3 Cert (June 2014)

This Page is Intentionally Left Blank for Notes/Workings

IAB L3 Cert (June 2014)

SECTION B

INSTRUCTIONS

There is **ONE** question in this section of the paper. You must complete **ALL TASKS** within the question.

QUESTION ONE

Trent Rowing Club

Workings – Calculation of Members' Accumulated Fund – For Use in Answering Question One Task A

Workings – Calculation of Accumulated Fund of Members of Trent Rowing Club as at 31 May 2013

£

Assets of Club:

Total Assets _____
....

Liabilities of Club:

Total Liabilities _____
....

Members Accumulated fund _____

IAB Level 3 answer booklet I

IAB L3 Cert (June 2014)

Trent Rowing Club

Members Subscriptions (Income) Account, Clubhouse Rent Account and Clubhouse Heat and Light Account – For Use in Answering Question One Task B

DR		Members Subscriptions (Income)		CR
Details	**£**		**Details**	**£**

DR		Clubhouse Rent		CR
Details	**£**		**Details**	**£**

DR		Clubhouse Heat and Light		CR
Details	**£**		**Details**	**£**

IAB Level 3 answer booklet I

IAB L3 Cert (June 2014)

Trent Rowing Club

Income and Expenditure Account – For Use in Answering Question One Task C

<table>
<tr>
<td colspan="3">Trent Rowing Club
Income and Expenditure Account for the Year Ended 31 May 2014</td>
</tr>
<tr>
<td>Income</td>
<td>£</td>
<td>£</td>
</tr>
<tr>
<td>Members subscriptions
Christmas disco income
  Less Christmas disco expenses
Surplus on Christmas disco</td>
<td></td>
<td></td>
</tr>
<tr>
<td>Expenditure
Clubhouse rent
Clubhouse heat and light
Clubhouse maintenance
Vehicle expenses
Boat repairs
Depreciation</td>
<td></td>
<td></td>
</tr>
<tr>
<td>Surplus of income over expenditure</td>
<td></td>
<td></td>
</tr>
</table>

IAB L3 Cert (June 2014)

Trent Rowing Club

Balance Sheet – For Use in Answering Question One Task D

Trent Rowing Club Balance Sheet as at 31 May 2014	£	£	£
Fixed Assets			
Clubhouse fixtures and fittings (net book value)			
Club boats and boating equipment (net book value			
Club vehicle (net book value)		_____	
Current Assets			
Members subscriptions in arrears			
Cash and Bank	_____		
Less Current Liabilities			
Clubhouse rent (accrued)			
Clubhouse heat and light (accrued)	_____		
		_____	
			_____
Represented by:			_____
Members opening accumulated fund			
Surplus in year		_____	
Members closing accumulated fund			_____

Page17

437

IAB Level 3 answer booklet I

IAB L3 Cert (June 2014)

This Page is Intentionally Left Blank for Notes/Workings

IAB Level 3 model answers I

June 2014 Examination
Model Answers

321 Exam ID

Model Answer Booklet for the following Qualifications:

300: Level 3 Certificate in Bookkeeping QCF: 50084793
320: Level 3 Certificate in Manual Bookkeeping QCF: 50092601
340: Level 3 Certificate in Applied Bookkeeping QCF: 50092765
3000: Level 3 Certificate in Bookkeeping QCF: 60107315
3030: Level 3 Diploma in Bookkeeping QCF: 60104843

Time Allowed 3 Hours
Paper No: 0040

FOR USE BY ASSESSOR ONLY:

IAB ID	Units covered	Possible marks
309	Record transactions and make accounting adjustments – M6010732	**100**
308	Prepare financial statements for a not for profit organisation – D6010757	**40**

International Association of Book-keepers, Suite 5, 20 Churchill Square, Kings Hill, West Malling, Kent ME19 4YU
Tel: 01732 897750, Fax: 01732 897751, email:education@iab.org.uk Website: www.iab.org.uk

SECTION A

QUESTION ONE

Marton Engineering

Marton Engineering – Purchase Ledger Control Account – Answer Tasks A, B and C

General Ledger (Extract)

DR				Purchase Ledger Control				CR
2014	Details		£	2014	Details			£
31 May	Purchase ret'ns day book	1	4,200	1 May	Balance b/f	1		189,240
31 May	Cash book - payments	1	104,300	31 May	Purchase day book	1		99,560
31 May	Cash book - discounts	1	1,540					
31 May	Balance c/d	2	178,760					
		½	288,800			½		288,800
				31 May	Balance b/d	1		178,760

9 marks

Marton Engineering

Schedule Reconciling the Purchase Ledger Control Account Balance at 31 May 2014, to the Personal Account Balances in the Subsidiary Purchase Ledger at that date - Answer Task D

Schedule Reconciling Purchase Ledger Control Account Balance to Total Creditors in the Subsidiary Purchase Ledger at 31 May 2014

		£	
Balance on the Purchase Ledger Control at 31 May 2014	½	178,760	(CR)
Total creditors in the subsidiary Purchase Ledger at 31 May 2014	½	178,760	(CR)
Difference	1	Nil	

---

2 Marks

IAB Level 3 model answers I

IAB L3 Cert (June 2014)

Marton Engineering

Schedule Amending Total Debtor Balances as at 31 May 2014 – Answer Task E

Schedule Amending Trade Debtor Balances in the Sales Ledger at 31 May 2014			
		£	
Trade debtors in the Sales Ledger at 31 May 2014	½	152,220	(DR)
Amendments			
(i) Invoice total transposed when posted to debtor personal account	½	(900)	(CR)
(ii) Bad debt not posted to debtor personal account	½	(2,400)	(CR)
(iii) Cheque received not posted to debtor personal account	½	(1,800)	(CR)
(iv) Trade debtor balance not included on list extracted from subsidiary Sales ledger	½	1,840	(DR)
Amended Sales Ledger balances	1	148,960	(DR)
Balance on Sales Ledger Control Account	½	148,960	(DR)

4 Marks

IAB L3 Cert (June 2014)

QUESTION TWO

Alpha-cabs

General Ledger Accounts Answer - Tasks A, B, C, F, H and J

DR			Vehicles (Cost)				CR
Date	Details		£	Date	Details		£
31/5/13	Balance b/f	1	81,000	31/5/14	Fixed assets disposal	1	26,000
1/11/13	Bank	½	30,000				

DR			Vehicles (Provision for Depreciation)				CR
Date	Details		£	Date	Details		£
31/5/14	Fixed assets disposal	1	12,688	31/5/13	Balance b/f	1	26,908
				31/5/14	Depreciation expense	1	14,160

DR			Depreciation Expense			CR
Date	Details		£	Date	Details	£
31/5/14	Vehicles dep.n	1	14,160			

DR			Fixed Assets Disposal				CR
Date	Details		£	Date	Details		£
31/5/14	Vehicles (cost) ½		26,000	31/5/14	Bank	1	11,500
				31/5/14	Vehicles depreciation	½	12,688
				31/5/14	Profit and Loss	2	1,812
			26,000				26,000

10½ Marks

Page 3

IAB Level 3 model answers I

Alpha-cabs
Fixed Asset Register (Extract)
Answer – Tasks B, C and D

Item Description	Date of Acquisition	Capitalised Cost £	Annual Depreciation £	Accumulated Depreciation £	Net Book Value £	Disposal Proceeds £	Disposal Date
Vehicles							
Vauxhall Vivaro BD08 ACS	1/8/10	26,000					
Depreciation – Year ended 31/5/11			5,200	5,200	20,800		
Depreciation – Year ended 31/5/12			4,160	9,360	16,640		
Depreciation – Year ended 31/5/13			3,328	12,688	13,312		
Disposed of year ended 31/5/14						½ 11,500	½31/5/14
Ford Mondeo BD60 ACS	1/9/11	20,000					
Depreciation – Year ended 31/5/12			4,000	4,000	16,000		
Depreciation – Year ended 31/5/13			3,200	7,200	12,800		
Depreciation – Year ended 31/5/14			1 2,560	½ 9,760	½ 10,240		
Mercedes BD12 ACS	1/7/12	35,000					
Depreciation – Year ended 31/5/13			7,000	7,000	28,000		
Depreciation – Year ended 31/5/14			1 5,600	½ 12,600	½ 22,400		
Vauxhall Movano BD13 ACS ½	½ 1/11/13	½ 30,000					
Depreciation – Year ended 31/5/14			1 6,000	½ 6,000	½ 24,000		

8½ Marks

IAB L3 Cert (June 2014)

Alpha-cabs

Journal – Answer - Tasks E, G and I

Journal

2014	Details	DR £	CR £
	Journal Task E		
31 May	Depreciation Expense 1/4 Vehicles (Provision for Depreciation) 1/4 Depreciation on vehicles for the year ended 31 May 2014 1/4	1 14,160	1 14,160
	Journal Task G		
31 Dec	Fixed Assets Disposal 1/4 Vehicles (Cost) 1/4 Vehicles (Provision for Depreciation) 1/4 Fixed Assets Disposal 1/4 Transfer of the cost and accumulated depreciation of vehicle disposed of to the Fixed Assets Disposal account at the year end 31 May 2014 1/2	1 26,000 1 12,688	1 26,000 1 12,688
	Journal Task I		
31 Dec	Profit and Loss 1/4 Fixed Assets Disposal 1/4 Transfer of loss on disposal of vehicle to the Profit and Loss Account at the year end 31 May 2014 1/4	1 1,812	1 1,812

11 Marks

Total Marks Question 2 = 30 Marks

IAB L3 Cert (June 2014)

QUESTION THREE

Sola-Tech

General Ledger (Extract) – Ledger Accounts Answer - Tasks B, D, F, I, K and L

General Ledger (Extract)

DR					Provision for Doubtful Debts		CR
Date	Details		£	Date	Details		£
31/5/14	Balance c/d	1	2,655	31/5/13	Balance b/f		2,145
				31/5/14	Profit and loss	2	510
			2,655				2,655
				31/5/14	Balance b/d	½	2,655

DR					Sales Ledger Control		CR
Date	Details		£	Date	Details		£
31/5/14	Balance b/f		178,500	31/5/14	Bad debts	1	1,500
				31/5/14	Balance c/d	1	177,000
			178,500				178,500
31/5/14	Balance b/d	½	177,000				

DR					Rates		CR
Date	Details		£	Date	Details		£
31/5/14	Balance b/f		26,400	31/5/14	Prepayments	1	6,000
				31/5/14	Profit and loss	2	20,400
			26,400				26,400

DR					Power Heat and Light		CR
Date	Details		£	Date	Details		£
31/5/14	Balance b/f		3,845	31/5/14	Profit and loss	2	4,565
31/5/14	Accruals	1	720				
			4,565				4,565

DR					Operating Expenses		CR
Date	Details		£	Date	Details		£
31/5/14	Balance b/f		7,540	31/5/14	Prepayments	1	900
31/5/14	Accruals	1	1,750	31/5/14	Profit and loss	2	8,390
			9,290				9,290

Page 6

445

IAB L3 Cert (June 2014)

General Ledger (Extract) Continued

DR   **Stock**   **CR**

Date	Details		£	Date	Details		£
1/6/13	Balance b/f		154,500	31/5/14	Trading	1	154,500
31/5/14	Trading	1	164,050	31/5/14	Balance c/d	1	164,050
			318,550				318,550
31/5/14	Balance b/d	1	164,050				

DR   **Bad Debts**   **CR**

Date	Details		£	Date	Details		£
31/5/14	Sales ledger control	1	1,500	31/5/14	Profit and loss	1	1,500

DR   **Prepayments**   **CR**

Date	Details		£	Date	Details		£
31/5/14	Rates	1	6,000	31/5/14	Balance c/d	1	6,900
31/5/14	Operating expenses	1	900				
			6,900				6,900
31/5/14	Balance b/d	½	6,900				

DR   **Accruals**   **CR**

Date	Details		£	Date	Details		£
31/5/14	Balance c/d	1	2,470	31/5/14	Power heat and light	1	720
				31/5/14	Operating expenses	1	1,750
			2,470				2,470
				31/5/14	Balance b/d	½	2,470

29 Marks

IAB Level 3 model answers I

IAB L3 Cert (June 2014)

Sola-Tech

Schedule Amending Closing Stock Valuation – Answer -Task G

Schedule Amending Closing Stock Valuation

Details		£
Original closing stock valuation		164,750
Amendment:		
Stock item damaged	1	(700)
Amended Stock Valuation at 31 May 2014	1	164,050

2 Marks

Page 8

447

IAB L3 Cert (June 2014)

Sola-Tech

Journal – Answer -Tasks A, C, E, H and J

Journal

2014	Details	DR £	CR £
31 May	**Journal Task A** Bad Debts Sales Ledger Control Balance on debtor account written off as bad debt	1 1,500	1 1,500
31 May	**Journal Task C** Profit and Loss Provision for Doubtful Debts Adjustment to increase the provision for doubtful debts at the year end	1 510	1 510
31 May	**Journal Task E** Prepayments Rates Power Heat and Light Accruals Prepayments Operating Expenses Operating Expenses Accruals Adjustments to account for rates prepaid, power heat and light accrued and operating expenses prepaid and accrued at the year end	1 6,000 1 720 1 900 1 1,750	1 6,000 1 720 1 900 1 1,750
31 May	**Journal Task H** Trading Stock (opening) Stock (closing) Trading Transfer of opening and closing stock to Trading Account at the year end	1 154,500 1 164,050	1154,500 1164,050

Page 9

448

IAB Level 3 model answers I

Sola-Tech

Journal (continued)

Journal

2014	Details	DR £	CR £
31 May	**Journal Task J** Profit and Loss Bad Debts	1 1,500	1 1,500
	Profit and Loss Rates	1 20,400	1 20,400
	Profit and Loss Power Heat and Light	1 4,565	1 4,565
	Profit and Loss Operating Expenses	1 8.390	1 8,390
	Transfer of expenses to Profit and Loss Account at the year end 31 May 2014		

24 Marks

Total marks question 3 = 55 Marks

Total This Unit = 100 Marks

Page 10

IAB Level 3 model answers I

SECTION B

QUESTION ONE

Trent Rowing Club

Members' Accumulated Fund as at 31 May 2013 – Answer Task A

		£
Assets of Club:		
Clubhouse fixtures and fittings (net book value)	½	4,800
Membership subscriptions (in arrears)	½	560
Cash and Bank	½	3,620
Club boats and boating equipment (net book value)	½	18,500
Club vehicle (net book value)	½	10,000
Total assets		37,480
Liabilities of Club:		
Clubhouse rent (accrued)	½	700
Clubhouse heat and light (accrued)	½	380
Total liabilities		1,080
Members accumulated fund	½	36,400

4 Marks

IAB Level 3 model answers I

IAB L3 Cert (June 2014)

Trent Rowing Club

Accounts – Answer Task B

DR	Membership Subscriptions (Income)		CR
Details		**£**	
Balance b/f	1	560	
Income & Expenditure	1	12,420	
		12,980	
Balance b/d	½	480	

Details		**£**
Receipts	½	12,500
Balance c/d	1	480
		12,980

DR	Clubhouse Rent		CR
Details		**£**	
Payments	½	5,100	
Balance c/d	1	800	
		5,900	

Details		**£**
Balance b/f	1	700
Income & Expenditure	1	5,200
		5,900
Balance b/d	½	800

DR	Clubhouse Heat and Light		CR
Details		**£**	
Payments	½	1,180	
Balance c/d	1	480	
		1,660	

Details		**£**
Balance b/f	1	380
Income & Expenditure	1	1,280
		1,660
Balance b/d	½	480

12 Marks

Page 12

451

IAB L3 Cert (June 2014)

Trent Rowing Club
Income and Expenditure Account – Answer Task C

Trent Rowing Club Income and Expenditure Account for the Year Ended 31 May 2014				
Income		**£**		**£**
Members subscriptions			1	12,420
Christmas disco income	1	2,680		
Less Christmas disco expenses	1	1,150		
Surplus on Christmas disco			1	1,530
				13,950
Expenditure				
Clubhouse rent	1	5,200		
Clubhouse heat and light	1	1,280		
Clubhouse maintenance	1	1,260		
Vehicle expenses	1	1,650		
Boat repairs	1	1,250		
Depreciation	1	2,980		
				13,620
Surplus of income over expenditure			2	330

12 Marks

IAB Level 3 model answers I

IAB L3 Cert (June 2014)

Trent Rowing Club

Balance Sheet – Answer Task D

<table>
<tr><td colspan="4">Trent Rowing Club
Balance Sheet as at 31 May 2014</td></tr>
<tr><td></td><td>£</td><td>£</td><td>£</td></tr>
<tr><td>Fixed Assets</td><td></td><td></td><td></td></tr>
<tr><td>Clubhouse fixtures and fittings (net book value)</td><td></td><td>1   4,320</td><td></td></tr>
<tr><td>Club boats and boating equipment (net book value)</td><td></td><td>1 23,000</td><td></td></tr>
<tr><td>Club vehicle (net book value)</td><td></td><td>1   9,000</td><td></td></tr>
<tr><td></td><td></td><td></td><td>36,320</td></tr>
<tr><td>Current Assets</td><td></td><td></td><td></td></tr>
<tr><td>Membership subscriptions in arrears</td><td>1   480</td><td></td><td></td></tr>
<tr><td>Cash and Bank</td><td>1 1,210</td><td></td><td></td></tr>
<tr><td></td><td></td><td>1,690</td><td></td></tr>
<tr><td>Less Current Liabilities</td><td>1   800</td><td></td><td></td></tr>
<tr><td>Clubhouse rent (accrued)</td><td>1   480</td><td></td><td></td></tr>
<tr><td>Clubhouse heat and light (accrued)</td><td></td><td>1,280</td><td></td></tr>
<tr><td></td><td></td><td></td><td>1   410</td></tr>
<tr><td></td><td></td><td></td><td>1 36,730</td></tr>
<tr><td>Represented by:</td><td></td><td></td><td></td></tr>
<tr><td>Members opening accumulated fund</td><td></td><td>1 36,400</td><td></td></tr>
<tr><td>Surplus in year</td><td></td><td>1   330</td><td></td></tr>
<tr><td>Members closing accumulated fund</td><td></td><td></td><td>1 36,730</td></tr>
</table>

12 Marks

Total This Unit = 40 Marks

Total Marks This Paper = 140 Marks

Page 14

**June 2014 Examination
Question Paper**

322 Exam ID

Question Paper for the following Qualifications:

300:   Level 3 Certificate in Bookkeeping QCF: 50084793
320:   Level 3 Certificate in Manual Bookkeeping QCF: 50092601
340:   Level 3 Certificate in Applied Bookkeeping QCF: 50092765
3000: Level 3 Certificate in Bookkeeping QCF: 60107315
3030: Level 3 Diploma in Bookkeeping QCF: 60104843

Units:
310:   Prepare financial statements for a partnership: Y6010742
311:   Prepare financial statements for a sole trader: A6010734

Time Allowed 3 Hours
Paper No:0041

General Instructions

1. Enter your IAB Student Number, Candidate Number and Name of Examination Centre
    in the spaces provided on the front cover of your Answer Booklet
2. All Answers to be written in blue or black ink
3. All Questions must be answered
4. Cross out errors neatly or use correcting fluid in moderation
5. Calculators are permitted
6. A blank page is provided in the Answer Booklet for workings if required
7. The Question Paper and Answer Booklet have information and data printed on both
    sides of the pages
8. Mobile phones are not permitted

International Association of Book-keepers, Suite 5, 20 Churchill Square, Kings Hill, West Malling, Kent ME19 4YU
Tel: 01732 897750, Fax: 01732 897751, email:education@iab.org.uk Website: www.iab.org.uk

IAB Level 3 question paper II

IAB L3 Cert June 2014 Paper 2

THIS PAPER CONSISTS OF TWO SECTIONS YOU MUST COMPLETE ALL THE QUESTIONS AND ALL TASKS WITHIN EACH SECTION

SECTION A – PREPARE FINANCIAL STATEMENTS FOR A PARTNERSHIP INSTRUCTIONS

There are **TWO** questions in this section of the paper. You must complete **ALL TASKS** within the questions.

QUESTION ONE

Alda and Bani have been in partnership for several years. The following Trial Balance has been extracted from the financial records of their business as at   31 May 2014:

Alda and Bani
Trial Balance as at 31 May 2014

	DR £	CR £
Capital – Alda		120,000
Capital – Bani		80,000
Current Account – Alda (31/5/ 2013)	1,220	
Current Account – Bani (31/5/ 2013)		1,650
Drawings – Alda	16,000	
Drawings – Bani	14,000	
Bank (current account)		2,450
Cash	200	
Premises (cost)	125,000	
Equipment (cost)	60,000	
Vehicles (cost)	30,000	
Provision for Depreciation (31/5/2013) – equipment		30,000
Provision for Depreciation (31/5/2013) – vehicles		6,000
Sales		740,480
Purchases	594,220	
Stock (31/5/2013)	45,560	
Wages and Salaries	64,340	
Heat and Light	5,440	
Rates	15,800	
Vehicle expenses	6,670	
Advertising	2,400	
Bank charges and interest	1,120	
Other expenses	2,750	
Trade debtors	40,680	
Trade creditors		44,820
	1,025,400	1,025,400

1

IAB L3 Cert June 2014 Paper 2

The following additional information is available as at 31 May 2014:

1 Stock as at 31 May 2014 was valued at cost of £48,430.

2 Heat and light of £1,620 is accrued.

3 Rates of £5,800 are prepaid.

4 Depreciation for the year ended 31 May 2014 is to be provided for as follows:

Equipment £12,000

Vehicles £6,000

A deed of partnership drawn up on behalf of the partnership includes the following details:

a Interest is to be charged on partners drawings. For the year ended 31 May 2014 interest to be charged is as follows:

	£
Alda	600
Bani	400

b Interest is to be given on partners capital at the rate of 2% per year.

c Remaining profits are to be shared equally between partners.

NB: Neither of the partners has introduced further capital to the business during the year ended 31 May 2014

REQUIRED

TASK A

Prepare the Trading and Profit and Loss Account of the partnership for the year ended 31 May 2014.

TASK B

Prepare the Profit and Loss Appropriation Account of the partnership for the year ended 31 May 2014.

TASK C

Prepare the Current Account of each partner for the year ended 31 May 2014.

TASK D

Prepare the Balance Sheet of the partnership as at 31 May 2014.

Total marks question 1 = 24

2

IAB L3 Cert June 2014 Paper 2

Note: The following proformas are provided for your use in completing the above tasks:

- Trading and Profit and Loss Account – see **page 1** of your **answer booklet**

- Profit and Loss Appropriation Account – see **page 2** of your **answer booklet**

- Current Accounts – see **page 3** of your **answer booklet**

- Balance Sheet – see **page 4** of your **answer booklet**

3

IAB L3 Cert June 2014 Paper 2

QUESTION TWO

Cara and Dee have been in partnership for several years. A Partnership Agreement drawn up on their behalf included the agreement that they would share profits and losses in ratio of Cara 60% and Dee 40%

As at 31 May 2013 the Capital and Current Accounts of Cara and Dee carried balances as follows:

	Capital Account	Current Account
Cara	£80,000	£800 (DR)
Dee	£50,000	£900 (CR)

It was agreed that as from 1 June 2013 Eve would be admitted to the partnership at which date she paid £60,000 into the business Bank Account in respect of her capital and share of goodwill.

As at 1 June 2013 the goodwill of Cara and Dee's business was valued at £40,000.

Following the admission of Eve to the partnership it was agreed that:

• A Goodwill Account would not be kept in the books of account of the partnership

• Partners would be given interest on capital at the rate of 3% per year

• Salaries would be paid to partners as follows:

- Cara £6,000 per year
- Dee £5,000 per year
- Eve £4,000 per year

• Remaining profits or losses would be shared Cara 40%, Dee 30% and Eve 30%

In the year ended 31 May 2014 the partnership business of Cara, Dee and Eve generated a net profit of £56,600. The partners took drawings from their business as follows:

Cara £20,000

Dee £18,000

Eve £16,000

4

IAB Level 3 question paper II

REQUIRED

TASK A

Prepare the Capital Accounts of each Partner as at 1 June 2013 to account for the admission of Eve the partnership. Balance off the Capital Accounts as at 1 June 2013 bringing down the account balances as at that date.

TASK B

Prepare the Profit and Loss Appropriation Account of the partnership (Cara, Dee and Eve) for the year ended 31 May 2014.

TASK C

Prepare the Current Accounts of Cara, Dee and Eve for the year ended 31 May 2014.

Total marks question 2 = 36

Note: The following proformas are provided for your use in completing the above tasks:

- Capital Accounts – see **page 6** of your **answer booklet**

- Profit and Loss Appropriation Account – see **page 7** of your **answer booklet**

- Current Accounts – see **page 8** of your **answer booklet**

Total marks this unit = 60

5

IAB Level 3 question paper II

SECTION B – PREPARE FINANCIAL STATEMENTS FOR A SOLE TRADER

INSTRUCTIONS

There is **ONE** question in this section of the paper. You must complete **ALL TASKS** within the question.

QUESTION ONE

    (A) The following list of balances has been extracted from the books of account of Comet Trading at the financial year end 31 May 2014.

    (B)

	£	
Bank	2,150	(DR)
Cash	500	
Sales	744,620	
Telephone	1,020	
Purchases	607,760	
Sales returns	2,650	
Purchase returns	1,920	
Discounts allowed	2,870	
Discounts received	3,650	
Stock (31 May 2013)	64,550	
Equipment (cost)	32,000	
Equipment (provision for depreciation 31 May 2013)	6,400	
Value added tax (VAT)	4,440	(CR)
Drawings	36,140	
Rent and rates	21,400	
Capital	104,250	
Wages	46,980	
Vehicles (cost)	45,000	
Vehicles (provision for depreciation 31 May 2013)	9,000	
Vehicle expenses	4,980	
Heat and light	2,960	
Trade debtors	47,790	
Trade creditors	45,550	
Sundry expenses	350	

REQUIRED

TASK A
List the balances given above on the Trial balance provided. You are to make the trial balance debit and credit column totals agree by adding any imbalance in the books as a Suspense Account balance.

TASK B
Post the imbalance in the books calculated in Task A above to the Suspense Account provided.

6

IAB Level 3 question paper II

IAB L3 Cert June 2014 Paper 2

Note: The following proformas are provided for your use in completing the above tasks:

- Trial Balance – see **page 10** of your **answer booklet**

- Suspense Account - see **page 11** of your **answer booklet**

(C) Since the list of ledger balances above were extracted from the books of account of Comet Trading the following bookkeeping errors have been discovered:

(D)

    (i)   The net goods total for purchases had been understated by £1,000 when posting the total from the Purchase Day Book to the Purchases Account at the end of May 2014

    (ii)   A transposition error had been made in balancing off the Sales Account as at 31 May 2014, resulting in the account balance being understated by £270.

REQUIRED

TASK C
Prepare the Journal entries necessary to correct the two errors given above.

TASK D
Post the Journal entries prepared in Task C above to the Suspense Account, thereby eliminating the difference in books balance. Your Journal entries should be dated 31 May 2014 and should include suitable narratives.

TASK E
Using the ledger account balances per the Trial Balance extracted from the books of Comet Trading at 31 May 2014, and the Journal entries prepared in Task C above list the balances (adjusted where necessary) on the Extended Trial Balance provided.

Note: The following proformas are provided for your use in completing the above tasks:
- Journal – see **page 11** of your **answer booklet**
- Suspense Account – see **page 11** of your **answer booklet**
- Extended Trial Balance – see **page 12** of your **answer booklet**

7

461

IAB L3 Cert June 2014 Paper 2

(C) You are provided with the following information relating to accounting adjustments to be applied in preparing financial statements on behalf of Comet Trading for the year ended 31 May 2014:

- Stock at 31 May 2014 was valued at £69,120

- Rent and rates of £7,200 were prepaid at 31 May 2014

- An accrual of £1,320 needs to be made at 31 May 2014 to account for heat and light bills unpaid at that date

- Depreciation for the year ended 31 May 2014 is to be provided for as follows:

  - Equipment £6,400
  - Vehicles £9,000

REQUIRED
TASK F
Process the adjustments given above through the Adjustments column of the Extended Trial Balance.

TASK G
Extend the Trial Balance, calculate net profit or loss in the year ended 31 May 2014 and balance the Balance Sheet columns.

TASK H
Use account balances extended to the Profit and Loss Account and Balance Sheet columns of the Extended Trial Balance to prepare the following financial statements on behalf of Comet Trading:
- Trading and Profit and Loss Account for the year ended 31 May 2014

- Balance Sheet as at 31 May 2014

Total marks question 1 = 40

8

IAB Level 3 question paper II

IAB L3 Cert June 2014 Paper 2

Note: The following proformas are provided for your use in completing the above tasks:

- Extended Trial Balance – see **page 12** of your **answer booklet**

- Trading and Profit and Loss Account – see **page 13** of your **answer booklet**

- Balance Sheet – see **page 14** of your **answer booklet**

Total marks this unit = 40

9

**June 2014 Examination
Answer Booklet**

322 Exam ID

IAB Student No: ....

IAB Candidate No: ....

Name of Exam Centre:..

Date of Exam:...

Answer Booklet for the following Qualifications:

300: Level 3 Certificate in Bookkeeping QCF: 50084793
320: Level 3 Certificate in Manual Bookkeeping QCF: 50092601
340: Level 3 Certificate in Applied Bookkeeping QCF: 50092765
3000: Level 3 Certificate in Bookkeeping QCF: 60107315
3030: Level 3 Diploma in Bookkeeping QCF: 60104843

Time Allowed 3 Hours
Paper No: 0041

FOR USE BY ASSESSOR ONLY:

IAB ID	Units covered	Possible marks	Actual marks	Pass or Fail
310	Prepare financial statements for a partnership: Y6010742	60		
311	Prepare financial statements for a sole trader: A6010734	40		

International Association of Book-keepers, Suite 5, 20 Churchill Square, Kings Hill, West Malling, Kent ME19 4YU
Tel: 01732 897750, Fax: 01732 897751, email:education@iab.org.uk Website: www.iab.org.uk

SECTION A

QUESTION ONE

Alda and Bani Trading in Partnership

Trading and Profit and Loss Account - for use in Answering Question One
Task A

Alda and Bani Trading and Profit and Loss Account for the Year Ended 31 May 2014	£	£	£

1

Alda and Bani Trading in Partnership

Profit and Loss Appropriation Account - for Use in Answering Question One Task B

Alda and Bani		
Profit and Loss Appropriation Account for the Year Ended 31 May 2014		
	£	£

Alda and Bani Trading in Partnership

Current Accounts - for Use in Answering Question One Task C

DR   Current Accounts   CR

Date	Details	Alda £	Bani £	Date	Details	Alda £	Bani £

Alda and Bani Trading in Partnership

Balance Sheet for Use in Answering Question One Task D

Alda and Bani Balance Sheet as at 31 May 2014			
	£	£	£

IAB Level 3 answer booklet II

This Page is Intentionally Left Blank for Notes/Workings

QUESTION TWO

Cara, Dee and Eve Trading in Partnership

Capital Accounts - for Use in Answering Question 2 Task A

DR   Capital Accounts   C

Date	Details	Cara £	Dee £	Eve £	Date	Details	Cara £	Dee £	Eve £

Workings – Goodwill Adjustment

Page   6

Cara, Dee and Eve Trading in Partnership

Profit and Loss Appropriation Account - for Use in Answering Question 2
Task B

Cara, Dee and Eve		
Profit and Loss Appropriation Account for the Year Ended 31 May 2014		
	£	£

Cara, Dee and Eve Trading in Partnership

Current Accounts for Use in Answering Question 2 Task C

DR   Current Accounts   C

Date	Details	Cara £	Dee £	Eve £	Date	Details	Cara £	Dee £	Eve £

This Page is Intentionally Left Blank for Notes/Workings

IAB Level 3 answer booklet II

QUESTION ONE – Comet Trading

Trial Balance – for use in Answering Question One Task A

Comet Trading Trial Balance as at 31 May 2014	DR £	CR £
Bank		
Cash		
Sales		
Telephone		
Purchases		
Sales returns		
Purchases returns		
Discounts allowed		
Discounts received		
Stock (31 May 2013)		
Equipment (cost)		
Equipment (provision for depreciation 31 May 2013)		
Value Added Tax (VAT)		
Drawings		
Rent and rates		
Capital		
Wages		
Vehicles (cost)		
Vehicles (provision for depreciation 31 May 2013)		
Vehicle expenses		
Heat and light		
Trade debtors		
Trade creditors		
Sundry expenses		
Suspense		
Totals		

IAB Level 3 answer booklet II

Comet Trading

Suspense Account - for Use in Answering Question One Tasks B and D

DR					Suspense Account			CR
2014	Details		£	2014	Details		£	

Journal - for Use in Answering Question One Task C

Journal

2014	Details	DR £	CR £

Comet Trading

Extended Trial Balance for Use in Answering Question One Tasks E, F and G

Comet Trading – EXTENDED TRIAL BALANCE AS AT 31 MAY 2014								
	Trial Balance		Adjustments		Profit & Loss		Balance Sheet	
Ledger Account	DR	CR	DR	CR	DR	CR	DR	CR
	£	£	£	£	£	£	£	£
Bank								
Cash								
Sales								
Telephone								
Purchases								
Sales returns								
Purchase returns								
Discounts allowed								
Discounts received								
Stock (31 May 2013)								
Equipment (cost)								
Equipment prov'n for dep'n								
Value Added Tax (VAT)								
Drawings								
Rent and rates								
Capital								
Wages								
Vehicles (cost)								
Vehicles prov'n for dep'n								
Vehicle expenses								
Heat and light								
Trade debtors								
Trade creditors								
Sundry expenses								
Totals								
Closing stock – P & L								
Closing stock – Bal Sheet								
Prepayment adjustment								
Accruals adjustment								
Depreciation expense								
Net profit								
Totals								

Comet Trading

Trading and Profit and Loss Account - for Use in Answering Question One
Task H

Comet Trading			
Trading and Profit and Loss Account for the Year Ended 31 May 2014			
	£	£	£
Sales			
Less Sales returns			
Less Cost of Goods Sold			
Opening stock			
Add Purchases			
Less Purchase returns			
Less Closing stock			
Cost of Sales			
Gross Profit			
Add Other Income			
Discounts received			
Less Expenses			
Telephone			
Discounts allowed			
Rent and rates			
Wages			
Vehicle expenses			
Heat and light			
Sundry expenses			
Depreciation			
Net profit			

Comet Trading

Balance Sheet - for Use in Answering Question One Task H

Comet Trading Balance Sheet as at 31 May 2014			
	£	£	£
Fixed Assets	Cost	Less Dep'n to Date	NBV
Equipment			
Vehicles			
Current Assets			
Stock			
Trade debtors			
Prepayment			
Bank			
Cash			
Less Current Liabilities			
Trade creditors			
Accrual			
Value Added Tax (VAT)			
Working capital			
Financed By:			
Capital			
Add Net Profit			
Less Drawings			

This Page is Intentionally Left Blank for Notes/Workings

June 2014 Examination
Model Answers

322 Exam ID

Model Answer Booklet for the following Qualifications:

300: Level 3 Certificate in Bookkeeping QCF: 50084793
320: Level 3 Certificate in Manual Bookkeeping QCF: 50092601
340: Level 3 Certificate in Applied Bookkeeping QCF: 50092765
3000: Level 3 Certificate in Bookkeeping QCF: 60107315
3030: Level 3 Diploma in Bookkeeping QCF: 60104843

Time Allowed 3 Hours
Paper No: 0041

FOR USE BY ASSESSOR ONLY:

IAB ID	Units covered	Possible marks
310	Prepare financial statements for a partnership: Y6010742	60
311	Prepare financial statements for a sole trader: A6010734	40

International Association of Book-keepers, Suite 5, 20 Churchill Square, Kings Hill, West Malling, Kent ME19 4YU
Tel: 01732 897750, Fax: 01732 897751, email:education@iab.org.uk Website: www.iab.org.uk

IAB Level 3 model answers II

Alda and Bani Trading in Partnership
Trading and Profit and Loss Account – Answer Task A

Alda and Bani			
Trading and Profit and Loss Account for the Year Ended 31 May 2014			
	£	£	£
Sales			1/4 740,480
Less Cost of Goods Sold			
Opening stock	1/4 45,560		
Add Purchases	1/4 594,220		
		639,780	
Less Closing stock		1/4 48,430	
Cost of Sales			1/4 591,350
Gross profit			1 149,130
Less Expenses			
Wages and salaries		1/4 64,340	
Heat and light (£5,440 + £1,620)		1/2 7,060	
Rates (£15,800 - £5,800)		1/2 10,000	
Vehicle expenses		1/4 6,670	
Advertising		1/4 2,400	
Bank charges and interest		1/4 1,120	
Other expenses		1/4 2,750	
Depreciation		1/2 18,000	
			112,340
Net profit			1 36,790

6 Marks

IAB L3 Cert June 2014 Paper 2

Alda and Bani Trading in Partnership
Profit and Loss Appropriation Account – Answer Task B

Alda and Bani		
Profit and Loss Appropriation Account for the Year Ended 31 May 2014		
	£	£
Net profit		1/2 36,790
Add Interest on drawings: Alda	1/2 600	
Bani	1/2 400	
		1,000
		37,790
Less Interest on capital: Alda	1/2 2,400	
Bani	1/2 1,600	
		4,000
		33,790
Less Share of profits: Alda	2 16,895	
Bani	2 16,895	
		33,790
		-

6½ Marks

IAB L3 Cert June 2014 Paper 2

Alda and Bani Trading in Partnership

Current Accounts – Answer Task C

DR   **Current Accounts**   CR

Date	Details	Alda £	Bani £	Date	Details	Alda £	Bani £
31/5/13	Balance b/f	¼ 1,220		31/5/13	Balance b/f		¼ 1,650
31/5/14	Interest on drawings	¼ 600	¼ 400	31/5/14	Interest on capital	¼ 2,400	¼ 1,600
31/5/14	Drawings	¼ 16,000	¼ 14,000	31/5/14	Share of profit	¼ 16,895	¼ 16,895
31/5/14	Balance c/d	½ 1,475	½ 5,745				
		19,295	20,145			19,295	20,145
				31/5/14	Balance b/d	¼ 1,475	¼ 5,745

4 Marks

IAB L3 Cert June 2014 Paper 2

Alda and Bani Trading in Partnership
Balance Sheet - Answer Task D

Alda and Bani Balance Sheet as at 31 May 2014			
	£	£	£
Fixed Assets	Cost	Less Dep'n to Date	NBV
Premises	125,000	-	¼ 125,000
Equipment	60,000	½ 42,000	¼ 18,000
Vehicles	30,000	½ 12,000	¼ 18,000
	215,000	54,000	½ 161,000
Current Assets			
Stock	¼ 48,430		
Trade debtors	¼ 40,680		
Prepaid expenses	¼ 5,800		
Cash	¼ 200		
		95,110	
Less Current Liabilities			
Trade creditors	¼ 44,820		
Accrued expenses	¼ 1,620		
Bank	¼ 2,450		
		48,890	
Working capital			½ 46,220
			1 207,220
Financed By:			
Capital – Alda	¼ 120,000		
Add Current account	¼ 1,475		
		121,475	
Capital – Bani	¼ 80,000		
Add Current account	¼ 5,745		
		85,745	
			1 207,220

7½ Marks

Total This Question = 24 Marks

IAB L3 Cert June 2014 Paper 2

QUESTION TWO

Cara, Dee and Eve Trading in Partnership

Capital Accounts – Answer Task A

DR   Capital Accounts   CR

Date	Details	Cara £	Dee £	Eve £	Date	Details	Cara £	Dee £	Eve £
1/6/13	Goodwill adjm't	-	-	2 12,000	31/5/13	Balance b/f	½ 80,000	½ 50,000	-
1/6/13	Balance c/d	1 88,000	1 54,000	1 48,000	1/6/13	Bank	-	-	½ 60,000
					1/6/13	Goodwill adjm't	2 8,000	2 4,000	-
		88,000	54,000	60,000			88,000	54,000	60,000
					1/6/13	Balance b/d	½ 88,000	½ 54,000	½ 48,000

12 Marks

Workings – Goodwill Adjustment

Partners	Goodwill Creation £	Goodwill Deletion £	Net Adjustment £
Cara	24,000 (CR)	16,000 (DR)	8,000 (CR)
Dee	16,000 (CR)	12,000 (DR)	4,000 (CR)
Eve	-	12,000 (DR)	12,000 (DR)
	40,000 (CR)	40,000 (DR)	-

IAB L3 Cert June 2014 Paper 2

Cara, Dee and Eve Trading in Partnership

Profit and Loss Appropriation Account – Answer Task B

<table>
<tr><th colspan="3">Cara, Dee and Eve
Profit and Loss Appropriation Account for the Year Ended 31 May 2014</th></tr>
<tr><td></td><td>£</td><td>£</td></tr>
<tr><td>Net profit</td><td></td><td>½
56,600</td></tr>
<tr><td>**Less** Interest on capital: Cara</td><td>2 2,640</td><td></td></tr>
<tr><td>Dee</td><td>2 1,620</td><td></td></tr>
<tr><td>Eve</td><td>2 1,440</td><td></td></tr>
<tr><td></td><td></td><td>5,700</td></tr>
<tr><td></td><td></td><td>50,900</td></tr>
<tr><td>**Less** Salaries: Cara</td><td>½ 6,000</td><td></td></tr>
<tr><td>Dee</td><td>½
5,000</td><td></td></tr>
<tr><td>Eve</td><td>½ 4,000</td><td></td></tr>
<tr><td></td><td></td><td>15,000</td></tr>
<tr><td></td><td></td><td>35,900</td></tr>
<tr><td>**Less** Share of profit: Cara</td><td>2 14,360</td><td></td></tr>
<tr><td>Dee</td><td>2
10,770</td><td></td></tr>
<tr><td>Eve</td><td>2
10,770</td><td></td></tr>
<tr><td></td><td></td><td>35,900</td></tr>
<tr><td></td><td></td><td>-</td></tr>
<tr><td></td><td></td><td></td></tr>
</table>

14 Marks

IAB L3 Cert June 2014 Paper 2

Cara, Dee and Eve Trading in Partnership

Current Accounts - Answer Task C

DR Date	Details	Cara £	Dee £	Eve £	Date	Details	Cara £	Dee £	CR Eve £
31/5/13	Balance b/f	½ 800	-	-	31/5/13	Balance b/f	-	½ 900	-
31/5/14	Drawings	½20,000	½18,000	½ 16,000	31/5/14	Interest on capital	½ 2,640	½ 1,620	½ 1,440
31/5/14	Balance c/d	½ 2,200	½ 290	½ 210	31/5/14	Salaries	½ 6,000	½ 5,000	½ 4,000
					31/5/14	Share of profit	½ 14,360	½ 10,770	½10,770
		23,000	18,290	16,210			23,000	18,290	16,210
					31/5/14	Balance b/d	½ 2,200	½ 290	½ 210

10   Marks

Total This Question = 36 Marks

Total This Unit = 60 Marks

IAB L3 Cert June 2014 Paper 2

SECTION B
QUESTION ONE
Comet Trading
Trial Balance – Answer Task A

<table>
<tr><td colspan="5" align="center">**Comet Trading**
Trial Balance as at 31 May 2014</td></tr>
<tr><td></td><td colspan="2" align="center">**DR**
£</td><td colspan="2" align="center">**CR**
£</td></tr>
<tr><td>Bank</td><td>1/4</td><td>2,150</td><td></td><td></td></tr>
<tr><td>Cash</td><td>1/4</td><td>500</td><td></td><td></td></tr>
<tr><td>Sales</td><td></td><td></td><td>1/4</td><td>744,620</td></tr>
<tr><td>Telephone</td><td>1/4</td><td>1,020</td><td></td><td></td></tr>
<tr><td>Purchases</td><td>1/4</td><td>607,760</td><td></td><td></td></tr>
<tr><td>Sales returns</td><td>1/4</td><td>2,650</td><td></td><td></td></tr>
<tr><td>Purchases returns</td><td></td><td></td><td>1/4</td><td>1,920</td></tr>
<tr><td>Discounts allowed</td><td>1/4</td><td>2,870</td><td></td><td></td></tr>
<tr><td>Discounts received</td><td></td><td></td><td>1/4</td><td>3,650</td></tr>
<tr><td>Stock (31 May 2013)</td><td>1/4</td><td>64,550</td><td></td><td></td></tr>
<tr><td>Equipment (cost)</td><td>1/4</td><td>32,000</td><td></td><td></td></tr>
<tr><td>Equipment (provision for depreciation 31 May 2013)</td><td></td><td></td><td>1/4</td><td>6,400</td></tr>
<tr><td>Value Added Tax (VAT)</td><td></td><td></td><td>1/4</td><td>4,440</td></tr>
<tr><td>Drawings</td><td>1/4</td><td>36,140</td><td></td><td></td></tr>
<tr><td>Rent and rates</td><td>1/4</td><td>21,400</td><td></td><td></td></tr>
<tr><td>Capital</td><td></td><td></td><td>1/4</td><td>104,250</td></tr>
<tr><td>Wages</td><td>1/4</td><td>46,980</td><td></td><td></td></tr>
<tr><td>Vehicles (cost)</td><td>1/4</td><td>45,000</td><td></td><td></td></tr>
<tr><td>Vehicles (provision for depreciation 31 May 2013)</td><td></td><td></td><td>1/4</td><td>9,000</td></tr>
<tr><td>Vehicle expenses</td><td>1/4</td><td>4,980</td><td></td><td></td></tr>
<tr><td>Heat and light</td><td>1/4</td><td>2,960</td><td></td><td></td></tr>
<tr><td>Trade debtors</td><td>1/4</td><td>47,790</td><td></td><td></td></tr>
<tr><td>Trade creditors</td><td></td><td></td><td>¼</td><td>45,550</td></tr>
<tr><td>Sundry expenses</td><td>1/4</td><td>350</td><td></td><td></td></tr>
<tr><td>Suspense</td><td>1/2</td><td>730</td><td></td><td></td></tr>
<tr><td>**Totals**</td><td>1/2</td><td>919,830</td><td>1/2</td><td>919,830</td></tr>
</table>

7½ Marks

Page 8

IAB L3 Cert June 2014 Paper 2

Comet trading

Suspense Account – Answer Tasks B and D

DR					Suspense Account		CR
2014	**Details**		**£**	**2014**	**Details**		**£**
31 May	Difference in books 1/2		730	31 May	Purchases 1/2		1,000
31 May	Sales 1/2		270				
			1,000				1,000

1½ Marks

Journal – Answer Task C

Journal

2014	Details	DR £	CR £
31 May	Purchases 1/4	½ 1,000	
	Suspense 1/4		½ 1,000
	Correction of error, purchases understated when transferred from Purchase Day Book 1/4		
31 May	Suspense 1/4	½ 270	
	Sales 1/4		½ 270
	Correction of transposition error understating balance on Sales Account 1/4		

3½ Marks

IAB L3 Cert June 2014 Paper 2

Comet Trading
Extended Trial Balance – Answers Tasks E, F and G

Ledger Account	Trial Balance DR £	Trial Balance CR £	Adjustments DR £	Adjustments CR £	Profit & Loss DR £	Profit & Loss CR £	Balance Sheet DR £	Balance Sheet CR £
	Comet Trading – EXTENDED TRIAL BALANCE AS AT 31 MAY 2014							
Bank	2,150						¼ 2,150	
Cash	500						¼ 500	
Sales		½ 744,890				¼ 744,890		
Telephone	1,020				¼ 1,020			
Purchases	½ 608,760				¼ 608,760			
Sales returns	2,650				¼ 2,650			
Purchase returns		1,920				¼ 1,920		
Discounts allowed	2,870				¼ 2,870			
Discounts received		3,650				¼ 3,650		
Stock (31 May 2013)	64,550				¼ 64,550			
Equipment (cost)	32,000						¼ 32,000	
Equipment prov'n for dep'n		6,400		¼ 6,400				½ 12,800
Value Added Tax (VAT)		4,440						¼ 4,440
Drawings	36,140						¼ 36,140	
Rent and rates	21,400			¼ 7,200	½ 14,200			
Capital		104,250						¼ 104,250
Wages	46,980				¼ 46,980			
Vehicles (cost)	45,000						¼ 45,000	
Vehicles prov'n for dep'n		9,000		¼ 9,000				½ 18,000
Vehicle expenses	4,980				¼ 4,980			
Heat and light	2,960		¼ 1,320		½ 4,280			
Trade debtors	47,790						¼ 47,790	
Trade creditors		45,550						¼ 45,550
Sundry expenses	350				¼ 350			
Totals	½ 920,100	½ 920,100	-	-	-	-	-	-
Closing stock – P & L				¼69,120		¼ 69,120		
Closing stock – Bal Sheet			¼69,120				¼ 69,120	
Prepayment adjustment			¼ 7,200				¼ 7,200	
Accruals adjustment				¼ 1,320				¼ 1,320
Depreciation expense			¼15,400		¼ 15,400			
Net profit					½ 53,540			½ 53,540
Totals			½93,040	½93,040	½ 819,580	½ 819,580	½ 239,900	½ 239,900

16½ Marks

IAB Level 3 model answers II

Comet Trading

Trading and Profit and Loss Account – Answer Task H

Comet Trading Trading and Profit and Loss Account for the Year Ended 31 May 2014		
	£	**£**	**£**
Sales		¼ 744,890	
Less Sales returns		¼ 2,650	
			742,240
Less Cost of Goods Sold			
Opening stock	1/4 64,550		
Add Purchases	1/4 608,760		
Less Purchase returns	1/4 1,920		
		671,390	
Less Closing stock		1/4 69,120	
Cost of Sales			½ 602,270
Gross Profit			½ 139,970
Add Other Income			
Discounts received			1/4 3,650
			143,620
Less Expenses			
Telephone		1/4 1,020	
Discounts allowed		1/4 2,870	
Rent and rates		1/4 14,200	
Wages		1/4 46,980	
Vehicle expenses		1/4 4,980	
Heat and light		1/4 4,280	
Sundry expenses		1/4 350	
Depreciation		1/4 15,400	
			90,080
Net profit			1 53,540

5¾ Marks

IAB L3 Cert June 2014 Paper 2

Comet Trading

Balance Sheet – Answer Task H

<table>
<tr><td colspan="4" align="center">Comet Trading
Balance Sheet as at 31 May 2014</td></tr>
<tr><td></td><td align="center">£
Cost</td><td align="center">£
Less Dep'n to Date</td><td align="center">£
NBV</td></tr>
<tr><td>**Fixed Assets**</td><td></td><td></td><td></td></tr>
<tr><td>Equipment</td><td align="right">32,000</td><td align="right">1/4 12,800</td><td align="right">1/4   19,200</td></tr>
<tr><td>Vehicles</td><td align="right">45,000</td><td align="right">1/4 18,000</td><td align="right">1/4   27,000</td></tr>
<tr><td></td><td align="right">77,000</td><td align="right">30,800</td><td align="right">1/4 46,200</td></tr>
<tr><td>**Current Assets**</td><td></td><td></td><td></td></tr>
<tr><td>Stock</td><td align="right">1/4 69,120</td><td></td><td></td></tr>
<tr><td>Trade debtors</td><td align="right">1/4 47,790</td><td></td><td></td></tr>
<tr><td>Prepayment</td><td align="right">1/4   7,200</td><td></td><td></td></tr>
<tr><td>Bank</td><td align="right">1/4   2,150</td><td></td><td></td></tr>
<tr><td>Cash</td><td align="right">1/4   500</td><td></td><td></td></tr>
<tr><td></td><td></td><td align="right">126,760</td><td></td></tr>
<tr><td>**Less Current Liabilities**</td><td></td><td></td><td></td></tr>
<tr><td>Trade creditors</td><td align="right">1/4 45,550</td><td></td><td></td></tr>
<tr><td>Accrual</td><td align="right">1/4   1,320</td><td></td><td></td></tr>
<tr><td>Value Added Tax (VAT)</td><td align="right">1/4   4,440</td><td></td><td></td></tr>
<tr><td></td><td></td><td align="right">51,310</td><td></td></tr>
<tr><td>Working capital</td><td></td><td></td><td align="right">1/4 75,450</td></tr>
<tr><td></td><td></td><td></td><td align="right">½ 121,650</td></tr>
<tr><td>**Financed By:**</td><td></td><td></td><td></td></tr>
<tr><td>Capital</td><td align="right">1/4 104,250</td><td></td><td></td></tr>
<tr><td>**Add** Net Profit</td><td align="right">1/4 53,540</td><td></td><td></td></tr>
<tr><td></td><td></td><td align="right">157,790</td><td></td></tr>
<tr><td>**Less** Drawings</td><td></td><td align="right">1/4 36,140</td><td></td></tr>
<tr><td></td><td></td><td></td><td align="right">121,650</td></tr>
<tr><td></td><td></td><td></td><td align="right">½ 121,650</td></tr>
</table>

5¼ Marks
Total This Question= 40 Marks
Total This Unit = 40 Marks

OCR Advanced Subsidiary GCE *Accounting Principles*
2005 Specimen Paper

Gemma Bay started business on 1 January 1998. The following information is available for the purchases of machinery and office equipment.

Machinery
1 January 1998 – three machines purchased, M1 and M2 costing £15,000 each, and M3 costing £20,000.

1 January 2000 – two machines purchased, M4 and M5 costing £12,000 each.

1 October 2000 – two machines purchased, M6 costing £15,000 and M7 costing £25,000.

Office equipment
1 January 1998 – office equipment purchased costing £25,000. Machinery is depreciated at the rate of 20% per annum by the reducing balance method. Office equipment is depreciated by the straight line method over an estimated life of 10 years, taking into account a residual value of 10% on cost price. Machine M2 was disposed of on 30 June 1999 for £10,200 and Machine M3 was disposed of on 30 September 2000 for £13,000. No office equipment was disposed of during the period.

A full year's depreciation is provided in the year that machinery is purchased. No depreciation is provided in the year of disposal. The financial year end is 31 December.

Required
(a) Prepare the following accounts for each of the years 1998, 1999
and 2000:
(i) Machinery Account
(ii) Provision for Depreciation of Machinery Account. [19]

(b) Prepare the Machinery Disposals Account for each of the years
1999 and 2000. [8]

(c) Prepare the Balance Sheet extract as at 31 December 2000 for
Machinery and Office Equipment. [4]

(d) Evaluate the choice of depreciation methods used by the business
for these types of fixed asset. [8]
[Total: 39]

© OCR 2000

OCR Advanced Subsidiary GCE Accounting *Accounting Principles*
2005 Specimen Paper

Dragon Ltd manufactures a single product. Its costs and sales for the year ended 30 November 2000 were as follows:

Units sold	21,000
Selling price per unit	£40
Variable costs per unit	
Wages	£8
Materials	£18
Overheads	£4
Fixed costs	£187,000

To improve profit for the year commencing 1 December 2000 the following changes are expected to take place.
Units to be sold are 22,500.
Selling price is to be maintained at £40 per unit.
Wages are to be increased by 5% per unit.
Material costs are to be reduced by 10% per unit, this being achieved by committing to a long-term contract with a single supplier only.
Variable overheads are to be reduced by £0.10 per unit.
Fixed costs are to increase by £20,000.

Required
(a) Using the data for the year commencing 1 December 2000, calculate:
    (i)   the break-even in units and sales value;
    (ii)   the profit for the year;
    (iii) the margin of safety in units and as a percentage;
    (iv) the sales in units required to maintain the profit level of the
    year ended 30 November 2000.   **[24]**

(b) Explain what you understand by the term 'margin of safety'.   **[4]**

(c) Evaluate its usefulness to a company.   **[4]**

(d) Briefly outline two advantages and two limitations of break-even
     analysis.   **[4]**

[Total: 36]

**OCR Advanced Subsidiary GCE Accounting *Final Accounts*
2502 Specimen Paper**

On 28 February 1999 the following balances were extracted from the books of
Barber Manufacturing, a local business solely owned by Ken Barber.

	£
Stocks – 1 March 1998	
Raw materials	38,300
Work in progress	40,200
Finished goods	58,590
Purchases – raw materials	573,000
Direct expenses	63,100
Direct wages	146,200
Indirect wages	38,300
Sales	1,163,400
Debtors	93,600
Loan interest	500
Rent and rates	16,100
Insurance	920
Sundry office expenses	15,760
Premises at cost	120,000
Provision for depreciation – premises	24,000
Plant and machinery at cost	80,000
Provision for depreciation – plant and machinery	52,560
Provision for unrealised profit and goods manufactured	2,790
Bad debts	720
Provision for doubtful debts	3,120
Loan (10% p.a. interest)	10,000

The following information is also relevant:

- Stocks as at 28 February 1999:
  - raw materials £35,40
  - work in progress £36,476
  - finished goods £74,340.

- The business transfers finished goods from the factory to the Trading Account
  at factory cost plus 5% profit on manufacture.

- A provision is to be made for unrealised profit on the stock of finished goods
  on 28th February 1999 of £3,540.

- The loan was taken out on 1 March 1997 and is for a five-year period.

- Rent and rates are apportioned between the factory and office on the basis 5:1.

- Rent of £1,900 is outstanding.

- Insurance, which includes a prepayment of £80, is apportioned between factory and office on the basis 6:1.

- Provision for depreciation is to be made as follows:
  - premises: 5% on cost, to be apportioned 5:1 between factory and office
  - plant and machinery: 30% on the reducing balance basis, to be apportioned 6:1 between factory and office
  - provision for doubtful debts is to be provided at 4% of debtors.

Required

(a) A Manufacturing, Trading and Profit and Loss Account for the year ended 28 February 1999 (for internal use only)   **[28]**

(b) An explanation of the advantages and disadvantages for Barber Manufacturing of changing from a sole trader business to a partnership in terms of ownership and finance.   **[8]**

[Total: 36]

© OCR 2000

**OCR Advanced Subsidiary GCE Accounting *Final Accounts*
2502 Specimen Paper**

Nick Morgan, a member of Sandfields Sports Club, has taken over the duties of Treasurer of the Club, the previous Treasurer having recently moved away from the area. The following statement has been prepared for presentation to members at the Club's annual general meeting.

Balance Sheet for the year end 31 December 1999

Balances for 1998	£		**Payments**	£
Premises	12,000		Equipment	1,100
Equipment	2,400		Donations	250
Bank	810		Rates and insurance	1,840
	15,210		Postage	235
			Depreciation and equipment	480
Subscriptions received			Part-time wages	2,707
1998	279			
1999	4,314			
2000	168	4,761		
			Balances to 2000	
			Premises	12,000
Life membership	600		Equipment	1,920
			Bank	1,439
Premises sub-let	1,300			
Premises sub-let				
advance payment	100			
		21,971		21,971

- A life membership scheme was introduced during 1999 and any such fees received are to be capitalised and transferred to income over five years by equal installments each year, commencing in the year received.

- Premises are not depreciated, while equipment is depreciated by 20% of the balance brought forward from the year before. Provision should be made on new equipment bought during the year. The depreciation rate is applied for the full year irrespective of date of purchase. No assets were disposed of during the year.

- At 31 December 1999 £40 was owing for part-time wages, and rates of £110 had been prepaid.

Required

(a) An Income and Expenditure Account for the year ending
31 December 1999, together with a Balance Sheet as at that date,
to good accounting format, for submission to members.   **[28]**

(b) Explain to the new Treasurer the differences between a
Receipts and Payments Account, and an Income and Expenditure
Account. Indicate when one would be used in preference to
the other.   **[12]**

[Total 40 marks]

© OCR 2000

OCR Advanced GCE Accounting *Company Accounts and Interpretation*
2505 Specimen Paper

The summarised Balance sheets at the end of the last two years for Tyler plc are shown below

	30 April 1998			30 April 1999		
	£'000	£'000	£'000	£'000	£'000	£'000
Fixed assets	Cost	Depreciation	Net	Cost	Depreciation	Net
Premises	100	–	100	100	–	100
Plant and machinery	80	18	62	105	24	81
Motor vehicles	30	12	18	30	16	14
	210	30	180	235	40	195
Current assets						
Stock		38			79	
Debtors		52			49	
Bank		56			25	
		146			153	
Current liabilities						
Trade creditors	62			71		
Corporation Tax	11			12		
Dividends	8	81	65	9	92	61
			245			256
Capital and reserves						
Ordinary shares			200			210
6% Redeemable preference shares			20			
Capital redemption Reserve			–			10
Profit and loss			25			36
			245			256

(i) Plant and machinery costing £25,000 was sold during the year at a loss of £3,000. The depreciation charge for the year on plant and machinery was £16,000. No motor vehicles were disposed of or bought during the year.

(ii) The 6% redeemable preference shares were redeemed at par on 1 May 1998.

(iii) Interest received from short term investments purchased and sold between 1 January to 31 March 1999 amounted to £2,000.

Required

(a) A Cash Flow Statement in accordance with FRS 1 (revised) for the year ended 30 April 1999. **[31]**

(b) A major shareholder is concerned about a reduction in the bank balance of Tyler plc although a profit has been made for the year. How would the directors explain this situation? **[4]**

[Total marks 35]

© OCR 2000

OCR Advanced GCE Accounting Company *Accounts and Interpretation* 2505 Specimen Paper

The issued share capital of Cowbridge plc consists of 400,000 Ordinary Share of £1 each, and 80,000 7% Preference Shares of £1 each. If offered a further 150,000 Ordinary Shares to the public at a price of £1.80 each.

The terms of the issue were:

	£
Payable on application	0.50
Payable on allotment (including the premium)	0.80
First call	0.50

Applications were received for 165,000 shares. It was decided to return application monies to applicants for 15,000 shares, and the remaining applicants were allotted shares to exactly the full issue amount.

All money due on allotment was duly received and the first call was to be made at a later date.

Required

(a) Prepare the following ledger accounts to record the above transactions. (Note: balancing of accounts is not required.)
   Bank Account
   Application and Allotment Account
   Ordinary Share Capital Account
   Share Premium Account   **[14]**

(b) Explain the term 'authorised share capital'. How is the authorised share capital of a company authorised? Why could this capital differ from the issued capital?   **[6]**

[Total: 20]

© OCR 2000

AQA GCE Accounting Foundation Tier Paper 2 3122/2F
24 June 2003

David Ford is an electrical wholesaler. Information about some of the businesses transactions for February 2003 is given below.

On 8 February 2003 David Ford sent two invoices to customers, the details were as follows:

	£
Invoice number 00121 to Melchester Electrical Supplies	
10 personal stereos model A43 at £40 each	400.00
plus VAT	70.00
	470.00
Invoice number 00122 to Town Traders Ltd.	
12 personal stereos model AT79 at £70 each	840.00
6 micro hi-fis model T24 at £90 each	540.00
	1,380.00
Less trade discount 20%	276.00
plus VAT	193.20
	1,297.20

(a) Record the information from the two invoices in the sales journal

Date	Customer	Invoice No	Goods		VAT		Total	
			£	p	£	p	£	p

PCD Manufactures Ltd is one of David Ford's suppliers. The following information relates to the account for this creditor.

Feb 1   Balance, amount owed to PCD Manufactures Ltd by David Ford £600

14   David Ford settled his account with PCD Manufacture Ltd by cheque £600

23   Invoice sent by PCD Manufactures Ltd to David Ford for goods £1,000 plus VAT £175

27   David Ford received a credit note from PCD Manufactures Ltd for £160 plus VAT £28, for goods returned.

(b) Record the above information in the account of PCD Manufactures Ltd. Bring down the balance on the account at March 2003.

PCD Manufacturing Ltd Account

Date			£	p	Date			£	p

(6 marks)

David Ford maintains a three-column cash book. The transactions for March 2003 have been recorded.

Date	Details	Folio	Discount £	Cash £	Bank £	Date	Details	Folio	Discount £	Cash £	Bank £
Mar 1	Balance	B/d		800		Mar 1	Balance	B/d			3,000
Mar 5	T Wolf		75		1,425	Mar 3	Cleaning			40	
Mar 8	Sales				2,025	Mar 8	A Kalifa		100		1,900
Mar 17	F Townsend		250		4,750	Mar 11	Motor expenses			30	
Mar 18	Cash	C			700	Mar 18	Bank	C		700	
Mar 30	Sales			55		Mar 20	Wages				350
						Mar 23	B Hughes		40		760
						Mar 27	Drawings				400
						Mar 31	Balance	C/d		85	2,490
			325	855	8,900				140	855	8,900
April	Balance	B/d		85	2,490						

(c) What does the balance b/d of £3,000 on 1 March represent? **(1 mark)**

(d) (i) Do the columns headed 'Discount' refer to cash discount or trade discount? **(1 mark)**

    (ii) Give a reason for your choice of answer in (d) (i) **(2 marks)**

(e) (i) Is the discount on 5 March discount allowed or discount received? **(1 mark)**

(ii) Give a reason for your choice of answer in (e) (i) **(2 marks)**

(iii) What percentage is the discount in (e) (i)? **(1 mark)**

(f) (i) Is the discount on 8 March discount allowed or discount received? **(1 mark)**

(ii) give a reason for your choice of answer in (f) (i) **(2 marks)**

(g) (i) What does the C in the Folio column on 18 March stand for **(1 mark)**

(ii) Explain why there are two entries in the Cash Book on 18 March **(1 mark)**

(h) What do the drawings on 27 march represent? **(2 marks)**

(i) Name and complete the following accounts to show where the totals of £325 and £140 will be transferred to at the end of March.

				Account			

Date		£	p	Date		£	p

				Account			

Date		£	p	Date		£	p

(4 marks)

AQA GCE Accounting Foundation Tier Paper 2 3122/2F
24 June 2003

The following list of balances appeared in the books of W. Boardman at 31 March 2003.

	£
Sales	492,700
Purchases	250,000
Carriage inwards	1,200
Carriage outwards	1,500
Discounts allowed	2,800
Discounts received	2,400
Returns inwards	7,000
Returns outwards	8,000
Vehicles at cost	70,000
Trade debtors	50,000
Motor expenses	24,000
Insurance	12,000
Stock at 1 April 2002	33,000
Electricity	16,000
Salaries	102,000
Sundry expenses	4,850
Rent received	7,000

The following additional information is also available.

- Stock at 31 March 2003 was £35,000.

- Provide for depreciation on cost as follows: vehicles 20% p.a.

- Electricity of £4,000 was outstanding at 31 March 2003.

- Insurance of £3,000 was prepaid at 31 March 2003.

Prepare W. Boardman's trading and profit and loss accounts for the year ended 31 March 2003. **(21 marks)**

© AQA 2003

AQA GCE Accounting Foundation Tier Paper 2 3122/2F
24 June 2003

RolHoMa Ltd has prepared the following balance sheet which contains a number of errors.

RolHoMa Ltd Balance Sheet
for the year ended 31 December 2002

	£		£
Share capital and reserves	123,000	Premises	110,000
Motor vehicles	28,000	Stock at 31 December 2002	11,000
Debentures	55,000	Stock at 1 January 2002	16,000
Cash	1,000	Machinery	40,000
Bank loan repayable 2005	6,000	Retained profit	23,500
Trade debtors	10,000	Balance at bank	4,000
		Expenses owing	500
		Trade creditors	7,000
		Fixtures and fittings	11,000
	223,000		223,000

(a) Explain briefly what is meant by:
  (i) Fixed assets (**2 marks**)
  (ii) Current assets (**2 marks**)
  (iii) Current liabilities (**2 marks**)
  (iv) Long-term liabilities (**2 marks**)

(b) Prepare a corrected balance sheet for RolHoMa Ltd. showing clearly:
  (i) Fixed assets
  (ii) Current assets
  (iii) Current liabilities
  (iv) Long-term liabilities
  (v) Share capital and reserve

(**22 marks**)

AQA GCE Accounting Higher Tier Paper 1 3122/1H
18 June 2003

The following information was taken from the accounting records of J. Bells Ltd.

Sales Journal (Day Books)

Date 2003	Customer	Goods £	VAT £	Net £
14 May	A. Dancer & Co Ltd	2,600	455	3,055

At 1 May 2003 A. Dancer and Co Ltd owed J. Bells Ltd £4,650.

On 18 May 2003 A. Dancer and Co Ltd sent a cheque for £4,570 to J. Bells Ltd claiming £80 discount.

Using the ledger account below write up the account for A. Dancer and Co Ltd as it would appear in the books of J. Bells Ltd. Bring down the balance on 1 June 2003.

A. Dancer and Co Ltd Account

Date	Details		Date	Details	

(6 marks)

A trial balance has been prepared but the following items have not been included:

	£
Purchases	235,000
Machinery	120,000
Bank overdraft	53,000
Provision for doubtful debts	4,000
Returns inwards	2,000
Carriage outwards	3,000
Rent received	25,000
Bad debts written off	10,000
Carriage inwards	20,000

From the list above complete and total the following trial balance by inserting the appropriate amount in the correct column.

Trial balance as at 31 March 2003

		Dr £	Cr £
Total of trial balance entries made so far		325,000	633,000
(a)	Purchases		
(b)	Machinery		
(c)	Bank overdraft		
(d)	Provision for doubtful debts		
(e)	Returns inwards		
(f)	Carriage outwards		
(g)	Rent received		
(h)	Bad debts written off		
(i)	Carriage inwards		

(9 marks)

© AQA 2003

AQA GCE Accounting Higher Tier paper 1 13122/1H
18 June 2003

Select the information required from the following list of balances to produce a Balance Sheet as at 31 May 2003 for United Boxes plc. The Balance Sheet should show a figure for working capital.

	£
Machinery (at cost)	80,000
Issued ordinary shares	75,000
Vehicles (at cost)	50,000
Opening stock	10,000
General reserve	25,000
Debtors	30,000
Closing stock	15,000
Bank overdraft	2,000
Creditors	17,000
Provision for depreciation	
Machinery	20,000
Vehicles	15,000
Provision for doubtful debts	500
Proposed dividends	10,000
Profit and Loss Account balance as at 31 May 2003	10,500

(17 marks)

© AQA 2003

AQA GCE Accounting *Unit 2 Financial Accounting: Introduction to Published Accounts of Limited Companies* **14 January 2004**

The following balances have been extracted form the books of Positive Advertising Plc at 31 December 2003.

	£000
Issued share capital	
Ordinary shares of £1 each fully paid	2,000
6% Preference shares of £1 each fully paid	500
Profit and loss account balance as at 1 January 2003	65
Revaluation reserve	70
Trade creditors and accrued expenses	35
Profit before tax for the year ended 31 December 2003	694
Taxation for the year ended 31 December 2003	208

The directors propose the following:

A full year's dividend on the preference shares.
An ordinary share dividend of 4% per share.

Required

(a) Prepare the profit and loss appropriation account for the year
ended 31 December 2003   **(8 marks)**

(b) Prepare the capital and reserves section of the balance sheet   **(5 marks)**

(c) Prepare the current liabilities section of the balance sheet   **(4 marks)**

When preparing a balance sheet it is important to distinguish between long-term and current liabilities.

(d) Give **one** example of a long-term liability   **(1 mark)**

(e) Explain why it is important to distinguish between long-term
and current liabilities.   **(4 marks)**

© AQA 2004

AQA Advanced Subsidiary GCE Accounting *Unit 2 Financial Accounting: Introduction to Published Accounts of Limited Companies* **14 January 2004**

The managing director of Supermarket Supreme Plc has asked you to prepare a short report explaining to shareholders the purpose of producing a cash flow statement each year.

To ....

From ....

Date ....

Subject ....

(Heading **1 mark**)
(Report **7 marks**)

© AQA 2004

AQA Advanced Subsidiary GCE Accounting *Unit 2 Financial Accounting: Introduction to Published Accounts of Limited Companies* **14 January 2004**

In the books of Jones and Simpson Ltd the following errors have been discovered after preparing the draft accounts for the year ended 31 October 2003.

1   The purchase of a machine costing £4,000 has been included in the total for purchases.

2   Returns inwards of £640 have been omitted completely from the accounts.

3   The sales day book was undercast by £7,800.

4   The wages were incorrectly stated as £89,000. The correct figure was £98,000.

The draft profit calculated was £67,000.

Required

(a) Calculate the corrected net profit for the year ended
     31 October 2003   **(6 marks)**

(b) State any changes, as a result of these corrections, which
     will have to be made to the balance sheet. Identify each
     sub-heading, item and amount involved.   **(6 marks)**

© AQA 2004

AQA Advanced Subsidiary GCE Accounting *Unit 2 Financial Accounting: Introduction to Published Accounts of Limited Companies* **14 Jan 2004**

Both directors and auditors have duties with regard to the accounts of limited companies. Explain what their duties are.

Directors' duties are ....
....
....
....
....
....

(3 marks)

Auditors' duties are ....
....
....
....
....
....

(3 marks)

© AQA 2004

AAT Sample examination papers

AAT NVQ/SVQ Level 2 in Accounting *Preparing Ledger Balances and an Initial Trial Balance (PLB)* (2003 standards) 30 November 2004

Task 2.1
The following document has been received by Special Events from its customer PKG Limited.

BACS REMITTANCE ADVICE	
To: Special Events	From: PKG Limited
Your ref: SE102	*Our ref:1650*

30 November 2004	BACS Transfer	£1,410
Payment has been made by BACS and will be paid directly into your bank account on the date shown above		

(a) What accounts in the main (general) ledger will be used to record this transaction?

(b) Give ONE advantage to Special Events of being paid by BACS transfer.

(c) Give ONE advantage to PKG Limited of paying by BACS transfer.

Task 2.2
What documents would Special Events send out:

(a) with a cheque to pay an account?

(b) to list unpaid invoices and ask for payment each month?

(c) to correct an overcharge on an invoice issued?

Task 2.3
Special Events keeps a small amount of petty cash in the office to purchase miscellaneous items during the month. The imprest level is £100. The following purchases were made during November.

15 November Window Cleaning	£30.00
22 November Postage	£25.00
29 November Stationery	£28.00

(a) Make the relevant entries in the petty cash control account showing clearly the balance carried down at 30 November (closing balance) and brought down at 1 December (opening balance).

(b) What will be the amount required to restore the imprest level?

(c) Name ONE precaution that should be taken to ensure the petty cash is safe and secure.

Task 2.4

Keith Boxley has just learned that a customer, Bibby and Company, has ceased trading and the outstanding amount on its account will have to be written off as a bad debt. What accounting entries must you make in the main (general) ledger to write off the net amount of £500 and the VAT?

Account name	Dr £	Cr £
_____	_____	_____
_____	_____	_____
_____	_____	_____

Task 2.5

Keith Boxley needs advice about the most efficient way of organising the filing system. Suggest one efficient way of filing each of the following documents, giving a different method for each.

(a) Sales invoices _____

(b) Purchase invoices _____

(c) Bank statements _____

Task 2.6

Within a computerised accounting system code numbers will be used, for instance customer account codes.

Give TWO other examples of the use of code numbers in a computerised accounting system.

Task 2.7

Keith Boxley is purchasing a computer and hopes to change from a manual to a computerised accounting system. He already has a keyboard and mouse.

Name ONE other item of hardware and one item of software that he will also need to operate the system.

Task 2.8

The following information has become available.

(a) An amount of £45 has been credited to the discounts allowed account instead of the discounts received account.

(b) An amount paid by cheque for insurance has been recorded as £120 instead of the correct amount of £180.

(c) A credit purchase of £600 plus VAT for stationery has been incorrectly recorded as £200 plus VAT.

Record the journal entries needed in the main (general) ledger, to deal with the above. Narratives are not required.

Task 2.9
This is a summary of transactions with suppliers during the month of November.

	£
Balance of creditors at 1 November 2004	30,260
Goods bought on credit	11,500
Money paid to credit suppliers	9,357
Discounts received	170
Goods returned to credit suppliers	125

(a) Prepare a purchases ledger control account from the above details. Show clearly the balance carried down at 30 November (closing balance) and brought down at 1 December (opening balance).
   The following closing credit balances were in the subsidiary (purchases) ledger on 30 November.

	£
Williams and Whale	15,400
Jacksons Limited	3,500
Conference Caterers	11,218
Fine Foods	1,900
J. Wilson	215

(b) Reconcile the balances shown above with the purchases ledger control account balance you have calculated in part (a).

(c) What may have caused the difference you calculated in part (b)?

Task 2.10
On 29 November Special Events received the following bank statement as at 22 November: The cash book as at 29 November is shown below.

CENTREPOINT BANK Plc
High Street, Bedford BF13 8RF

To Special Events   Account No 34287280   22 November 2004

STATEMENT OF ACCOUNT

Date 2004	Details	Paid out	Paid in	Balance	
01 Nov	Balance b/f			10,4000	C
05 Nov	Cheque 006165	3,500		6,900	C
08 Nov	Cheque 006166	2,100		4,800	C
11 Nov	Bank Giro Credit				C
	L Smith		5,000	9,800	C
11 Nov	Bank Giro Credit				C
	B Roberts		7,500	17,300	C
12 Nov	Cheque 006168	380		16,920	C
15 Nov	Direct Debit				C
	Bedford CC	186		16,734	C
19 Nov	Direct Debit				C
	Myers Insurance	45		16,689	C
22 Nov	Overdraft facility fee	40		16,489	C
22 Nov	Bank charges	50		15,599	C

CASH BOOK

Date 2004	Details	Bank £	Date 2004	Cheque number	Details	Bank £
01 Nov	Balance b/f	10,400	01 Nov	006165	LLB Limited	3,500
11 Nov	L Smith	5,000	01 Nov	006166	Down and Daly	2,100
11 Nov	B Roberts	7,500	05 Nov	006167	Hobbs Limited	4,600
15 Nov	G Brown	1,700	05 Nov	006168	H & H Limited	380
22 Nov	B Singh	4,550	22 Nov	006169	Eddies Bar	500

(a) Check the items on the bank statement against the items in the cash book.

(b) Update the cash book as needed.

(c) Total the cash book and clearly show the balance carried down at 29 November (closing balance) and brought down at 30 November (opening balance). Note: you do not need to adjust the accounts in Section 1.

(d) Using the information prepare a bank reconciliation statement as at 29 November.

© AAT 2004

AAT NVQ/SVQ Level 3 in Accounting *Recording and Evaluating Costs and Revenues (ECR)* **(2003 standards) 29 November 2004**

China Ltd manufactures and sells pottery made from clay. You work as an accounting technician at China Ltd, reporting to the Finance Director. The company operates an integrated absorption costing system. Stocks are valued on a first in first out (FIFO) basis. The Finance Director has given you the following tasks.

Task 1.1

Complete the following stock card for clay using the FIFO method for valuing issues to production and stocks of materials.

STOCK CARD									
Product: Clay									
	Receipts			Issues			Balance		
Date	Quantity kgs	Cost per kg £	Total cost £	Quantity kgs	Cost per kg £	Total cost £	Quantity kgs	Cost per kg £	Total cost £
B/f at 1 Nov							15, 000	0.50	7,500
8 Nov	60,000	0.45							
9 Nov			45,000						
16 Nov	40,000	0.55							
17 Nov			50,000						

Additional data

The company's production budget requires 25,000 kgs of clay to be used each week. The company plans to maintain a buffer stock of clay equivalent to one week's budgeted production. It takes between one and two weeks for delivery of clay from the date the order is placed with the supplier.

Task 1.2

Calculate the reorder level for clay.

© AAT 2004

AAT NVQ/SVQ Level 3 in Accounting *Maintaining Financial Records and Preparing Accounts (FRA)* **(2003 standards) 1 December 2004**

Frank Khan owns Fixit, a business that repairs and maintains properties. There are no credit sales. The business operates from small rented premises where the plant and equipment are stored. Frank Khan does not keep a double entry book-keeping system. You are an accounting technician at Harper and Co., the accounting firm that prepares the final accounts for Fixit. You are working on the accounts for Fixit for the year ending 30 September 2004. Your colleague has already summarised the cash and bank accounts.

Fixit
Cash and bank summary for the year ended 30 September 2004

	Cash £	Bank £		Cash £	Bank £
Balance b/d	560	2,310	Rent		2,600
Sales	17,400	32,000	Wages	20,500	
Bank	10,000		Materials	2,600	
			Creditors for materials		11,005
			Travel expenses	2,470	
			Administration expenses	1,990	
			Cash		10,000
			Balance c/d	400	10,705
	27,960	34,310		27,960	34,310

The following balances are also available:

Assets and liabilities as at:	30 September 2003 £	30 September 2004 £
Plan and equipment at cost	19,000	19,000
Plant and equipment accumulated depreciation	5,600	Not yet available
Stocks of materials at cost	2,890	1,940
Prepayment for rent	550	Not yet available
Creditors for materials	1,720	1,835
Accrual for travel expenses	380	425

Task 1.1
Calculate the figure for capital as at 30 September 2003.

Task 1.2
Calculate the total sales for the year ended 30 September 2004.

Task 1.3
Prepare the purchases ledger control account for the year ended 30 September 2004, showing clearly the credit purchases of materials.

Task 1.4
Calculate the total purchases of materials for the year ended 30 September 2004.

Task 1.5
Depreciation is provided at 25% per annum on a reducing balance basis.

(a) Calculate the depreciation charge for the year ended 30 September 2004.

(b) Calculate the revised accumulated depreciation as at 30 September 2004.

Task 1.6
Calculate the travel expenses for the year ended 30 September 2004.

Task 1.7
The figure for rent in the cash and bank summary includes £650 for the quarter starting 1 October 2004.

Prepare the rent account for the year ended 30 September 2004, showing clearly the rent for the year.

Task 1.8
Frank Khan has given you a closing stock figure of £1,940 at cost. He has also told you that he has a supply of bricks which he acquired free of charge. He is confident that he will be able to sell these bricks for at least £500. These are not included in the stock valuation of £1,940. What figure for closing stock should be included in the accounts of Fixit? (Circle only one answer.)

£1,440 / £1,940 / £2,440 / None of these

Task 1.9
Complete the following trial balance as at 30 September 2004, taking into account your answers to the above tasks, and all the other information you have been given.

Fixit

Trial balance as at 30 September 2004

	Dr £	Cr £
Plant and equipment		
Plant and equipment accumulated depreciation		
Opening stock		
Prepayment		
Creditors for materials		
Accrual		
Bank		
Cash		
Capital		
Sales		
Purchases		
Wages		
Depreciation charge for the year		
Travel expenses		
Rent		
Administration expenses		
Closing stock – profit and loss account		
Closing stock – balance sheet		
Total		

Task 1.10

Frank Khan has told you he is concerned about the figure in the trial balance for fixed assets. He knows that it includes all the plant and equipment that he has bought over a number of years but he does not have a list of the items. It is possible that some are broken or missing. He needs your advice. Write a memo to Frank Khan:

- List SIX items of information that a fixed assets register should contain.

- Give THREE reasons why he should keep a fixed assets register.

© AAT 2004

AAT NVQ/SVQ (2003 standards) 1 December 2004

Henry and James are the owners of HJ Cleaning, a partnership business that sells industrial cleaning equipment. You are an accounting technician at Harper and Co., the accounting firm that prepares the final accounts for HJ Cleaning.

- The financial year end is 30 September.
- The partners maintain an integrated accounting system consisting of a main ledger, a purchases ledger, a sales ledger and a stock ledger.
- Stock records are maintained at cost in the stock ledger which is updated every time a sale or stock purchase is made.
- HJ Cleaning is registered for VAT.
- The proforma extended trial balance for the year ended 30 September 2004 is shown below.

At the end of the financial year on 30 September 2004, the following trial balance was taken from the main ledger:

	Dr £	Cr £
Administration expenses	88,014	
Bank	106,571	
Capital account – Henry		50,000
Capital account – James		50,000
Cash	165	
Closing stock	69,580	69,580
Current account – Henry		3,600
Current account – James		4,200
Depreciation charge for the year	8,750	
Opening stock	75,150	
Purchases	185,400	
Purchases ledger control account		16,200
Rent	14,000	
Sales		450,800
Sales ledger control account	53,000	
Selling expenses	43,970	
VAT		10,200
Vehicles at cost	35,000	
Vehicles accumulated depreciation		25,000
Total	679,600	679,600

Additional data

Most of the year-end adjustments have been entered, but there are some adjustments you now need to make:

(a) Accountancy fees of £1,900 need to be accrued. Ignore VAT.

(b) A provision for doubtful debts of 1.5% of the value of the sales ledger control account needs to be introduced.

(c) The total value of a purchase invoice for electricity for £329, including VAT of 17.5%, was debited to selling expenses. Electricity should be charged to administration expenses.

(d) A credit note from a supplier for purchases was entered into the ledgers as a purchase invoice. The credit note was for £470 including VAT at 17.5%.

Task 2.1
Prepare journal entries to account for the above. Dates and narratives are not required.

Task 2.2
Enter your journal entries into the adjustment columns of the extended trial balance.

Task 2.3
Extend the profit and loss and balance sheet columns of the extended trial balance. Make entries to record the net profit or loss for the year ended 30 September 2004.

HJ Cleaning Extended trial balance as at 30 September 2004

	Ledger balances		Adjustments		Profit and loss account		Balance sheet	
	Dr £	Cr £	Dr £	Cr £	Dr £	Cr £	Dr £	Cr £
Administration expenses	88,014							
Bank	106,571							
Capital account – Henry		50,000						
Capital account – James		50,000						
Cash	165							
Closing stock	69,580	69,580						
Current account – Henry		3,600						
Current account – James		4,200						
Depreciation charge for the year	8,750							
Opening stock	74,150							
Purchases	185,400							
Purchases ledger control account		16,200						
Rent	14,000							
Sales		450,800						
Sales ledger control account	53,000							
Selling expenses	43,970							
VAT		10,220						
Vehicles at cost	35,000							
Vehicles accumulated depreciation	25,000	679,600						
	TOTAL	679,600						

Additional data

Henry and James share the profits of the partnership equally.

Task 2.4

Update the partners' current accounts to account for the profit or loss for the year ended 30 September 2004. Balance off the accounts and bring the balances down.

Current accounts

	Henry £	James £			Henry £	James £
			30 September 2004	Balance b/d	3,600	4,200

Task 2.5

Prepare a balance sheet for HJ Cleaning as at 30 September 2004.

HJ Cleaning Balance sheet as at 30 Septmber 2004				
Workings		£	£	£
	Fixed assets			
	Vehicles			
	Current assets			
	Stock			
	Debtors			
	Bank			
	Cash			
	Current liabilities			
	Creditors			
	VAT			
	Accruals			
	Net current assets			
	Net assets			
	Capital employed	Henry	James	Total
	Capital accounts			
	Current accounts			
	Total			

Additional data

On 1 October 2004 Charles was admitted to the partnership.

- He introduced £100,000 to the bank account.
- Goodwill was valued at £220,000 on 30 September 2004.
- Goodwill is to be eliminated from the accounts.
- The new profit sharing percentages are:
  Henry 40%
  James 40%
  Charles 20%

Task 2.6

Update the capital accounts for the partnership, showing clearly the introduction and elimination of goodwill. Balance off the accounts.

Capital accounts

		Henry £	James £	Charles £			Henry £	James £	Charles £
					1 October 2004	Balance b/d	50,000	50,000	

Note the style difference between the OCR and AQA papers in displayed maximum marks for each question is deliberate and reflects the differences in styles on the actual papers. AAT papers do not display maximum marks.

© AAT 2004

Glossary

Accounting ratios. Statistical measures taken from the accounts of a business to aid financial assessment and control.

Accruals. Expenses incurred, but not yet billed to the firm.

Amalgamation. Joining two firms into one.

Assets. The term comes from the word 'assez', meaning 'enough'. It is used because the property of a proprietor is judged in terms of whether it is sufficient to discharge his/her liabilities, i.e.: to settle his/her debts.

Assets: fixed and current. Assets are classified into fixed assets and current assets. The former are those which will be retained in the business, e.g.: machines, motor vehicles, etc; the latter, it is assumed, will be consumed in the business within the fiscal year and includes: stock, debtors, cash in hand and cash at bank.

Average cost method. A method of stock valuation in which remaining stock values are averaged out every time a withdrawal is made.

Bad debts. Debts which a firm regards as uncollectable.

Balance. This term is used in 3 different ways in double entry bookkeeping.
1. For the debit and credit column totals
2. For the balancing item required to equalise the two column totals (balance c/d)
3. For that balancing item transferred as the opening figure for the subsequent accounting period (balance b/d).

Balance sheet. A listing of the ledger balances remaining after compilation of the revenue account. (It is not, as some think, called a balance sheet merely because it balances.)

Bank reconciliation. A standardised format statement explaining a discrepancy between the bank statement balance and the cash book balance.

Bought ledger. That division of the ledger which contains personal accounts of suppliers. It is also sometimes referred to as the purchase ledger or creditors account.

Cash book. The book in which records of cash and banking transactions are made.

Credit note. A document which reverses the effect of an invoice.

Creditors. People or firms to whom the business owes money.

Capital. This term derives from the latin words 'Capitalis', meaning 'chief' and 'capitali', meaning 'property', giving us the combined meaning of 'property of the chief'. The chief of a business is, of course, the proprietor.

Control account. An account in a ledger division which amounts to a mini trial balance for that division. It consists of aggregates of each type of posting therein, e.g.: the sales ledger control account will be posted with the aggregate value of cheques received, the aggregated invoice totals for the month, and so on. It is used both as a check on the accuracy and as a means of making the compilation of the overall trial balance easier.

Debtors. People or firms who owe money to the business.

Depreciation. The writing down of an asset's value in the books of a business to allow for wear and tear.

Dividends. Shares of profit paid to shareholders.

Drawings. The retrieval of capital by a proprietor or partners for private use.

Early settlement discount. A discount allowed to customers as an enticement to pay their bills on time.

Expenses. Purchases of goods or services for consumption by the business within the financial year. They do not enhance the value of any fixed assets though they may include repairs to them. Examples are: goods for resale, wages, repairs, heat and lighting costs, petrol and professional fees.

FIFO. First In First Out. A method of stock valuation based on the assumption that the latest cost prices prevail.

Final accounts. The revenue accounts and balance sheet of a firm at a particular moment in time and covering a particular financial period, e.g.: a financial year.

Goodwill. The intangible fixed asset of a business's reputation.

Gross profit. Sales revenue minus cost of sales.

Gross profit margin. Gross profit as a percentage of sales.

Imprest system. A system of managing petty cash in which a fund is regularly replenished to a set amount by the cashier.

Income and expenditure account. A non-profit-making club's equivalent of a business's profit and loss account.

Input tax. VAT charged by a supplier on goods or services it has supplied and which will be subsequently reclaimed by the business from HM Revenue and Customs.

Interim accounts. Revenue accounts and balance sheet drawn up at intervals more frequent than each financial year and used for management purposes.

Invoice. A bill for goods or services rendered.

Journal. A book of prime entry in debit and credit format used for initial entries of a miscellany of transactions for which no other book exists. E.g.: the intial recording of opening figures, bad debt, depreciation and the correction of errors. However, some people refer to the day books as journals too, e.g.: sales journal, purchase journal, etc. and the journal as defined above is then referred to as the 'Journal Proper'.

Ledger. The ledger is the essential double entry accounting system and consists of a number of divisions, e.g.: the general ledger, personal ledger, cash book and petty cash book. Since each of these divisions is often kept in a separate bound book it is not surprising that people tend to think of them as separate ledgers, but this is not truly the case, they are all divisions of the one ledger system.

Liabilities. Financial obligations to others – debts owed out. Capital too is listed under liabilities in the balance sheet since it is owed to the proprietor by the business.

LIFO. Last In First Out. A method of stock valuation based on the assumption that the earliest cost prices prevail.

Limited company. A business entity which has its own rights and obligations under the law. Its capital is divided into shares and the liability of the shareholders in the event of a liquidation is limited to the value of shares held.

Liquidity. The ability of a firm to pay its debts.

Net profit. Gross profit minus overhead expenses.

Nominal ledger. That division of the ledger in which impersonal accounts are kept.

Output tax. VAT charged to customers by a business and which it will have to subsequently remit to HM Revenue and Customs.

Overhead expenses. Expenses which cannot be directly related to turnover.

Partnership. An unlimited business unit owned by more than one proprietor.

Personal ledger. That division of the ledger which contains personal accounts of suppliers and customers. It is divided into 2 sub-divisions – bought ledger and sales ledger.

Petty cash book. The book of prime entry in which records of small cash transactions are kept.

Postage book. A book in which records of stamps purchased and used are made.

Private ledger. A separate division of the ledger in which capital items are posted.

Private limited company. A limited liability company whose share dealings are restricted and cannot be quoted on the stock exchange. It only has to have two shareholders and one director to comply with company law, though that director could not also act as company secretary.

Profit. The reward to the proprietor, partners or shareholders for the business risk they have taken.

Profit and loss account. That section of the revenue accounts which shows the calculation of net profit, by deduction of overhead expenses from gross profit.

Profit and loss appropriation account. That part of the revenue accounts of a partnership or limited company which explains how the net profit is to be appropriated.

Provision for bad debts. A suitable provision set against the value of debtors to allow for some which will become uncollectable.

Provision for depreciation. An allowance set against an asset for wear and tear.

Public company. A limited liability company which is empowered to sell its shares freely and have them quoted on the stock exchange. It must have a minimum of 7 shareholders and 2 directors.

Purchase day book. A book of prime entry in which the inital record of purchases is made prior to posting to the ledger.

Purchase returns day book. A book of prime entry in which the intial record of goods returned to suppliers is made prior to posting to the ledger.

Receipts and payments book. The main accounting book used by many club stewards in non-profit-making clubs.

Revenues. Inflows of money or money's worth to the firm, e.g. sales figures, rents, discounts received, etc. They must be distinguished from proceeds of sale of fixed assets, which is capital income rather than revenue income and is ultimately shown in the balance sheet rather than the trading, profit and loss account.

Revenue accounts. The set of accounts which shows the net profit earned by a business, how it is calculated and how it is to be distributed. Typically they include the trading account and the profit and loss account. For a partnership or limited company they will also include an appropriation account, for a manufacturing business, they will include the manufacturing account and for a club they will include an income and expenditure account.

Sales day book. The book of prime entry in which the initial record of all sales is made prior to posting to the ledger.

Sales ledger. That division of the ledger which contains personal accounts of customers. It is also sometimes referred to as the debtors ledger.

Sales return day book. The book of prime entry in which the initial record of goods returned by customers is made prior to posting to the ledger.

Share capital.

Authorised share capital The amount of capital a company is permitted to raise by means of issuing shares.

Issued share capital The nominal value of shares actually issued by a company.

Ordinary shares Shares in a company which earn the holders a percentage of profits. In the event of a liquidation this category of investors will be the last in the queue for recovery of their investment.

Preference shares Shares which entitle the holders to a fixed rate of dividend on profits. Their claim on profits comes before ordinary shareholders as would their claim on residual assets in the event of a liquidation.

Redeemable shares Shares which the company is empowered to buy back.

Sole proprietorship. An unlimited firm owned solely by one person.

Statement of affairs. A description and valuation of the assets and liabilities of a business and the way the net assets are represented by capital at a particular moment in time. In effect, it is the same as a balance sheet, but not called so because the source used for compilation is not the ledger balances, but rather a series of inventories.

Stock. Goods for resale or for use in a manufacturing process for the production of goods for resale.

Suspense account. An account into which a value equal to an error can be posted temporarily in order to make the books balance while the source of the error is being sought.

Trading account. That section of the revenue accounts which explains the calculation of gross profit.

Trial balance. A listing and summing of all the ledger balances at a particular moment in time to confirm that the total debits equal the total credits and, thus, provide some measure of confidence in the accuracy of the ledger posting.

Value Added Tax (VAT). A tax on goods and services. Businesses act as sub-collectors by charging VAT on goods they sell and remitting it to HM

Revenue and Customs after deducting the VAT they, themselves, have been charged on their purchases from other firms.

Working capital. The difference between current assets and current liabilities.

Index

Index